# REINVENTING HISTORY
The Enlightenment Origins
of Ancient History

'I used to say some people make money and some make history – which is very funny until you find you can't afford to keep yourself alive.' Anthony H. Wilson (1950–2007)

# REINVENTING HISTORY
## The Enlightenment Origins of Ancient History

*Edited by*
James Moore, Ian Macgregor Morris
and Andrew J. Bayliss

Centre for Metropolitan History, Institute of Historical Research
School of Advanced Study, University of London
2008

Published by
UNIVERSITY OF LONDON
SCHOOL OF ADVANCED STUDY
INSTITUTE OF HISTORICAL RESEARCH
CENTRE FOR METROPOLITAN HISTORY
*Senate House, London WC1E 7HU*


Editorial matter © James Moore, Ian Macgregor Morris
and Andrew J. Bayliss 2008
All remaining chapters © their respective authors 2008
All rights reserved


ISBN 978 1 905165 37 7


Printed by Cromwell Press Group Ltd, Trowbridge, Wiltshire


*Jacket illustration:* The Temple of Minerva at Sunium [now thought to be the Temple of Poseidon] (E. Dodwell, *Views in Greece* (London, 1821), courtesy of the Joint Library of the Hellenic and Roman Societies)

# Contents

| | |
|---|---|
| List of Illustrations | vii |
| Notes on Contributors | ix |
| Acknowledgements | xi |

INTRODUCTION

1. History in Revolution? Approaches to the Ancient World in the Long Eighteenth Century
   *James Moore and Ian Macgregor Morris* — 3

PART ONE: HISTORICAL CONTROVERSIES AND HISTORICAL CONSCIOUSNESS

2. Xenophon and the Greek Tradition in British Political Thought
   *Doohwan Ahn* — 33

3. William Young and the *Spirit of Athens*
   *Peter Liddel* — 57

4. 'The deadly principles of fanaticism': Puritans and Dissenters in Gibbon's *Decline and Fall of the Roman Empire*
   *John Seed* — 87

PART TWO: METHODS AND INTERPRETATIONS

5. The Battle of Actium and the 'slave of passion'
   *Carsten Hjort Lange* — 115

6. History as Theoretical Reconstruction? Baron D'Hancarville and the Exploration of Ancient Mythology in the Eighteenth Century
   *James Moore* — 137

7. Colonel Leake and the Historical Geography of Greece
   *Malcolm Wagstaff* — 169

PART THREE: THE POLITICS OF HISTORIOGRAPHICAL DEVELOPMENT

8. The Rise and Fall of the Roman Historian: The Eighteenth Century in the Roman Historical Tradition
   *Gareth Sampson* ............................................................. 187

9. Greek, but not Grecian? Macedonians in Enlightenment Histories
   *Andrew J. Bayliss* .......................................................... 219

10. Navigating the *Grotesque*; or, Rethinking Greek Historiography
    *Ian Macgregor Morris* .................................................. 247

Bibliography of Primary Material ........................................ 291

Bibliography of Secondary Material .................................... 301

Index ............................................................................... 309

# List of Illustrations

*Jacket:* The Temple of Minerva at Sunium [now thought to be the Temple of Poseidon] (E. Dodwell, *Views in Greece* (London, 1821), courtesy of the Joint Library of the Hellenic and Roman Societies)

Fig. 1. The octagonal Tower of Winds, Athens (J. Stuart and N. Revett, *The Antiquities of Athens* (London, 1762–1816), courtesy of the Joint Library of the Hellenic and Roman Societies) — 12

Fig. 2. The Athenian Acropolis (E. Dodwell, *Views in Greece* (London, 1821), courtesy of the Joint Library of the Hellenic and Roman Societies) — 20

Fig. 3. The modern (early nineteenth-century) agora of Athens (E. Dodwell, *Views in Greece* (London, 1821), courtesy of the Joint Library of the Hellenic and Roman Societies) — 20

Fig. 4. Map of Thermopylae by Robert Wood, 1751 (Wood, *Diaries* (unpublished manuscript), courtesy of the Joint Library of the Hellenic and Roman Societies) — 26

Fig. 5. Plan of Sparta [detail] (W.M. Leake, *Travels in the Morea* (London, 1830), courtesy of the Joint Library of the Hellenic and Roman Societies) — 171

Fig. 6. Detail of Macedonia and the Greek mainland (T. Stanyan, *The Grecian History* (2nd edn., London, 1739), courtesy of Ian Macgregor Morris) — 246

# Notes on Contributors

**Doohwan Ahn** is a doctoral candidate in eighteenth-century intellectual history at the University of Cambridge.

**Andrew J. Bayliss** is Lecturer in Greek History in the Institute of Archaeology and Antiquity at the University of Birmingham.

**Carsten Hjort Lange** recently completed his PhD thesis on Apollo, Actium and the Triumvirate in the Department of Classics at the University of Nottingham.

**Peter Liddel** is Lecturer in Greek History in the School of Arts, Histories and Cultures at the University of Manchester.

**Ian Macgregor Morris** is a Research Fellow in the Department of Classics and the Centre for Spartan and Peloponnesian Studies at the University of Nottingham.

**James Moore** is Deputy Director of the Centre for Metropolitan History at the Institute of Historical Research, London.

**Gareth Sampson** recently completed his PhD thesis on the Tribunate and the Roman Republic in the Department of Classics and Ancient History at the University of Manchester.

**John Seed** is Senior Lecturer in Modern History in the School of Arts at Roehampton University.

**Malcolm Wagstaff** is Emeritus Professor of Historical Geography at the University of Southampton.

# Acknowledgements

This volume was conceived in Manchester but has arrived into the world in its present form thanks to friends and colleagues in many university departments around Britain and Europe. We would like to thank Tim Cornell, Steve Rigby, Stephen Hodkinson and Peter Lowe for their encouragement in our early endeavours and Kevin King, Catherine Tite, Kostas Vlassopoulos, Carsten Lange and Gareth Sampson for helping develop our ideas into this book. Thanks are also due to the British Society for Eighteenth-Century Studies and the Classical Association for facilitating several of our conference sessions on the historiogaphy of the ancient world in the eighteenth century and for supporting the development of the subject area.

We would also like to thank those who participated in our eighteenth-century historiography colloquium at the University of Nottingham and the recent 'Making History' conference at the Institute of Historical Research, London. Several of the papers from these events have provided the basis for chapters in this book. We are very grateful for the assistance of Anastasia Bakogianni at the Institute of Classical Studies, London and to the many library and archive staff who have helped us to obtain rare publications – in particular those at the ICS, Joint Library of the Hellenic and Roman Societies, London and at the British School of Athens. We would also like to acknowledge the support of the Arts and Humanities Research Council. Ian Macgregor Morris' contributions to the volume have been part of his postdoctoral fellowship on the AHRC-funded project, 'Sparta in Comparative Perspective, Ancient to Modern'.

Finally, the editors are very grateful to the Institute of Historical Research, London for supporting the publication of this work and, in particular, to Olwen Myhill, for all her hard work in preparing the draft material and seeing it through to final production.

*Andrew J. Bayliss*
*Ian Macgregor Morris*
*James Moore*

November 2008

# INTRODUCTION

1. History in Revolution? Approaches to the Ancient World in the Long Eighteenth Century

*James Moore and Ian Macgregor Morris*

*Neither common sense nor intuition can replace a critical knowledge of past historians.*[1]

The eighteenth century is often viewed as a critical phase in the transition to the modern world. Whether one is a student of state formation, politics, theology, the history of ideas or industrial economics there is good reason to see the century as a turning point in the history of Western civilisation.[2] Yet this period of modernisation was one in which the past, and ideas about the past, loomed large in everyday culture. It was an era in which the built form of many cities increasingly emulated the architecture and decorative styles of the classical world and when political revolutions created new governments and constitutions based upon the models of Greece and Rome. Even the literature of this era was shaped by classical preconceptions, with the 'Battle of the Books' illustrating just how self consciously the early eighteenth century viewed itself in relation to the great civilisations of the classical period.[3] This volume attempts to re-evaluate the impact of these complex trends and preoccupations on the writing of history, and ancient history in particular. For many years the influence of Arnaldo Momigliano has, with some justification, dominated debates about the eighteenth-century historiography of the ancient world. Momigliano focused historians' attention on how revolutionary the eighteenth century was in the process of historical scholarship, bringing together, he argued, the traditions of antiquarian scholarship and historical erudition to produce new modes of research

---

[1] A. Momigliano, *Studies in Historiography* (London, 1966), vii.
[2] For aspects of this debate, see P. Gay, *The Enlightenment: An Interpretation* (London, 1973); D. Spadafora, *The Idea of Progress in Eighteenth-Century Britain* (Yale, 1990); N. Aston, *Religion and Revolution in France* (Basingstoke, 2000), J.E. Bradley (ed.), *Religion and Politics in Enlightenment Europe* (Notre Dame, 2001).
[3] J. Levine, *The Battle of the Books. History and Literature in the Augustan Age* (London, 1991).

and writing. This facilitated a more critical, non-linear approach to the development of historical narrative allowing the use of a wider range of sources and providing a framework for more effective source criticism and synthesis.[4]

Momigliano stressed the importance of historians understanding both ancient and modern contexts in order to obtain an effective appreciation of any piece of historical scholarship. The current volume develops that approach, bringing together classicists, ancient historians and eighteenth-century specialists in order to re-evaluate important aspects of historiographical development. In doing so it becomes clear that some of the traditional assumptions about the progress of historical method are invalid, that some key historical approaches were actually pioneered before the start of the eighteenth century, and that history was more heavily influence by related scholarly disciplines than is sometimes supposed. Moreover this volume will stress how the practice of history-writing became much more diverse in the eighteenth century, highlighting how other literary genres, particularly the novel, the travel journal and the epic poem, came to shape the way history was written. This in turn was partly due to the changing nature of the audience and the growth of a consumer society focused around the culture of the book and of public reading. The purpose of this volume is not to provide a thorough-going explanation of how history was shaped by these processes of cultural deepening and diffusion but it will suggest new avenues for exploring the eighteenth-century 'revolution' in historiography. Momigliano emphasised the way in which antiquarianism and erudition came together; we emphasise the way in which eighteenth-century historians occupied many different scholarly worlds, drawing on the particular traditions of which they were a part. In the case of Nathaniel Hooke, the celebrated historian of the Roman republic, it was the rich tradition of French Catholic scholarship, 'grand tour' antiquarianism and English republican political tradition.[5] In the case of Baron D'Hancarville, the historian of classical myth, it was one rooted in the experimental philosophy of Diderot and the proto-anthropology of early American explorers.[6] William Gell came from

---

[4] For recent overviews of Momigliano's work, contrast K. Christ, 'Arnold Momigliano and the History of Historiography', *History and Theory*, 30 (1991), 5–12 with R. Ridley, 'Leges Agrariae: Myths Ancient and Modern', *Classical Philology*, 95 (2000), 459–67.

[5] Hooke's work was heavily influenced by the work of Catrou. Compare F. Catrou and P. Rouillé, *Histoire Romaine* (Paris, 1725–37) with N. Hooke, *The Roman History* (London, 1738–71).

[6] F. Haskell, 'The Baron D'Hancarville; An Adventurer and Art Historian in Eighteenth-Century Europe', 31–45, in F. Haskell (ed.), *Past and Present in Art and Taste* (Yale, 1987).

a background of academic classicism but was strongly influenced by emerging methods of geographical survey.[7] Above all it is important to map the way in which scholastic traditions overlapped, not only through international contacts and literary dissemination, but also through the actions of individuals. Men such as Robert Wood occupied many worlds. Wood was a man who led expeditions to Troy and Palmyra, developed a detailed treatise on the original genius of Homeric literature and, in his spare time, served as a government minister at a time of radical political turmoil.[8]

In many cases the writing and interpretation of history was to have very direct political consequences. At one point the American constitutional convention descended into a historical debate about the fall of the Roman republic, with historical models being used to defend specific republican traditions.[9] Following the French revolution, Charles Dupuis, the historian of myth, found himself in a key role in the directory advising on the philosophical nature of religion and influencing the secularist movement of the post-revolutionary period.[10] Even in England, apparently the model of a stable political regime, the historian played a key part in the politics of the state. The historical contributions of Adam Smith and Edmund Burke are well known and documented but others also reached positions of prominence. Indeed, not only were scholars such as Wood embedded in establishment circles, historians also provided the intellectual basis for much anti-establishment politics. Hooke, for example, was long-suspected of being a Jacobite spy, blackmailing one of the most powerful aristocratic houses in England and organising networks for the Pretender. The explanation for the prominence of historians in positions of power is not straightforward but it does demonstrate the importance of history as a cultural canon – and particularly ancient history as this represented the fundamental historical reference points for much political debate. The eighteenth century may have been a time of rapid modernisation but it was also one in which the historicisation of cultural forms and political arrangements was seen as fundamental to developing a critical understanding of human thought, motivation and activity. History provided validation and justification. History mattered.

---

[7] W. Gell, *The Itinerary of Greece* (London, 1810).
[8] Wood was MP for Brackley MP between 1761–71 and served as an under secretary of state.
[9] W. Gribbin, 'Rollin's Histories and American Republicanism', *The William and Mary Quarterly*, 29 (1972), 611–22.
[10] C. Dupuis, *The Origin of All Religious Worship* (New Orleans, 1872).

To talk of a revolution in historical methodology and process, however, may be a little misleading. If a revolution did take place it was one which had its roots in the political preoccupations and historical debates of the seventeenth century and one that was not complete until the development of more systematic and 'scientific' techniques of philological and archaeological investigation in the middle of the nineteenth century. Indeed one might argue that the emergence of classics and archaeology as separate university disciplines undermined process of convergence between antiquarianism and historical erudition. It not only created immediate institutional divisions and a separate methodological focus but also separated the specialist professional scholar from the amateur. There is certainly some evidence that university historians, classicists and archaeologists very self-consciously attempted to distance themselves from the amateur gentleman scholars of the previous era.[11] Even today few undergraduate courses expect students to look back to the generation of historians who preceded Grote. Therefore, rather than seeing the methodological changes of historical scholarship as a sudden convergence, it may be better to view it as one which was the culmination of a process in which a range of historical trends and scholastic approaches came together in an attempt to write empirically-validated comprehensive accounts of the past that could meet the more rigorous demands for truth than had become prevalent in the era of the *philosophes*. However the ambition and wide-ranging nature of these accounts could be said to have proved their undoing. In the era of the full-time historian, anthropologist and archaeologist they inevitably became vulnerable to specialist critiques drawing upon more 'scientific' methods. Arguably this produced histories that were more narrowly focused or embedded in particular national historical traditions. One might say that in recent years the wheel has turned full circle with aspects of eighteenth-century methodology and approach being rediscovered as a model for future scholarship. The increasing emphasis on comparative history is one which most eighteenth-century historians would have recognised, especially those such as Volney and D'Hancarville who worked on the creation and diffusion of religious belief across cultures.[12] The concept of

---

[11] More work is required on the impact of the 'professionalisation' of the historical community. Archaeology is beginning to receive attention. See S. Marchand, *Down From Olympus: Archaeology and Philhellenism in Germany 1750–1970* (Princeton, 1996).

[12] Anon, *Christianity A Form of The Great Solar Myth From the French of Dupuis* (London, n.d.), C. Volney, *The Ruins, or a Survey of the Revolution of Empires* (London, 1819 edition), see esp. 228–33.

'interdisciplinary' would not have been recognised by this generation but the borrowing of methodological approaches from ancient sources, travel literature, natural philosophy and proto-anthropology was common in the landmark histories of the time. Moreover the scholarly community was a genuinely international one, with Anglo-French connections remarkably close, aided by the fact that the British Roman Catholic community often sent its children to leading French seminaries for their education. The eighteenth-century 'revolution' in historical method may, then, have had more profound and lasting consequences than those identified by Momigliano. In some important respects, eighteenth-century patterns of historical scholarship can appear more 'modern' that those of the nineteenth.

However before exploring these methodological changes it is important to explore the broader culture trends that saw a fundamental reshaping of historical writing in this period. The sources of this change cannot be linked to one particular philosophical tradition or political movement, although it is clear that it is closely related to changes in cultural production that took place in the latter half of the seventeenth century. The nature of historical writing was, of course, bound by national traditions and preoccupations but similar debates about constitutionalism emerged in both Britain and France. In Britain debates about the legitimacy and extent of kingly authority culminated in the so-called Glorious Revolution of 1688 that brought William of Orange to the throne. The long term consequences of this revolution on British political ideas have been explored by many historians but perhaps most fundamentally it highlighted debates about the nature of English Liberty and the Anglo-Saxon constitution which found resonance amongst political theorists schooled in the classics. Famously, for Shaftesbury, great cultural endeavour could only flourish in a free society – a principle that was as valid for the modern society as it was for the ancients. Later, of course, this was a dictum, taken up by Winkelmann to emphasise the connection between Greek freedom and excellence in Greek art – and by implications the dangers to civilisation that were inherent in suppressing liberty. In this view the roots of liberty were the roots of civilisation itself. This encouraged thinkers from Thomas Paine to Adam Smith to search for the sociological causes that underpinned liberty and provided the preconditions for the security of civil society – and in doing so ancient models were the models to be consulted.[13] Such was

---

[13] H. Weisinger, 'The English Origins of the Sociological Interpretation of the Renaissance', *Journal of the History of Ideas*, 11 (1950), 321–38.

the importance of classical exemplars that British cabinet ministers were even known to consult prominent historians on the intimate workings of the Roman Republican Constitution.[14] Both Whigs and Tories utilised historical precedents to support their own contemporary constitutional positions.[15]

Consequently much eighteenth-century history was taken up with the search for general laws that would explain the rise and fall of liberty and of civilisation. This, in turn, led to politics losing its primacy as the explanatory source for historical change and culture increasingly being seen as the root of historical transformation. The Quarrel between the Ancient and Moderns, so popular in seventeenth-century France had, by the mid-eighteenth century, developed into a broader debate about the uniformity of human development and natural potential.[16] Most thinkers followed Descartes in believing that human nature and the natural laws of God operated uniformly throughout all historical periods. This served to emphasise the importance of historical incidents and circumstances that created the discontinuities of history, such as the eclipse of Athens and the decline of the Roman Empire. Similarly one can read Hume's account of human nature as reflecting a pattern of very gradual progress, interrupted by breaks that overturn the natural order. The difficulty is that few, if any, thinkers produced a coherent theory of accident or incident that destroyed patterns of progress or development.[17] It was only with Ferguson's *Essay on the History of Civil Society* that a broader comparative theory of stagnation began to emerge. Decline, for Ferguson, was the product of:

> ... those revolutions of state that remove, or withhold, the objects of every ingenious study or liberal pursuit; that deprive the citizen of occasions to act as the member of a public; that crush his spirit; that debase his sentiments, and disqualify his mind for affairs.[18]

The revolutions were not natural or inevitable processes, but rather the product of apathy, neglect and corruption. Thus moral actions, culture

---

[14] F.M. Turner, 'British Politics and the Demise of the Roman Republic: 1700–1939', *Historical Journal*, 29 (1986), 577–99. See, for example, J. Stanhope, *A Memorial Sent from London by the Late Earl Stanhope, to the Abbot Vertot at Paris. Containing the following questions, relating to the constitution of the Roman Senate* (London, 1721).
[15] Turner, 'British Politics', 577–99.
[16] Levine, *The Battle of the Books*, J.B. Bury, *The Idea of Progress: An Inquiry into its Origin and Growth* (London, 1928), R.F. Jones, *Ancients and Moderns* (London, 1936).
[17] K. Bock, 'Theories of Progress, Development, Evolution', in T. Bottomore and R. Nisbit, *A History of Sociological Analysis* (London, 1979), 55–7.
[18] A. Ferguson, *An Essay on the History of Civil Society*, fifth edition (London 1782), 384, also cited in Bottomore and Nisbit, *History*, 57.

and institutions could guard against decline. Ferguson's approach to civic republicanism, with its focus on enlightened citizenship, clearly owed much to Cicero and Tacitus. His concern for neglect and corruption reflected both contemporary constitutional debate surrounding the Hanoverian constitution and recent Roman historiography, notably Hooke's work on the Roman Republic and Gibbon's work on luxury and political decline. Indeed since De Beaufort's 1737 *Treatise on Liberty in Civil Society* historians had generally followed Polybius and Tacitus in identifying personal ambition and corruption as the major destructive force in political commonwealths.[19] Historians were, then, embedding classical republican concepts in modern narratives in order to convey a specific moral and didactic purpose. Theirs was an attempt to identify fundamental laws that would be of value to the modern legislator that would either validate or challenge existing political arrangements.

A similar process can be observed in France, although the nature of French absolutism and dynamics of French politics meant that the terms of the debate and cultural reference points differed. The *histoire raisonée* movement probably contributed significantly to the moral and didactic nature of British history writing even though its original concerns were focused on the specific problems of French political life and governance. In many respects it was a transitional movement, drawing on an earlier tradition of sixteenth-century *érudits*, constitutional and legal scholars who argued that history was to be understood in scientific terms, and emphasising the important of accuracy and critical understanding of sources. The new movement, however, combined a desire for literary excellence with the belief that historical writing should have a broader didactic and social role.[20] In effect it liberated cultural history from a subordinate role and gave it explanatory power – the power to explain particular patterns of governance and institutional behaviour. This, then, was a 'history from below' long before the term was invented in the twentieth century. The specific objects of research varied, although some of the most famous works tended to focus on the national cultural history of France and the cultural history of French government. Much of this work seems remarkably 'modern' – even 'postmodern' – in its concentration on the heterogeneous nature of human cultures and the subjective nature of the nation state and national historical identity.

---

[19] W. Velema, 'Ancient and Modern Virtue Compared: De Beaufort and Van Effen on Republican Citizenship', *Eighteenth-Century Studies*, 30 (1997), 437–43.

[20] P.K. Leffler, '"The Histoire Raisonée", 1660–1720: A Pre-Enlightenment Genre', *Journal of the History of Ideas*, 37 (1976), 219–40.

This approach is particularly evident in the work of Fénelon, the most famous proponent of this school, who emphasised the importance of understanding the subtleties of cultural evolution in order to map the long term process of historical causation.[21] Similarly Henri de Boulainvilliers argued for a detailed understanding of the cultural history of France in order to understand the problems and complexities of contemporary French politics. For Boulainvilliers, and those working in a similar school, history represented a fundamental challenge to the power of Louis XIV and French Absolutism, demonstrating that despotism emerged from the collapse of the ideal political order of aristocracy and feudal order.[22] Although this work focused primarily on modern, or at least post-classical, subject matter it was important both for his methodological innovation and the classical parallels that were drawn. Gabriel Daniel drew explicit comparisons between modern France and the nature of Greek and Roman civilisation while Louis Le Gendre compared the art, poetry, music and culture at the time of Charlemagne with that the classical world.[23] However this genre of work was not simply a reaction of a privileged group to Absolutism, it also had wider religious and international connotations. The presence of a growing body of Huguenot historians attacking French despotism gave the controversy an international dimension, invoking broader debates about constitutionalism that would echo throughout the century.[24]

In Britain there was no movement like the *histoire raisonée* but historical debates about liberty and constitutionalism took what may be described today as a 'cultural turn'. Interest in the Roman republic began to focus not merely on the increasingly autocratic nature of political personalities and military leaders but on the structural problems of the Roman state and society which resulted in the collapse of the Republic and the creation of the Empire. In particular, attention was focused on the office and holders of the tribunate, men such as the Gracchi, Saturninus and Clodius. Interest in the tribunate as the popular and democratic element of the constitution grew, with scholars arguing as to its role in this process.[25] Central to this process was Hooke, who argued, against

---

[21] Leffler, 226, 229.
[22] V. Buranelli, 'The Historical and Political Thought of Boulainvilliers', *Journal of the History of Ideas*, 18 (1957), 475–94.
[23] P.K. Leffter, 'French Historians and the Challenge to Louis XIV's Absolutism', *French Historical Studies*, 14 (1985), 1–22.
[24] Leffler, 'French Historians', 16.
[25] For example, Seran de la Tour, *Histoire du tribunat de Rome, depuis sa creation jusqua la reunion de sa puissance a celle de l'empereur Auguste*, 2 vols. (Amsterdam, 1774).

mainstream scholarly opinion, that the tribunate had a positive role to play in the reformation of a decaying system.

Over the next century this aspect of Roman republican history became central to historical debates about the stability of republican constitutions and was used by both radical and conservatives to defend their own political positions.[26] Other celebrated Roman histories also highlighted popular culture as an important explanatory force for constitutional decay and collapse. A satirist once remarked that Gibbon once offered over one hundred different reasons for the fall of Rome. This may or may not be true but it was certainly the case that many of the primary causes were located not in 'high politics', personal morality or political leadership, but rather in the fratricidal nature of political culture, the divisive nature of religion and the social and economic problems of imperial management. By the end of the eighteenth century, both the growth of Roman autocracy and the collapse of imperial power were being explained primarily in cultural terms.

Yet perhaps the most striking change to British scholarship on the ancient world was the steadily growing interest in Greek, as opposed to Roman, history – a change clearly evident by the end of the Napoleonic wars. Integral to this was a growing interest in the political forms of the Greek city-states, igniting fierce debate over the relative merits of Athens and Sparta. While radicals turned to a utopian vision of the latter, moderate reformers fostered a preference for the distinctly commercial Athens. It was only later in the nineteenth century, however, that the gradual belief arose in the supremacy of Athenian democracy as the model for modern constitutions rather than those of the Roman republic or Sparta.[27] For much of the eighteenth century Periclean Athens was a model to be deplored rather than celebrated, and historians tended to follow Aristotle and Plato in condemning Greek models of democracy as rule by the mob or the dispossessed. Far preferable was the republican virtue of Sparta, and when Greek democracy was celebrated at all it was in its Spartan form or in the form of moderate Solonian democracy. Periclean democracy was often regarded as a warning against

---

[26] For a detailed study, see Turner, 'British Politics', 577–99.
[27] On these reputations and debates, see: E. Rawson, *The Spartan Tradition in European Thought* (Oxford, 1969); J. Roberts, *Athens on Trial the Antidemocratic Tradition in Western Thought* (Princeton, 1994); I. Macgregor Morris, 'The Paradigm of Democracy: Sparta in Enlightenment Thought', in T. Figueira (ed.), *Spartan Society* (Swansea, 2004), 339–62; and 'The Refutation of Democracy? Socrates in the Enlightenment', in M.B. Trapp (ed.), *Socrates From Antiquity to the Enlightenment* (Aldershot, 2007), 209–27.

Fig. 1. The octagonal Tower of Winds, Athens
(J. Stuart and N. Revett, *The Antiquities of Athens* (London, 1762–1816),
courtesy of the Joint Library of the Hellenic and Roman Societies)

The publication of views like this illustrated just how much 'history' in Athens remained to be explored and the possibilities that existed for the traveller. The building was also to be the inspiration behind James Stuart's tower of the same name at Shugborough, Staffordshire.

popular rule – a demonstration of how popular rule would only collapse into tyranny and autocracy.[28] This was in dramatic contrast to the late nineteenth century when Periclean models were used to explain and justify the coming of mass democracy in Britain and when art galleries and cultural institutions were erected in honour of the Periclean idea.[29] Admiration of Greek society came first, not so much through a celebration of its politics, but its literature, with the likes of Dryden, Fénelon, Pope and Glover consciously emulating and reworking classical texts. This fostered a wider interest in Greek politics, fusing with the Greek element of the classical republican tradition.[30] Related to this process was a growing awareness of Greek art.[31] Winckelmann followed Shaftesbury in arguing

[28] M. Herman Hansen, 'The Tradition of Athenian Democracy', *Greece and Rome*, 39 (1992), 14–30.
[29] 'Periclean Preston – Public Art and the Classical Tradition in Nineteenth-Century Lancashire', *Northern History*, 40 (2003).
[30] On the Greek republican tradition, see E. Nelson, *The Greek Tradition in Republican Thought* (Cambridge, 2004).
[31] For a recent discussion of the role of classical (and neo-classical) art in Britain, see D. Kurtz, *The Reception of Classical Art in Britain* (Oxford, 2000).

that cultural achievement can only be fostered in a free society, and helped to make fifth-century art particularly fashionable – a fashion that encouraged a re-evaluation of Greek, and particularly Athenian constitutional forms. Athens increasingly became the focus of scholarly attention partly because of the availability of literary sources and the fashion for translation. However much of the explanation for this trend must be due to the work of travellers and artists who 'rediscovered' the remains of Athens in the seventeenth and eighteenth century. In Britain the expeditions of the Society of Dilettanti were particularly influential, especially the publications of Stuart and Revett, which provided the first detailed depictions of key classical sites in Athens.[32] Not only did they change fashions in British architecture towards a distinctively 'neo-Grec' style, they helped encourage an increasing body of scholarly literature on ancient Greece. History was still written largely as a didactic art. Successful models were celebrated and tyrannical ones critiqued. The growth of popular sympathy for the Greek national cause encouraged historians and poets to consider whether great cultural achievements of the past could be revived. Parallels were drawn with the Persian wars and modern-day Ottoman oppression.[33] This movement is most closely associated with the 'Byronic Revolution', but literary and political philhellenism had a long history, one which constantly made reference to fifth- and fourth-century achievement in support of modern Greek nationalism.[34] Inevitably this meant that some periods in Greek history were neglected. The Hellenistic period was almost entirely overlooked. Alexander received little interest until the nineteenth century. Greece in the Roman period barely received any attention until a gradual growth in interest in early church history and the period of Constantine. This focus is partly explained by source availability, but the interest in the social and cultural basis of civic life meant that there was a close relationship between artistic fashions and the direction of historical scholarship. Historians had become preoccupied with understanding the cultural basis for human achievement.

[32] J. Stuart and N. Revett, *Antiquities of Athens*, 4 vols. (London, 1762–1816); D. Watkin, *Athenian Stuart, Pioneer of the Greek Revival* (London, 1982); J.M. Crook, *The Greek Revival* (London, 1972); D. Stillman, *English Neo-classical Architecture*, 2 vols. (London, 1988); D. Watkin, *The Life and Work of C.R. Cockerell* (London, 1974).
[33] For background, see: T. Spencer, *Fair Greece, Sad Relic* (London 1954); T. Kaiser, 'The Evil Empire? The Debate on Turkish Despotism in Eighteenth-Century French Political Culture', *Journal of Modern History*, 72 (2000), 6–34.
[34] D. Constantine, *Early Greek Travellers and the Hellenic Ideal* (Cambridge, 1984); T. Webb, *English Romantic Hellenism* (Manchester, 1982); I. Macgregor Morris, 'To Make a New Thermopylae: Hellenism, Greek Liberation, and the Battle of Thermopylae', *Greece & Rome*, 47 (2000), 211–30.

The focus of history writing had changed. Gone was the Renaissance preoccupation with revealing the moral strengths and weaknesses of individual leaders and instead there was a focus on the moral and cultural health of the broader community. However this focus on cultural history and the conditions of freedoms raised some problems for traditional notions and conceptualisations of Providence. Firstly the idea of Providence was, of course, used to justify Absolutism. Therefore those attacking notions of kingly rule also had to attack prevailing notions of Providence. This was at a time when existing theological doctrines surrounding Providence were under epistemological attack and, at least in Protestant circles, being fundamentally reinterpreted. Indeed, by the second half of the eighteenth century it was not uncommon for the notion of Providence to be satirised, or even used to demonstrate the alleged primitive and unsophisticated nature of Islamic or Roman Catholic systems of belief.[35] Students of historiography, however, should be cautious about viewing the eighteenth century as a triumph of rationalism over religion or Providence. Some historians and *philosophes* did, of course, eventually come to reject Christian theology entirely. These were, however, in a minority and the majority of prominent eighteenth-century historians retained Christian belief while rejecting Christian chronologies, events or patterns of causation. Similarly most of the major literary, scientific and philosophers of the time – Dryden, Cowper, Boyle, Locke, Berkeley – remained committed Christians. The fundamental questioning of the historicity of the New Testament did not necessarily undermine the faith of leading scholars.[36]

Moreover, in the British context, it was empiricism, rather than rationalism and abstract philosophy, which represented the most fundamental attack on the established order of knowledge.[37] This reflected the British empiricist tradition of philosophy but also the increasingly important British traditions of popular antiquarianism that were prevalent in aristocratic circles. Ideas from rationalist philosophy may have been utilised in the process of source criticism but this was history driven by sources not abstract ideas. This can best be seen in the work of Nathanial Hooke.[38] Like his French contemporaries in the

---

[35] See R. Chandler, *Travels in Asia Minor* (London, 1775).
[36] G. Wells, 'Stages of New Testament Criticism', *Journal of the History of Ideas*, 30 (1969), 147–60.
[37] D. Greene, 'Augustinianism and Empiricism: A Note on Eighteenth-Century Intellectual History', *Eighteenth-Century Studies*, 1 (1967), 33–68.
[38] I. Macgregor Morris, J. Moore, G. Sampson, 'Nathanial Hooke, Roman Historian', *Dictionary of Literary Biography, British Eighteenth-Century Historians* (New York, 2006).

*histoire raisonée*, his was a political history that made direct reference to contemporary political conditions. Yet it was driven by the desire to reconstruct Roman Republican sources drawing upon consul lists and the syntheses of earlier scholars, to compose an account of political decay.

Like the earlier French schools Hooke wrote in the annalistic tradition while gradually moving to a more non-linear model of historical interpretation and, in particular, focusing on the cultural processes which rendered key political disputes, such as the land question, of such great long-term importance. Approaches that embedded themselves in the detail of cultural history and emphasised geographical diversity naturally made it difficult to adopt a strictly linear and chronological approach to narrative writing. This is evident in Gibbon where the need to write a cultural history which encompasses the complexity of the Mediterranean World forces him, in the latter stages of the *Decline and Fall*, to move to a history organised conceptually and geographically rather than strictly chronologically. The move to non-linear histories was, therefore, partly due to cultural history approaches of the *histoire raisonée*, partly the traditions of English Empiricism and party changing literary fashions that favoured sweeping epic over focused narrative. This can be most obviously seen in the 'cult of Homer' in the mid-eighteenth century when Homeric literature reached its apogee of popularity and when many authors attempted to emulate epic forms by way of popular fiction or poetry.[39] Some produced fictive epic accounts based upon historical adaptation. Glover's *Leonidas* was a particularly popular and widely celebrated example of this genre, rendering Glover at least as popular as any contemporary historian.[40] It is not surprising therefore that the structural nature of historical writing changed as epic forms that emphasised digression and complex plot structure grew in popularity. This, in a sense, was the victory of Herodotus over Thucydides. A history limited, in the main, to a narrative of recent politics, disputes and conflicts was being replaced by one which sought to preserve and understand the complexity of cultural history, understand its geographic and ethnographic nature and attempt a rationalised synthesis to understand the web of causation. This decentring of politics was one

---

[39] K. Simonsuuri, *Homer's Original Genius – Eighteenth-Century Notions of the early Greek Epic* (Cambridge 1979), esp. chs. 11–12; D.M. Forster, *Homer in English Criticism: the Historical Approach in the Eighteenth Century* (Yale, 1947).

[40] R. Glover, *Leonidas* (London, 1737). See I. Macgregor Morris, *The Age of Leonidas: Hellenism and the Classical Tradition in the Enlightenment* (forthcoming).

which Momigliano recognised but, arguably, failed to explain. Only by understanding the broader literary culture of the eighteenth century and its distinctive modern preoccupations are we likely to arrive at a satisfactory answer. Eighteenth-century writers may have framed their ancient histories using classical models but their preoccupations with republicanism, empire, tyranny and trade were not identical to those of the ancients, however much classical precedents shaped everyday cultural behaviour. Momigliano was correct in emphasising the importance of understanding past historians but past historians can only be understood in the context of their own material worlds and the changes that take place within them. This provides them with their specific orientations and goals and allows the trajectory of historiography to be plotted against the broader intellectual history of the period.

In many respects reconstructing the material world of the past historians is difficult. In the case of some of the most celebrated, such as Gibbon, substantial collections of private papers allow for a forensic examination of his life and activities. However, for other landmark historians such as Hooke and Mitford no such collections are available and reconstruction of their broader social connections can be difficult. In the case of Hooke there is considerable uncertainly about many aspects of his life, including the details of his religious belief, whether all his children were brought up in the Catholic tradition and the extent to which he was involved in Jacobite agitation in Britain before the rebellion of 1745.[41] His work may have been financed through the personal affection of his patroness or he may have been blackmailing her because of her late husband's associations with the Jacobite movement. There is even some uncertainty as to how many of the four volumes of his history of the Roman republic he actually wrote. The third volume is written in an eclectic style suggesting that it may have been heavily edited before publication. The final volume, published long after his death, is a much weaker tome taking a somewhat different political stance and may have been written by his son from his father's notes. These are some of the problems that beset the student of historiography – and Hooke is a relatively well-known figure featuring in a number of biographical studies. Many historical scholars were much less well known and rarely engaged in the circles of major literary groups or celebrated aristocratic societies such as the Society of Dilettanti. Therefore there are some methodological problems in assembling the

---

[41] At least of one of this children, Luke, was brought up as a Catholic, see T. O' Connor, *An Irish Theologian in Enlightenment Europe: Luke Joseph Hooke 1714–96* (Dublin, 1995).

scholarly worlds in which leading historians inhabited.[42] In France the world of scholarship tended to be more institutionalised than in Britain. The tradition of Catholic scholarship in major religious houses across the country continued. Antiquarian groups flourished and in some cases received state patronage. Germany had a wide network of universities which, by the end of the eighteenth century, had established schools of philology and classics. In England there were, of course, only two ancient universities and few of the country's most celebrated historians were attached to them. There were some significant exceptions. Robert Wood was a fellow at Cambridge but his Cambridge networks seem to have had only limited influence over his major research projects and scholarly interests.[43] His celebrated expeditions to Palmyra, Baalbec and Troy were organised privately and owed little to his Cambridge associations.[44] For Wood, like many British scholars, private money and aristocratic scholarly networks provided the basis for his work.[45] By the end of the eighteenth century, universities and scholarly societies were becoming more important for the dissemination of research findings. Scottish universities were particularly important in this respect. Le Chevalier, for example, chose the University of Edinburgh as the place to announce his 'discovery' – erroneous as it turned out – of Troy and an English translation of his finding was published by the learned society he addressed. However for most celebrated historians of the period it is essential to unravel the web of private scholarly connections that an individual enjoyed. This is not an easy task and may explain why historiographical studies of British subjects often explore the work of the historian but rarely the historian and his intellectual network.

Despite the limitations of detailed private sources one can still, however, reconstruct something of the material and cultural world in which eighteenth-century historians operated. Momigliano's observation about the incorporation of antiquarian techniques and material culture into the process of writing history is clearly important. At one level the

---

[42] Classical scholarship – that is the study of classical languages – has received more systematic attention in this respect, see for example: R. Pfeiffer, *History of Classical Scholarship* (Oxford, 1976); C. Brink, *English Classical Scholarship* (Cambridge, 1985); R. Bolgar, *The Classical Heritage and its Beneficiaries* (Cambridge, 1954); M.L. Clark, *Greek Studies in England, 1700–1830* (London, 1945).

[43] J. Butterworth, 'Robert Wood and Troy: A Comparative Failure', *Bulletin of the Institute of Classical Studies*, 32 (1985).

[44] R. Wood, *The Ruins of Palmyra* (London, 1753), *The Ruins of Baalbec* (London, 1757), *Essay on the Original Genius and Writings of Homer* (London, 1775).

[45] T. Spencer, 'Robert Wood and the Problem of Troy in the Eighteenth Century', *Journal of the Warburg and Courtauld Institutes*, 20 (1957), 75–105.

desire to use material evidence as an antidote to scepticism and to validate events can be seen as a natural response of the historical pyrrhonism of the time.[46] Some mid eighteenth-century writers took literary scepticism to the extreme. Père Hardouin, finding contradictions between numismatic sources and ancient sources, concluded that all the ancient texts, with the exception of Cicero, Pliny, Horace's *Satires* and *Epistles*, and Virgil's *Georgics*, were late fourteenth-century Italian forgeries.[47] Material evidence appeared to offer, in the words of Francesco Bianchini 'symbol and proof of what happened'.[48] However this shift towards interest in material culture cannot merely be seen as a philosophical response to the methodological problem of validating literary evidence. There are few examples of specific texts being validated by a particular archaeological discovery or synthesised numismatic collection. Rather material evidence supplied additional material to fuel historical debates and, sometimes, offer re-evaluation of the contexts of particular literary evidence. The new historians of the eighteenth century were keen to utilise material evidence because it appeared to offer the prospect of a more complete history, one that went beyond a Thucydidean historical narrative of political events towards a more complex history of culture and society.[49] Sometimes new evidence, such as the discovery of the Capitoline marbles in the 1540s, helped a broader understanding of politics and society by revealing the names – and potentially the social connections – of a range of forgotten public figures who played a critical role in the state.

In other cases, such as the discovery of Pompeii and Herculaneum, excavation revealed a complete society, almost frozen in time, engaged in its daily business and with its key elements of artistic achievements largely intact. These types of discoveries not only offered the opportunity to explore the social context of political history, they offered the opportunity to write a new type of history that did not necessarily give primacy to the political. New evidence meant social and cultural factors could be given greater explanatory power in new accounts of long term historical change.

It would be wrong, however, to assume that the historical scholar was the primary force in stimulating interest in the material culture of

---

[46] A. Momigliano, 'Ancient History and the Antiquarian', in *Studies in Historiography* (London, 1966), first published in the *Journal of the Warburg and Courtauld Institutes*, 13 (1950), 285–315.
[47] Momigliano, *Studies*, 16.
[48] Cited in Momiglaino, *Studies*, 14–15.
[49] M. Phillips, 'Reconsiderations on History and Antiquarianism: Arnaldo Momigliano and the Historiography of Eighteenth-Century Britain', *Journal of the History of Ideas*, 57 (1996), 297–316, esp. 300–1.

the ancient world. In reality the fashion for archaeological investigation was rooted in deeper antiquarian and artistic traditions.[50] The collecting of antique marble sculpture had a long history across Europe and its relationship with antiquarian research has been well documented. The roots of this tradition are deep and complex, with the Papacy itself playing some role in stimulating renewed Renaissance interest in classical Roman statuary and, of course, classical inscriptions. In Britain the cultural activities of Charles I and rivalries between Lord Arundel and the Duke of Buckingham help establish collecting as a popular fashion amongst aristocratic circles.[51] This process was accelerated by the growing popularity of the Grand Tour at the end of the seventeenth century.[52] By the middle of the eighteenth century, Rome had a network of dealers in antiquarian objects to cater for the tourist market. Rising prices acted as a stimulus for the break-up of many of the Italian collections and the dissemination of classical statuary across Europe, with Britain, France and Russia being the most prominent destinations for major pieces.[53] In some cases the dealers were foreigners, with British and French dealers being particularly prominent. Often they would not only deal in antiquities but sponsor artists and even new excavations. In Rome the most prominent British dealer was Gavin Hamilton, who commissioned digs to enhance the emerging collection of the young Charles Townley.[54] These included celebrated excavations at Hadrian's Villa and Pantanello Lake.[55] Even in Athens, a city far beyond the traditional European Grand Tour, commercial dealers began to emerge to cater for the more adventurous tourist. The expedition and publications of Stuart and

[50] R. Sweet, *Antiquaries: The Discovery of the Past in Eighteenth-Century Britain* (Cambridge, 2004).
[51] J. Scott, *The Pleasures of Antiquity British Collectors of Greece and Rome* (Yale, 2003), esp. 11–30.
[52] J. Black, *The British Abroad: the Grand Tour in the Eighteenth Century* (Stroud, 1992), E. Chaney, *The Evolution of the Grand Tour* (London, 1998), C. Hornsby, *The Impact of Italy: the Grand Tour and Beyond* (London, 2000), H. Tregaskis, *Beyond the Grand Tour: the Levant Lunatics* (London, 1979). The Grand Tour was progressively 'democratised' in the later eighteenth century with important implications for cultural history, see L. Withey, *Grand Tours and Cook's Tours* (London, 1998).
[53] A. Clark, 'The Development of the Collections and Museums of 18th-Century Rome', *Art Journal*, 26 (1966–7), 136.
[54] G. Vaughan, 'The Collecting of Classical Antiquities in England in the 18th Century: a Study of Charles Townley (1737–1805) and His Circle', University of Oxford D.Phil. thesis (1988), 176.
[55] For a description of the excavations, see A.H. Smith, 'Gavin Hamilton's Letter to Charles Townley', *Journal of Hellenic Studies*, 21 (1901), 306–21. D. Irwin, 'Gavin Hamilton: Archaeologist, Painter and Dealer', *Art Bulletin*, 44 (1962).

Fig. 2. The Athenian Acropolis
(E. Dodwell, *Views in Greece* (London, 1821), courtesy of the
Joint Library of the Hellenic and Roman Societies)

This interesting view of the Acropolis, from the period of Elgin's expedition, shows the residence of the Ottoman governor of Athens and other Ottoman dwellings that were cleared shortly after the creation of the modern Greek state.

Fig. 3. The modern (early nineteenth-century) agora of Athens
(E. Dodwell, *Views in Greece* (London, 1821), courtesy of the
Joint Library of the Hellenic and Roman Societies)

This illustrates the prominent Islamic presence and the cosmopolitan nature of the town's population before the Greek War of Independence. Views like this appealed to both 'classical' and 'oriental' tastes and helped popularise interest in Greek history.

Revett made it a popular destination for a new generation of explorer, keen to obtain original works of Greek art rather than Roman copies. By the time the generation of Gell, Dodwell and Byron visited Athens, the French consul Fauvel had established an apparently lucrative trade in antiquities and assisted Elgin in obtaining permission to remove the marbles from the Parthenon.[56] The public excitement surrounding the display of the marbles in London demonstrates just how much popular interest there was in the material culture of the classical past and how an aristocratic fashion had become an important cultural canon. Moreover major collections were not just limited to a few great townhouses of London. The fashion for collecting meant that many of the great provincial families had sculpture collections and some had even reconstructed their homes – and sometimes their gardens – to imitate the work of classical, and particularly, Greek sculpture. Collectors often established networks and even those without family collections or a classical education began to ape the great collections of the time. In Lancashire Charles Townley developed a major collection of statuary, mainly from Rome, locating it both in his London town house and his Burnley mansion. This had a major impact on Henry Ince Blundell, a relatively ill-educated man whose family money had been made from the mineral wealth of their estates. Soon Blundell was not only using Townley's agents in Rome to acquire items for a new collection for himself but asking Townley to help him construct a dedicated sculpture gallery in the style of a miniature Pantheon to display these works.[57] Both collections contributed to the broader dissemination a taste for collecting. Blundell's collection was opened to the public and became a major centre of attraction in north Lancashire. Townley also sought to establish a public museum in north-west England but ultimately his legatees donated the works to the British Museum, where they became the foundational collection of today's Department of Greek and Roman Antiquities.[58]

Interest in material culture was not, however, just limited to collecting elements of 'high' cultural production such as statuary. Items of statuary in good condition commanded very high prices and were limited in availability, and many items in Italian collections were heavily mutilated and over-restored. Even well-preserved items did not always accord with eighteenth-century notions of taste – Blundell has become notorious

---

[56] For background on Athens around this time, see C. Eliot, 'Gennadeion Notes III: Athens in the time of Lord Byron', *Hesperia*, 37 (1968), 134–58.
[57] See J. Fejfer, *The Ince Blundell Collection of Classical Sculpture* (Liverpool, 1997).
[58] H. Ellis, *The Townley Gallery of Classical Sculpture in the British Museum* (London, 1846).

for demanding that a hermaphrodite be 'restored' and turned into a Venus.[59] Many collectors struggled to fund excavations and meet the very high prices being demanded for antique marbles in the second half of the eighteenth century. Townley appears to have run out of money in the 1770s, buying large amounts on account and struggling to pay Hamilton's bills. It is not surprising then that interest began to turn to other material objects of the classical world, particularly those that were plentiful, transportable and could offer a narrative about their origin and their creators. Coins were probably the most popular object to collect and the history of coin collecting had deep roots in Renaissance antiquarian traditions. As Momigliano points out they could sometimes form the foundation stones of historical writing, with numismatics playing a central part in both Bianchini's ecclesiastic histories and Valliant's history of the Ptolemies and Seleucids.[60] In Britain the antiquarian tradition of collecting coins from Roman sites was particularly strong, not least because literary evidence provided few clues about many locations and the only possibility of accurate dating of particular earthworks often came through an examination of coin finds. The dissemination of information about coin collections was also relatively straightforward, with even primitive printing technology and modest artistic skills being able to reproduce such objects in a tolerably accurate way.

Coins provided a variety of data for the historian. At a most fundamental level they offered the possibility of dating particular camps, buildings or roads to specific periods. They often offered a modicum of literary evidence and, sometimes, cult or religious symbolism. They also offered portraiture and, occasionally, the depiction of historical or mythical events. However in this respect coins were somewhat limited simply because their size and shape provided for little detail or elaboration. Pottery could be much more valuable and offered more detailed and sophisticated depictions of events, stories, or individuals. It could also contribute to debates about the development of particular artistic styles and techniques – and possibly, when there were sufficient numbers over a large enough period of time, even a history of the chronological development of those styles and techniques. Moreover, by comparing them to other material forms, particularly sculpture, there was the possibility of writing a new art historical account of classical times, taking into account the 'popular' visual culture of pottery and the 'high'

---

[59] H. Blundell, *Engravings and Etchings of Sepulchral Monuments, Cinery Urn, Gems, Bronzes, Prints, Greek Inscriptions, Fragments Etc in the Collection of Henry Blundell at Ince*, vol. I (London, 1809), 41. See also Fejfer, *Ince Blundell Collection*.

[60] Momigliano, *Studies*, 8.

public culture of statuary. This particular development, however took some time not least because there was reluctance to accept pottery as having the same status as other objects of classical material culture. By the end of the eighteenth century, major archaeological excavations had revealed the wealth of historical evidence to be found on pottery and earthenware but there were still only a limited number of collectors. Of these Sir William Hamilton was probably the most famous and his desire to publish his collection in a major multi-volume work did much to give this collecting genre respectability.[61] Josiah Wedgewood's production of modern pottery in a mock Grecian style demonstrated that popular taste for these classical forms was widely shared but its impact on historical research was limited until the nineteenth century.[62] This suggests that the new history of the eighteenth century, while turning its focus towards a history of the social and cultural, was still a little conservative in its reading of material culture. Sources which had high contemporary cultural value, such as statuary, or which were embedded in existing antiquarian traditions, such as coins, were integrated into new historical narrative. Evidence from sources such as pottery took more time to diffuse into the historical consciousness. More work is required on this process of diffusion but the uneven nature of the process may help explain the growing institutional and methodological division between historians and archaeologists as the nineteenth century progressed.

It is important, however, to remember that archaeology was not merely concerned with the removal of material objects from historical sites. Napoleon's archaeological exploits in Egypt and Elgin's work in Greece are often seen as symbolic of a 'heroic' age of archaeology concerned with the large-scale removal and preservation of historic remains.[63] Yet some of the most famous and high-profile expeditions saw the removal of remarkably few material remains other than those that were easily portable. Spon and Wheeler were primarily concerned with establishing that significant ruins of ancient Athens existed and describing their nature and extent.[64] Stuart and Revett were concerned with recording the dimensions and architectural characteristics of specific monuments and their place in the current topography of Athens and its surroundings.[65]

---

[61] I. Jenkins and K. Sloan (eds.), *Vases and Volcanoes Sir William Hamilton and his Collection* (London, 1996).
[62] M. Vickers, 'Value and Simplicity: Eighteenth-Century Taste and the Study of Greek Vases', *Past and Present*, 116 (1987), 98–137.
[63] For a study of the 'acquisitive culture' of this age in Greece, see C. P. Bracken, *Antiquities Acquired The Spoliation of Greece* (Newton Abbot, 1975).
[64] G. Wheeler, *A Journey into Greece, in Company of Dr Spon of Lyons* (London, 1682).
[65] Stuart and Revett, *Antiquities*.

Wood's expeditions to Palmyra and Baalbec focused on actually finding the cities, mapping their geographical location and recording key architectural fragments. His expedition to the Troad was also one that concentrated on the correct identification of the basic historical geography of the area, attempting to separate history from myth and to validate the accuracy of Homeric topography.[66] Chandler's work in Asia Minor followed a very similar pattern and, even much later, Leake was primarily focused on the identifying the correct historical geography of particular sites and recording inscriptions, not on the removal of material objects.[67] It was not until the 1840s that there were serious attempts to 'recover' major architectural trophies from southern Asia Minor. Charles Fellows' work in Lycia and the Xanthus valley was celebrated precisely because this type of expedition was unusual.[68] Therefore for much of the eighteenth century classical archaeology was as much concerned with the re-assembly of historical geography and the accurate identification of particular sites than the assembly of material remains. This was partly because ancient geographies, particularly Strabo, were often positively misleading in their detail and it was clearly essential to accurately identify a site before expensive and time-consuming excavations could take place. Greece and Asia Minor were part of the Ottoman Empire whose provincial governors were often cautious about permitting Frankish 'treasure hunters' to explore too freely. Much of the countryside was lawless with the possibility of bandit attack all too common. Most archaeological travellers and explorers donned Turkish dress for protection and travelled in small groups in order not to draw attention to themselves. Even when the authorities were co-operative, transporting bulk loads of antiquities could be prohibitively expensive – as Lord Elgin found out to his cost.[69] Much archaeological exploration therefore tended to involve the copying and collection of particular inscriptions, the opening of readily-available tombs, the sketching of major monuments and the delineation of local geography.

---

[66] For details of his and other early expeditions to the Troad, see J. Cook, *The Troad An Archaeological and Topographical Study* (Oxford, 1973), 14–44.

[67] W. Leake, *Journal of a Tour in Asia Minor* (London, 1824); J.M. Wagstaffe, 'Colonel Leake and the Classical Topography of Asia Minor', *Anatolian Studies*, 37 (1987), 23–35.

[68] C. Fellows, *A Journal Written during an Excursion in Asia Minor* (London 1839), *An Account of Discoveries in Lycia, being a Journal kept during a Second Excursion in Asia Minor* (London, 1841); *An Account of the Ionic Trophy Monument Excavated at Xanthus* (London, 1848).

[69] The best study of the Elgin controversy is W. St. Clair, *Lord Elgin and the Marbles* (Oxford, 1998).

Thus a major archaeological innovation in the second half of the eighteenth century was not only the emergence of new historical geographies of the eastern Mediterranean but the emergence of historical geography as a distinctive historical genre. It was a genre that combined traditional literary techniques, drawing on Strabo and Pausanias in particular, forms of archaeological explanation and methods of geographical and cartographical survey. However it was also linked to a particular literary fashion of the eighteenth century – that of travel writing. The development of this fashion was assisted by the growth of the Grand Tour but also by the increasing globalisation of travel opportunities and trade. Many reports on archaeological explorations of Greece and Asia Minor were heavily influenced by this genre. The accounts of Wood and Chandler frequently spend as much time discussing the experience of travel and incidents on the way as the classical sites themselves. Figures such as Bruce, who explored the Nile delta and sought the source of the Blue Nile, wrote dramatic romantic accounts of their ventures – so dramatic and romantic that in the case of Bruce some doubted whether the expedition had ever actually taken place.[70] Even studious and somewhat staid characters such as William Gell provided documentary details about the events experienced on the journey and the personal experience of the site itself. Far from pursuing cold objectivity the traveller and historical geographer often became caught in the excitement of the moment.[71] This was particularly the case with Troy, where bitter debate reigned over the location of the site and the accuracy of Homer's topography. Sitting atop Mount Ida William Franklin constructed the entire scene in his imagination:

> In the plain below, every circumstance as described by Homer is minutely recognized; the city and tower of Ilium below our feet, the sources of Scamander, the rich and fertile plain of Troy watered by the Simios and the Scamander whose sight is obscured by its deep and sedgy banks, the barrow of Aesyetes, the Sigaean and Rhoetean promontories, and the situation of the Grecian fleet, present a succession of pleasing and interesting objects, while the picture is bounded with a double view of the Hellespont and Aegean sea, and the islands of Lemnos, Imbros and Samothracia. In short nothing is wanting to complete the scene, and the enthusiasm of the moment is perhaps excusable when the exulting traveller shall exclaim, 'Troy exists'.[72]

---

[70] J. Bruce, *Travels to Discover the Source of the Nile, In the Years 1768, 1769, 1770, 1771, 1772 and 1773* (London, 1790); M. Bredin, *The Pale Abyssinian: A Life of James Bruce, African Explorer and Adventurer* (London, 2001).
[71] W. Gell, *The Topography of Troy and its Vicinity* (London, 1804), 10. Also see Gell, *Itinerary*.
[72] Franklin, *Remarks*, 26.

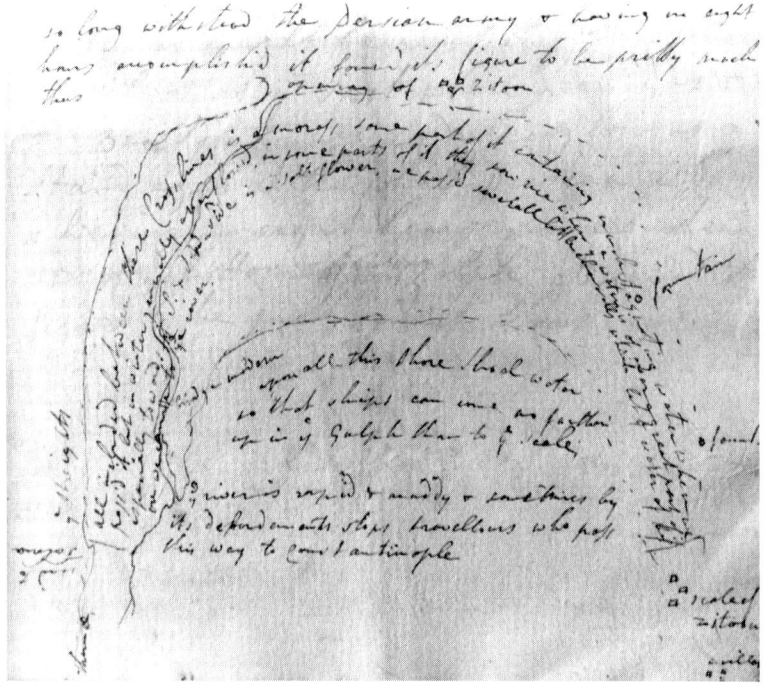

Fig. 4. Map of Thermopylae by Robert Wood, 1751
(Wood Diaries (unpublished manuscript), courtesy of the
Joint Library of the Hellenic and Roman Societies)

Franklin was not the only one to get carried away by landscape. There were similar romantic and sentimental attachments to the battlefields of the Persian war. When Byron wrote the famous lines at Marathon "standing on the Persian grave, I cannot think myself a slave", he was invoked widespread cultural perceptions of the site as a place of pilgrimage. Thermopylae also became a place of pilgrimage, assisted by travel literature and popular accounts of Leonidas' sacrifice, not least Glover's celebrated poem of the early eighteenth century.[73] By the end of the eighteenth century, authors were beginning to attempt comprehensive guides to Greece. The guide that most classical travellers used was, of course, Pausanias' survey of the second century A.D. that, despite its sometimes obtuse content, allowed explorers a reasonable opportunity to identify the relative locations of major cities and, sometimes, particular

---

[73] I. Macgregor Morris, 'Shrines of the Mighty: Rediscovering the Battlefields of the Persian Wars', in E. Bridges, E. Hall and P.J. Rhodes (eds.), *Cultural Responses to the Persian Wars: Antiquity to the Third Millennium* (Oxford, 2007), 231–64.

sites within cities. Guides produced by Edward Dodwell and later Christopher Wordsworth partly mimicked the structure and approach of Pausanias, while adding anecdotes and modern historical observations.[74]

The significance of this type of exploratory travel literature was the impact it had on the writing of histories. Names and places were given material form and brought alive for the historical scholar even if he was unable to visit the places mentioned. History took a distinctly geographical and topographical turn. This was necessitated by the desire of some historians to write in epic form but it was also heavily influenced by popularity of a new travel literature. The later chapters of Gibbon's *Decline and Fall*, demonstrate the importance of comparative geographical and spatial histories in understanding long-term historical change. Spatial and geographical issues also became crucial to understanding military campaigns and the collapse of the Roman republic into imperial despotism. It was not until the later nineteenth century that historical geography emerged as a clearly identifiable discipline but by the time William Leake published his accounts of the cities of Greece and Asia Minor, methods of historical geography and historical survey had become an established form of historical analysis.[75] This work could not only reveal more about classical literature – whether it be Homer, Strabo or Pausanias – but it could contribute to a broader understanding of specific historical events, politics or warfare.

Yet the cultural and geographical turns were not the only ones of significance. Alongside the rigorous empiricism of traditional archaeologists, historians and travellers was the growth of conceptual, comparative history that attempted to 'read' beyond the immediate sources to develop long-term theories of historical change. It attempted to theorise where existing histories were silent often by drawing comparisons with primitive societies of the present day. This trend was also assisted by the growth of travel and exploration literature and particularly the proto-anthropological texts examining the cultures of India and the Americas. It facilitated the writing of new histories of 'barbarian races' or those who left no literary evidence of their existence. The discovery in 1653 of the grave of Childeric, a fifth-century A.D. Merovingian ruler, was just one example of how material and visual evidence offered apparently exciting

---

[74] E. Dodwell, *A Classical and Topographical Tour through Greece* (London, 1819), C. Wordsworth, *Greece* (London, 1839).

[75] Even Leake's formalistic style of reporting and analysis contained elements of the travel literature genre. See W. Leake, *Travels in the Morea* (London, 1830), *Travels in Northern Greece* (London, 1835), *The Topography of Athens* (London, 1841).

opportunities to explore history beyond the received text.[76] It took time for historians and antiquarians to develop systematic ways of interpreting this category of evidence and the process of diffusion into historical accounts was uneven. Yet they did bring with them more theoretical approaches and, arguably, more methodological sophistication in the comparative treatment of evidence. These approaches often attempted to read the visual evidence and symbols of societies in order either to explain universal factors in human development or the diffusion of cultural ideas across peoples and continents. Something of this approach can be seen in Winkelmann who attempts to classify and organise cities and cultures according to the types of artistic work they produce.[77] Later D'Hancarville, under the influence of the philosophical approaches of both Diderot and English empiricism, attempted to take the approach one step further by using artistic styles to plot the growing sophistication of human development and thus date particular sites or material evidence. In D'Hancarville's case this approach was undermined by a tendency to assume that all crude works were of early date and more sophisticated works later, regardless of the context in which they were found. However D'Hancarville's real significance lies in his attempt to write a history of signs and symbols and explain through them the emergence of similar religious beliefs, motifs and practices from civilisations many thousands of miles apart. Many then, and now, consider this an unconvincing form of pyscho-history but its importance was the way in which it pointed to the opportunity to study classical civilisations in comparative perspective.

Far from ignoring non-Western peoples, many historians attempted to understand documented Western history within a universal historical framework – one that postulated a common path of human development while recognising the different meanings of religious and cultural practice in particular historical contexts. This type of reasoning was not only one which found favour in the eighteenth century – notably with Volney and Dupuis – but was to have longer term historical significance with thinkers from Fraser to Freud adopting aspects of this type of historical reasoning. This form of conceptual and comparative history did not find universal favour but it contributed to the growing methodological tool box of the eighteenth-century historian who had already embraced cultural history and historical geography to open up new avenues of

---

[76] P. Burke, 'Images as Evidence in Seventeenth-Century Europe', *Journal of the History of Ideas*, 64 (2003), 273–96, esp. 284–6.

[77] For the context of Winckelmann's contribution, see A. Potts, *Flesh and the Ideal: Winckelmann and the Origins of Art History* (London, 1994).

historical explanation. The comparative history of civilisations could be one that was driven by tradition empiricism, in the style of Ferguson's histories and proto-sociology of civil society, or one that drew on the psychological and epistemological approaches that were to be influential in the development of anthropology. The eighteenth century may have been a period when the traditions of antiquarianism and historical erudition came together but historians of the period did much more than simply combine and enhance existing traditions. They changed the focus of history to one that gave prominence to culture, embraced geographical and spatial questions and developed interdisciplinary and comparative techniques. In many respects they established the key elements of historiographical modernity.

# PART ONE

Historical Controversies and Historical Consciousness

## 2. Xenophon and the Greek Tradition in British Political Thought*

### Doohwan Ahn

### I

In spite of the recent rehabilitation of Xenophon (431–355 B.C.) as a key political theorist of Greek antiquity, primarily in American political science by disciples of the late university of Chicago professor Leo Strauss,[1] his name has seldom figured in the study of the history of political thought.[2] This is quite surprising given that nearly all the major political authors whose writings we readily include in the so-called 'Western canon', from Marcus Tullius Cicero and Niccolò Machiavelli through to Montesquieu and Jean-Jacques Rousseau, had shown no hesitation at all in expressing publicly their intellectual debts to this all-round student of Socrates.[3] As Strauss perceptively noted in his influential trilogy on Xenophon's Socratic learning, 'Xenophon was generally considered as a wise man and a classic in the precise sense until the end of the eighteenth century'.[4] Though Strauss's prime objective was to excavate the genuine Socratic

---

* The second section on kingship is partly reprinted from my article entitled 'The Politics of Royal Education: Xenophon's Education of Cyrus in Early Eighteenth-Century Europe', appearing in *The Leadership Quarterly*, 19 (2008), 439–52, © 2008, with permission from Elsevier.
[1] See C. Nadon, *Xenophon's Prince: Republic and Empire in the* Cyropaedia (Berkeley, 2001); J. Howland, 'Xenophon's Philosophic Odyssey: On the *Anabasis* and Plato's *Republic*', *The American Political Science Review*, 94 (2000), 875–89.
[2] Take for example, E. Nelson's *Greek Tradition in Republican Thought* (Cambridge, 2004), 128, 134.
[3] Cicero, 'Letter 114 (IX. 25) Cicero to Papirius Paetus', in *Letters to Friends*, vol. II, ed. and trans. D. R. Shackleton Bailey (Cambridge, Massachusetts, 2001), 2–3; Machiavelli, *The Prince*, ed. Q. Skinner and R. Price (Cambridge, 1988), 53–4; Montesquieu, *The Spirit of the Laws*, eds. A.M. Cohler, B.C. Miller, and H.S. Stone (Cambridge, 1989), 12, 39–40, 49–50, 112–14, 348–9, 362–4; Rousseau, *Emile or On Education*, trans. A. Bloom (New York, 1979), 343.
[4] *On Tyranny: An Interpretation of Xenophon's* Hiero (Ithaca, 1968), 25. The other two volumes are *Xenophon's Socrates* (Ithaca, 1972) and *Xenophon's Socratic Discourse: An Interpretation of the* Oeconomicus (Ithaca, 1970). For more on Strauss's Xenophon, see J. Clay, 'The Real Leo Strauss', *The New York Times* (7 June, 2003).

synthesis of theory and practice from Xenophon's three recollections of the Greek sage, *The Memorabilia*, *Apology*, and *Symposium*, which, he believed, were less tainted by metaphysics than those left by Plato, he also provided vital clues to why Xenophon had somewhat suddenly vanished from the pantheon of great thinkers at the threshold of modernity. He conjectured that our interest in Xenophon declined as we began to compare him with Plato as a philosopher and as a historian with Thucydides. When set against Plato's theoretical complexity and sophistication, Xenophon seemed too 'simple-minded and narrow-minded or philistine' to comprehend 'the core or depth of Socrates's thought'.[5] And when read against Thucydides's *History*, Xenophon's *Hellencia* and *Anabasis* appeared to be too 'unadorned' and rustic.[6] From this, it may be surmised that the enduring legacy of Xenophon across Europe until the turn of the nineteenth century conversely owed much to the simplicity and practicality of his teachings and writing style.

The aim of this essay is to investigate ways in which Xenophon's variegated works from *Ways and Means* to *Cyropaedia* had been exploited by eighteenth-century Britons with a view to advancing their discrete political agendas and causes, taking Strauss's speculation as a frame of reference. First and foremost, it is to do justice to Xenophon's hitherto overlooked influence, thereby casting new light on the Greek tradition in British political thought without discrediting the Roman heritage which has lately come into vogue thanks largely to the Cambridge school of intellectual history.[7] In this regard, it is my suggestion that if Greek antiquity had played any part in transforming the ideological topography of eighteenth-century Britain, it is less through Plato and Aristotle, whose ideas are at any rate too philosophical, if not pedantic, to be deployed for urgent purposes, than through Xenophon's prudence. It was primarily his hands-on approach to important issues of political society, ranging

---

[5] Strauss, *Xenophon's Socrates*, 83.
[6] Strauss, *Xenophon's Socrates*, 83.
[7] Interestingly, neither J.G.A. Pocock nor Quentin Skinner, two eminent leaders of the contextual movement, acknowledges the popularity of Xenophon. This is understandable to a certain extent because both James Harrington and Thomas Hobbes, their respective heroes, had rarely quoted Xenophon's writings. But their common idol Machiavelli was somewhat different. Xenophon's *Cyropaedia* was the only book that Machiavelli recommended to his royal audience in his advice book, see *The Prince*, eds. Q. Skinner and R. Price (Cambridge, 1988), 53–4. As said above, and will be pointed out later, Cicero, too, spoke highly of the *Cyropaedia* despite his aversion to its celebration of the monarchical form of the government. See 'On the Republic' 1.27.43 (*De Re Publica/De Legibus*, trans. C.W. Keyes (Cambridge, Massachusetts, 2006), 67–9).

from economic policy to virtuous kingship, with a flavour of the Socratic wisdom that had caught the attention of our ancestors. In other words, they read Xenophon principally because they could easily draw various historical parallels between his world and theirs without spending too much time and energy trying to navigate the labyrinth of theoretical abstraction, as was the case with his fellow pupil Plato's *Republic*. He was, in a word, a man of historical prudence.[8] Besides, unlike Cicero and, to a lesser degree, Machiavelli, Xenophon examined different forms of government, from Sparta to the Persian Empire, on their own merits. Whether he preferred Athens or Sparta is a cause of contention only for us. Hardly anyone had felt the need to identify Xenophon's political allegiance before the birth of modern historical scholarship.[9] Instead, readers praised him for being so adventurous as to join the army of the Cyrus the Younger as a mercenary officer, for it not only resulted in the *Anabasis* but also gave him first-hand experience of Persian society with which he embellished the *Cyropaedia*. Furthermore, it was believed to have equipped him with an unusual degree of objectivity, rendering his discussion of Greek affairs at least as credible as those made by Herodotus and Thucydides.[10] With this in mind, I revisit the three closely connected issues of kingship, commercial rivalry, and foreign affairs, which had swept the British political scene particularly since the settlement of 1688, from the perspective of British devotees of Xenophon, 'one of the greatest men of antiquity'.

## II

Among the myriad of writings of the Tory leader Henry St. John, Viscount Bolingbroke, one that stood out in its popularity, influence, and depth of thinking, not only during his life time but, perhaps more so, after his death in 1751, is doubtlessly his advice book for princes, *The*

---

[8] In this regard, it is not an exaggeration to say that Xenophon is the Greek equivalent of Tacitus, see A. Momigliano, 'Tacitus and the Tacitist Tradition', in *The Classical Foundations of Modern Historiography* (Berkeley, 1990), 109–31.
[9] A rare exception is Algernon Sidney, *Discourses concerning Government*, ed. T.G. West (Indianapolis, 1996), 175–95. It was against Sir Robert Filmer's critique of Athens's democratic political system that Sidney wanted to refute, see 'Patriarcha', in *Filmer: Patriarcha and Other Writings*, ed. J.P. Sommerville (Cambridge, 1991 [2004]), 27–9 (2. 15).
[10] See, for instance, John Hawkey's preface to his translation of Xenophon's *Anabasis* entitled *The Ascent of Cyrus the Younger; the Retreat of the Ten Thousand Greeks* (Dublin, 1738), iii–xxxvi.

*Idea of a Patriot King*.[11] Written in 1738 on the eve of the War of Jenkin's Ear and originally addressed to George Lyttelton, the then secretary of Frederick, Prince of Wales, this highly evocative political tract successfully summarised all he had been hankering after through various political and intellectual activities for decades. Some of these activities had fortunately earned him enduring esteem in the blossoming European republic of letters, but others had, contrary to his good intentions, besmirched the high reputation of his country as a leading member of the League of Augsburg against France under the Sun King Louis XIV.[12]

Bolingbroke's *Idea of a Patriot King*, however, occupies a somewhat enigmatic place in the British tradition of civic humanism because of the immensity of stress it had put on the role of a prince as a Godlike, moral safeguard against national corruption.[13] It is true that not a few pamphlets had appeared well before Bolingbroke's treatise, urging the Crown to take the non-partisan position mindful of the public interest at all times. Bolingbroke himself had previously touched on this issue of non-partisan leadership of a sovereign on several occasions. But his main focus so far had been given to the urgent necessity of achieving national unity under the guidance of the patriotic Country party, which he deemed to have the quality and capacity to become the single defender of the free and mixed constitution, truly representing the British people.[14] This sudden change of topic and direction within his political thinking, not unexpectedly, has left many to wonder what had inspired him to concentrate on kingship at this juncture, and who had helped him in taking this new approach towards the traditional republican conundrum of the unending conflict between civic virtue and moral degeneration.

---

[11] D. Armitage, 'Introduction', in *Bolingbroke: Political Writings*, ed. D. Armitage (Cambridge, 1997), xxi–xxiii, xli–xliv; 'A Patriot for Whom? The Afterlives of Bolingbroke's Patriot King', *The Journal of British Studies*, 36 (1997), 397–418.

[12] I. Kramnick, *Bolingbroke and His Circle: The Politics of Nostalgia in the Age of Walpole* (Ithaca, 1968 [1992]), 163; H.T. Dickinson, *Bolingbroke* (London, 1970), 247–313; 'Bolingbroke: *The Idea of a Patriot King*', *History*, 20 (1970), 13–19. On the recipient of Bolingbroke's counsel, see S. Varey, 'Hanover, Stuart and the *Patriot King*', *British Journal of Eighteenth-Century Studies*, 6 (1983), 163–72. On Bolingbroke's intellectual influence across the English Channel, see R.A. Barrell, *Bolingbroke and France* (Lanham, 1988); B. Channel, *Bolingbroke: Exile et Ècriture au Siècle des Lumière – Angleterre-France (Vers 1715–Vers 1750)*, 2 vols. (Paris, 1992).

[13] S. Burtt, *Virtue Transformed: Political Argument in England, 1688–1740* (Cambridge, 1992), 87–109.

[14] For example, see 'A Dissertation upon Parties', in *Bolingbroke: Political Writings*, 30–7, 76–8, 122–31, 162–8.

To begin with, it has been widely acknowledged that Bolingbroke's patriot king was basically derived from Machiavelli's prince. Felix Raab, for example, has argued in his classic work on the English reception of the Florentine author, 'Bolingbroke, the next great English Machiavellian used the ruler with *virtù* as a model for an English king who would be able to rise above the new factionalism'.[15] There is no question that Bolingbroke read and studied Machiavelli with utmost care. However, Bolingbroke's Machiavelli was wearing a new garb which was markedly different from the ones that his predecessors had weaved for the Florentine writer in the sixteenth and seventeenth centuries, as Raab himself has admitted.[16] Bolingbroke was in fact extremely critical of what Machiavelli had proposed to princes:

> Machiavel is an author who should have great authority with the persons likely to oppose me. The only difference between us, is I would have the virtue real: he requires no more than the appearance of it.[17]

In every aspect, Bolingbroke's *Idea of a Patriot King* took an overtly anti-Machiavellian posture. Unable to identify its place in the tradition of classical republicanism, a leading British intellectual historian has recently jumped to the conclusion that Bolingbroke's patriot king is simply 'a republican oxymoron'.[18] We are also told that Bolingbroke had modelled himself on Cicero, and that his mirror-for-princes might be defined as a misguided travesty of his great Roman republican hero's magnum opus, *De Officiis*.[19] This interpretation, however, fails to take into account the fact that Cicero himself was a great admirer of Xenophon's *Cyropaedia*, though he did not endorse the monarchical form of government. He had even written to Quintus that Xenophon 'created a matchless blend of firmness and courtesy' in Cyrus, telling his brother that 'with good reason our Roman Africanus used to keep that book always in his hands'.[20]

---

[15] Raab, *The English Face of Machiavelli: A Changing Interpretation, 1500–1700* (London, 1964), 254. Also, Kramnick, *Bolingbroke and His Circle*, 163; J. Hart, *Viscount Bolingbroke: Tory Humanist* (London, 1965), 144–63.
[16] Raab, *The English Face of Machiavelli*, 261.
[17] Bolingbroke, 'The Idea of a Patriot King', 241.
[18] Armitage, *The Ideological Origins of the British Empire* (Cambridge, 2000 [2004]), 187; 'Empire and Liberty: A Republican Dilemma', in *Republicanism: A Shared European Heritage – vol. II The Values of Republicanism in Early Modern Europe*, 29–46.
[19] Armitage, 'Introduction', in *Bolingbroke: Political Writings*, xxii.
[20] 'Letters to Quintus', I. I. I. 23. See *Letters to Quintus and Brutus*, ed. and trans. D.R. Shackleton Bailey (Cambridge, Massachusetts, 2002), 25.

In contrast, the Archdeacon William Coxe came to a very different conclusion in his much celebrated biography of Sir Robert Walpole at the end of the eighteenth century. Notwithstanding his blatant endorsement of the conventional Whiggish prejudice against the ambitious and untrustworthy Tory anti-Machiavellian thinker, Coxe was able to detect that Bolingbroke was simply transcribing the *Cyropaedia* of Xenophon and his French inheritor Archbishop Fénelon's *Telemachus, Son of Ulysses*:

> In this extraordinary attempt to reconcile the ideas of a government by prerogative, with those of liberty and happiness, he [Bolingbroke] endeavours to bribe the imagination instead of convincing the judgement, by an artificial and brilliant display of all those scenes of splendour and domestic felicity which are so lavishly and exquisitely pourtrayed in the *Cyropaedia* of Xenophon, and Fénelon's *Telemachus*; scenes which adorn the page of the speculative philosopher, but must be considered as mere puerilities from a practical politician.[21]

The tradition of political discourse that Bolingbroke had resorted to was, as is well known, neither the Filmerian divine right of kings nor the Lockean social contract theory.[22] It was instead the Renaissance humanist idea of kingship, a political ideology that is believed to have miserably failed to find a proper place in England even in its heyday of the late sixteenth and early seventeenth centuries, due in part to the prevalence of a mystical belief in the common law and the ancient constitution, and to the growing extremist tendencies on both sides of the government: regicidal republicanism on the part of the Parliament and French-style absolutism and Hobbes's civil science on the side of the Crown.[23] Worse still, there exists a tacit, yet firmly institutionalised Whiggish consensus that such a political doctrine had become completely extinct by the time of, or at least by, the Revolution Settlement.[24] And understandably it has also never been considered as a serious issue in the history of the neo-Harringtonian ideology. It therefore comes as no surprise that Maurice Ashley, younger brother to the Third Earl of Shaftesbury, dedicated his 1728 English translation of the *Cyropaedia* to his sister and not to his

---

[21] *Memoirs of the Life and Administration of Sir Robert Walpole, Earl of Orford*, vol. 1 (London, 1978), 213.
[22] Kramnick, *Bolingbroke and His Circle*, 84–187.
[23] J. Figgis, *The Divine Right of Kings*, second edition (Cambridge, 1922), 137–76; Pocock, *The Machiavellian Moment*, 333–400; Raab, *The English Face of Machiavelli*, 8–254.
[24] H.T. Dickinson, *Liberty and Property: Political Ideology in Eighteenth-Century Britain* (London, 1977 [1979]), 13–192.

master George II.²⁵ For him, Xenophon's *Cyropaedia* was essentially a moral story of anti-Epicureanism, a pseudo-historical lesson of the culture of politeness, not a mirror-for-princes.²⁶ In view of the long history of the denigration of the humanist conception of princely rule in England, it is hardly surprising that Bolingbroke's *Idea of a Patriot King* has been characterised as a belated and far misguided intellectual and political venture.²⁷

Nevertheless it is still questionable whether Bolingbroke's project was too far-fetched and thus doomed to fail either in theory or in practice. Theoretically, to start with, there is nothing inherently contradictory and entirely new in his visualisation of 'a king on who the eyes of a whole people are fixed, filled with admiration, and glowing with affection'.²⁸ For Bolingbroke's description of a patriot prince who is 'possessed of absolute power, neither usurped by fraud, nor maintained by force, but the genuine effect of esteem, of confidence, and affection' matches seamlessly with Xenophon's image of Cyrus.²⁹ Cyrus, according to Xenophon, 'believed that he could in no way more effectively inspire a desire for the beautiful and the good than by endeavouring, as their sovereign, to set before his subjects a perfect model of virtue in his own person'.³⁰ 'He thought that it was not possible for him to incite others to good and noble deeds, if he were not himself such as he ought to be'.³¹ 'He practiced what he preached' and galvanised 'in his people a

---

²⁵ *Cyropaedia, or the Institution of Cyrus* (London, 1728). For more on Ashley's translation, see I. Macgregor Morris, 'Creating the Enlightenment Prince: Maurice Ashley's Translation of the *Cyropaedia* of Xenophon', in M. Zebrowski (ed.), *Ancient Greece in Eighteenth-Century Britain: Translation and Commentary in a Tradition of Philosophy, Politics, Culture* (a special edition of the *Annals of Scholarship*) (forthcoming, 2008). However, the initial reception of Xenophon's *Cyropaedia* was not inhospitable at all, see J. Grogan, 'Many Cyruses': Xenophon's *Cyropaedia* and English Renaissance Humanism' (forthcoming). I would like to thank Grogan for showing me her insightful article.
²⁶ See L.E. Klein, *Shaftesbury and the Culture of Politeness: Moral Discourse and Cultural Politics in Early Eighteenth-Century England* (Cambridge, 1994), 43–6, 108–11.
²⁷ Hart, *Viscount Bolingbroke*, 83–116. The fact that the preface of the English translation of one of Xenophon's Socratic works, *Hiero*, which mainly concerns the nature of tyranny, unusually has no political overtones can also be mentioned here. Xenophon, *Hiero, or the Condition of Tyrant*, second edition (London, 1713), A2–A6.
²⁸ Bolingbroke, 'Patriot King', 293.
²⁹ Bolingbroke, 'Patriot King', 293.
³⁰ *Cyropaedia* 8.1.21; see also 8.1.26. Translated by W. Miller, *Cyropaedia: Books V–VIII* (Cambridge, Massachusetts, 1914 [2000]), 317.
³¹ *Cyropaedia* 8.1.12; trans. Miller, *Cyropaedia 5–8*, 311.

spirit of emulation in what was beautiful and good'.³² As the paragon of virtue, wielding absolute moral authority over his people, Cyrus, was, in other words, Xenophon's patriot king.³³ Not only did Bolingbroke share Xenophon's emphasis on the pedagogical role of sovereigns, but he even concurred with his Greek teacher that popularity of a monarch was also determined by his or her appearance.³⁴ As Cyrus held the opinion that he ought to 'cast a sort of spell upon' his subjects through his clothes and manners, Bolingbroke's English Cyrus, Queen Elizabeth, 'saw how much popularity ... depended on the decorum, the decency, the grace, and the propriety of behaviour'.³⁵ Both Cyrus and Elizabeth understood that 'the sole true foundation of that sufficient authority and influence' was 'popularity', and that to acquire it they needed 'to excel his subjects not only in point of being actually better than they', but at the same time 'should observe the decorum necessary to preserve the esteem'.³⁶

It is commonly held that since Elizabeth was essentially a limited monarch under the rule of law, whilst Cyrus was at best a benevolent oriental despot unrestrained by any form of legal or constitutional procedures, bracketing them together is to blur the most crucial difference between tyranny and a free state. Indeed, this was one of the points that Bolingbroke took great pains to stress throughout his booklet, making a detailed comparison between Elizabeth and Louis XIV, in fear of mounting public accusation of Jacobitism.³⁷ However, it is wrong to juxtapose hurriedly the neo-Roman theory of a free state, in particular its overriding principle of non-domination, with Cyrus's Persia, categorising the latter as fundamentally oppressive and autocratic.³⁸ 'We must

---

[32] *Cyropaedia* 8.2.23, 16; trans. Miller, *Cyropaedia* 5–8, 345, 347.

[33] Recently there have been some attempts to read the *Cyropaedia* as a work of political theory, expanding and deepening Strauss's classic interpretation, see C. Nadon, *Xenophon's Prince: Republic and Empire in the* Cyropaedia (Berkeley, 2001); W. Newel, 'Xenophon's *Education of Cyrus* and the Classical Critique of Liberalism', unpublished Ph.D. dissertation (Yale, 1981).

[34] Machiavelli also stressed the appearance of a royal figure, but his argument rests on a different understanding of moral politics, see Newell, 'Machiavelli and Xenophon on Princely Rule', 108–30.

[35] *Cyropaedia* 8.1.40; trans. Miller, *Cyropaedia* 5–8, 325; Bolingbroke, 'Patriot King', 287.

[36] *Cyropaedia* 8.1.40; trans. Miller, *Cyropaedia* 5–8, 325; Bolingbroke, 'Patriot King', 289.

[37] Bolingbroke, 'Patriot King', 286–9.

[38] On the neo-Roman theory of non-domination and its logical consequence, the rule of law, see Skinner, *Liberty before Liberalism* (Cambridge, 1998); P. Pettit, *Republicanism: A Theory of Freedom and Government* (Oxford, 1997).

distinguish ourselves from slaves in this way', announced Chrysantas, Cyrus's faithful lieutenant, 'that, whereas slaves serve their masters against their wills, we, if indeed we claim to be free, must do of our own free will all that seems to be of the first importance'.[39] This Hellenic idea of 'absolute rule over free and willing subjects', to use Erasmus' succinct summarising of Xenophon's *Oeconomicus*, is also emphatically pointed out by Cyrus's father, Cambyses.[40] While teaching his son that 'people are only too glad to obey the man who they believe takes wiser thought for their interests than they themselves do', Cambyses clearly drew a line between 'compulsory obedience' and 'willing obedience'.[41] His wife even went further. She cautioned her son Cyrus during his sojourn at his grandfather's court in Media not to confuse the Persian ideal of justice with the Median and return with a knowledge acquired from his grandfather, enunciating that 'in Persia equality of rights is considered justice' and his father's standard 'is not his will but the law'.[42] Furthermore, one of the key principles of the Persian education was 'the equal freedom of speech'.[43] Although expelled from Athens for voluntarily serving under the ally of its foremost rival, Sparta, Xenophon was well versed in his teacher's celebrated distinction of kingship and despotism, 'a government of men with their consent and in accordance with the laws of the state' and 'a government of unwilling subjects and not controlled by laws, but imposed by the will of the ruler'.[44] Thus, even the staunch Whig such as Sidney approvingly referred to the practice of justice that Cyrus had shown.[45]

Last but not least, it must be remembered that aside from his Persian origin, there is nothing in Xenophon's description of Cyrus that is

---

[39] *Cyropaedia* 8.1.4; trans. Miller, *Cyropaedia* 5–8, 307.
[40] *The Education of a Christian Prince*, ed. L. Jardine (Cambridge, 1997), 1. It must be pointed out that Erasmus, nevertheless, did not like Xenophon's *Cyropaedia*, arguing that Xenophon was a pagan and Cyrus was 'the worst image of a prince'. His dislike of Xenophon and his advice book can be explained by his emphasis on peace among Christian rulers, see ibid., 62–3.
[41] *Cyropaedia* 1.6.21; trans. Miller, *Cyropaedia*, *Books I–IV* (Cambridge, Massachusetts, 1914 [2001]), 107.
[42] *Cyropaedia* 1.3.18; trans. Miller, *Cyropaedia* 1–4, 43.
[43] *Cyropaedia* 1.3.10; trans. Miller, *Cyropaedia* 1–4, 37.
[44] *Memorabilia* 4.6.12. Trans. E. C. Marchant and O. J. Todd, *Memorabilia / Oeconomicus / Symposium / Apology* (Cambridge, Massachusetts, 1923 [2002]), 345 (4. 6. 12). Newell has argued that Xenophon's lifelong intellectual project was to come up with a new type of tyrannical rule, see his 'Tyranny and the Science of Ruling in Xenophon's *Education of Cyrus*', *The Journal of Politics*, 45 (1983), 889–906.
[45] *Courtly Maxims*, eds. H.W. Blom, E. Mulier, R. Janse (Cambridge, 1996), 34.

fundamentally at odds with Christianity. Quite to the contrary, the Bible had high opinion of the Persian emperor, eulogising his sacred role as the saviour of the oppressed Jews.[46] Although the Jewish episode of his philanthropic prince recorded in the Bible was not included in Xenophon's account, his pagan idea of leadership was in accord with the biblical portrayal of Cyrus as God's shepherd.[47] 'The duties of a good shepherd and of a good king', wrote Xenophon, registering some of the central tenets of Cyrus's patriotic rule, were 'very much alike; a good shepherd ought, while deriving benefit from his flocks, to make them happy, and in the same way a king ought to make his people and his cities happy, if he would derive benefits from them'.[48] He also stated that 'a good ruler is not at all different from a good father', anticipating Bolingbroke's famous depiction of a free people governed by a patriot king as 'a patriarchal family'.[49] In light of the fact that this kind of political imagination, described by Michel Focault as 'the shepherd-king model', had dominated the biblical minds of Catholics for centuries, it is no coincidence that the Archbishop of Cambrai François de Salignac de la Mothe-Fénelon whose acclaimed political novel, *Telemachus*, Bolingbroke cherished and perused when composing his advice to Frederick, also took its cue from the same Greek source.[50]

Originally written for the education of his prematurely deceased pupil Duke of Burgundy, eldest grandson of Louis XIV, Fénelon's *Telemachus* shared the same sense of public responsibility with its British counterpart.[51] Fénelon's Cyrus, Telemachus, was the very antithesis of Louis XIV who in pursuit of his own personal glory and ambition had not only ruined his own country but, more importantly, shattered the highly vulnerable

---

[46] Ezra, 1: 1–2, 6: 3–22.
[47] Isaiah, 44:28. For a succinct discussion of this model of government and its lasting legacy in the eighteenth century, see Michel Foucault, '*Omnes et Singulatim*: Towards a Critique of Political Reason', in *Essential Works of Foucault, 1954–84: vol. III – Power*, ed. J.D. Faubion and trans. R. Hurley (New York, 2000), 298–325.
[48] *Cyropaedia* 8.2.13; trans. Miller, *Cyropaedia 5–8*, 339.
[49] *Cyropaedia* 8.1.1; trans. Miller, *Cyropaedia 5–8*, 305; Bolingbroke, 'Patriot King', 257–8.
[50] Tatum, *Xenophon's Imperial Fiction*, 27–8; M. Bizos, 'Notice', in *Xénophon: Cyropédie*, tome I (Paris, 1971), 53–4, n. 6.
[51] On Fénelon's intellectual influence in the formation of French aristocratic patriotism after the death of Louis XIV, see A. Chérel, *Fénelon au XVIII siècle en France (1715–1820): Son Prestige, Son Influence* (Geneva, 1970); L. Rothkrug, *Opposition to Louis XIV: The Political and Social Origins of the French Enlightenment* (Princeton, New Jersey, 1965), 179–457; J.M. Smith, *Nobility Reimagined: The Patriotic Nation in Eighteenth-Century France* (Ithaca, 2005), 26–103; J. Shovlin, *The Political Economy of Virtue: Luxury, Patriotism, and the Origins of the French Revolution* (Ithaca, 2006), 1–79.

system of balance in Europe, necessitating a series of secretive diplomatic manoeuvres and financially exhausting military conflicts, to restore the equilibrium by means of various defensive alliances and partition treaties.[52] Not unexpectedly, Salentum, Fénelon's reformed France, values above all else 'the love of virtue, the fear of the gods, a natural goodness towards our neighbours', and abhors 'that brutality which, under the gaudy names of ambition and glory, madly ravages whole provinces, and sheds the blood of men who are all brothers'.[53] Despite the fact that Cyrus was essentially a military hero, and that he was inherently virtuous and courageous, while Telemachus had a judicious mentor throughout his long voyage in search of his missing father Ulysses, it is not difficult to draw a parallel between Fénelon's Salentum and Xenophon's Persia.[54] In addition to their common insistence on implementing draconian measures to rejuvenate public spirit under the patriotic monarch, Telemachus and his ancient predecessor never advocated, let alone attempted to defend, hereditary right to rule as God's gift. Fénelon was a vehement critique of Bossuet, Louis XIV's dutiful religious chaperon, who strove to guard the rapidly crumbling Filmerian justification of absolute kingship with his *Politics drawn from Holy Scripture*.[55]

The extent of Xenophon's intellectual influence on Fénelon can also be felt in the works of his Scottish disciple and first biographer Chevalier Andrew Michael Ramsay. In point of fact Ramsay was much more forthright about his espousal of Xenophon's Hellenic conception of princely rule than Fénelon and Bolingbroke. Cleverly taking advantage of Xenophon's silence about Cyrus's education in his adolescence, just as his French Archbishop had done with Homer's similar silence about much of Telemachus' life, Ramsay came up with his own version of a patriot king with a stronger religious flavour, reflecting his Freemasonic devotion and distaste for atheism, and entitled his philosophical romance, *A New Cyropaedia or the Travels of Cyrus*.[56] Published in 1727, it entertained extraordinary popularity, running through ten editions in France by the end of the eighteenth century. More importantly, this close

---

[52] I. Hont, *Jealousy of Trade: International Competition and the Nation-State in Historical Perspective* (Cambridge, Massachusetts, 2005), 24–30.
[53] Fénelon, *Telemachus, Son of Ulysses*, ed. and trans. P. Riley (Cambridge, 1994), 131.
[54] Fénelon, *Telemachus*, 129–49; *Cyropaedia* 7.5.72–85; trans. Miller, *Cyropaedia* 5–8, 293–301. See also, C. Nadon, 'From Republic to Empire: Political Revolution and the Common Good in Xenophon's *Education of Cyrus*', *The American Political Science Review*, 90 (1996), 361–74.
[55] Chérel, *Fénelon au XVIII siècle en France (1715–1820)*.
[56] Tatum, *Xenophon's Imperial Fiction*, 27–8.

friend of two leading philosophers of the Scottish Enlightenment, Hume and Francis Hutcheson, was once tutor to Charles Edward, the Young Pretender. Although his tenure ended abruptly only after a year of service due to internal conflicts of the exiled Stuart court, it is not unreasonable to think that if his education had any bearing on the Jacobite movement, particularly its strikingly liberal and reformist political platform, it must have been chiefly through his Socratic reading of Xenophon's *Cyropaedia*.[57] On the other hand, Ramsay's lifelong preoccupation with Xenophon's *Cyropaedia* can be seen as a testimony to his unflinching loyalty towards the Stuarts. For, ever since James VI and I had chosen to draw on its concept of ideal kingship for his own advice book for princes, *Basilicon Doron*, Xenophon's *Cyropaedia* had always remained at the heart of the Stuart royalist ideology, withstanding both the English Civil War and the Dutch invasion in 1688.[58] And this might be one of the reasons why Bolingbroke was so keen to conceal his intellectual indebtedness to Xenophon's *Cyropaedia* in his *Idea of a Patriot King*, and also why he castigated the most eminent student of Xenophon James I, so relentlessly for leaning towards the divine right of kings to disguise his personal failings and vices.[59]

## III

'Trade was never esteemed an affair of state till the last century; and there scarcely is any ancient writer on politic, who has made mention of it'.[60] So wrote down David Hume in his seminal essay on civil liberty published in 1741 amidst of the Austrian War of Succession which continued the entrenched animosity between Britain and Spain in the Spanish West Indies. The main objective of this highly controversial essay was to make revise the traditional republican distinction between free states and absolute monarchies, taking into consideration the changing historical conditions. But before turning to his main subject Hume decided to make a small, but

---

[57] Ramsay, *Observations on a New Plan of Education of a Young Prince* (London, 1732). On Ramsay's influence across the French aristocratic society, see Smith, *Nobility Reimagined*, 48–9.

[58] King James VI and I, 'Basilicon Doron' in *King James VI and I: Political Writings*, ed. J.P. Sommerville (Cambridge, 1994 [2001]), 1–61. Further, see J. Cramsie, *Kingship and Crown Finance under James VI and I, 1603–1625* (Woodbridge, Suffolk, 2002), 13–66. The seventeenth-century English translation of the *Cyropaedia* was dedicated to Charles I on the eve of the English Civil War.

[59] Bolingbroke, 'Patriot King', 288–9.

[60] Hume, 'Of Civil Liberty' in *Hume: Political Essays*, 52.

not insignificant correction to what he had just uttered. In his footnote to the above quotation Hume admitted that there was one exception to the pre-modern negligence of commerce and overseas trades: Xenophon. Strangely, however, his reference was Xenophon's *Hiero*. Xenophon's main focus in the *Hiero*, as is well known, is neither commerce nor public revenues. Rather it is in effect the story of Socrates persuading the despot Hiero to become a virtuous and loving prince. However, Hume was well aware of Xenophon's discussion of the Athenian economy after the Peloponnesian War in his *Ways and Means*, which was already translated into English, and even mentioned it favourably a few paragraphs later. It is impossible to know why Hume referred to the *Hiero* and not the *Ways and Means* on this occasion as he left no explanation, but it is not difficult to surmise that he wanted to underline the historic importance of the commercial revolution. Hume's effort to draw a sharp demarcation between the ancients and the moderns notwithstanding, many contemporary commentators of commerce found Xenophon's economic analysis of the war-stricken economy of Athens of immense help in understanding the situation of their country.

In 1697, Walter Moyle, a renowned commonwealthman, who spearheaded the anti-standing army campaign in cooperation with John Trenchard against their new Dutch master, William III, translated Xenophon's *Ways and Means* at the request of Charles Davenant. Davenant was one of the most active Tory critics of William III's wartime economic policy that was deemed to have created the moneyed interest. He had written several important political satires and numerous economic tracts which laid out the ideological grounds upon which the Country coalition between the Old Whigs and their Tory allies were formed.[61] Moyle's translation of the *Ways and Means* was published along with Davenant's scathing treatise on the ill consequences of the newly established public debt system, epitomised in the foundation of the Bank of England in 1694, making a compelling historical parallel between eighteenth-century Britain and Athens. As he himself had enunciated in his preface, Davenant, by inserting Xenophon's *Ways and Means*, wished to 'shew the public, how ancient the true notions were, concerning revenues and trade'.[62] In his dedicatory letter to his Tory friend, Moyle articulated why he found it necessary to render this particular essay into English at this juncture:

---

[61] Robbins, *The Eighteenth-Century Commonwealthman* (Indianapolis, 1987), 101.
[62] Davenant, 'Discourses on the Publick Revenues, and on the Trade of England, Part I', in *The Political and Commercial Works of Charles Davenant*, ed. Sir Charles Whitworth (London, 1771), 149.

> [I]t is to Trade we owe the Rise and Progress of the English Greatness, that has enabled us to support so tedious a War against the most formidable Power which has been known in Europe for these many Ages and that alone can enable us to discharge the vast Debts we have contracted by the War … The general Rules for the Increase of Riches and Trade, are either directly advanc'd, or may be very naturally deduc'd from this Discourse. That admirable Maxim *That the true Wealth and Greatness of a Nation, Consists in Numbers of People, well employ'd*, is every where inculcated throughout the whole course of the Treatise.[63]

This was also the maxim that Francis Grant, a Country gentleman, extolled and capitalised on when putting forward his complaints against the Whig government for neglecting the British fishing industry across the Atlantic in 1734.[64] Following Xenophon's teaching, Grant asserted that 'nothing can so much, nor so advantageously imploy our Poor and increase our People, as the Herring fishery', and 'it's Trade that begets Trade, as Fire begets Fire; and the more that Trade encreaseth, the more will industrious People from all Parts flock to us'.[65] Neither Machiavelli nor Harrington featured in Grant's pamphlet. Instead, it was Xenophon who received the highest praise from Grant. He claimed that 'the only ancient author, who has wrote of the true interest of a state, in a manner adopted to the principles and circumstances of latter ages' was Xenophon.[66]

Next, both Moyle and Davenant were fulsome in their praise for Xenophon's extensive use of numbers and figures in his policy suggestions. At the end of his preface of the English translation of the *Ways and Means*, Moyle paid tribute to both Xenophon and Davenant for their contributions:

> I believe Xenophon was the first Author that ever argu'd by Political Arithmetick, or the Art of Reasoning upon things by Figures, which has been improv'd by some able Heads of our own Nation, and carry'd to the highest Perfection by your own successful Inquiries.[67]

The popularity of political arithmetic among the Country opposition is not very difficult to comprehend. The physician and polymath John Arbuthnot, for example, who created the figure of John Bull, stated in 1701, while complementing the statistical works of Sir William Petty

---

[63] Moyle, 'To the AUTHOR of the ESSAY upon *Ways and Means*', in *A Discourse upon Improving the Revenue of the State of Athens* (London, 1697), 4–5, 7–8.
[64] Grant, *The British Fishery recommended to Parliament* (London, 1734), 11.
[65] Grant, *The British Fishery*, 12–13.
[66] Grant, *The British Fishery*, 11.
[67] Moyle, 'To the Author of the ESSAY upon *Ways and Means*', 8.

and Gregory King, both of whom Moyle mentioned in his preface, that 'political arithmetic is not only the great instrument of private commerce, but by it are (for ought to be) kept the public accounts of a nation … This is the true political knowledge'.[68] Davenant who had published numerous statistical reports while working as Inspector-General of Imports and Exports concurred with Arbuthnot.[69] He insisted, 'such a political arithmetic as could distinguish in all the different parts which compose a nation's wealth, must be very useful and do public service'.[70] It therefore comes as no surprise that the anonymous editor of the 1751 Scottish edition of Sir William Petty's *Political Arithmetic* decided to include Xenophon's *Ways and Means*, and that Davenant used the same title, *Ways and Means*, for his essay on the public revenues of Britain after the Nine Years' War.

Xenophon's stress on the benefits of state initiated silver mining also had not passed unnoticed. He had suggested to his fellow Athenians who were left destitute by the Peloponnesian War that 'the silver mines … if a proper system of working, were introduced, a vast amount of money would be obtained from them apart from our other sources of revenue'.[71] As a matter of fact, what had inspired Davenant to support the exportation of bullion in exchange for cheap raw materials, taking it as a central tenet of his free trade belief, was Xenophon's *Ways and Means*.[72]

> It is so strange, Xenophon, so long ago, should see that exportation of bullion, in the way of Traffic, could not be prejudicial to a country; and yet that we, who are a trading nation, should startle at it, to whom experience should have given better lights … This wise statesman, long versed in affairs, … not only saw that bullion, but that coined money might be

---

[68] Arbuthnot, 'Essay on the Usefulness of Mathematical Learning', in *Life and Works of John Arbuthnot* (London, 1892), 421–2.
[69] Davenant, 'Discourses on the Public Revenues, and Trade of England, Part II', in *The Political and Commercial Works of Charles Davenant*, vol. I, 127–49.
[70] Davenant, 'Discourses', vol. I, 142.
[71] Xenophon, 'Ways and Means', in *Xenophon: Scripta Minora*, trans. E. C. Marchant and G. W. Bowersock (Cambridge, Massachusetts, 1968), 205 (4. 1).
[72] This is not to say that the Roman example that Cicero had handed over to Machiavelli had no influence on Davenant. He had put forward the Roman system, instead of the Athenian, as the ideal public revenue model to be followed by Britain, see his 'A Discourse upon Grants and Resumptions', in *The Political and Commercial Works of Charles D'Avenant*, vol. III, 30–57. On Xenophon's work, see P. Gauthier, *Un Commentaire Historique des Poroi de Xénophon* (Geneva, 1976); J. Dillery, 'Xenophon's Poroi and Athenian Imperialism', *Historia*, 42 (1993), 1–11. I am grateful to Professor Dillery for kindly sending me a copy of his insightful article.

exported with safety, when a gainful return did arise from the commodity purchased.⁷³

The immediate objective of Davenant's critique of the bullionist position was to vindicate the East India Company that had long been scolded for draining the nation's wealth, most recently by John Pollexfen, a leading member of the Whig Council of Trade and one of the Commissioners of Trade. In point of fact, the section was a lengthy rejoinder to Pollexfen's point-by-point rebuttal of his earlier tract on the subject, *An Essay on the East-India Trade*, which was entitled *England and East-India Inconsistent in Their Manufactures* and published in 1697. To those, like Pollexfen, who worried that England had a negative effect on her environment unlike, her ancient predecessor, referring to Xenophon's stress on restoring silver mining in Laurion, Davenant brought the recent debacle of the Spanish Empire to their attention.⁷⁴ His diagnosis was that 'what rendered their treasure useless to the body of the people' was 'the strict prohibition to export the species'.⁷⁵ It was, in a nutshell, 'an early bar to industry'.⁷⁶ 'Had the Spaniards added conduct and industry to their good fortune', Davenant even surmised, 'peradventure they might have compassed the universal monarchy they aimed at'.⁷⁷ His conclusion was that 'all countries thrive or decline by trade, as they well or ill manage their product and manufactures'.⁷⁸ The East India trade, on this understanding, was doubly advantageous to Britain. For it not only promoted the growth of industry at home but also enabled her manufacturers to undercut their foreign competitors in the international market.

The legacy of Xenophon, however, did not last long. By the time Adam Smith conceived of his magnum opus, *An Inquiry into the Nature and Causes of the Wealth of Nations*, the mercantilist interpretation of Xenophon's economic writings of Moyle and his Tory colleague Charles Davenant was rapidly fading. The popularity of the *Ways and Means* as one of the most important essays on commerce and overseas trades dwindled as the mercantile system came under fire for instigating 'the

---

[73] Davenant, 'Discourses on the Publick Revenues, and on the Trade of England, Part II', in *The Political and Commercial Works of Charles Davenant*, vol. II, 107.
[74] See, Xenophon, *Ways and Means* 4.1–4.18; trans. Marchant and Bowersock, in *Xenophon: Scripta Minora* (Cambridge, Massachusetts, 1968), 205–11.
[75] Davenant, 'Discourses on the Publick Revenues, and on the Trade of England, Part II', vol. II, 108.
[76] Davenant, 'Discourses', vol. II, 108.
[77] Davenant, 'Discourses', vol. I, 383.
[78] Davenant, 'Discourses', vol. II, 227.

spirit of jealous emulation' between the nations, as well as for sacrificing the interest of the public to the growth of a small coterie of monopolies. Of course, Athens was still admired for its remarkable commercial prosperity, but it was ascribed chiefly to its policy of laissez faire and not to its interventionist economic policy of development. This changing trend of interpretation can be seen in an anonymous pamphlet published in 1753 when the prolonged issue of naturalisation was heatedly disputed once more in Parliament.

> The whole Tenor of his [Xenophon's] Reasonings upon the state of the *Athenian* Affairs, tends to *sap* the very Foundation of all *Monopolies* and *Exclusions*. To imagine he favour'd any *Exclusions*, would be to suppose him inconsistent with himself ... Like a judicious *Artist*, he touche'd their *Botches* and *corrupt Parts* with a lenient and gentle Hand, as the Pride of the *Democracy* would not permit him to probe their *Sores* to the Quick, without Clamour.[79]

Despite desperate efforts by William Young to revive the spirit of Athens in Britain at the turn of the eighteenth century, it was, however, in France that the first maritime empire in history met the most enthusiastic audience.[80] Benjamin Constant, who led the intellectual assault upon Napoleon's military-despotic imperialism, found Xenophon's idealised image of reformed Athens extremely helpful in setting out his celebrated notion of a commercial society infused with individual liberty.

> Athens ... was as of all the Greek republics the most closely engaged in trade: thus it allowed its citizens an infinitely greater individual liberty than Sparta and Rome. If I could enter into historical details, I would show you that, among the Athenians, commerce had removed several differences which distinguished the ancient from the modern peoples. The spirit of the Athenian merchants was similar to that of the merchants of our days. Xenophon tells us that during the Peloponnesian War, they moved their capitals from the continent of Attica to place them on the islands of the archipelago.[81]

---

[79] Anon., *Reflections upon Naturalisation, Corporations, and Companies; Supported by the Authorities of both Ancient and Modern Writers* (London, 1753), 13.
[80] On William Young, see Peter Liddel's contribution to this volume; on Constant, see Ian Macgregor Morris in this volume.
[81] Constant, 'The Liberty of the Athenians Compared with that of the Moderns: Speech given at the Athénée Royal in Paris', in *Constant: Political Writings*, ed. Biancamaria Fontana (Cambridge, 1998 [2002]), 315. Further, 'The Spirit of Conquest and Usurpation and Their Relation to European Civilization', in ibid., 103.

But even this celebration of Xenophon's free and commercial Athens diminsihed as the century wore on. Thus, for Karl Marx, Xenophon was simply a contemporary of Plato 'who with his characteristic bourgeois instinct already comes closer to the division of labour within the workshop'.[82] The Xenophon who worried about public debt and overseas commerce disappeared, and in his place a new Xenophon who advocated economic freedom and enunciated the division of labour emerged.

## IV

In 1755 the renowned political satirist and Jacobite John Shebbeare began to publish a series of political essays on the present state of national affairs in the form of epistolary novel, allegedly written by an Anglicised Italian Jesuit to stress the impartiality of his views and interpretations. His foremost objective was to explain the rapid deterioration in Anglo-French relations, both in Europe and America, which was instigating a radical realignment of the European powers. More important, Shebbeare concentrated his oppositional criticism on 'the Hanoverian preoccupation of the crown', claiming that it sacrificed Britain's maritime interest.[83] In fact, ever since the accession of George I, Hanover had been the greatest bugbear of British ministers and diplomats. At the centre of Shebbeare's characteristic disparagement of the Hanoverian connection, which, in his opinion, had dragged Britain into the European quagmire, was a striking comparison of Athens and Britain.

> What an Eye so dim that cannot distinguish the Analogy so manifest between the *Athenians* of his Time and the *English* of ours? What Mind so stupid as not to foresee the same Events?[84]

Early eighteenth-century Britain was a land in turmoil. Not only was the newly established dynasty under threat from recurrent Jacobite insurrections in support of the exiled Stuart kings, but, more importantly, its relationship with major powers on the other side of the English Channel remained extremely volatile. As a matter of fact, the much acclaimed Protestant succession was secured at the expense of the isolationist foreign policy which, many still believe, underpinned the unprecedented

---

[82] Marx, *Capital: A Critique of Political Economy*, vol. 1, trans. B. Fowkes (London, 1976 [1990]), 488. See *Cyropaedia* 8.2.5–6; trans. Miller, *Cyropaedia* 5–8, 333.
[83] B. Simms, 'Hanover: The Missing Dimension', in B. Simms and T. Riotte (eds.), *The Hanoverian Dimension in British History, 1714–1837* (Cambridge, 2007), 1.
[84] Shebbeare, *A Letter to the People of England, on the Present Situation and Conduct of National Affairs. Letter I*, second edition (London, 1755), 4.

economic progress leading to the Industrial Revolution. Doubtlessly no one questioned what Josiah Child, Governor of the East India Company, succinctly verbalised in the late seventeenth century that 'foreign trade produces riches, riches power, power preserves our trade'.[85] There were, however, other issues which were considered to be much more pressing and important than those concerning commerce and overseas trade by the makers of foreign policy. What characterises early eighteenth-century Britain is a constant search for a harmony between the dynastic interest fixated on Europe and the mercantile interest longing for immediate cessation of international hostilities as well as more colonies and open markets. And it is this cacophony which accounts for the popularity of the anti-Machiavellian patriot king discourse in early eighteenth-century Britain.

In this respect, it is not difficult to understand that the first and foremost goal of Davenant and Moyle in translating Xenophon's *Ways and Means* was to criticise the Williamite foreign policy that had dragged England into a military and diplomatic quagmire across the Channel under the banner of the Protestant succession and the European balance of power. In reasoning that the Nine Years' War had introduced the Bank of England and caused the Financial Revolution, giving rise to the unpatriotic and corruptive moneyed interest, Davenant pressed Parliament to cease engaging in the continental affairs without considering the economic situation of the nation. Peace, in his principled opinion, would bring what Britain had lost in the course of the expensive war and much more. Thus, Xenophon's advice given to his fellow Athenians after their tragic defeat in the Peloponnesian War was of particular relevance to the British situation.

> If it seems clear that the state cannot obtain a full revenue from all sources unless she has peace, is it not worth while to set up a board of guardians of peace? … For I presume that those states are reckoned the happiest that enjoy the longest period of unbroken peace; and of all states Athens is by nature most suited to flourish in peace.[86]

Closely related to Davenant's longing for an immediate cession of war was his strong advocacy of an empire of the seas. As is well known, the blue water policy became predominant with the so-called Standing Army debate during the last years of the reign of William III. With a view to reinforcing their argument that a standing army was fundamentally incompatible with a free government, many began to point out that it

---

[85] Child, *A Treatise concerning the East-India Trade* (London, 1681), 29.
[86] *Ways and Means* 8.1–2; trans. Marchant and Bowersock, in *Xenophon: Scripta Minora*, 225.

was absolutely unnecessary for a country surrounded by the seas. Not only the changing nature of international competition, but also its geographical location as well as constitutional structure, indicated that Britain was to become the empire of the seas. The eyes of a myriad of analysts of commerce, regardless of their different political positions, were consequently fixed upon the image of the Royal Navy as the protector of England from both 'the fears of invasion from abroad' and 'the dangers of slavery at home'.[87]

Given this, it is not surprising that the Country pamphleteers like Davenant constantly argued against the Whig ministry throughout the first half of the eighteenth century that Britain should follow the footsteps of the Athenian Empire, especially in her policy of neutrality and dedication to overseas trades and commerce. Specifically, to the disgruntled landed interest who had been suffering from the continuous wars, Xenophon's suggestion that Athens should always take advantage of her semi-insular location and aspire to become a maritime trading empire rather than an aggressive territorial state, the point emphatically put forward also by Pericles in his famous reply to the Spartan ultimatum, was therefore a very alluring story. According to Thucydides, Pericles had thundered to his fellow Athenians that,

> Sea-power is of enormous importance ... Suppose we were an island, would we not be absolutely secure from attack? As it is we must try to think of ourselves as islanders; we must abandon our land and our houses, and safeguard the sea and the city.[88]

Bolingbroke's main contention in his *Idea of a Patriot King* was also indistinguishable from what Shebbeare suggested. He wanted once and for all to set the mind of Frederick, who as the heir to the throne was already gathering an entourage of oppositional M.P.s, on his new island realm.[89] At the very heart of Bolingbroke's teaching was Britain's insularity. After criticising Machiavelli's model of an amoral prince, Bolingbroke argued that,

> Great Britain is an island; and, whilst nations on the continent are at immense charge in maintaining their barriers, and perpetually on their guard, and frequently embroiled, to extend or strengthen them, Great Britain may, if her governors please, accumulate wealth in maintaining hers; make herself secure from invasions, and be ready to invade others when her own immediate

---

[87] See Armitage, *The Ideological Origins of the British Empire*, 125–98.
[88] Thucydides 1.143; trans Warner, *History of the Peloponnesian War* (London, 1972), 122.
[89] For more on the popularity of Frederick among the Country gentlemen, see G. Young, *Poor Fred: The People's Prince* (Oxford, 1937).

interest, or the general interest of Europe requires it ... By a continual attention to improve her natural, that is her maritime strength, by collecting all her forces within herself, and reserving them to be laid out on great occasions, such as regard her immediate interests and her honour, or such as are truly important to the general system of power in Europe; she may be the arbitrator of differences, the guardian of liberty, and the preserver of that balance, which has been so much talked of, and is so little understood.[90]

Again, this was exactly what Xenophon told Athenians who were deeply concerned about their international status should Athens follow the isolationist foreign policy that he recommended. Xenophon wrote in his *Ways and Means* that,

> He will find that in old days a very great amount of money was paid into the treasury in time of peace, and that the whole of it was spent in time of war; he will conclude on consideration that in our own time the effect of the late war on our revenues was that many of them ceased, while those that came in were exhausted by the multitude of expenses; whereas the cessation of war by sea has been followed by a rise in the revenues, and has allowed the citizens to devote them to any purpose they chose ... But some one may ask me, Do you mean to say that, even if she is wronged, the state should remain at peace with the offender? No, certainly not; but I do say that our vengeance would follow far more swiftly on our enemies if we provoked nobody by wrong-doing; for then they would look in vain for an ally.[91]

It may therefore be stated that the philosophical basis of the celebrated Tory blue water policy set forth most famously in Bolingbroke's *Idea of a Patriot King* should be sought not in the preface of Harrington's semi-utopian tract where the importance of naval supremacy was mentioned sporadically and rather vaguely, though critical philosophically, in relation to Venice, but rather in this much more historically pointed and nuanced criticism of the Williamite-Hanoverian continental commitments. What James Harrington wanted to emphasise in his famous statement that 'the sea giveth law unto the growth of Venice, but the growth of Oceana giveth law unto the sea' is less the seaborne nature of Oceana than its adherence to the agrarian law.[92] More specifically, the reason why Oceana was capable of imposing its rule on the sea was not because it encouraged commerce and overseas trades but because its constitution was hinged on the immovable property, that is to say, land. As a faithful Aristotelian, Harrington

---

[90] Bolingbroke, 'Patriot King', 277–8.
[91] *Ways and Means* 8.1–3; trans. Marchant and Bowersock, in *Xenophon: Scripta Minora*, 229.
[92] 'The *Commonwealth* of *Oceana*', in *The Commonwealth of Oceana* and *A System of Politics*, 7.

firmly believed that *nomos* was inseparably linked to land and its orderly distribution among citizens.[93] Venice, on the contrary, was unable to withstand corruptive luxury from the sea because it loosened its agrarian law. This arguably accounts for and is substantiated by the fact that no leading exponent of the blue water foreign policy in the early eighteenth century referred to Harrington's tract, *The Commonwealth of Oceana*.[94]

As a matter of fact, Bolingbroke himself wrote a short commentary on Thucydides's *History of the Peloponnesian War* entitled *On the Policy of the Athenians*. Investigating the causes of the decline of Athens' empire after the war with Sparta, Bolingbroke lamented that if only 'the whole of their policy' was 'consisted in interposing their force in cases of necessity only, to prevent the weak from being unjustly oppressed by their more powerful neighbour; and in avoiding, as much as possible, to make themselves parties, much less principals in their quarrels'.[95] The centrality of Xenophon in the Tory conception of Britain as a new Athens was also confirmed by Montesquieu in his *Spirit of the Laws*. After quoting at length Xenophon's discussion of Athens's empire on the sea that 'if the Athenians lived on an island and had also empire on the sea, they would have the power to harm others and no one would be able to harm them, so long as they remained masters of the sea', Montesquieu emphatically added that 'you might say that Xenophon intended to speak of England'.[96]

How, then, could we explain the pseudo-republican coupling of empire and liberty that Bolingbroke set forth in his portrait of a patriot king? Although Bolingbroke only mentioned the Roman emperor Nerva as his ideal model in his advice-book for princes, it is also possible to interpret Xenophon's *Cyropaedia* as a political recipe for empire.[97] At least that was how Shebbeare read the book. In his caustic pamphlet published on the eve of the Seven Years' War, Shebbeare, while urging a fundamental revision of British foreign policy, proclaimed that:

> Was it not by means of the happy Union of those superior Qualifications in the first *Cyrus*, that he extended his Empire from the little Realm of *Persia*

---

[93] See C. Schmitt, *The Nomos of the Earth in the International Law of the Jus Publicum Europaeum*, trans. G. L. Ulmen (New York, 2006), 67–79.

[94] Armitage, *The Ideological Origins of the British Empire*, 170–98; E.H. Gould, *The Persistence of Empire: British Political Culture in the Age of the American Revolution* (Chapel Hill, 2000), 1–71.

[95] 'On the Policy of the Athenians', in *A Collection of Political Tracts* (Dublin, 1748), 169. This pamphlet was published under the pseudonym Phil-Athenus.

[96] Montesquieu, *The Spirit of the Laws*, eds. A.M. Cohler, B.C. Miller, and H.S. Stone (Cambridge, 1989), 362.

[97] Bolingbroke, 'Patriot King', 293.

over Nations, almost too distant to be visited, and whose Languages were unintelligible to each other, as *Xenophon* has described them?[98]

However, as Xenophon had fully acknowledged in his short, yet highly controversial afterthought to his *Cyropaedia*, causing much confusion and doubts as to its authorship, Bolingbroke had to admit that even the most virtuous patriotic monarch was unable to vouch for the qualities of his heir.[99] 'The royal mantle', he lamented, 'will not convey the spirit of patriotism into another king'.[100] 'Our Patriot King must be a patriot from the first'.[101] After unwillingly accepting that his seemingly innovative and visionary solution to the ill consequences of the Revolution Settlement and the subsequent Hanoverian Succession had a major inherent defect, Bolingbroke, as Xenophon had already done to his Persian friends, therefore, decided to appeal to the British people to act together and remain frugal and virtuous. 'If they do not', Bolingbroke warned, 'they will have none but themselves to blame'.[102] The fate of Xenophon's *Cyropaedia*, at least as the quintessence of the mirror-for-princes literature, was sealed as the royal chamber gradually receded from the central stage of politics with the advent of parliamentary democracy and the concurrent formation of modern bureaucracy. Thus what Coxe remarked in respect of the nature of the text at the end of the eighteenth century – 'it must be considered as mere puerilities from a practical politician' – can be read as a reflection of the historic transformation towards what we call modernity, a transformation with which our British devotees of Xenophon were struggling to come to terms.[103] What is more revealing perhaps is that the end result of George III's ambitious attempt to become a Bolingbrokean patriot king with vigorous maritime expansionist foreign policy was the independence of the thirteen colonies in America.[104]

---

[98] *A Letter to the People of England, on the Present Situation and Conduct of National Affairs. Letter I*, second edition (London, 1755), 5.
[99] *Cyropaedia* 8.8.1–27; trans. Miller, *Cyropaedia* 5–8, 439–53; P. Windsor Sage, 'Dying in Style: Xenophon's Ideal Leader and the End of the *Cyropaedia*', *The Classical Journal*, 90 (1994–5), 161–74. Miller argues that the last chapter of the *Cyropaedia* on the fall of the Persian Empire after the death of Cyrus is not written by Xenophon, see his footnote in his Loeb translation of the *Cyropaedia*, 438–9.
[100] Bolingbroke, 'Patriot King', 252.
[101] Bolingbroke, 'Patriot King', 247.
[102] Bolingbroke, 'Patriot King', 252.
[103] *Memoirs of the Life and Administration of Sir Robert Walpole*, vol. 1 (London, 1978), 213.
[104] Armitage, 'A Patriot for Whom? The Afterlives of Bolingbroke's Patriot King', *The Journal of British Studies*, 36 (1997), 397–418.

# 3. William Young and the *Spirit of Athens**

## *Peter Liddel*

A number of approaches have emerged in the contemporary study of the modern historiography of ancient Greece. On the one hand there are intellectual biographies of individual modern (or early-modern) scholars, institutions and movements; on the other, there are histories of the reception of ideas, places, individuals and institutions. In this paper I shall attempt to combine the biographical approach with an analysis of the ways in which the work of William Young presented his interpretation of ancient Athenian history in the light of contemporary political thought. It will become clear that despite his claims at originality and innovation in drawing on the work of Montesquieu, Young's work owed a great deal to a wide range of Enlightenment approaches to antiquity. In so doing, I hope to highlight a problem that has blighted modern historiographical scholarship: the tendency to evaluate eighteenth-century studies of Greek history according to modes of analysis developed in the mid-nineteenth century for thinking about the post-French Revolution party histories and narratives.[1] I want also to suggest that it is necessary to read eighteenth-century histories in a way which takes more notice of their relationship to contemporary developments not only in historiography but also in other literary genres.

---

* I am grateful to Dr James Moore and Dr Ian Macgregor Morris for their guiding me towards a better contextualisation of Young's work, and to Dr Laurence Brown for discussing the Caribbean context of William Young. I am also grateful to the participants at the 2007 Nottingham Historiography colloquium and the Institute of Historical Research 2007 'Making History' colloquium.

[1] This has a great deal to do with the way in which nineteenth-century reviewers tended to dismiss the works of their predecessors: for instance, see Macaulay's reading of Mitford's history as a Tory history: T. Macaulay, 'On Mitford's History of Greece', in H. Trevelyan (ed.), *Miscellaneous Works of Lord Macaulay*, 5 vols. (New York, [1873]), vol. IV, 470–94, first published in *Knight's Quarterly Magazine*, November 1824. For an early twentieth-century occurrence of the term, see T. Peardon, *The Transition in English Historical Writing, 1760–1830* (New York, 1933). Also see Ian Macgregor Morris' article, 247–90 below.

## 1. Introduction: William Young, Second Baronet (1749–1815)

William Young, the son of a colonial governor of the same name, was deeply involved in national and colonial administration: he was a Whig MP for St Mawes in Cornwall from 1784–1806, and a governor of Tobago from 1807–15.[2] Politically, he is remembered as an advocate of slavery who argued that abolition would damage the prosperity of Britain, the colonies themselves, and suggested that it was unlikely to relieve the condition of Africa.[3] His publications on the Caribbean and the British Constitution reflected his administrative and political activity,[4] but he had antiquarian interests too. In 1786 he became a fellow of the Royal Society and in 1791 a fellow of the Society of Antiquaries. Indeed, his first publication was *The Spirit of Athens* of 1777[5] which, according to Sheridan, won him fame. However, the work is rarely cited in later histories of Greece, and little certain is known about its reception, other than the remarks that the author himself makes on others' approval of it in the preface to the editions of 1786 and 1804.[6]

---

[2] For the life of Young, see E.I. Carlyle, revised by R. Sheridan, Oxford *DNB* s.v. 'Young, Sir William, second baronet (1749–1815)'. On the role of Young and his father, William Young, first baronet (1724/5–1788) in the adminstrative organisation of Tobago and in the Anglo–French struggle for domination of the island, see J.-C. Nardin, *La mise en valeur de l'Isle de Tabago (1763–83)* (The Hague, 1969).

[3] For his views on the slave-trade and the treatment of slaves, see R. Sheridan, 'Sir William Young (1749–1815): Planter and Politician, with special reference to slavery in the British West Indies', *Journal of Caribbean History*, 33 (1999), 1–26. He opposed Wilberforce's motion of 28 February 1805 for the second reading on the bill on the abolition of the slave trade: see P. Hogg, *The African Slave Trade and Its Suppression: A Classified and Annotated Bibliography of Books* (London, 2006), 194. For Young's opposition, see also D.B. Gaspar, 'Ameliorating Slavery: The Leeward Islands Slave Act of 1795', 241–58, in R. L. Paquette and S. L. Engerman (eds.), *The Lesser Antilles in the Age of European Expansion* (Gainesville, 1996), at 245–6. On landed anti-abolitionists, see also D. Davis, *The Problem of Slavery in the Age of Revolution* (New York, 1999), 101–2.

[4] For a list of his works, see Sheridan, Oxford *DNB* s. v. 'Young, Sir William'.

[5] Full title: *The Spirit of Athens, being a Political and Philosophical Investigation of the History of that Republic*, second and third editions (London, 1786 and 1804) used the title *The History of Athens; Including a Commentary on the Principles, Policy, and Practice, of Republican Government; and on the Causes of Elevation and of Decline, which operate in every free and commercial state*.

[6] The preface to the 1786 edition sets out to correct errors and deficiencies of the 1777 edition, with a view to 'a more considerate and mature enquiry' (1786, xi). He claims in the preface to the 1804 edition that his style and language were criticised but 'its matter and substance were approved of by many thinking and learned men, and their approbation was expressed in terms which have encouraged me to suppose, that my book was that a *corrected edition* might be acceptable' (1804, x). His praise of Republicanism clearly drew criticism: he defended his use of the term as in 'the ancient sense of the word' (1804, xiv).

Young was a late voice in the Quarrel of the Ancients and Moderns, and, like others, he expressed hope that antiquity offered models and lessons to the modern world.[7] Those who have commented on his work have drawn quite different conclusions.[8] Loraux and Vidal-Naquet saw Young as an advocate of a commercial view of a modernist Athenian city-state. Demetriou interprets Young's moderate political viewpoint as characteristic of a section of parliamentary Whigs with conflicting loyalties. Roberts, meanwhile, sets him up as a critic of democratic Athens.[9] Accordingly, there is no consensus on him and there exists no full portrayal of him or his significance in Greek historiography. The tendency to fit him into sharply-dichotomised democratic or anti-democratic pigeonholes has however been surpassed: for Macgregor Morris, Young was an Athenophile who worried that her political system was subject to mob rule; he advocated a form of democracy which would feature the Spartan characteristics of rule of law and limited equality (see below section 6).[10]

In this paper I shall investigate Young's claim that his interpretation of Athens was grounded in the theories of Montesquieu; but I shall suggest that he shares many themes with near-contemporary studies of Greece (in particular those of Rollin, Mably) and also other writers such as Bolingbroke and Glover. Several lines of argument will run through

---

[7] See P. Gay, *The Enlightenment: An Interpretation. The Rise of Modern Paganism* (New York, 1966), 31–71.

[8] Many serious studies of historiography do not mention Young, often because they focus on the post-Gillies or Victorian periods: see A. Momigliano, 'George Grote and the study of Greek history', in A. Momigliano (ed.), *Studies in Greek Historiography* (London, 1969), 56–74; F. Turner, *The Greek Heritage in Victorian Britain* (New Haven; London, 1981); O. Murray, 'Introduction', in O. Murray (ed) *Athens: Its Rise and Fall* by E. Bulwer Lytton (London and New York, 2004), 1–34.

[9] N. Loraux, and P. Vidal-Naquet, 'The Formation of Bourgeois Athens', in P. Vidal-Naquet (ed.), *Politics Ancient and Modern* (Cambridge, 1995), 82–140; J. Roberts, *Athens on Trial: The Antidemocratic Tradition in Western Thought* (Princeton, NJ, 1994), 188 and 202; K. Demetriou, *George Grote on Plato and Athenian Democracy: a Study in Classical Reception*. Koinon, 2 (Frankfurt am Main, 1999), 43–4. Another work has suggested that he conceived of England in his own age as undergoing a 'Demosthenic moment', a time when commercial interests and party struggles threatened the prosperity that gave rise to them: see A. Potkay, *Fate of Eloquence in the Age of Hume* (Ithaca and London, 1994), 32.

[10] I. Macgregor Morris, 'The Paradigm of Democracy: Sparta in Enlightenment Thought', 339–58, in T. Figueira (ed.), *Spartan Society* (Swansea, 2004), at 353–5; I. Macgregor Morris, 'The Refutation of Democracy? Socrates in the Enlightenment', 209–27, in M. Trapp (ed.), *Socrates from Antiquity to the Enlightenment* (London, 2007), at 223–4.

this paper: I shall argue that, like other eighteenth-century writers on Greece, Young set out not to write a conventional narrative history but one which demonstrated political lessons for his contemporaries; that in order to do this he introduced to an interpretation of Athens the political sociology of Montesquieu (and in particular the ideas of spirit and national character: see section 2). I will discuss the deployment of four key phenomena in his history (the nature of ancient virtue, the rise and fall of empire, the role of the individual, and his interpretation of democracy: see sections 3–6) and the ways in which these corresponded to Young's own involvement in contemporary colonialism and the interests and achievements of his literary predecessors and contemporaries. I shall suggest that the toning down of the rhetoric of democracy in the later editions of his work may be seen as a response to contemporary political events (see sections 6 and 7).[11] My first step, however, will be to investigate Young's presentation of his own interpretation of the past, his engagement with notions central to the work of Montesquieu, and their broad intellectual background, which was not always acknowledged in his work.

## 2. *History* and *Spirit* and Young's Athens

Young's work on Athens went through three publications; the 1786 and 1804 editions changed the title from *Spirit of Athens* to *History of Athens*, perhaps a concession to the trend among his contemporaries.[12] But the titles and subtitles used by Young suggest not a narrative, but rather a 'political and philosophical investigation' or a 'commentary on principles'.[13] In all three editions, Young presented a self-consciously selective approach to historiography:

> The design of the following treatise, is from the annals of men and things to extract the spirit of character and event; with the narrative to interweave the moral, and in the history enfolding its comment, to render each political lesson explicit and applicable.[14]

One clear effect of this focus was to make his accounts of the military details of the great conflicts of the fifth century B.C. sparse: moral and

---

[11] Demetriou, *George Grote*, 44 notes the shift in Young's expressed political values.
[12] Histories of Greece were published with the title 'A History of Greece', or similar, by Temple Stanyan (1707–39), Robertson (1768), Goldsmith (1774), Gillies (1786) and Mitford (1784).
[13] For the full titles of Young's work, see above n. 6.
[14] 1786, ix (= 1804, vii (rephrased from 1777, viii–ix)).

political rather than the military spheres of history were emphasised. But while his history did not set out to be comprehensive, his statements recognised a tension which demanded that, if history was to be teaching by example, it should be conceived as forming contiguous blocks: anecdotes, accounts of events and biographies were deemed to do little to give a fair impression, and Young warned against the danger of using free-standing examples as a ground for lessons:

> My book may be of some use to the young, or to the superficial student; – it may teach him that the ancient Greek history is fraught with something more than apothegm and anecdote, – that to know the names of Marathon and Salamis, of Codrus, or of Cimon, (to pursue a metaphor of Mr Burke's) is merely to know the land-marks of history, and not the country … in my course many a flower have I disregarded, that others have stayed to pluck, and perchance, sometimes a simple have I culled, which another hath neglected.[15]

In a later edition, he elucidated this line of thinking, and proposed that a subject matter should be 'kept entire' and history should be written 'in some complete series'.[16] Like many others in the eighteenth century, this conception of connected Greek history was dominated by the rise and fall model of change, and, as we shall see throughout this paper (especially in sections 4 and 5), the notion of decline loomed large. But this system allowed Young, in philosophical mode, to pinpoint a peak of Athenian civilisation, the moment at which the thoughtful reader should stop and take stock:[17] for him the acme of history was the point at which enthusiasm for public interests was at its most vigorous. This took place in Athens, he suggested, in the period immediately after the close of the Persian wars (from 479 B.C.): the state, as he conceived

---

[15] Young 1777, ix.
[16] 1804, iv: 'A selection of instances from general history can never form grounds of certain inference, or afford a safe lesson for human policy and conduct, even if the designs of the compiler are most pure and impartial'; 1804, v: 'If history is truly defined 'to be philosophy teaching by example', it cannot be unworthy the leisure of the wisest man, to examine the example, and elucidate the lesson it contains: but to this effect, a subject-matter should be taken and kept entire, and the reference touch it, in all its parts'; 1804, vi: 'History, then, should be taken in some complete series, with all the relations of successive character and vicissitude'.
[17] 1804, 10: 'In this history of intellect, manners, and society, I presume to suggest, that there has, at some time, been an epoch, at which the philosophic reader may pause; and note the character of man sufficiently developed and matured, for the conferring and enjoying all practical advantages in society, and yet clear from the vices and corruptions, which attend a more general and advanced intercourse'.

of the Athenian polis, its citizens and its statesmen combined wealth, patriotism, experience, vigour and calmness with readiness for public activity.[18]

Another aspect of his view of historiography was his repudiation of objectivity. In a challenge to Aristotle's claim that poetry is more philosophical than history, he claimed poetic licence in his 1777 and 1786 editions by talking about his 'free mode' of writing history and the possible exaggerations and anachronisms that it introduced:

> Poetry may perhaps show the scene to a dim eye, in larger quarries, and in stronger colours; – to gain this advantage likewise over to history, and to pair a forcible and expressive picture of my subject, – I have changed the attitudes of some figures, I have transposed others, and have approximated them to a stronger contrast, or to a more glaring light. Some few Anachronisms are the result of this free mode of treating history – I trust they are the few.[19]

This 'free mode' of writing history was nothing new: it echoed the philosophical historiography of Rollin and others.[20] Ultimately, however, it was a mode that he abandoned: in his third edition, the claim that subjectivity makes history more worthwhile was replaced with a more direct stance in later editions of 1786 and 1804: the idea (see below n. 34) that Athens provided a parallel to Britain just as the fall of Rome would have provided a model to the French.

Young's bold statements about the originality of what he was doing are striking though ultimately the rhetoric is sometimes misleading. He showed in his 1804 edition that he was aware of the value of claiming,

---

[18] 1804, 166: 'The *state* was become most wealthy; its people were become numerous and inured to war; and from the habits of a naval war were become bold and expert on the seas, and suited to the purposes and enterprise of trade. Its citizens were become versed in public business, whether touching exterior policy or domestic management. – Its statesmen and military leaders were experienced in each department; and its vigour was yet hitherto unimpaired by corruption, and its constitution unbroken by popular frenzy, or by the intrigues which individuals, distinguished by riches and ability, might be supposed to create'. Cf. 1804, 264: 'In the moral, as in the physical world, the point of maturity is but that of a moment, whilst increase and decrease have their periods, and in general of reciprocal duration'.

[19] 1786, viii–ix (=1777, viii).

[20] Rollin, in his preface, wrote that his work was intended to be one for 'instruction of the youth', he strived to 'avoid the dry sterility of epitomes', and wrote of the 'liberty' he had taken to make alterations to ancient accounts of events: see C. Rollin, *The Ancient History of the Egyptians, Carthaginans, Assyrians, Babylonians, Medes and Persians, Macedonians, and Grecians*, eighth edition (London, 1788) vol. I, 13–15.

albeit retrospectively, that writing the history of Athens was a deliberate step in a new direction.[21] That particular claim was well-founded: histories of individual city states were rare at this point, and a less surprising choice for such a study would have been Sparta, the city that Mably and Rousseau had focused upon, but whose mores Young rejected.[22] It was indeed the case that in the first half of the eighteenth century the centrality of Athens in the emergence of classical culture led the likes of Winckelmann and Voltaire to say approving things about Athens,[23] and the pro-Athenian rhetoric was picked up again in de Pauw's 1788 *Philosophical Dissertations on the Greeks*.[24] But enthusiasm for Athens and her political systems was far from the norm among Anglophone historians.

I will now turn to Young's claims about the significance of political thought to his work. From early on in his history, Young aligned himself with Aristotle's theory of constitutional change and enthused about his interest in eudaimonism.[25] The preface to the third edition introduces the reader to the significance for historical understanding of Machiavelli, Montesquieu, Harrington and others.[26] Montesquieu

---

[21] 1804, vii: 'In the choice of subject-matter, I was in the first instance directed by an observation that the History of Athens had in each previous instance been implicated in that of Greece, and that a distinct and separate account of that most distinguished republic of antiquity had by no historian been treated at large'.

[22] On the Spartan example, see J. K. Wright, *A Classical Republican in Eighteenth-Century France: the Political Thought of Mably* (Stanford, 1997); E. Rawson, *The Spartan Tradition in Western European Thought* (Oxford, 1969); P. Cartledge, 'The Socratics' Sparta and Rousseau's', in S. Hodkinson and A. Powell (eds.), *Sparta: New Perspectives* (Swansea, 1999), 311–37. Young, on the other hand, was dismissive of the value of the Spartan example, for she was unenlightened (1804, 93 n.), her policies motivated only by self interest (1804, 96); and the Lycurgan laws restricted the movement of their citizens (147–8).

[23] Voltaire: see P. Vidal-Naquet, *Politics*, 143; Winckelmann: M. Hansen, *The Tradition of Ancient Greek Democracy and Its Importance for Modern Democracy* (Copenhagen, 2005), 14.

[24] de Pauw: Macgregor Morris, 'The refutation', 220–3.

[25] At 1804, 101, he suggested that happiness is the end of all political ordinances or arrangements. All three editions contain a chapter on the principles of happiness: see (1804, 152 ff. = 1777, 131 ff.). He praises Athens as the state best designed for happiness (1804, 85). His enthusiasm for Aristotle expanded beyond his ideas about happiness: early on in his history, he aligns himself with Aristotle's theory of constitutional decay, with *politeiai*, for instance, being perverted into a democracy (54). Aristotle, he claimed, was the 'most correct writer on political subjects I have read' (132).

[26] 1804, iv–vi. The work contains many other direct and passing references to political thinkers: Bolingbroke at 1804, 4; Bacon at 1804, 108; Harrington at 1804, 298–9.

emerges as the most important guide to the interpretation of history, and is particularly prominent in the preface to the 1786 and 1804 editions but also in the first half of all three editions. Indeed, the title of the 1777 edition surely provides the reader with the immediate intellectual context of the work: that context was Montesquieu's 1748 *Spirit of the Laws*, published in France but well known and welcomed in some circles in Britain; its plaudits included both Whigs and Tories.[27] It combined an analysis of the main forms of government with a consideration of the corresponding historical, ecological, religious and commercial conditions, in other words their 'Spirit'. Montesquieu drew on Graeco-Roman examples especially the first books of the *Spirit*, showing a preference for Rome and Sparta, but drawing occasionally on Athens; his typology of government was deeply influenced by that of Aristotle's *Politics*.[28] Central to Montesquieu's analysis of politics was the definition of the three kinds of government (republic, monarchy, and despotism) according to 'nature' and 'principle'. The 'nature' of government referred to the number of individuals possessing sovereignty; the 'principle' was the sentiment that motivated men within the collectivity. The 'principle' of a republic was virtue.

Young shared Montesquieu's view that a populace expressed virtue through its political activity (on virtue, see below, section 3).[29] He also shared Montesquieu's conceptualisation of Britain as a republic, claiming, in the preface to the 1804 edition, that Britain was a 'regal republic' which

---

[27] Mitford cited it in his history: *The History of Greece* (London, 1829), vol. II, 249, III, 462. On the reception of Montesquieu's work among English and Scottish thinkers, see A. Cohler, 'Introduction', xi–xxviii, in A. Cohler, B. Miller and H. Stone (eds.), *Montesquieu, The Spirit of the Laws* (Cambridge, 1989), at xxiv–xxvi and xxxii; F. Fletcher, *Montesquieu and English Politics* (London, 1939). Montesquieu's *Spirit* was of particular interest to British thinkers of a Whig persuasion because of the author's collusion with British thinkers like Bolingbroke and also because it offered up the English government of his time as one whose end was political liberty (*Spirit*, 11.6, 19.27). For Montesquieu's stay in England and his association with Bolingbroke, see E. Nelson, *The Greek Tradition in Republican Thought* (Cambridge, 2004), 129. On its critics, see R. Romani, *National Character and Public Spirit in Britain and France, 1750–1914* (Cambridge, 2002), 31–7.

[28] Montesquieu was the author of *The Considerations on the Causes of The Greatness of the Romans and Their Decline* of 1734. On his view of Rome, see R. Oake, 'Montesquieu's Analysis of Roman History', *Journal of the History of Ideas*, 16 (1955), 44–59. For his views on Athens, see C. Mossé, *L'Antiqueteé dans la Révolution française* (Paris, 1989), 55–61; Roberts, *Athens*, 172.

[29] For an exploration of the connection between concepts of good, virtue and classical republicanism, see P. Miller, *Defining the Common Good: Empire, Religion and Philosophy in Eighteenth-Century Britain* (Cambridge, 1994).

was an example of regulated liberty and power.³⁰ The notions of nationhood and *caractère national* important to Montesquieu's work resurface in the history of Young. ³¹ Central to Young's decision to concentrate on the history of one city state was the idea that meaningful, philosophic, history was that which was able to elucidate 'national characteristics'.³² But why choose Athens? His decision to concentrate on Athens owed a great deal to contemporary developments in perceptions of that city: on the one hand, there was the growing consensus, already noted, that the cultural achievements of classical Athens made her worthy of attention (in Young's own words, Athens was 'a school to all nations for the liberal arts, eloquence and philosophy')³³. But there was also a sense that Athens, as a commercial and victorious 'nation', offered a model of modernity: this sentiment was expressed in a remark of Montesquieu, repeated in the preface to Young's later editions, and suggested that Athens, as an imperial power, offered the most attractive parallel to the emerging imperial state of England.³⁴

---

³⁰ 1804, xv: 'Tacitus yet praised in theory, that of which he doubted in effect. Could the political genius of this learned Roman now rise from the grave, and looking back to the revolutions and wreck of communities and states which during the last twelve years, have spread disorder and desolation throughout civilized Europe, including his own great city of Rome; – then turn his regard to the West, and observe the Regal Republic of Great Britain standing firm and untouched, – a bright example of regulated liberties and power to correct a distracted world'. Young's concept of the republic could not stand in clearer contrast to the rhetoric of the dedication to George III that stood at the head of Gillies' 1786 *History of Greece*, promising that the history of Greece illustrates the turbulence of democracy and the incurable evils in every form of republican policy and shows the benefits of the 'lawful dominion of hereditary kings', J. Gillies, *History of Greece* (London, 1786).

³¹ See R. Romani, *National Character*, 9–62. On traditions about the interplay of freedom and national character upon which Montesquieu drew, M. Meehan, *Liberty and Poetics in Eighteenth-Century England* (London, 1986), 13–23.

³² 1777, vii: 'National characteristics, as much, or more than private character, should be clearly deducible from this kind of work; and if treated with such view (and with such view it should be treated) history may teem with as much philosophic theory as poetry'.

³³ Young, 1804, 389.

³⁴ Montesquieu, *Spirit*, 21.7. The passage was cited by Young, 1786, x–xi; 1804, viii: 'The treatise of Montesquieu on the greatness and decline of the Roman empire, was founded on a subject which might have supplied a forcible lesson to the kingdom, and at the time in which he wrote. That author, in another, and greater work, remarking on a passage of Xenophon relative to the naval power of the Athenians says, "one would imagine almost that Xenophon was speaking with allusion to England". I seem therefore to pursue the idea of Montesquieu, when I investigate the History of the Great Grecian Republic; assuming that "its arts, its sciences, its liberty, its commerce, its colonies, and its empire of the seas, render the subject peculiarly our own"'; cf. 1804, 367. In making Athens a commercial state he was reacting to Hume's rejection of the idea of Athens as a commercial power: Vidal-Naquet, *Politics*, 90, 114; D. Hume, *Essays. Moral, Political and Literary*, ed. E. F. Miller (Indianapolis, 1985), 256–8, 416–7.

One theme of Montesquieu's work was to consider the ways in which the laws of a constitution are related to both the climate and the nature of the terrain[35] and the populousness of a state.[36] These and a wider group of factors give rise to the general spirit of a nation: 'Many things govern men: climate, religion, laws, the maxims of the government, examples of past things, mores and manners; a general spirit is formed as a result.'[37] Montesquieu was not the first to theorise about the significance of physical conditions in the development of political principles or national character: he was pre-empted by Temple and Blackmore, and also travellers like Robert Wood,[38] but Montesquieu, as Meehan has argued, provided an 'authoritative endorsement' of the idea which made it appear more intellectually coherent.[39] These principles resemble closely those which Young identified as contributing to the spirit of Athens: in his opening chapter, he sets out to investigate the springs that lead to the social and spirited principles of public actions.[40] It quickly emerges, in chapters 2 and 3, that these are the nature of the population, its soil, climate, its deities, the reciprocal ties of the family, the nature of early government and contact with other communities.[41] For both writers, it wasn't just the physical sense of an environment that had an impact on the nature of men and the state, but the mental world, the pre-established order of society, and the form of political constitution: this was the essence of *Spirit*. The significance of the development of the mind for the course of Greek history had already been brought out by Tourreil in his preface to his translation of Demosthenes'

---

[35] The theme of books 14 to 18 of the *Spirit of the Laws*.
[36] The theme of book 23.
[37] Montesquieu, *Spirit*, 19.4.
[38] Wood took the idea in a different direction, suggesting 'the notion that a locale, through association with events and ideas, attained an almost mystical power': see I. Macgregor Morris, '"Shrines of the Almighty": Rediscovering the Battlefields of the Persian Wars', in E. Bridges and P. Rhodes (eds.), *Cultural Responses to the Persian Wars. Antiquity to the Third Millennium* (Oxford, 2007), 231–64 and D. Constantine, *Early Greek Travellers and the Hellenic Ideal* (Cambridge, 1984), 66–84.
[39] On British writers' hypotheses about the links between national character and climate, see Meehan, *Liberty*, 17.
[40] 1804, 11–12.
[41] 1804, 14–31. The same sentiment is expressed in the first edition, 1777, 163: 'Whoever would develop a national character, let him contemplate it in the laws and regulations of the state, the nature of its dominion abroad, and the tenor of its constitution at home; let him reflect on their combination with the arts, with the religion, – nay, with the very face, and climate of the country; with these let him compare historical facts, and if he hath candidly and acutely pursued the speculation, he will have a set of manners before him very near the truth, and which should cautiously cede even a contemporary opinion, and however respectable'.

speeches as early as 1691.[42] Young held up the history of the Persian wars as an example which substantiated Montesquieu's theories, suggesting that both constitution and climate made their outcome a foregone conclusion: the Persians were unable to foment republican virtue.[43] Young's interpretation of the notion of spirit led him to encompass in his work the history of intellect, of manners, and society,[44] and accordingly he introduced non-political scholarship to his analysis of Athens. In a chapter dedicated to the development of art in Athens and its relationship to republican virtue, he repeated Winckelman's view that 'free states are the best nursery-bed of the arts'.[45] In so doing Young linked up with those writers, such as Shaftesbury, who located a culture of freedom in ancient Athens, expressed through its literature and arts, and who suggested that antiquity offered a serious alternative to the Christian-based culture and politics of modern Europe.[46] It is clear, therefore, that while Young's emphasis was on his use of Montesquieu's work, he in fact drew on ideas circulated in the work of a wide range of eighteenth-century writers: this was also the case in his deployment of the notion of virtue in the history of Athens.

## 3. Virtue, Ancient and Modern

For Montesquieu, virtue was a characteristic of a good republican form of government; it was conceptualised simply as the individual's love of the republic. It consisted of the sacrifice of individual passions for the sake

---

[42] See J. de Tourreil, *Several Orations of Demosthenes, to Encourage the Athenians to Oppose the Exorbitant Power of Philip of Macedon. English'd from the Greek by several hands. To which is prefix'd the historical preface of Monsieur Tourreil* (London, 1702), esp. 14 and 23.

[43] 1804, 110: 'Montesquieu hath entered into a disquisition concerning physical effects on the constitution of men and states: throughout the annals of mankind, I know not a period more fully demonstrative of his theories, and of the influence of government on men, and of climate on both, than the times of contest betwixt Greece and Persia. If history is philosophy teaching by example, never did it teach in a more nervous strain, the lesson of contempt for tyranny, and of love and admiration for a state of freedom'. Young's choice of Persia was in tune with Montesquieu's orientalist stance as it emerged in his *Persian Letters*.

[44] Young, 1804, 10, cf. 310. On the Whig notion of the science of manners, see Romani, *National Character*, 159–200.

[45] 1804, 189: 'free states (it hath by many been observed) are the best nursery-bed of the arts; and other states (it will be observed) have ran a career somewhat similar to that of Athens; and have known a period when emulation, sickening in the stagnation of public services and duties, might be supposed to invigorate in others scenes of employment.'

[46] See L. Klein, *Shaftesbury and the Culture of Politeness. Moral Discourse and Cultural Politics in Early Eighteenth-Century England* (Cambridge, 1994), 199–206; for the broader context, see Macgregor Morris, 'Shrines', 231–2.

of the interests of the community.[47] For Young too, true virtue was to be separated from private profit, and he worried that even the kind of virtuous behaviour which was inspired by a desire for self-adulation was corrupting: 'it is a mark of general depravity when a self-adulation exalts the mere duties of life'.[48] In these words, Young appears to follow Montesquieu's line, taking up his idea that political virtue consists of a painful renunciation of oneself.[49]

Young translated Montesquieu's notion of virtue into patriotism; indeed, his expressed justification for writing a history of Athens (as well as accounts of early Rome) was to study 'ancient patriotism and virtue', which would animate and urge the reader to a noble course.[50] Young, however, was coinciding with a broader tendency, visible also in the work of Bolingbroke and in the poetry of the era, namely Richard Glover's epic poem *Leonidas* of 1737, to deploy ancient models of virtuous activity as a way of bringing together virtue and patriotism.[51] But it is clear that Young perceived a significant difference between ancient and modern virtue, especially as one moved back in time: in the heroic age, patriotism was 'characterised by a wild and impetuous generosity, by an enthusiastic patriotism, and daring love of freedom … virtues were indebted to the passions for more, than, ever since, the boasted aid of reason could afford

---

[47] Montesquieu, *Spirit* 5.2, cited by Young 1804, 95. The love of the common good was a notion shared by many thinkers in the context of the post-Reformation state before the revolutionary epoch of the 1770s: see Miller, *Defining*, 413–21.

[48] Young, 1804, 118.

[49] Montesquieu, *Spirit*, 4.5 (35). There was however some dispute about the nature of virtue: for Young, virtue was a moral quality as it was linked to both public and private behaviour. He objected to Montesquieu's claim that virtue was political but not moral (Young, 1804, 132 n.). Montesquieu, of course, was keen to distance his system from that of Christian morality: it is possible that Young was keen to distance himself from the secularist reputation of Montesquieu's work that had led it to be put on the Vatican's Index of Prohibited Books: see C. Betts, 'Introduction' to Montesquieu, *The Persian Letters* (Harmondsworth, 1973), 19.

[50] 1804, 8: 'If the student may ever reach to the excellence which he thus admires; if the idea of imitation which hath thus enraptured his fancy, may at a time useful for his country, give spirit to his will, suggest resources to his mind, and supply new energies for all his actions: if these may be the effects on a mind suited to engage in the study, 'of ancient patriotism and virtue,' what other chapter in history is to be valued above that, which may thus animate a man, and urge him to noble services, in a good and public cause?'.

[51] Bolingbroke, especially in *The Idea of A Patriot King* of 1749: see I. Kremnick, *Bolingbroke and his Circle. The Politics of Nostalgia in the Age of Walpole* (Harvard, 1968), 30–8; Glover: see Macgregor Morris, 'The paradigm', 350–1 and E. Clough, 'Loyalty and Liberty: Thermopylae in the Western Imagination', 363–84, in T. Figueira (ed.), *Spartan Society* (Swansea, 2004), esp. 365–71.

them',[52] and even in the fifth century virtue was inspired rather than taught.[53] Ancient Athenian society also placed more emphasis on the centrality of the community to individual identity:

> *Then* individuals formed a community; *now*, more properly it may be said, that a community consists of individuals. Then the interest of the whole was deemed that of each; now the inverse is adopted, and each would operate on the whole. The genius of patriotism, which animated every breast, no longer exists; nay, the very instances of its existence are questioned: we wonder at past transactions and ancient stories; we doubt that the Greek Codrus, or Roman Decii devoted themselves.[54]

We get the impression that for Young, as for Mably and Rousseau, ancient virtue was elusive:[55] the Athenians were deeply virtuous beyond the reaches of modern states: not just in their achievement of giving primacy to the community through their genius of patriotism, but also by virtue of their resistance of the Persian invasion. His account of the ancient notion of virtue suggests particularly strongly the depth of his feeling that the modern world ought to recreate the ancient form. However, Athenian imperial expansion, and its corollaries of commercialism and luxury, undermined virtue.

### 4. Empire and History

It was common practice in eighteenth-century discourse to draw parallels between ancient and modern imperial structures as a way of warning about the dangers of imperial expansionism.[56] Indeed, in *Considerations on the Rise and Fall of Rome* Montesquieu argued at length that Rome fell because of her excessive expansionism. The impact of Young's personal preoccupations on his perception of history became most clear in his analysis of the fifth-century Athenian empire: the comparison that Young drew (see note 34) between Athenian and contemporary English sea power was one deeply attractive to someone whose family was very involved in the imperial consequences of that sea-power. As the son of a colonial governor, sugar plantation owner and a governor in waiting, Young's

---

[52] Young, 1804, 7.
[53] Young, 1804, 94–5.
[54] Young, 1804, 11 (=1777, 9).
[55] On the unattainability of ancient (particularly military) virtue, see J. Rousseau, *Social Contract*, 4.8; Mably, 'Observations on the Greeks', in *Translations from the French by D.Y.* (Lynn, 1770), 25.
[56] F. Turner, 'British Politics and the Decline of the Roman Republic: 1700–1939,' *Historical Journal*, 29 (1986), 577–99; C. Ataç, 'Imperial Lessons from Athens and Sparta', *History of Political Thought*, 27 (2006), 642–60.

account of Athens highlighted some of the benefits offered by empire for the imperial ruler. He believed that the European nations' exploration of the world gave rise to diverse forms of character and led to 'the furtherance of every art of utility or entertainment'.[57] To prove the desirability of European colonialism, he contrasted it with the 'vast but sequestered empire' of China which he claimed had been outstripped in the perfection of arts and knowledge by the 'infant colonies of the west'.[58] His defence of the Athenian empire was also based on a view of its consequences, which amounted to a form of harmonious cosmopolitanism which reflected that which he claimed existed in Britain's Caribbean colonies:

> The dominion of the seas, and the connections of trade, must have habituated many citizens to foreign excursions; many too, from other countries, became their guests in return; national prejudices were thus broken in upon; the minds of men became more knowing and enlarged; and the people were taught to comprize others, as well as Greeks, within the circle of their benevolence: their very slaves partook of that benevolence; they bore no badge of servitude, but were clothed as citizens; the laws protected them equally from insults and blows.[59]

The expansion of Athenian sea power after the Persian wars therefore led to the development of a national intelligence and a universal benevolence. But once this combined with growing wealth and commercialism, it deeply corrupted patriotic virtue. While he felt that the combination of commerce

---

[57] His first pronouncement on Greek colonies was introduced alongside Montesquieu's principle that soil and climate have a significant effect on the development of individual character (1804, 25–6). From this followed the theory that the impact of commerce and intercourse is beneficial as the variety of national character forced new combinations on that of individuals: 'Italian fancy, French wit, English penetration, and German assiduity, have from divers and distant habitations, met and united their common labours, and connected and modified their several qualities and powers for the furtherance of every art of utility or entertainment'.

[58] 1804, 26. On the use of China in Anglophone eighteenth-century writings as an 'allegory of the spatial difference that provides critical perspective', see R. Batchelor, 'Imagining the British Nation through China', 79–92 in F. Nussbaum (ed.), *The Global Eighteenth Century* (Baltimore and London 2003), 82.

[59] 1777, 132. Such a view should be tied in with Young's sentiments about slaves and his anti-abolitionism – in Young's accounts of his tours of the West Indies, he claimed to have been: 'greeted wholeheartedly by his slaves, and he reciprocated by granting them extra holidays and gifts of herrings and rum, holding balls in the great house, and at Christmas feasting, drinking, dancing, and exchanging gifts. He was pleased that he discovered little evidence of harsh treatment of his and other planters' slaves. In all of the islands he visited he was observant of the methods of feeding, housing, clothing, disciplining, providing medical care, and religious instruction of the slaves' (reported in Sheridan, *Oxford DNB*, s.v. 'Young, Sir William').

and liberty made Athens prosper,[60] he also felt that once commercial interests were put in front of all others they became pernicious. Accordingly, he held that enthusiasm for the Athenian expedition to Sicily (415–413 B.C.) was a sign that naval and commercial interests were dictating military policy. In short, naval power was an 'over-nutritious stimulative to greatness', while commerce accelerated the downfall of Athens given the immutable rule that '*with the same haste a commercial nation accedes to empire, it speeds to dissolution*': application and frugality, the promoters of trade, he suggested, were the victims of the success of the enterprise, as 'the importation of luxuries enervates the industry that is in pursuit of them'.[61]

This line of thought allowed Young to reconcile his views on the greatness of the Athenians with the predominant contemporary interpretation of Athenian history based on those of Plutarch and Polybius: the failure of Athenian citizens to appropriately allocate their labour meant that Athenian cultural skill outlived her political greatness.[62] Part of Young's explanation of the decline of Athenian virtue was that concern for art and commerce supplanted the virtuous love of patriotism: the prosperity of the arts fell out of step with the decline of her constitution as virtue became concentrated on culture rather than patriotic activity. His explanation of Athenian decline echoed very strongly Mably's claim, in his *Entretiens de Phocion* of 1763, that foreign conquests lead to wealth, luxury, and can soften a nation.[63] This view is closely related to the 'luxury' debates of the eighteenth century, which saw critics of luxury and commerce (such as Bolingbroke) look towards ancient texts for warnings about the pernicious effect of luxury.[64] But whereas Montesquieu concluded that Rome fell not owing to luxury but owing to excessive conquest and

---

[60] 1804, 263 n.
[61] 1804, 264–5, 268. Elsewhere, Young conceived of commercialism as the cause of decline of both Athens and Aegina: 1804, 41, 111.
[62] It endured in a period when 'emulation, sickening in the stagnation of public services and duties, might be supposed to invigorate in other scenes of employment' (1804, 189). The reality and reputation of Athenian greatness, once famed for liberty, commerce, her republic, and the empire of the seas, was sustained in the fourth century only through arts and commerce, and she was thereafter not less famous as a school to all nations for the liberal arts, eloquence and philosophy!' (1804, 389).
[63] G. Mably, *Entretiens de Phocion sur le rapport de la morale avec la politique; traduits du grec de Nicoclès, avec des remarques* (Amsterdam, 1763), 94.
[64] See I. Hont, 'The Luxury Debate in the Early Enlightenment', in M. Goldie and R. Wokler (eds.), *The Cambridge History of Eighteenth-Century Political Thought* (Cambridge, 2006), 379–418. For Bolingbroke's view, citing Rome to link luxury with commerce, see I. Kramnick, *Bolingbroke and His Circle. The Politics of Nostalgia in the Age of Walpole* (Harvard, 1968), 170.

war,[65] Young suggested that empire, commerce, and luxury were deeply connected. Young's views were highly derivative of the Whig critique of commercialism that had surfaced in Roman historiography, which took the view that it was potentially corrosive of republican liberty.[66] Young's reflections on the role of commercialism in the decline of the Athenian empire and republican virtue, while they reflected a view (against that of Hume: see note 34) of Athens as a modernist city-state, might seem to be at odds with his own family's commercial interests in the West Indies. But Young's position should be seen as a set of reservations about the dangers raised by rampant commercialism rather than as an outright condemnation of commerce.[67]

Young held the view that empires should be conceived of as communities arranged in pursuit of the common good. He expressed firm views on the rights and obligations of colonists, suggesting that settlers who land on an unappropriated spot of land reserve the right to adopt the form of association that 'their prejudices or wisdom may suggest'[68] – perhaps casting back a thought to his own father's involvement in the formation of an administrative plan for island of Tobago.[69] Still, he followed the line of thought that said that the notion of virtue should be extended to the treatment of the diverse interests of far-flung colonial possessions.[70] He insisted, citing Montesquieu, that dependencies ought to be founded in the spirit of mutual interests and reciprocal benefit: such a foundation would encourage acquiescence.[71] Moreover, he insisted that it was important to allow subject cities to partake in peace, revenue and regulations of dominion, and the free constitution of a superior state, but warned that even with such treatment subjects are likely to 'imbibe the high spirit and force which distinguish the donors ... Will they not, as they savour liberty, disrelish command?'.[72] Conversely, he held that 'a

---

[65] *Considerations on the Causes of the Greatness of the Romans and Their Decline*, trans. D. Lowenthal (Indianapolis, 1999).
[66] See Turner, 'British Politics', 579.
[67] Ideologues of empire had much to say on good and bad imperial practices, see A. Pagden, *Lords of all the World. Ideologies of Empire in Spain, Britain and France c.1500–c.1800* (New Haven and London, 1985).
[68] 1804, 102.
[69] See above, note 3.
[70] Miller, *Defining*, 159–79, 414.
[71] 1804, 396–7. This notion (that there was a reciprocal relationship between colonist and colony: obedience in exchange for protection), was one held up in Barron's *History of the Colonization of the Free States of Antiquity* (London, 1777), 32, in which he argued such a process was absent in the Greek era of colonisation.
[72] 1804, 156.

contrary demeanour must be of equally destructive tendency'. He clearly believed that imperialism in the Athenian context brought with it an influx of money and consequent moral decline, which, in the Athenians' case, was accelerated by their neglect of virtuous rule: the empire fell into decay as they demanded more money and used it for the ornament of their city.[73] The oppressiveness of Athens in peace and her harshness and cruelty in war meant that her power was bound to disintegrate after the Sicilian expedition: one of his most rhetorically powerful passages stated that '*despotism is but the gigantic phantom of power; good-will and the sense of national welfare, interest, and protection give it genuine substance*'.[74]

Like the other phenomena contingent with democracy, the Athenian empire contributed to her decline. Indeed, for Young, as it was for other republican writers since Macchiavelli, the whole story of ancient history amounted to a moral explanation of the decline of ancient republican virtue.[75] Another factor in his analysis of decline was the role of the individual. Citing Montesquieu's *Considerations on the Rise and Fall of Rome*, he suggested that the brevity of office drove generals and admirals to over-exertion and extension of empire,[76] as statesmen were more likely to attempt to satisfy and conciliate the people by pressing on with expansionist enterprises.[77] This was one strand of his wider uneasiness about the pernicious effect of great men on the history of the republic.

## 5. The Individual in History

For Young, virtue, as we have noted, was a form of patriotism that necessitated the sacrifice of one's own selfish passions (though not necessarily one's true interests); this was a view common in eighteenth-

---

[73] 1804, 149, 159.
[74] 1804, 280. He held the view that fourth-century Athens became a tyrant city (390) and one that was unsuitable for an empire: 'the passions of domination, of avarice, and of pride, have too often given up the ear of a sovereign people to the voice of an interested demagogue' (396–7).
[75] See F. Turner, 'British Politics', 578. There is one significant difference however: while Machiavelli felt strongly that commerce undermined liberty in the ancient world, Young thought that commerce and liberty sometimes sustained and fostered each other: 1804, 263 n.
[76] 1804, 85: 'To gain the favour of their fellow-citizens, they pressed on each moment of their employ for new occasions of signalizing themselves, urged enterprise on enterprise, and the final result was conquest and dominion for their sovereigns, the republic'.
[77] Young, 1804, 85.

century rhetoric.[78] This was a view that pervaded his narrative of Athenian history: the decline of patriotism and virtue saw pursuit of personal power supplant the desire to serve the common good. The degeneracy of Athens led to the growing prominence of great men who changed the course of her history and undermined her free state: Pericles was the politician he identified as undermining the patriotic virtues of the Athenian community. Reliant upon a combination of corruption and party faction for his power, Young claimed that he substituted 'art for strength' by encouraging the development of arts and sciences and military reliance on the fortification of the city and the fleet; his introduction of military and political pay corrupted the Athenians and made them less patriotic; Pericles conciliated the people with empty eloquence and payment.[79] His obituary on Pericles stands in resounding contrast to that of Thucydides:

> Perhaps it had been well for the republic, had he never been born! But his death was equally fatal to it, as his life, for none other knew how to redress the evils which he had occasioned. He had accustomed the people to the voice of a demagogue ... on his death a thousand pretenders arose, and with rival arts and equal weakness perplexed the public councils, disunited the people and led them to ruin and destruction.[80]

Pericles was not the only 'demagogue' who ruined the functioning of the Athenian free state: Theramenes (see below, section 7) was guilty of a crime still worse: usurpation. Young's emphasis on the role of individuals in the decline of Athens gives rise to some tension with his principles of investigation: his complaints about those historians who 'make public events secondary to private characters', and who, 'instead of attempting to absorb the attention in the weal and fortunes of a collective state, take the easier task of painting a single figure in life' suggests a disregard for biographical approaches to historiography: the danger of such an approach was to make the reader focus unduly on the vices and the virtues of an individual, but without full consideration of the actions of a combined society.[81] Whereas those historians appeal to men's preference

---

[78] In the eighteenth-century discourse, patriotism could be defined as the recognition that personal and common interests are the same. See Macgregor Morris, 'The paradigm', 350.
[79] Young, 1804, 240–4, 254–5.
[80] Young, 1804, 255. It is of no surprise that Young held deep contempt for Alcibiades (1804, 277–82), and for those demagogues who he thought with their flattery and corruption led Athens to disaster and shattered the compact and union of democracy (1804, 373–6) and destroyed the 'collective self-regard' – in other words the virtue of the people (1804, 373–6, 432).
[81] Young, 1804, 137.

for sentiment over thought, his aim, he says, is not to entertain, but 'to rouse public principles and public virtue, whilst I conjoin causes and effects, and note each progressive step to elevation, and towards decline by the republic of Athens'.[82] But towards the end of his history, Young admitted that as his history went on, and as the Athenians became less collectively virtuous, it became increasingly hard to focus on the people and more appropriate to focus on individuals, as the account 'became a constellation of lesser and of greater stars, which in proportion to the dimness of the whole, have shone out conspicuous to the view'.[83] The tension revealed here suggests that Young's principles on the writing of history coincide with what he thinks of as virtue: virtue is republican and should be about patriotism and communities working together; accordingly, historiography should be about the history of communities, not of individuals. The state of Athens from the time of Pericles (the most important Athenian politician of the period from around 454 to 429 B.C.) was able only to illustrate the greater role of the individual in the history of the degenerate and declining nation.

---

[82] Young, 1804, 138. The meditation on the damage that an individual can do is rather reminiscent of Montesquieu's *Considerations on Rome*, where the usurpation of wealthy and corrupt men rid the society of virtue: see Montesquieu, *Considerations*, 121. The disunity of the people reminds us of Montesquieu's theory that (92) the fall of Rome was caused by conquest and over-extension, which led to the destruction of the single spirit of the love of liberty and hatred of tyranny; Rome accordingly became stricken by factions and dissension (93–5).

[83] Full quotation (1804, 349): 'In discoursing of the prior times of the republic, I have cautiously refrained from the stories in history, and rejected the apothegms and anecdotes of distinguished individuals, as ill-suited to the purpose of the work. Nay, I testified my disapprobation of the writer who should degrade a community by a selected instance; and drawing the attention of his reader from the characteristics of a great nation to the character of a great man, seem to bid him remark transcendent virtue as an exception, and not a rule. The spirit of those ancient times warranted the remark; – the whole people of Athens, during the Persian wars, seemed to be so united in their pursuit of what was good, and what was great, that to praise one, seemed injustice to all. But this galaxy of bright and excellent qualities, wherein to distinguish and fix on any one, more bright and more excellent than the rest, was so difficult for the eye, gradually lost its indiscriminate lustre, and became a constellation of lesser and of greater stars, which in proportion to the dimness of the whole, have shone out conspicuous to the view, and have attracted our attention to their superior brilliancy and magnitude. Thus my regard hath of late unwarily been drawn from a consideration of the whole to its more particular and luminous spots. Looking back on my comment, I find it from time to time, attending more and more to individual names, and to characters. The further I proceed, the more I forsee I shall thus deviate from the principle I at first laid down: but doth not such deviation originate in the changeable nature of man and things, and make part of the very subject which I have undertaken to discuss'.

## 6. Democracy and Republicanism

Young's comments on the part played by Pericles in the downfall of Athens entailed some criticism of mid fifth-century Athenian democracy. But it would be too simplistic to class him as just a critic of democracy. Young, like other classical republicans, certainly has room for some praise for popular political activity. But his reading of Athenian democracy placed emphasis on its less radical characteristics, such as its use of elections for selection of generals: he overlooked the more controversial aspects of direct democracy. Indeed, he followed Montesquieu's view that the people are capable of competently electing magistrates owing to the fact that they are able to perceive merit, even if they are unable to manage public affairs by themselves.[84] He even expanded this idea, suggesting that 'constant attention to public affairs forms the minds of many', that the people learn well to judge statesmen and generals, and that the people who elect magistrates and leaders are more likely to vote in the interests of the commonwealth than any other group.[85] But explicit praise for 'democracy' was limited in Young's work. In the first edition he heaped praise on the democracy of Solon's era (Solon was archon of Athens in 594 B.C.) as the government that was the quickest route to happiness:

> A warm advocate for the liberties of mankind (liberties, which political institution ought surely to medicate with the tenderest hand, nor wantonly corrode or amputate) I may perhaps appear bold in asserting that a democracy in the high perfection of its establishment, is the state best calculated for general happiness.[86]

Revealingly, this passage was retained in the later editions, but by 1786, 'free state' had replaced 'democracy'.[87] Indeed, the notion of democracy is never explicitly praised without reservation in later editions. In his 1786 edition, he suggested that the democratic form of government offered value only if it is modified by law, institutions and the

---

[84] Young holds the view that a greater number of people engaged in the political sphere 'adds natural force and consequence in themselves' (1804, 54; cf. pp. 80–2; Montesquieu, *Spirit* 2.2). There is debate in modern scholarship about whether Montesquieu was an advocate of the republican form of government above all others: the alternative explanation is that as a proto-sociologist, he was also a relativist who took the line that different forms of government suited different physical and mental environments: see Nelson, *Greek Tradition*, 163.
[85] Young, 1804, 80, 83–4.
[86] Young, 1777, 63.
[87] Young, 1786, 63; Young, 1804, 85.

'best principles';[88] Solon's constitution was described rather as not a 'democracy'[89] but as an 'as it has been called democracy', and was better defined as a republic.[90] As Macgregor Morris has pointed out, Young held a positive view of Athenian democracy as long as it was limited and there was 'equality of power … as far as nature will admit': in some ways it was founded, like the Athens of de Pauw, on a constitutional system that Mably had read into the evidence for classical Sparta.[91] Young reassured his readers in terms that would appeal to them, telling them that even though Solon legislated with the intention of promoting equality,[92] his constitution was a mixed republic, and one which guaranteed the rights

---

[88] Young, 1786, 60. This coincides with a wider tendency: in the period c.1790 to c.1840, the term 'democracy' was most frequently used to refer to the radical, direct, form of democracy, rather than its modern, representative form: see M. Hansen, 'Direct democracy, ancient and modern', 135–49 in P. McKechnie (ed.), *Thinking like a Lawyer. Essays on Legal History and General History for John Crook on his Eightieth Birthday* (Leiden, 2002).

[89] Young, 1786, 39 (=1804, 52): 'The Democracy, *as it has been called*, of Solon, when re-established by Clisthenes, was of the best kinds of republic; and the evils that ensued, in the course of Athenian history, from the flux of morals, and the concomitant innovations on the original polity, and not to be placed to the account of the first institution'.

[90] He went on to elaborate: whatever Isocrates' meant by 'democracy', Solonic Athens was a republic, resembling the *politeia* of Aristotle, which decayed into a more democratic form. 1804, 53: 'From the great authorities above cited, it appears to have been both his and their meaning, that the commonwealth of Athens was originally a mixed republic. That it had a tendency, however, to become, in process of time, a more popular and democratic state, will appear from a summary review of the powers vested in the people by their great legislator'.

[91] Macgregor Morris, 'The paradigm', 353–4.

[92] 1804, 53. Young's analysis of Solon's census classes argued that its distinctions did not affect the spirit of patriotism which was the virtue of the republican constitution of Athens. Instead, he suggested that his reforms introduced a 'virtual equality' in the sense that its citizens' rights and freedoms were watched over, indiscriminately of their background (1804, 43). To support this analysis, he cited Montesquieu's own comments on the notion of equality in a democracy: 'It suffices to establish a census [cites Plutarch, *Life of Solon* 18] that reduced differences or fixes them at a certain point, after which it is the task of particular laws to equalize inequalities, so to speak, by the burdens they impose on the rich and the relief they afford to the poor'. (*Spirit*, 5.5) In its original context, Montesquieu commented no further on whether laws did indeed undermine inequality in Athens, though he took Plutarch (*Solon*, 18.2) to say that Solon excluded the *thetes* from all burdens. Young's substantiation of Montesquieu's statement takes it in a different direction, adding in citations of Isocrates' *Antidosis*, and [Xenophon]'s *Constitution of the Athenians*, which suggest that the regulation of liturgies was the system that minimised inequality. What we see here is that Young's analysis is providing an extension and substantiation of Montesquieu's comments on Greece in order to support his case that Solon introduced an appropriate level of equality to Athens.

and future property security of its subjects.[93] It appears to be the case that Young became more cautious about his praise of democracy in the period between 1777 and 1786: Young introduced to the second edition an account of the treatment of the generals after Arginusae which ends with the statement 'the democracy was become tyrant'.[94] Significantly, his move away from praise of democracy began before the French revolution, but coincided with both the Patriot Revolt of the Dutch Republic and the revolutionary period in America.[95] I shall return at a later point (section 7) to the ways in which Young's work marks the commencement age of revolution in historiographical thought.

One reservation about the Athenian republic was the way in which it allowed for statesmen to get carried away in expansionist enterprises. But a further element of the corruption that afflicted Athens was her deviation from Montesquieu's ideal of the separation of the powers. This doctrine, that the separation of judicial, executive and legislative powers is necessary for the survival of good government, is striking in its enduringness and in the legacy it left for the American constitution. It was one which he derived from a number of tracts, among them Bolingbroke, but it is a doctrine most commonly associated with Montesquieu.[96] Young attempted to introduce the theory to his vision of Solonian Athens. He envisaged that executive power lay in the hands of 'the higher order or ranks of men', legislation and deliberation in the hands of the people and the judicial in the hands of an Areopagus consisting of men of irreproachable morals.[97] In his discussion of Athens after the Pisistratids (the Pisistratid tyranny at Athens lasted from

---

[93] 1804, 47–8: 'The happiness and rights of men were Solon's objects, and having provided for them by a wise and impartial legislation, he adopted other regulations necessary to the giving vigour and perpetuity to his system. With a view of precluding an inordinate increase of landed estate, on which unconstitutional influence might be supposed to build, as on its proper basis; he made a new distribution of lands of Attica, and by agrarian institutions obviated any future infringement on that distribution'.

[94] Young, 1786, 188.

[95] On the significance of the rhetoric of democracy in the American revolutionary era and the Patriot Revolt of the Dutch Republic, see J. Dunn, *Setting the People Free. The Story of Democracy* (London, 2005), 77–88. It is likely that that the aftermath of the French revolution made Young yet more cautious in his use of democratic terminology. See below, section 7, on his description of the era of the Thirty Tyrants with the revolutionary era of France. In a work of 1793 entitled *The Rights of Englishmen*, Young distinguished the British republican constitution from the forms of democracy that existed in Greece and in the revolutionary situation of France. This work however drew only negative examples to be drawn from Athens: W. Young, *The Rights of Englishmen* (London, 1793), 8, 10, 11, 24.

[96] See I. Kramnick, 'Bolingbroke', 145–50.

[97] Young, 1804, 43–6.

546 to 510 B.C.), the terminology changes but the idea of separation was the same: he envisaged a distinction between executive power and primary authority, suggesting that in a free commonwealth, primary authority – the determination and promulgation of popular will – can be resident in the many but executive power should belong to the few:

> A free commonwealth hath too seeds of dissolution proper to itself. In such state, the primary authority is resident in the many; but of course, the executive power must be delegated to the few. The first is in the hands of the people, whose will being once determined and promulgated, necessity from day to day more rarely calls for their interposition: the second, entrusted to their agents, requires unremitted exertion. As the one power becomes dormant, the latter increases in vigilance; till at length the importance of the state yields to the consequence of private men, and the servant of the public directs the legislation he should obey.[98]

The Athenians, he suggested, attempted to remedy the problem of the increasing power of the executive by introducing the device of ostracism.[99] However, this system was undermined by Pericles, who, out of desperation to retain ministerial power, corrupted the people by using new extents of flattery. The downfall of Athens was cemented by the decision of the upper classes to relinquish political activity; they instead concentrated on developing their private fortunes through commercial interests, and left all the general concerns of the state to the demagogues.[100]

The resulting situation meant that, instead of leaders co-operating with a virtuous and patriotic people to the good of the community, Athens struggled by with a situation with demagogues who corrupted and flattered a degenerate mob while the wealthy, with commercial interests, looked after themselves and their lives of luxury. The harmonious republicanism

---

[98] Young, 1804, 86.

[99] 1804, 88–9. Again, he followed Montesquieu's opinion (*Spirit* 29.7, 605) on the institution, and praised both the fact that it could be introduced against one individual at a time and that the large quorate meant that it was 'difficult for any one to be exiled unless his absence was necessary'.

[100] 1804, 236: 'When wealth began to distinguish the fortunate from war or trade: and when art had suggested enjoyments, which the passions of men are ever ready to meet half way, and which wealth alone could procure; progressively gain became the substitute for each worthier motive of action, and the sense of public duties yielded to pleasures and to self-interest. Some citizens, relinquishing to the demagogues all general concerns of state, were absorbed in voluptuous habits of life; others in the lucrative course of trade; and some solicited a participation of riches from the patronage, and others from the apprehensions of able, opulent, and enterprising men, who were beneficent from ambition, or from the sense of responsibility; who wished to possess, or who had possessed, the executive offices of government'.

and virtuous patriotism of the Athenians of the era immediately after the Persian wars was destroyed. Finally, I want to pursue two lines of thought: the ways in which Young's history offered a corrective to the political reality of the day and also the ways in which socio-political upheavals at the end of the eighteenth century led him to revise the political views expressed in his history.

## 7. History as a Lesson in the Age of Revolution

It has emerged that Young was an original thinker in few senses: his work does however illustrate a clear link between political events and the production of historiography. Young made no secret of the fact that his interpretation of history was anchored in contemporary political developments. In his 1804 edition, he says 'the present crisis' – a reference to the age of revolutions in which he lived and the Napoleonic Wars – has led him to republish his work, claiming that the truth of his conclusions had been proved by the period of revolutions and popular commotion.[101] But a closer look suggests that events had changed his views not just on democracy (as was noted in section 6) but also on the significance of history: this is the impression he gives in the changing epigraphs, written in Greek, on the frontispiece of the works. Both are drawn from the works of the fourth-century orator Isocrates:

> 1777 edition: 'Every polity is the soul of a state, having as much power over it as the mind over the body' (*Panathenaikos*, 138).[102]

> 1786 and 1804 editions: 'Reflect on the fortunes and accidents which befall both common men and kings, for if you are mindful of the past you will plan better for the future' (*To Nicocles*, 35).[103]

These epigraphs are indicative of Young's apparent reconsideration of the meaning of history in the eleven-year period after the first edition. Whereas the first edition assumed that the notion of spirit is central to adducing historical lessons, the later editions enunciated more clearly the idea that actual parallel events can offer lessons to the present. His comparison of Athenian and British sea power in the preface to the second and third editions makes this message even more stark,[104] and

---

[101] Young, 1804, x.
[102] πᾶσα πολιτεία ψυχὴ πόλεώς ἐστι, τοσαύτην ἔχουσα δύναμιν ὅσηνπερ ἐν σώματι φρόνησις.
[103] Θεώρει τὰ γιγνόμενα καὶ τὰ συμπίπτοντα καὶ τοῖς ἰδιώταις καὶ τοῖς τυράννοις ἀπ' αὐτῶν· ἂν γὰρ τὰ παρεληλυθότα μνημονεύῃς, ἄμεινον περὶ τῶν μελλόντων βουλεύσει.
[104] Moreover, the statement that history's purpose, as Bolingbroke believed, 'to teach philosophy by example' is announced only in the third edition: 1804, 4.

the development of his ideas is suggested by his withdrawal of the claim made at the end of his first preface that he had written his history only because he had the leisure.[105]

The second edition also clarified Young's vision of the intended audience of these lessons: in that book he introduces the idea that the purpose of writing history was to furnish maxims of state.[106] History, given his attempt to focus on the broader picture (see above, section 2), was aimed not just at statesmen but at anyone who was interested in notions of virtue and republicanism and the historical experience of corruption and decline. Indeed, it seems likely that Young took so much time to emphasise the didactic nature of his history because he had concluded by the time of his second edition (1786, by which time he was an MP) that there was little other point in academic pursuits.[107] Such a belief emerges yet more strongly in his preference for the Socrates of Xenophon's *Memorabilia* over the Socrates of Plato's dialogues because he thought that the former was more interested in principles of duty, religion and morality than contemplating the nature of abstract beauty.[108]

The lesson that Young's history offers is clear: it is that luxury, naval power, commerce and democracy threaten republican virtue. He was writing a warning to his contemporaries about the dangers that would arise if imperial, commercial and political interests were held by rival groups: this of course was the spirit of Whig supremacy. But it warned also about the threat that vainglorious individuals wielded against the spirit of virtue and patriotism and about the dangers of an inadequate separation of governmental powers. But the precise nature of the message that he offered appears to have changed in the period from 1777 to 1786; it had developed yet further by 1804.

The biggest change that he made to his history between 1786 and 1804 was the introduction of an entire chapter on the 'Usurpation of Thirty Tyrants',[109] the regime that held power in 404 B.C. after the Spartan defeat

---

[105] 'I wrote the following book to beguile an idle time, and I knew no better reason for publishing, than because – I have wrote, it', 1777, x.
[106] 'As the constitution of government becomes first perfect and then corrupt; as the arts of government become complicated and then depraved, the history will in its due course furnish maxims of policy, and lessons of state', 1786, 9.
[107] Young took the view that history, in order for it to be worthwhile, was obliged to offer lessons for the harmonisation of society, 1786, 29; if study does not offer a contribution to an understanding of civic duties and statecraft, it is mere vanity (1804, 336–8).
[108] Young, 1786, 195.
[109] Noted in his preface: 1804, xii; cf. 1804, 296–328.

of Athens in the Peloponnesian War. In his first two editions he had held that such an event was uninteresting to the modern reader as 'the polish and lenity of the modern age have rendered such subject unnecessary and uninteresting'.[110] But in the final edition, he suggested the tyranny that emerged during the course of the French revolution meant that an account of 'usurpation by demagogues of the people, and of the certain misconduct of a despotism so created' would provide a lesson 'at once interesting and useful'.[111] What was significant was that for Young, the terrors of the French revolution resembled not the periodic instability of classical Athenian democracy, but an imposition that was brought upon them owing to the selfish devices of the demagogue Theramenes.[112] Young's choice of the word 'usurpation' is significant: according to the Lockean definition, this refers not to the transformation the form of government but rather a change in leadership.[113] Young was quite clear that the Thirty transpired owing to the emergence of a self-seeking form of democratic leadership.

Young's history began its life therefore as a work that was political in the sense that it engaged with the republican tradition of investigating the idea of republican virtue and introduced it to the Athenian example. In its later editions that line was never abandoned, but the work becomes political in a different way, as it was re-written with the relationship between the immediate political past, present, and future put more clearly in focus.

## 8. Conclusion

It has emerged that the legacy that Young drew on was not the exclusive intellectual property of Montesquieu, but that of a range of writers including Bolingbroke, Rollin, and Mably. His introduction of Montesquieu's interpretation of republicanism gave rise to a reading of Athens which resembled Mably's Sparta inasmuch as it employed an ancient example in a construction of republicanism, but one which anticipated some of the pro-Athenian conclusions of Cornelius de Pauw.[114] He conceived of a history of Athens as a parable on the contemporary condition of England

---

[110] Young, 1804, xiii = 1777, 214.
[111] Young, 1804, xiii. He probably means Robespierre's Committee of Public Safety of 1793–5; less likely is it a reference to Napoleon Bonaparte.
[112] Stress on Theramenes' role: Young, 1804, 302–4.
[113] See Locke, *Second Treatise*, chapter 17.
[114] G. Mably, *Observations sur l'Histoire de la Grèce* (Paris, 1766); C. de Pauw, *Recherches philosophiques sur les Grecs* (Paris, 1788).

with a more positive tone than that of his predecessors. The first edition maintained that the eliciting of a notion of spirit in a historical context could lead to the possibility of drawing lessons from the past. Athens in the period of the Persian wars was held up as an ideal republican constitution, which combined concerns for liberty and limited equality with a pervading spirit of patriotism, a quality which he views as the historical embodiment of virtue. The later editions, published in the context of heightening political tension, present Athens more explicitly as an example which holds lessons for England. Young's adjustments to his history of Athens in its 1786 and 1804 editions confirm that an age of political revolution was also an age of historiographical fluctuation.

By drawing out Young's use of Montesquieu's political theory, I have emphasised Young's aim, to place his work within the tradition of political thought which came later to be known as Classical Republicanism. In doing so I hope to extricate his history from the dichotomising analysis designed for, and more suited to, analysing the Liberal and Tory histories of the era after the French Revolution. There may be more to say on how his work fits in with the picture of Classical Republicanism in the longer term, in particular Machiavelli's *Discourses* or the 1656 *Commonwealth of Oceana* of James Harrington.[115] There may be more to say on his views on the relationship of history to divine providence;[116] nor have I considered the relationship of his account of Athens to his works on the history and ethnography of the West Indian colonies.[117]

Finally, I want to engage with two further questions: first of all, why did Young claim to draw so heavily on the ideas of Montesquieu? Many of the ideas that he gleans from Montesquieu were hardly novel. But the continuous citation of Montesquieu gives Young an exact and authoritative intellectual reference point. What is striking is the claim (for the most part, a misleading claim) to do something new: not only by introducing the history of Athens to political thought, but by

---

[115] James Harrington the author of the tract called *Oceana* of 1656 which found much to praise in Athens: he held up institutions such as the use of lot and the large popular assembly as useful devices, defended the Athenian decision to ostracise Aristides, and sanctioned the use of the institution of ostracism as a matter of public security; however, even Harrington saw that a measure of aristocracy was necessary to retain sensible governance: he thought that Athenian aggression brought down Greek civilisation. Note, however, Young's dismissive remarks on that author (1804, iv).

[116] E.g. Young, 1777, 42 and 1804, 55. Rollin's preface to his *Ancient History* emphasised the ways in which ancient history gives insight into the workings of the Almighty.

[117] On his work on the Black Caribs, a writing up of his father's notes, see M. Craton, 'The Black Caribs of St. Vincent: A Reevaluation', in R.L. Paquette and S.L. Engerman (eds.), *The Lesser Antilles in the Age of European Expansion* (Gainesville, 1996), 71–85.

introducing political thought to the cultural and political history of Athens. By framing the first edition of his *Spirit of Athens* in this way Young was trying to prove worthiness for a public life: he recognised that to show himself a successor to his father he needed to demonstrate not only a grasp of history, an awareness of intellectual developments on the continent but also his ability to compose an analysis which demonstrated that he understood the nature of virtue, patriotism, happiness and the science of politics in a way that would address the artistic, political, diplomatic and intellectual predicaments of his day. His way of parading this was to show that he was able to understand the 'spirit' of a different age. This was his intention even if, as has been suggested, his work can be understood only in the broader contexts of eighteenth-century literary culture.

Secondly, why should we, scholars today, bother with William Young's work? How, if at all, can it contribute to our understanding Greek history? It is worth reading because it shows how Young, like other figures in the eighteenth century, addressed key problems in the writing of history and its use. Young offers interesting insights on historical methodology and the tensions between comprehensiveness and selectivity – he wants to use examples but he is aware that they can distort the general picture; he is aware of the problem in pitching correctly the role of the individual in ancient history, particularly in situations where ancient sources tend to centre explanation around the concept of the great man. Moreover, his history disproves the misconception that narrative was the only way of writing history before the invention of social history. This history, and in particular in its first edition, presented itself as sociological history. It was a way of writing history that predated the narrative histories of the city state, but one which perhaps contributed to the growing notion that the Athenians were modern.[118] Young's history is also an interesting reflection on the perceived relationship of political thought and ancient historical example in the eighteenth century: they occupied an overlapping intellectual space, and historiography drew on theory as the theory drew on ancient example.

My closing suggestion is that Young's history reminds us that there exist two very different encounters of historiography with political thought: on the one hand the form which is concerned with the allocation of power across the social hierarchy of the citizen-body: it therefore deals with

---

[118] For the classic statement of Athenian modernism, see Constant, B., 'On the Liberty of the Ancients Compared with that of the Moderns', in B. Fontana (ed.), *Constant: Political Writings* (Cambridge, 1992), 307–28.

notions of aristocracy, democracy, popular government, the quantity and quality of participation and the ideologies attached to that distribution of powers: it is an Aristotelian understanding of political change and refers to what Montesquieu thought of as the 'nature' of government. The histories of Mitford, Grote and Grundy, but also those of Ste Croix and Hansen exhibit a particular tendency to concentrate on that vein of political historiography. The other, corresponding to what Montesquieu thought of as the 'principle' of government deals with the negotiation and division of power among in the spectrum of institutions and the broader notions of character, spirit, happiness, virtue, and duty which underlay the working of those institutions: the concepts dealt with in varying depths in the work of Leo Strauss, Karl Popper and Hannah Arendt. Young's history, owing to its close engagement with both ancient and contemporary political thought, was able to encompass both streams of thought: this was the achievement of his *Spirit of Athens*.

# 4. 'The deadly principles of fanaticism': Puritans and Dissenters in Gibbon's *Decline and Fall of the Roman Empire**

## John Seed

In this essay I want to propose a reading of *The History of the Decline and Fall of the Roman Empire* which links some of its themes about religion in the ancient world, to a very different history – the history of Britain in the seventeenth century – and to a very different context, the opposition of religious Dissenters to the contemporary political establishment in the 1780s and the political crisis surrounding the French Revolution. I will suggest that *The Decline and Fall of the Roman Empire* transposes the terms of Hume's critical history of the English puritans to the early Christians. At the same time, especially in his later volumes, Gibbon strengthens the more conservative inflections of his religious scepticism, conferring an ironic legitimacy on the Hanoverian Church of England, in terms converging to Edmund Burke's *Reflections on the Revolution in France*. I will take his disputes with Joseph Priestley in the 1780s as a focus for some of these wider questions about the political ramifications of Gibbon's *History*.

## I

Contemporary churchmen and Dissenters were generally confident that they could identify a bedrock of scepticism, hostile to the Christian religion, beneath the shifting sands of Gibbon's prose. Joseph Priestley was particularly forthright in his criticisms of what he saw as Gibbon's deliberate obfuscation, speaking of 'the mask he has affected to wear, by pretending to believe in christianity, when he evidently does not'.[1] More

---

* Earlier versions of this essay were given at conferences at Roehampton University London (May 2007), the Institute of Historical Research, University of London (July 2007) and the British Society for Eighteenth-Century Studies (Oxford, January 2008). I'd like to thank James Moore and Peter Weston for comments on an earlier draft.

[1] J. Priestley, *Letters to a Philosophical Unbeliever. Part II. Containing a state of the evidence of revealed religion, with animadversions on the two last chapters of the first volume of Mr. Gibbon's History of the Decline and Fall of the Roman Empire* (Birmingham, 1787), xvii.

recently, historians have developed more complex understandings of Gibbon's religious formation. Statements in *The Decline and Fall*, in the *Memoirs* and in his correspondence seem to support positions as various, and as incompatible, as outright atheism, a gentlemanly deism, a rationalist protestantism, or even that of an old-fashioned high churchman. At the same time, the complexity of his writing resists easy incorporation into any straightforward doctrinal position or '-ism'. The notorious 15th and 16th chapters of the first 1776 volume of *Decline and Fall* are now taken to be merely an early formulation of positions which were explored in more subtle forms in later volumes and other writings.[2]

A comment at the very beginning of *The Decline and Fall* is helpful in disentangling at least some of Gibbon's complexities and ambiguities. It occurs in the important introductory chapter two, 'Of the Union and internal Prosperity of the Roman Empire in the Age of the Antonines': 'The various modes of worship, which prevailed in the Roman world, were all considered by the people, as equally true; by the philosopher, as equally false; and by the magistrate, as equally useful'.[3] The established religion of the ancient world may have been polytheist and riddled by superstition but, in Gibbon's account, it was tolerant, worldly, even polite and civilised. 'The superstition of the people was not embittered by any mixture of theological rancour', he noted. It was open to, and tolerant of, all the different religions of the world. The educated elites of the ancient world looked at the superstitions of the vulgar 'with a smile of pity and indulgence', but they treated them with respect, at least in public:

> they diligently practised the ceremonies of their fathers, devoutly frequented the temples of the gods; and sometimes condescending to act a part on the theatre of superstition, they concealed the sentiments of an Atheist under the sacerdotal robes. [I, 59]

Successive governing elites knew and valued the political uses of popular religion and encouraged the public festivals which, Gibbon says, 'humanize the manners of the people'. And they saw that the various kinds of religious practice developed in different parts of the Empire

---

[2] There is a huge secondary literature on Gibbon's *History*, much of it by John Pocock and much of it unavoidably concerned with the interpretation of religion. For two useful discussions see: D. Wootton, 'Narrative, Irony and Faith in Gibbon's *Decline and Fall*, *History and Theory*, 33, 4 (December 1994), 77–105; B. W. Young, '"Scepticism in Excess": Gibbon and Eighteenth-Century Christianity', *The Historical Journal*, 41, 1 (March 1998), 179–199.

[3] E. Gibbon, *The History of the Decline and Fall of the Roman Empire*, ed. David Womersley, 3 vols. (Harmondsworth, 1994), vol. I, 56. Subsequent references to this edition are in parentheses within the text.

served these 'salutary purposes' equally well. They were convinced, he says, 'that, in every country, the form of superstition, which had received the sanction of time and experience, was the best adapted to the climate, and to its inhabitants'. [I, 59] At the centre of this multi-faith empire, Rome became the common temple of all people and 'the freedom of the city was bestowed on all the gods of mankind'. [I, 60–1] Elsewhere in the first volume of *The Decline and Fall* Gibbon spoke of 'the religious harmony of the ancient world, and the facility with which the most different and even hostile nations embraced, or at least respected, each other's superstitions'. [I, 447]

This ancient religious system was not merely a set of speculative doctrines confined to the temple. It was part of the common culture of the period:

> The innumerable deities and rites of polytheism were closely interwoven with every circumstance of business or pleasure, of public or of private life; and it seemed impossible to escape the observance of them, without at the same time, renouncing the commerce of mankind, and all the offices and amusements of society. [I, 460]

Gibbon speaks of 'the cheerful devotion of the Pagans' and their 'convivial entertainments' when 'friends, invoking the hospitable deities, poured out libations to each other's happiness'. In the remains of antiquity, Gibbon says, we can see how polytheism creatively influenced every aspect of civilised life:

> the elegant forms and agreeable fictions consecrated by the imagination of the Greeks, were introduced as the richest ornaments of the houses, the dress, and the furniture of the Pagans. Even the arts of music and painting, of eloquence and poetry, flowed from the same impure origin. [I, 461]

A single people remained uncompromisingly hostile to every variant of paganism and refused to share in the religious harmony and civilised life of the ancient world: the Jews. 'The sullen obstinacy with which they maintained their peculiar rites and unsocial manners, seemed to mark them out as a distinct species of men, who boldly professed, or who faintly disguised, their implacable hatred to the rest of human-kind.' [I, 447–8] The first generations of Christians retained this 'inflexible perseverance' and 'intolerant zeal'. They too were hostile to every other group. They rejected not just the doctrines, but also the ceremonies, the customs and the traditions of their neighbours. Whether it was a marriage, a funeral or one of the great public spectacles, the early Christians, because of their scruples about idolatry, held themselves apart from the common culture around them. 'The ties of blood and friendship were frequently torn asunder by the difference of religious faith', Gibbon says, ascribing this to the 'rigid sentiments' and unsocial, even unnatural, attitudes of the Christians. Not even property was safe from these fanatics. Leaving all they owned to the Church, the 'unfortunate children' of some of these early Christians 'found themselves beggars, because their parents had been saints'. [I, 491] Nothing was more guaranteed to send a shudder down the spine of Gibbon's gentlemanly readers.

This contempt for the natural order, for the sanctities of property and family, were linked to the early Christian's contempt for the moderate and civilised pleasures of polite society:

> The unfeeling candidate for heaven was instructed, not only to resist the grosser allurements of the taste or smell, but even to shut his ears against the profane harmony of sounds, and to view with indifference the most finished productions of human art. Gay apparel, magnificent houses, and elegant furniture, were supposed to unite the double guilt of pride and of sensuality; a simple and mortified appearance was more suitable to the Christian who was certain of his sins and doubtful of his salvation. [I, 478–9]

Gibbon itemises particular objects of anathema, underlining the absurdity of this asceticism:

> false hair, garments of any color except white, instruments of music, vases of gold or silver, downy pillows (as Jacob reposed his head on a stone), white bread, foreign wines, public salutations, the use of warm baths, and the practice of shaving the beard, which, according to the expression of Tertullian, is a lie against our own faces, and an impious attempt to improve the works of the Creator. [I, 478–9]

This is an inventory of some of the accoutrements of civilised life for the propertied classes of Hanoverian England. Christian virtue involves a rejection not just of the ordinary comforts of civilised life, but of art and good taste. It is not just ascetic. It is also philistine. The point is underlined when Gibbon goes on to note that the virtue of these first Christians was generally protected by their poverty: 'it is always easy, as well as agreeable, for the inferior ranks of mankind to claim a merit from the contempt of that pomp and pleasure which fortune has placed beyond their reach'. [I, 479] In other words, this austere puritanism was not a matter of virtue and principle but of social envy.

Uncompromising zeal, or bigotry, was for Gibbon a key factor in Christianity's success in undermining the established polytheism of the ancient world. But once in the ascendant it spread division, factional struggles, provincial disputes and civil war everywhere across the Roman Empire. And it was the nomenclature of the eighteenth-century English establishment in church and state which Gibbon exploited to portray these early Christians: 'a recent and obscure sect', 'this mischievous sect', 'these unfortunate sectaries', 'obstinate and perverse enthusiasts', 'a sect of enthusiasts', 'a blind and furious enthusiasm', 'deluded fanatics', 'desperate fanatics', 'daring fanatics', 'savage fanatics', 'conscientious fanatics', and so on and so on. This is the vocabulary of anti-puritanism found everywhere among eighteenth-century English churchmen – a vocabulary which shaped successive histories of the seventeenth century from Clarendon to Hume. Sectary, enthusiast, zealot and fanatic are all synonyms for puritan and the puritan had a living exemplar: the Dissenter.

It is impossible to read Gibbon's account of the early Christians and their hostile relations to the Roman state and the wider society without being constantly reminded of the history of the Tudors and Stuarts in David Hume's *History of England*. Gibbon's counterposing of a worldly, sociable, tolerant, superstitious established religion to a sect of anti-social fanatics and enthusiasts is also the central binary opposition which shapes Hume's narratives of the sixteenth and seventeenth centuries. Here, for instance, is Hume's picture of the world of pre-reformation Rome in the opening chapters of his *History*, first published in 1754:

> That delicious country, where the Roman pontiff resides, was the source of all modern art and refinement, and diffused on its superstition an air of politeness, which distinguishes it from the gross rusticity of the other sects. And tho' policy made it assume, in some of its monastic orders, that austere mien, which is acceptable to the vulgar; all authority still resided in its prelates and spiritual princes, whose temper, more cultivated and humanized, inclined them to every decent pleasure and indulgence.[4]

Rome was 'the source of all modern art and refinement' and under its aegis 'the admiration of antient literature' and 'the inquiry after new discoveries' were encouraged. But, confronted by the protestant reformers, 'politeness' dissolved and 'the furious controversies of theology took the place of the calm disquisitions of learning'.

> From the admiration of antient literature, from the inquiry after new discoveries, the minds of the studious were every where turned to polemical science; and, in all schools and academies, the furious controversies of theology took place of the calm disquisitions of learning.[5]

It was the zeal of protestant fanatics which transformed Rome into a brutal spiritual despotism and gave rise to the massacres, assassinations and

---

[4] D. Hume, *The History of Great Britain. The Reigns of James I and Charles I*, ed. D. Forbes (Harmondsworth, 1970), 98–9.
[5] Hume, *History of Great Britain*, 97.

inquisitions which disturbed Europe for generations. In Hume's version the burden of responsibility for all this lay with the protestant reformers.

Similar antinomies are highlighted in Hume's account of early Stuart England. The Church in England was an established body which was part of the common culture of English society. Its language, its traditions, its ceremonies were integral to the daily life of the whole population. But with the emergence of the puritans in the sixteenth century a very different kind of religious body began to play a role in the state. Full of abstract anger and enthusiasm, puritanism was profoundly anti-social in its rejection of all authority, custom and common sense. The puritan enemies of Church and court were also the enemies of refinement, polite culture and learning:

> The wretched fanaticism which so much infected the parliamentary party was no less destructive of taste and science, than of all law and order. Gaiety and wit were proscribed; human learning despised; freedom of inquiry detested; cant and hypocrisy alone encouraged.[6]

Hume's account of the antagonism between the Laudian Church of England and the puritans in Stuart England is mirrored in Gibbon's account of the antagonism between the established polytheism of the ancient world and the early Christians.

There are two dimensions of Hume's historical critique of protestantism which deserve attention here, because of the light they throw on Gibbon's *Decline and Fall of the Roman Empire*. The first concerns the proper role of religion in society. In a lengthy footnote added to the second volume of his *History of England*, Hume went some way towards disarming the critics of the first volume – and especially of its negative account of religion as either superstition or enthusiasm. 'The proper office of religion', Hume says, 'is to reform men's lives, to purify their hearts, to inforce all moral duties, and to secure obedience to the laws and civil magistrate'. As long as religion is doing this, it is more or less invisible to the historian. Only 'the abuse of religion' surfaces in historical narrative: 'The adulterate species of it alone, which inflames faction, animates sedition, and prompts rebellion, distinguishes itself on the open theatre of the world, and is the great source of revolutions and public convulsions'. Partaking of the weaknesses of human nature, actually-existing Christianity too easily slips into this extreme – or to its opposite, supersition. The Church of England is, he says, 'perhaps the best medium between these extremes', though even this institution under

---

[6] Hume, *History of Great Britain*, 436. For a much fuller account of Hume on the English puritans, see John Seed, 'The spectre of Puritanism: forgetting the seventeenth century in David Hume's "History of England"', *Social History*, 30.4 (November 2005).

Archbishop Laud was 'somewhat infected with a superstition, resembling the popish'.[7] So the historian can legitimately criticise the real forms and effects of organised religion, without being misunderstood as an enemy of religion per se.

The second significant argument in Hume's *History* is about how religious sectarianism generates philistinism and provincialism. Throughout the chapters on Charles I's reign the refinement and civility of the king and his court are counterpointed to the grim-faced and anti-social hostility to the arts exemplified by the puritans. The king is admired for his taste and his encouragement of painting, architecture and writing. 'Before the civil wars, learning and the fine arts were favoured at court, and a good taste began to prevail in the nation'.[8] The puritan enemies of the court were also the enemies of refinement, polite culture and learning:

> The wretched fanaticism which so much infected the parliamentary party was no less destructive of taste and science, than of all law and order. Gaiety and wit were proscribed; human learning despised; freedom of inquiry detested; cant and hypocrisy alone encouraged.[9]

Gibbon discovered in Hume especially, but also in a wider enlightened historical narrative, a cosmopolitanism which moved beyond the narrow national boundaries of English protestantism with its intense sectarian divisions. Gibbon, like Hume before him, felt more sympathy for a cultured European Catholicism than for the narrow provincial protestantism which, he thought, was in the ascendant in England and Scotland. Hence their distaste for the prevailing anti-popery of Whigs and reformers of every stripe, both among churchmen and Dissenters. Hume's eulogy on the unformed church of Rome, cited above, was a provocative gesture of solidarity with a wider European civilisation. According to Gibbon:

> It is the duty of the patriot to prefer and promote the exclusive interest and glory of his native country: but a philosopher may be permitted to enlarge his views, and consider Europe as one great republic, whose varied inhabitants have attained almost the same level of politeness and civilization. [II, 511]

---

[7] D. Hume, *The History of Great Britain*, vol. II (1757), 450n. This is a much shortened version of a draft preface, reprinted in E.C. Mossner, *The Life of David Hume*, second edition (Oxford, 1980), 306–7.

[8] D. Hume, *The History of England from the Invasion of Julius Caesar to the Revolution of 1688. A New Edition with the Author's Last Corrections and Improvements*, vol. V (London, 1848), 435.

[9] Hume, *History of England*, V, 436.

Note that the attainment was of 'politeness and civilization'. An English Whig and an English (or Scottish) protestant might have judged that there were more important *differences,* in the achievement of political and civil liberties, between the constitutional monarchy of Britain and the absolutist regimes in much of Europe. But Gibbon is following the lead of Hume here in seeking to transcend religious and political faction. It was precisely this facet of the *Decline and Fall* which impressed Hume as unexpected in any English intellectual of his day. In his congratulatory letter of March 1776, Hume said: 'if I had not previously had the happiness of your personal acquaintance, such a performance from an Englishman in our age would have given me some surprize'. And he went on to comment on how Englishmen, 'for almost a whole generation, have given themselves up to barbarous and absurd faction, and have totally neglected all polite letters…'.[10] Gibbon's formation was hardly typical of Englishmen of his day. Had it not been for his five formative years in Lausanne, he later wrote, he would have spent years 'steeped in port and prejudice among the monks of Oxford': 'I should have grown to manhood ignorant of the life and language of Europe…'. In Lausanne, he said, 'I insensibly lost the prejudices of an Englishman'.[11] But this cosmopolitanism also put him out of touch with the real dispositions of those who had stayed behind at Oxford.

This brings us closer to the precise political contexts in which successive volumes of the *Decline and Fall* were drafted and published. The standard Everyman edition of Gibbon's *History*, edited by J.B. Bury in six volumes, ignored the divisions between the different volumes, manufacturing a single historical work that floated free of the period in which it was written and published. The new three-volume Penguin edition, edited by David Womersley, enables us now to read the History in much more complex and historically-specific ways. It is quite clear that Gibbon's conception of the work changed, as he worked on it for over twenty years. It changed too in the light of responses to the published volumes. And it is clear too, that his writing was sometimes inflected by the pressure of contemporary events. Gibbon was explicit that the actions and events he is describing in the pages of his history were relevant to the present. His aim was, he said, 'to connect the ancient and modern history of the World'. For instance, Constantine's alliance with the Church of Rome had continuing ramifications:

> a considerable portion of the globe still retains the impression it received from the conversion of that monarch; and the ecclesiastical institutions of

---

[10] *Miscellaneous Works of Edward Gibbon…*, ed. John Lord Sheffield, 2 vols. (1796), vol. I, 148. This first edition of his Memoirs and correspondence, in two volumes, is cited as *Miscellaneous Works*.
[11] *Miscellaneous Works*, I, 75–6.

his reign are still connected, by an indissoluble chain, with the opinions, the passions, and the interests of the present generation. [I,725]

Gibbon was keen that his readers should draw contemporary parallels. The purpose of historical writing was to record the past 'for the instruction of the present'. In one of his letters to Priestley he represented himself as the straightforward historian, 'who, without interposing his own sentiments, has delivered a simple narrative of authentic facts'.[12] But throughout the pages of the *Decline and Fall* his writing was full of pointed remarks, witty comments, ironic asides, judgements, which were intended to provoke agreement or disagreement among contemporary readers.

Gibbon thought that he was representing 'the sober discretion of the present age', as he put it in the first volume of the *Decline and Fall*. But he was finding out that his perspective on the present age was more limited than he had first thought. Hume had warned him in March 1776 that, despite his 'prudent temperament' in the chapters on religion, 'it was impossible to treat the subject so as not to give grounds of suspicion against you, and you may expect that a clamour will arise'.[13] And he softened and modified some of his comments in a second edition in June 1776 and a third edition in 1777. The first volume of the *Decline and Fall* was remarkably successful. It sold in large numbers and was enthusiastically reviewed. 'We do not remember any work published in our time, which has met with a more general approbation', the *Annual Register* commented in 1776: 'We are happy in adding our suffrage to the public voice, which has so justly declared in its favour'.[14] But if Gibbon was surprised by its prodigious success, he was also surprised by the hostile reaction to chapters 15 and 16. 'Let me frankly own that I was startled at the first discharge of ecclesiastical ordnance'.[15] In his *Memoirs* Gibbon seems to suggest that the attacks from within the Church of England peaked in the later 1770s and faded after their effective rebuttal in the pages of his *Vindication* in 1779. In fact they persisted throughout the 1780s.[16]

---

[12] *Miscellaneous Works*, I, 564.
[13] *Miscellaneous Works*, I, 149.
[14] *Annual Register* 1776 (1777), 236.
[15] *Miscellaneous Works*, I, 155.
[16] See for instance: J. Milner, *Gibbon's Account of Christianity Considered: together with some strictures on Hume's dialogues concerning natural religion …* (York, 1781); H. Taylor, *Thoughts on the Nature of the Grand Apostacy. With reflections and observations on the XVth chapter of Mr. Gibbon's History …* (1781); J. Chelsum, *A Reply to Mr Gibbons Vindication of some Passages in the Fifteenth and Sixteenth Chapters of the History of the Decline and Fall of the Roman Empire* (1785); E. Ryan, *The History of the Effects of Religion on Mankind; in countries, ancient and modern, barbarous and civilized …* (1788); W. Disney, *A Sermon Preached before the University of Cambridge, on Sunday, June 28, 1789 …* (Cambridge, 1789).

In the context of a profound political crisis they not only persisted but in some ways deepened, so that Gibbon became increasingly sensitive to the political contexts within which successive volumes of the *Decline and Fall* were being read in the 1780s. His repeated attacks on Joseph Priestley were strategic in trying to realign himself with the political establishment – to persuade his readers that enthusiasts like Priestley, and everything he represented, were the real threat to civilisation. This was in part a matter of anxious concern for his own reputation and political career, though after 1783 he had pretty much abandoned any expectation of public office. It was also a genuine attempt to rebalance his argument about superstition and enthusiasm in the early volumes of *The Decline and Fall* in the light of deepening political anxieties.

## II

The third volume of *The Decline and Fall,* published in 1781, concludes with a short essay, 'General Observations on the Fall of the Roman Empire in the West'. It summarises the reasons why the fate of Rome was not the inevitable future for Hanoverian England or for Europe as a whole. Gibbon takes it as a question that needed answering and he assumes the existence of an anxious readership in need of reassurance. The threat from outside was remote, possibly at some future date coming from 'some obscure people, scarcely visible in the map of the world'. But for Gibbon there was a potential internal threat too. 'Enthusiasm' figured as a perennial danger and he looked again at the negative effects of Christianity on the Roman empire – and in particular 'the flame of theological discord':

> the church, and even the state, were distracted by religious factions, whose conflicts were sometimes bloody, and always implacable; the attention of the emperors was diverted from camps to synods; the Roman world was oppressed by a new species of tyranny; and the persecuted sects became the secret enemies of their country. [II, 511]

Again, this sounds like nothing so much as Hume's history of Stuart England. And Gibbon had recently been shocked by the unexpected reactivation of that bloody history. He had been in London during the Gordon riots in June 1780 when a large demonstration of the Protestant Association in Westminster, petitioning against popery, had turned into several days of rioting and violence, leaving several hundred persons dead and areas of the West End and the City as smoking ruins. For Gibbon, as for other observers, the ghosts of the seventeenth century once more haunted the streets of London. In their immediate aftermath he wrote:

'forty thousand Puritans, such as they might be in the time of Cromwell, have started out of their graves; the tumult has been dreadful…'.[17] And the next day in another letter Gibbon again ascribed the riots to the revenants of old puritanism:

> Our danger is at an end, but our disgrace will be lasting, and the month of June 1780 will be marked by a dark and diabolical fanaticism, which I had supposed to be extinct, but which actually subsists in Great Britain, perhaps beyond any other country in Europe.[18]

This was precisely the language of Hume, shocked by the political disturbances of the 1760s. In the calls of 'Wilkes and Liberty!' he heard the rantings of seventeenth-century puritans. Just below the surface of the ordered polity of Hanoverian England smouldered the old flames of puritan enthusiasm:

> the present fury of the people, though glossed over by pretensions to civil liberty, is in reality incited by the fanaticism of religion; a principle the most blind, headstrong, and ungovernable, by which human nature can possibly be actuated. Popular rage is dreadful, from whatever motive derived: But must be attended with the most pernicious consequences, when it arises from a principle, which disclaims all controul by human law, reason, or authority.[19]

Threatening the fragile balance between authority and liberty in the Britain of the 1760s, Wilkite rhetoric was a destructive passion; a 'Frenzy of Liberty', he called it. Hume the historian saw the parallels with the civil war of the 1640s. The Cromwells and Pyms of the seventeenth century had reappeared in secular form with demands which were similarly unrealisable.

Contemporary assessments went some way towards exonerating Dissenters from any significant degree of involvement in the Gordon Riots. *The New Annual Register* of 1780 claimed that the ranks of the Protestant Association were 'chiefly Methodists and bigoted Calvinists of the lower ranks of life'. Other contemporaries said much the same. But an alleged identity between Gordon's Protestant Association and reforming religious Dissenters like Price and Priestley was gradually formed during the 1780s. From 1788, especially, churchmen countered the Dissenting campaign for repeal of the Test and Corporation Acts by

---

[17] *Miscellaneous Works*, I, 546.
[18] *Miscellaneous Works*, I, 547.
[19] 'Of the Coalition of Parties', in D. Hume, *Essays Moral, Political and Literary*, ed. E.F. Miller (Indianapolis, 1985), 500.

exploiting fears of a revival of popular protestantism and a repeat of the Gordon Riots. In his *Memoirs* at this time Gibbon commented on the political lesson of the Gordon riots: 'the flames of London, which were kindled by a mischievous madman, admonished all thinking men of the danger of an appeal to the people'.[20]

Gibbon's waspish exchanges with Joseph Priestley in 1783 are worth exploring further in the light of this renewed fear of puritan fanaticism.[21] In December 1782 Joseph Priestley sent his new two volume work, *The History of the Corruptions of Christianity*, to Gibbon. An accompanying note drew his attention to the conclusion, where, at the close of some 900 pages of detailed discussion, Gibbon was challenged to public debate. On 23 January 1783, some six weeks later, Edmund Gibbon wrote back acknowledging receipt of the weighty work – acknowledging but not exactly thanking:

> Sir,
> As a mark of your esteem, I should have accepted with pleasure your History of the Corruptions of Christianity. You have been careful to inform me, that it is intended not as a gift but as a challenge, and such a challenge you must permit me to decline.[22]

A brief flurry of letters followed – three on each side in the next four weeks. Gibbon declined the challenge and opposed publication of the correspondence.

In the only examination of this semi-public squabble, Paul Turnbull has drawn attention to the delicate situation of Gibbon's faltering political career at this juncture. From 1774 to 1781 Gibbon had sat as member of parliament for a Cornish borough in the gift of a family relation. By 1778 he was apparently aligned with the opposition. He voted against North and the government on a couple of occasions and moved in Foxite circles at Brook's. However, he burned his bridges with the Foxites in 1779 when he suddenly accepted from Lord North a lucrative appointment to the Board of Trade. Henceforth Gibbon had a reputation as cynical and untrustworthy, a mercenary and a turncoat. From June 1781 Gibbon sat for the safe government seat of Lymington in Hampshire, which again he owed to government patronage. In the spring of 1782 North's government fell and soon afterwards Gibbon lost

---

[20] *Miscellaneous Works*, I, 158.
[21] The letters were first published by Priestley, shortly after Gibbon's death, as an appendix to: J. Priestley, *Discourses on the Evidence of Revealed Religion* (1794), Appendix IV, 412–20. They were also printed in *Miscellaneous Works*, I, 564–70.
[22] *Miscellaneous Works*, I, 564.

his comfortable sinecure. As different factions jockeyed for position in the autumn of 1782 and the spring of 1783, the last thing Gibbon needed was public controversy about his alleged religious infidelity. As he well knew, George III had been unhappy about sanctioning his appointment to the Board of Trade three years earlier because of his notoriety as an infidel and had only relented after considerable pressure from North. Gibbon had then failed to get an appointment to the Paris embassy in 1782. So Priestley's challenge came at a moment when Gibbon was particularly sensitive about his public reputation. And his spiky response to Priestley was, Turnbull suggests, 'a careful attempt to protect his diminished claim to political preferment'.[23]

This ill-tempered exchange also enacts *social* differences between Gibbon and Priestley – and more broadly between the patrician culture within which Gibbon moved and the world of middle-class urban and provincial Dissenters. This points to a different kind of political contextualisation of Gibbon's hostility to Priestley – one which should help make sense of some important passages in the *Decline and Fall*. From his first letter to Priestley, Gibbon posed as the refined gentleman-scholar whose privacy has been rudely disturbed by a disputatious Dissenting minister, an enthusiast, a zealot and a fanatic. 'The behaviour which is reckoned polite in England', Adam Smith advised his Glasgow students, 'is a calm, composed, unpassionate serenity noways ruffled by passion'.[24] Note the terms Gibbon applies to Priestley: he is a disputant who 'proudly rejects', 'overthrows', and 'condemns'. In his second letter Gibbon declines further correspondence in view of 'the style and temper' of the letters he had received. That Priestley was not a gentleman, accustomed to the manners of polite society, is insinuated in Gibbon's little jibe about letters being a private matter between men of honour:

> If Dr Priestley consults his friends, he will probably learn that a single copy of a paper addressed under a seal to a single person, and not relative to any public or official business, must always be considered as private correspondence ....[25]

This is both patronising, in its patient explanation of the obvious – what a private correspondence is – and waspish in its insinuation that Priestley's friends may share his own failure to understand basic social etiquette.

---

[23] P. Turnbull, 'Gibbon's Exchange with Joseph Priestley', *British Journal for Eighteenth-Century Studies*, 14 (1991), 148.
[24] A. Smith, *Lectures on Rhetoric and Belles Lettres, The Glasgow Edition of the Works and Correspondence of Adam Smith*, vol. 4, ed. J.C. Bryce (Oxford 1983), 198.
[25] *Miscellaneous Works*, I, 569.

Gibbon further distances Priestley from polite society, placing him beyond the limits of civilised Europe, since he 'condemns the religion of every Christian nation'; 'you glory in outstripping the zeal of the Mufti and the Lama', he says.[26]

In his *Memoirs*, which he was revising during 1789–90, Gibbon resumed this condescending tone and subtle insult. Priestley, he said, returning to their exchanges of 1783, had ignored his advice to concentrate on his scientific studies: 'the dauntless philosopher of Birmingham continued to fire away his double battery against those who believed too little, and those who believed too much'. By what right does Gibbon assume the right to advise Priestley about anything? There is a further social snub intended, I think, in the description, 'philosopher of Birmingham'. Late eighteenth-century Birmingham was not just an unfashionable manufacturing town, far from the centres of European civilisation.[27] The name was synonymous at this time with cheap, poor-quality or counterfeit goods. Gibbon must have known the recent anecdote about Richard Rigby MP. When he heard that Gibbon's closest friend and posthumous editor, John Holroyd, had been made Lord Sheffield (in 1781), Rigby complained to the king about the lack of reward for his own political services. He suggested his title might be Lord Mistly, after his estates. The king rejoined that since Holroyd had become Lord Sheffield, then Rigby must become Lord Birmingham: 'which royal witticism so disconcerted Dick, that he instantly dropped the subject; and his Majesty relates the joke to every one at court'.[28]

Registering the snooty tones of Gibbon's letters to Priestley it is difficult to overlook contemporary anecdotes about the historian's foppish public manner. The playwright George Colman graphically counterposed Gibbon and Dr Johnson at some social gathering:

> Their manners and taste both in writing and conversation, were as different as their habiliments. On the day I first sat down with Johnson, in his rusty brown suit, and his blue worsted stockings, Gibbon was placed opposite me in a suit of flowered velvet, with a bag and a sword.[29]

And he contrasted the powerful and stately, if sometimes pedantic speech of Johnson to the mannered elegance and polish of Gibbon's. Boswell

---

[26] *Miscellaneous Works*, I, 564.
[27] Burke has similar fun with Richard Price's association with the Dissenting academy at Hackney, juxtaposed as a centre of learning to Oxford and the Sorbonne. E. Burke, 'An Appeal from the New to the Old Whigs' (1791), in *Further Reflections on the Revolution in France*, ed. D.E. Ritchie (Indianapolis, 1992), 172–3.
[28] *Hal's Looking-glas; or the R\*\*\*l Exhibition ...*, sixth edition (1783), 76.
[29] G. Colman, *Random Records* (1830), vol. I, 121.

recalled Johnson pronouncing on Lord Chesterfield's *Letters*: 'Every man of education would rather be called a rascal, than accused of deficiency in the graces'. To which Gibbon responded with a clever aside to a woman friend – 'in his quaint manner, tapping his box', according to Boswell: 'Don't you think, Madam (looking towards Johnson) that among all your acquaintance, you could find one exception?'[30] The blunt Yorkshireman, practical scientist and black-coated Dissenting minister Dr Priestley was hardly more gifted than Dr Johnson in what Gibbon, at least, would have seen as 'the graces'.

These issues surrounding 'manners' and polite society in Gibbon's exchanges with Priestley are politically significant. Gibbon's letters to Priestley and some of his other remarks invoke the vocabulary of enthusiasm and thus play into a powerful contemporary prejudice against religious Dissenters and against a whole provincial and middle-class culture. Enthusiasm, Hume suggested, is a characteristic of rising men, of the upwardly-mobile, of the uneducated parvenu, stemming 'from prosperous success, from luxuriant health, from strong spirits, or from a bold and confident disposition'. The enthusiast was a social embarrassment. He was also a dangerous bigot and a threat not just to authority but to society itself:

> The violence of this species of religion, when excited by novelty, and animated by opposition, appears from numberless instances; of the *anabaptists* in Germany, the *camisars* in France, the *levellers* and other fanatics in England and the *covenanters* in Scotland. Enthusiasm being founded on strong spirits, and a presumptuous boldness of character, it naturally begets the most extreme resolutions: especially after it rises to that height as to delude the inspired fanatic with the opinion of divine illuminations, and with a contempt for the common rules of reason, morality, and prudence.[31]

Thus enthusiasm produced 'the most cruel disorders in human society', overturning every established authority. It was the antithesis and the enemy of polite culture and the established order of Hanoverian England.[32]

It is striking how often in these years, confronted by Priestley's polemical energy, the subtleties of polite discourse are replaced by the repressive instruments of the state – the prison and the madhouse. In the 1783 exchange of letters Gibbon goes no further than to insinuate that, like all zealots, Priestley cultivates martyrdom. 'Remember the end

---

[30] J. Boswell, *The Life of Samuel Johnson, LL.D …*, vol. II (1791), 71–2.
[31] Hume, *Essays*, 76–7.
[32] See the important study by Jon Mee: *Romanticism, Enthusiasm and Regulation. Poetics and the Policing of Culture in the Romantic Period* (Oxford 2003).

of your predecessor Servetus, not of his life (the Calvins of our days are restrained from the use of the same fiery arguments), but, I mean, of his reputation', Gibbon pointedly warns. Of course he is referring precisely to what he says he isn't – implying that seeking martyrdom, Priestley may find other enthusiasts, some latter-day Calvin, to realise his death-wish for him.[33] In his second letter Gibbon disclaimed any interest in 'how far you are inclined to suffer, or inflict, martyrdom'.[34] But he does not at this stage go so far as to suggest the intervention of the magistrate. The other recipient of Priestley's *History of the Corruptions* in 1783 was the Whiggish bishop of Worcester, Richard Hurd. He commented privately that Priestley's 'impertinence' in sending him the book and calling on him to respond, 'shews him to be out of his head'.[35] William Jones, chaplain and biographer of Bishop Horne went further. He was uncomfortable about cooperating in his master's polemic with Priestley at this time: 'it always appeared to me, that Priestley was a person of too coarse a mind to be the proper object of a serious argument'. An adversary 'inflamed with hatred' against the church and avowing his intent to undermine its foundations should, Jones said, 'be considered (if a gentleman) as a person of unsound mind; if not a gentleman, then as an object of the penal laws of this country, if it should have any against such offenders'.[36] By the late 1780s this was pretty much Gibbon's view too.

## III

Gibbon and Priestley continued to growl at each other. In 1787 Priestley sent Gibbon the second part of his *Letters to a Philosophical Unbeliever* in which he returned to Gibbon's chapters 15 and 16. He did so, he explained, because these chapters were said to have created more unbelievers in recent years than any other publication. It was uncompromising in its criticisms, especially of what he saw as Gibbon's deliberate obfuscations. For instance, he makes this cutting remark on Richard Watson's *An Apology for Christianity*, for its polite and restrained criticisms of Gibbon:

> I am sorry to see him affect to believe Mr Gibbon to be sincere in the regard he professes for christianity. This I think to be unworthy of a

---

[33] *Miscellaneous Works*, I, 565.
[34] *Miscellaneous Works*, I, 568. Gibbon succinctly commented on Cranmer's martyrdom: 'the flames of Smithfield, in which he was afterwards consumed, had been kindled for the Anabaptists by the zeal of Cranmer'. W, III, 438.
[35] Quoted Turnbull, 'Gibbon's Exchange with Joseph Priestley', 148.
[36] W. Jones, 'The Life of Bishop Horne' (1795), reprinted in *The Theological, Philosophical and Miscellaneous Works of Rev. William Jones*, vol. XII (1801), 167–8.

christian bishop; as I think Mr Gibbon's pretenses are unworthy of a man.[37]

Gibbon responded in the fifth volume of *The Decline and Fall*. Chapter LIV ends with a couple of bewilderingly complex paragraphs, which outline the long-term effects of the reformation and which conclude with a brief but bitter attack on Priestley.[38] Here the danger from religious enthusiasts is specified more precisely. So too is the threat of legal sanctions. First Gibbon points out that Luther and Calvin were somewhat limited reformers. They did not question some of the core doctrines of the Church – Gibbon specifically refers to the Trinity and the Incarnation. And they retained many of the traditions of Rome. 'After a fair discussion we shall rather be surprised by the timidity, than scandalised by the freedom of our first reformers'. 'The philosopher' must nevertheless acknowledge his obligation to 'these fearless enthusiasts'. They levelled to the ground 'the lofty fabric of superstition', much of it inherited from paganism, which Gibbon says, had 'nourished' the 'credulity of the people'. A straightforward protestant reading of this passage might take this as a standard criticism of the ways in which Catholicism was little better than a set of semi-pagan rituals and superstitions. But was this disenchantment of the world – the disappearance from everyday life of saints and angels, images and relics, miracles and visions – an unalloyed good? A more critical reading, bearing in mind Gibbon's support for the social benefits of paganism in the first volume of *The Decline and Fall*, would note the author's doubts about 'whether the vulgar, in the absence of all visible objects, will not be inflamed by enthusiasm, or insensibly subside in languor and indifference'. [III, 437] In other words, the rituals and supersitions of the unreformed Church of Rome had preserved the lower orders from the equally dangerous alternatives of religious indifference or religious enthusiasm. But the reformation's destruction of ecclesiastical authority had undermined these stabilising effects:

> The chain of authority was broken, which restrains the bigot from thinking as he pleases, and the slave from speaking as he thinks: the popes, fathers,

---

[37] J. Priestley, *Letters to a Philosophical Unbeliever. Part II. Containing a state of the evidence of revealed religion, with animadversions on the two last chapters of the first volume of Mr. Gibbon's History of the Decline and Fall of the Roman Empire* (Birmingham, 1787), xix.

[38] Gibbon's correspondence enables us to be very precise about timings here. Gibbon was writing this fifth volume of the *Decline and Fall* between July 1784 and May 1786. It was sent to the press, along with the fourth and sixth volumes, in August 1787. We can be less sure about the timing of Part 2 of *Letters to a Philosophical Believer*. Priestley's preface is dated 1st February 1787.

and councils, were no longer the supreme and infallible judges of the world; and each Christian was taught to acknowledge no law but the scriptures, no interpreter but his own conscience. [III, 437–8]

Even a casual protestant reading could hardly miss the ambiguities here. The decline of religious authority has freed not only the Christian and the philosopher but also the bigot and the slave from restraint. Erasmus now makes his first and only appearance, at the head of a different tradition, one that passes down to the English latitudinarians:

> Since the days of Luther and Calvin, a secret reformation has been silently working in the bosom of the reformed churches; many weeds of prejudice were eradicated; and the disciples of Erasmus diffused a spirit of freedom and moderation. [III, 438]

This has led to the benefits of liberty of conscience and, in Holland and England, a degree of religious toleration which Gibbon calls prudent and humane.

But it had also led to 'languor and indifference'. The private beliefs of protestants now diverge from the official doctrines of the churches and 'the forms of orthodoxy, the articles of faith, are subscribed with a sigh or a smile by the modern clergy'. Gibbon, sounding like a high-church bishop, concludes the chapter by aligning himself not with this worldly scepticism but with the religious faith that has been lost:

> Yet the friends of Christianity are alarmed at the boundless impulse of enquiry and superstition. The predictions of the Catholics are accomplished: the web of mystery is unravelled by the Arminians, Arians, and Socinians, whose numbers must not be computed by their separate congregations. And the pillars of revelation are shaken by those men who preserve the name without the substance of religion, who indulge the licence without the temper of philosophy. [III, 439]

And so these pages travel from Luther and Calvin to Priestley and the congregations of Socinians; in other words, to the rational Dissenters of late eighteenth-century England.

These paragraphs at the end of Chapter LIV can be read at a number of different levels but they make sense, I think, if we track carefully the different constituencies which connect with these complex historical shifts in organised religion since the reformation. On the one hand there was the philosopher and the educated friends of Christianity (Erasmus, latitudinarian churchmen and, it is implied, Gibbon himself). These have benefited from the reformation and the intellectual freedom which it has brought. On the other hand there were 'the vulgar', the uneducated populace, who have lost the images, superstitions and ceremonies which shaped their everyday lives. This has left them bereft of a common culture and vulnerable to socially disruptive forces – crime, enthusiasm, and so on. Worse still, the reformation has let loose the fanatic and the bigot: 'those men who preserve the name without the substance of religion, who indulge the licence without the temper of philosophy.' In other words, pointing back once more to Hume, Gibbon identifies a dangerous fusion of philosophy and organised religion.

And the real sting in the tail is Gibbon's final footnote. Here he recommends to 'public animadversion' two passages from Priestley's *History of the Corruptions of Christianity* – the book which Priestley had sent him in 1783. These, Gibbon says, 'betray the ultimate tendency of his opinions'. At one, he says, the priest, at the other the magistrate may 'tremble!' [III, 439n.] What are these terrifying passages? The first, near the close of the lengthy section on 'The history of the opinions relating to the doctrine of the atonement', focuses on the slow process by which the corruptions of Christianity became the orthodoxy of the church. In the same way, these doctrines are now slowly dissolving: 'Great buildings do not often fall at once, but some apartments will still be thought habitable, after the rest are seen to be in ruins.' So too with 'great *systems of doctrine*': some parts are easily given up, others only gradually, until at last the whole system is abandoned:

> the detection of one falsehood prepares us for the detection of another, till, before we are aware of it, we find no trace left of the immense and seemingly well compacted system. Thus by degrees we can reconcile ourselves to abandon all the parts, when we could never have thought of giving up the whole.[39]

By chipping away at specific doctrines on a piecemeal basis – the atonement, the trinity, the immacualte conception, and so on – rational dissenters like Priestley are undermining the foundations of the Church, leading inexorably to the collapse of its whole doctrinal system.

The second passage, coming at the very end of Priestley's two volumes, is in apocalyptic rather than gradualist mode. It argues that the corruptions of primitive Christianity were brought about and maintained by political control:

> It is nothing but the *alliance* of the kingdom of Christ with the kingdom of this world (an alliance which our Lord expressly disclaimed) that supports the grossest corruptions of Christianity; and perhaps we must wait for the fall of the civil powers before this most unnatural alliance be broken. Calamitous,

---

[39] J. Priestley, *An History of the Corruptions of Christianity, in Two Volumes*, vol. I (Birmingham 1782), 275–6.

no doubt, will that time be. But what convulsion in the political world ought to be a subject of lamentation, if it be attended with so desirable an event. May *the kingdom of God*, and of Christ … truly and fully *come*, though all the kingdoms of the world be removed, in order to make way for it!'[40]

This passage – to which Gibbon had perhaps first directed his attention – was seized on by Burke a couple of years later in his *Reflections on the Revolution in France*. Quoting from it, he commented that these reformers are 'so heated with their theories' that the destruction of church and state with all the accompanying 'mischiefs' is quite acceptable: 'You see with what a steady eye these gentlemen are prepared to view the greatest calamities which can befall their country!'[41] Gibbon does not make explicit why the magistrate's attention should be called to this passage, but his very silence leaves his readers to imagine the worst.

To expose the intellectual absurdities of religion in the role of philosopher for a cultivated readership, such as Gibbon had done, was one thing. But to attack the established church as a political institution and to challenge the ascendancy of the manners of polite society, as Priestley and the Dissenters were doing, was something altogether different and more dangerous. It was this potential junction of the fanatic and the rabble, for Gibbon as for Burke, that warranted the intervention of the state.

It is worth noting the sharpness of the review of the final three volumes of the *Decline and Fall* in the *New Annual Register*. Set up as a reforming alternative to the increasingly conservative *Annual Register*, its editor was the rational Dissenting minister Andrew Kippis, friend of both Priestley and Dr Richard Price. One of its regular contributors in these years was William Godwin. Gibbon's second and third volumes had been given a laudatory review in its pages in 1781, though tempered with some reservations about its accounts of the early Christian church.[42] The same reviewer of the final volumes in 1788, while acknowledging 'proofs of astonishing industry, acute penetration, and fertility of genius', was more hostile. He commented on 'impure allusions' and 'indecent anecdotes' which should be cut from future editions. And without mentioning Gibbon's call to the magistrate to prosecute Priestley, it responded in kind:

---

[40] J. Priestley, *An History of the Corruptions of Christianity, in Two Volumes*, vol. II (Birmingham 1782), 484.
[41] E. Burke, *Reflections on the Revolution in France…* (1790), in *Burke: Select Works*, ed. E.J. Payne, 2 vols. (Oxford 1898), II, 67–8. Burke's Victorian editor notes that, published in the aftermath of 'a religious enthusiasm which had already reduced much of the metropolis to ashes' (the Gordon riots), the 'obloquy' which this passage subsequently brought on Priestley was hardly surprising or undeserved: 329n.
[42] *New Annual Register* for 1781 (1782), 223.

The faults to which we chiefly confine our observation are, the prejudices and sarcasms against Christianity which he has so frequently and so unnecessarily introduced, and the immoral tendency of many parts of his fascinating and seductive work. Against Christianity Mr Gibbon discovers all the bitterness and descends to practise the artifices of a malignant and seditious adversary.[43]

Seditious?

## IV

In his *Memoirs*, redrafted at the end of the 1780s, Gibbon threatened legal sanctions against Priestley once more, joining his voice to that of the established church in the form of Samuel Horsley, a high church cleric currently locked in polemical battle with Priestley:

> From my replies he has nothing to hope or fear: but his Socinian shield has been repeatedly pierced by the spear of Horsley, and his trumpet of sedition may at length awaken the magistrates of a free country.[44]

This might be read as a simple case of my enemy's enemy. But if we look closely at Horsley's political criticisms of Priestley and of religious Dissent more broadly, certain affinities become apparent. Expressing his alarm at 'how eminently the State hath lately been endangered, and the protestant cause disgraced, by a combination of wild fanatics, pretending to associate for the preservation of the reformed religion', Horsley identifies the Gordon riots as just one expression of a profounder malaise.[45] What he termed 'the irregular zeal of self-constituted teachers of religion', had destroyed the unity of the church and had encouraged both scepticism and fanaticism – the Scylla and Charybdis of the reformation's breakdown of ecclesiastical authority, which Gibbon had also identified. Horsley addresses Priestley directly:

> the root of all these evils hath been the prevalency of a principle, of which you seem to be disposed to be an advocate, that every man who hath credit enough to collect together a congregation, hath a right, over which the magistrate cannot without tyranny exercise controul, to celebrate divine worship according to his own form, and to propagate his own opinions.[46]

---

[43] *New Annual Register* for 1788 (1789), 238.
[44] *Miscellaneous Works*, I, 154.
[45] S. Horsley, *Letters from the Archdeacon of St.Albans, in Reply to Dr. Priestley* (1784), 171.
[46] Horsley, *Letters*, 171.

In other words, the problem was the civil liberties of the religious dissenter, who had no authority higher than his own bible and his own conscience. 'The chain of authority was broken, which restrains the bigot from thinking as he pleases, and the slave from speaking as he thinks', as Gibbon was to put it in the penultimate volume of the *History of the Decline and Fall of the Roman Empire*. [III, 438–9]

At the beginning of 1787 the Dissenters had launched a powerful campaign for the repeal of the Test and Corporation Acts which was polarising political debate in England. Gibbon well knew that Priestley, and the Dissenters as whole, were being subjected to an onslaught of virulent propaganda from within the Church of England and the political establishment. This assault on Dissenters was most influentially articulated in Burke's *Reflections on the Revolution in France*, published in 1790. 'I thirst for Mr Burke's Reflections on the revolution in France', Gibbon told his publisher in November 1790, asking for it to be sent to him in Lausanne as quickly as possible.[47] According to Horace Walpole, writing in February 1791, 'Gibbon admires Burke to the skies, even the religious parts he says'.[48] Gibbon himself commented in a letter at this time:

> Burke's book is a most admirable medicine against the French disease, which has made too much progress even in this happy country. I admire his eloquence, I approve his politics, I adore his chivalry, and I can even forgive his superstition.[49]

This comment is repeated almost verbatim in Gibbon's posthumously-published memoirs – though significantly he changes the final clause: 'I can almost excuse his reverence for Church establishments.'[50] When told of this remark, by Arthur Young, Burke is reported to have said that the historian had 'heartily repented of the anti-religious part of his work for contributing to free mankind from all restraint on their vices and profligacy, and thereby aiding so much the spirit which produced the horrors which blackened the most detestable of all revolutions'.[51]

---

[47] *The Letters of Edward Gibbon*, ed. J.E. Norton, vol. III: 1784–1794 (1956), 210. Hereafter cited as *Letters*.
[48] *The Letters of Horace Walpole*, ed. P. Cunningham, vol. IX (1859), 292.
[49] *Miscellaneous Works*, I, 238.
[50] 'I beg leave to subscribe my assent to Mr Burke's creed on the Revolution of France. I admire his eloquence, I approve his politics, I adore his Chivalry, and I can almost excuse his reverence for Church establishments.' *Miscellaneous Works*, I, 181.
[51] *The Autobiography of Arthur Young*, ed. M. Betham-Edward (1898), 258.

In Burke's view then, Gibbon had recanted the religious scepticism of the first volume of the *Decline and Fall*. There is some substance to this. Burke and Gibbon had mixed socially for many years but in the early 1790s they had become quite intimate, spending hours in each other's company on several occasions. Burke may well have been repeating here what Gibbon had said to him. Yet in fundamentals Gibbon already agreed with Burke without needing to recant in the lurid light of the French Revolution. Whether or not churchmen found the tone and language offensive, Gibbon had nevertheless asserted at several points in the first volume that religious scepticism was for the educated minority, not for the lower orders. 'A state of scepticism and suspense may amuse a few inquisitive minds. But the practice of superstition is so congenial to the multitude, that if they are forcibly awakened, they still regret the loss of their pleasing vision.' [I, 498–9] The spread of religious indifference in the ancient world, Gibbon warned, flowed from the philosopher, to the educated elite and the man of business, from the noble to the plebian, from the master to the servant and the slave. As a consequence, the lower orders were exposed 'to the danger of a painful and comfortless situation'. It was dangerous because it made them vulnerable to fanatical preachers whose enthusiasm offered security and certainty. Gibbon was as anxious as Burke or any churchman about the consequences of weakening the religious restraints on popular superstition and vice. Despite its chilly tone, the remark in the *Memoirs* on the controversy provoked by the first volume of the *Decline and Fall*, is a sincere concession to the manners of polite society:

> Had I believed that the majority of English readers were so fondly attached even to the name and shadow of Christianity; had I foreseen that the pious, the timid, and the prudent would feel or affect to feel with such exquisite sensibility; I might, perhaps have softened the two invidious chapters, which would create many enemies and conciliate few friends …[52]

When Gibbon had praised Burke and drily remarked that he could 'almost excuse his reverence for Church establishments', he pointedly added: 'The primitive Church which I have treated with some freedom, was itself at that time, an innovation, and I was attached to the old pagan establishment'.[53] Dissenters had frequently argued that the defence of the establishment by churchmen would equally have served as a justification of the pagan establishment against the early Christians. Priestley made precisely this point to Burke about his defence of prescription and tradition: 'On this principle, Sir, had you been a Pagan at the time of the

---

[52] *Miscellaneous Works*, I, 153.
[53] *Miscellaneous Works*, I, 214.

promulgation of Christianity, you would have continued one. You would also have opposed the reformation'.[54]

Churchmen, unsurprisingly, misread Gibbon. They failed to recognise themselves in the worldly, tolerant, polytheist pagans of the ancient world, who smiled indulgently at the superstitious rituals of the vulgar and who, in Gibbon's words, 'concealed the sentiments of an Atheist under the sacerdotal robes'. But this kind of polite religious scepticism was quite acceptable among gentlemen. And it is worth noting that one of Gibbon's critics, Bishop Richard Watson was something of a religious sceptic himself, adhering more or less to the same Unitarian position as Joseph Priestley, as did a number of prominent Cambridge churchmen in the 1770s and 1780s. But Watson was discrete about his heretical religious views and in public supported the established church. He was not just a Bishop but also Regius Professor of Divinity at Cambridge University. He was then a gentleman and was addressed as such by Gibbon in their courtly exchange of letters in 1776, as later in his *Vindication*, where he contrasted 'the keen and well-tempered weapon' of the Bishop with the 'rustic cudgels' of some of his other, 'staunch and sturdy' but less exalted, clerical critics. [III, 1160][55]

'Who', Burke asked in 1793, questioning the prognostic value of historical precedents, 'could have imagined that atheism could produce one of the most violently operative principles of fanaticism?' The answer was – Edward Gibbon. Precisely because he understood that religious scepticism could be conservative, gentlemanly, part of the ruling order, he also understood how it could fuse with enthusiasm to produce a potent and destabilising political force. Priestley, Price and the ranks of rational Dissent embodied just such a fusion. Gibbon identified in the French revolution 'the deadly principles of fanaticism' – just as Hume's *History of England* had in the English revolution, a century before. He spoke of 'zealous' 'Jacobin Missionaries'.[56] And in one of the later notes added to his *Memoirs* he warned: 'The fanatic missionaries of sedition have scattered the seed of discontent in our cities and villages'.[57] In another letter, early in 1793, he applauded the opening of war with France because Britain was 'now armed in the common cause against the most dangerous fanatics that

---

[54] J. Priestley, *Letters to the Right Honourable Edmund Burke, Occasioned by his Reflections on the Revolution in France, &c., ...*, third edition (Birmingham, 1791), 113.

[55] The reference is to Watson's *An Apology for Christianity in a Series of Letters Addressed to Edward Gibbon Esq* (Cambridge, 1776).

[56] *Letters*, III, 283.

[57] *Miscellaneous Works*, I, 181.

have ever evaded the peace of Europe'.[58] Here we have precisely the anti-puritan and anti-Dissenting lexicon utilised not just in Hume's *History of England* and Burke's *Reflections* but in contemporary polemics against the Dissenters in a thousand tracts, speeches and newspaper articles.

There is, I am arguing, a deep affinity between Gibbon and Burke. They are Hume-the-historian's two most important disciples and share a common vocabulary.[59] There is a striking instance of this in a letter of Gibbon's on 15 December 1789. Here, before Burke had even set pen to paper, Gibbon rehearses some key sections of the *Reflections*, down even to the vehement attack on the Dissenting minister Richard Price (whose 1789 sermon to the Revolution Society he seems to have read). There were abuses of government in France that cried out for reform Gibbon says. However, the French were wasting 'a glorious opportunity':

> If they had been content with a liberal translation of our system, if they had respected the prerogatives of the crown and the privileges of the Nobles, they might have raised a solid fabric on the only true foundation, the natural Aristocracy of a great Country.[60]

But France was moving in a very different direction. Gibbon pointed to the dramatic moment which Burke was to highlight in the *Reflections*: 'Their King brought a captive to Paris after his palace had been stained with the blood of his Guards: the Nobles in exile, the Clergy plundered in a Way which strikes at the root of all property …'. These 'flames of discord' were, he went on, 'kindled by the worst of men':

> a set of wild Visionaries (like our Dr Price) who gravely debate and dream about the establishment of a pure and perfect Democracy of five and twenty millions, the virtues of the Golden Age and the primitive rights and equality of mankind which would lead in fair reasoning to an equal partition of lands and money.[61]

Gibbon, no less than Burke, had identified in the 1780s how rational dissenters like Joseph Priestley and Richard Price were eroding the authority of the Church of England, unsettling the world of polite letters, threatening property and undermining the whole social and political order.

---

[58] *Letters*, III, 321.
[59] On Burke's appropriations from Hume's *History of England*, see John Seed, *Dissenting Histories: Religious Division and the Politics of Memory in Eighteenth-Century England* (Edinburgh, 2008), 157–60.
[60] *Letters*, III, 183–4.
[61] *Letters*, III, 184.

## V

When Gibbon commented in 1776 that 'the various modes of worship, which prevailed in the Roman world, were all considered by the people, as equally true; by the philosopher as equally false; and by the magistrate, as equally useful', he was not fully sensitive to the political ramifications of Hume's interpretation of institutional Christianity. But during the 1780s the complacent scepticism of the philosopher, secure in the circles of the polite world, gave way to a more uncertain situation in which the perspectives of the philosopher had to be reconciled with the responsibilities of the magistrate. Gibbon sharpened and focused the conservative dimensions of his religious scepticism. Increasingly his attack was not on Christianity as such than on a particular variant – enthusiasm – which, whether in the form of the primitive Christians, the Tudor and Stuart puritans, the eighteenth-century English Dissenters or the French revolutionaries, was socially and politically destabilising. Superstition, on the other hand, had positive benefits for the disciplining of the lower orders. Gibbon's scepticism, like Hume's before him, became part of the defence of the established social, political and ecclesiastical order. Hence the apparent paradox in the 1780s of a notorious religious sceptic aligning himself with a Tory high-church Bishop in defence of the Church of England against religious Dissenters. As Priestley ruefully commented, in the immediate aftermath of the 1791 Birmingham riots in which the magistrate, the clergyman and the mob cooperated to destroy the chapels and the houses of Dissenters:

> had I been an open enemy of all religion, the animosity against me could not have been greater than it is. Neither Mr Hume nor Mr Gibbon was a thousand part so obnoxious to the clergy as I am; so little respect have my enemies for Christianity itself, compared with what they have for their emoluments from it.[62]

---

[62] J. Priestley, *An Appeal to the Public on the Subject of the Riots in Birmingham, Part II ...* (1792), 111.

# PART TWO

Methods and Interpretations

# 5. The Battle of Actium and the 'slave of passion'*

*Carsten Hjort Lange*

In *Antony and Cleopatra* Shakespeare dramatically recalls Antonius' (Mark Antony) wish to fight the battle of Actium against Octavian (later Augustus) at sea 'For that he dares us to't'. Domitius Ahenobarbus suggests that this might not be a good idea after all (3.7):[1]

> Your ships are not well mann'd;
> Your mariners are muleters, reapers, people
> Ingross'd by swift impress; in Caesar's fleet
> Are those that often have 'gainst Pompey fought:
> Their ships are yare; yours, heavy: no disgrace
> Shall fall you for refusing him at sea,
> Being prepared for land.

In the end the battle at sea is lost, less because of the factors mentioned by Domitius Ahenobarbus, than because of the fleeing of Cleopatra (3.10). This is then recalled in Domitius Ahenobarbus' answer to Cleopatra, when she asks him who is to blame for the defeat at Actium (3.13):

> Antony only, that would make his will
> Lord of his reason. What though you fled
> From that great face of war, whose several ranges
> Frighted each other? why should he follow?
> The itch of his affection should not then
> Have nick'd his captainship; at such a point,
> When half to half the world opposed, he being
> The meered question: 'twas a shame no less
> Than was his loss, to course your flying flags,
> And leave his navy gazing.

---

* I am very grateful to Dr Andrew Bayliss, dr.phil Jacob Isager and Dr Ian Macgregor Morris for useful comments and suggestions. Furthermore, I would like to thank Dr James Moore and Dr Ian Macgregor Morris for the opportunity to participate in the colloquium 'Making History. Writing the History of the Ancient World in the Long Eighteenth Century. A Colloquium at the Institute of Historical Research'.

[1] The text used is that of the Oxford World Classics: Shakespeare (edited by M. Neill), *The Tragedy of Anthony and Cleopatra* (Oxford, 1994).

Shakespeare uses Plutarch superbly, to explain why, when Cleopatra abandoned the scene of battle, Antonius followed her, leaving his navy and army behind to fend for itself (*Ant.* 66, 68). Importantly, even though Cleopatra fled, it was when Antonius followed her that the battle was lost. This Shakespearean view, due to the influence of Plutarch, was also the most common view of the battle of Actium in the eighteenth century, the main focus of this article. The French historian Charles Rollin describes the scene from the point of view of the army of Antonius: 'But seeing themselves abandoned by their generals, they surrendered to Caesar, who received them with open arms'.[2]

Plutarch and the majority of the ancient sources agree that Cleopatra betrayed Antonius by fleeing and that he followed her, leaving his fleet and army behind. Most eighteenth-century scholars follow Plutarch and the ancient evidence on this issue. Johannes Kromayer, a German military historian rejects this evidence, in a famous article from 1899, arguing instead that this was all in accordance with a prearranged plan, as mentioned by Cassius Dio, a Roman senator and historian writing in the early third century A.D.[3] Yet as will be shown this idea, supported almost universally by modern scholars, does not fit the ancient evidence.[4]

This article will focus mainly on what today might be described the alternative eighteenth-century view of the battle of Actium. Its purpose

---

[2] C. Rollin, *The Roman History from the Foundation of Rome to the Battle of Actium: By Mr. Rollin*, vol. VI, eighteenth edition (London, 1841), 405. See Plutarch *Ant.* 68.3.

[3] J. Kromayer, 'Kleine Forschungen zur Geschichte des Zweiten Triumvirats VII. Der Feldzug von Actium und der sogenannte Verrath der Cleopatra', *Hermes*, 34 (1899).

[4] For the consensus, see Kromayer, *Hermes* 34, 33; T. Rice Holmes, *The Architect of the Roman Empire* (Oxford, 1928), 253–8, disagreeing with A. Ferrabino, 'La battaglia d'Azio', *Rivista de Filologia e di Istruzione Classica*, 52 (1924); G.W. Richardson, 'Actium', *Journal of Roman Studies*, 27 (1937), 158–9; J.M. Carter, *The Battle of Actium. The Rise and Triumph of Augustus Caesar* (London, 1970), 213; M. Grant, *Cleopatra* (London, 1972), 208, 211; J.R. Johnson, *Augustan Propaganda: The Battle of Actium, Mark Antony's Will, the Fasti Capitolini Consulares, and Early Imperial Historiography*, Ph.D. diss. (University of California, 1976), 48–9, 55; H. Bengtson, *Marcus Antonius. Triumvir und Herrscher des Orients* (Munich, 1977), esp. 230; C.B.R. Pelling, 'The Triumviral Period', in A.K. Bowman et al. (eds.), *CAH 10²*, *The Augustan Empire, 43 B.C.–A.D. 69* (Cambridge, 1996), 57; D. Kienast, *Augustus. Princeps und Monarch*, second edition (Darmstadt, 1999), 7; K. Bringmann, *Augustus* (Darmstadt, 2007), 100; M. Reinhold, *From Republic to Principate. An Historical Commentary of Cassius Dio's Roman History Books 49–52 (36–29 B.C.)* (Atlanta, 1988), 104–5, with more scholarship.

is twofold: it will demonstrate that Kromayer's ideas are already found in earlier scholars from the long eighteenth century and, importantly, there is an alternative that has wrongly been ignored for a long time. The alternative is the betrayal of Antonius by Cleopatra.[5] In this article I will not go into great detail on the battle itself, but mainly concentrate on its historiography, although it will be suggested that Plutarch (especially *Ant.* 66, 68) is more credible than Cassius Dio. The battle of Actium was most likely decided by the Cleopatra's treachery and the subsequent flight of Antonius.

**Crevier and Actium: a Case Study**

Jean Baptiste Louis Crevier, a student of Rollin and for twenty years professor of rhetoric in the college of Beauvais, completed *The Roman History From the Foundation of Rome to the Battle of Actium*, the work of his former teacher. This section will look closely at Crevier's description of the battle of Actium, as an example of the alternative eighteenth-century view of the battle.[6] The main evidence used by Crevier on the battle of Actium is Plutarch (*Ant.* 61–68).

Crevier rightly stresses that this conflict was of such a magnitude that 'the whole Roman Empire was shaken by this war'.[7] He continues to give a detailed account of the troops and ships involved in the battle. He concludes: 'By the account which I have given of the forces of the two parties, it appears that both generals had grounds to hope for victory'.[8]

He carries on to give an account of the preliminaries of war and rightly suggests that at this point in time Antonius was already in distress, due to desertions and famine amongst his troops.[9] But importantly, in the judgement of Crevier Antonius could still hope to win. As a result of the problematic situation, Antonius summoned a grand council. Crevier explains:

---

[5] Cleopatra's betrayal has found some support in the twentieth century, but A. Domaszewski, *Geschichte der Römischen Kaiser* (Leipzig, 1909), 154–5; M. Beike, *Kriegsflotten und Seekriege der Antike* (Berlin, 1990), 145 seem to be exceptions.
[6] J.B.L. Crevier, *The Roman History From the Foundation of Rome to the Battle of Actium: That is, To the End of the Commonwealth (By Mr. Crevier, Professor of Rhetorick in the College of Beauvais, being the Continuation of Mr. Rollin's Work)*, vol. XVI, second edition (London, 1754).
[7] Crevier, *Roman History*, 35.
[8] Crevier, *Roman History*, 36.
[9] Crevier, *Roman History*, 42–5.

Dio assures us, that Cleopatra's advice was to march back all the troops into Egypt, leaving only garrisons in the most considerable posts and towns in the countries they were to quit. A shameful and foolish advice, which I cannot believe even Cleopatra herself durst propose to Antony. Mean while this historian adds, that the Roman general consented to it, and that the battle of Actium, which followed soon after, happened in spite of Antony, when he had an intention to retire, and not to fight.[10]

Crevier interprets the ancient evidence on the battle of Actium, the same material modern scholars look at today. He continues:

> This account, of which I do not find the least hint in any other author, appears to me very improbable, and I rather chuse to follow that of Plutarch, according to whom, the resolution of giving battle having been taken and confirmed, they only deliberated whether they ought to fight by land or sea.[11]

Crevier rightly stresses that Cassius Dio is the only source that mentions this alleged prearranged plan to flee Actium. As a result he concludes that the scenario mentioned by Plutarch is much more likely. Crevier suggests that Antonius had every reason to have confidence in his 'battle-hardened' legions, even when disease and famine are taken into account.[12] This is fascinating and suggests, even though Crevier does not spell it out, that an oddity at Actium is the missing battle on land. He also mentions the suggestions by Antonius' generals to send Cleopatra back and make for Macedonia.[13] It should be remembered though that this would hardly have been possible without Antonius losing his fleet. At the same time Crevier is right in stressing that the legions would most likely be lost if this prearranged plan would be carried out. This is deemed very unlikely by the eighteenth-century historian, as it does not fit his understanding of Antonius and interpretation of the ancient evidence. He sums up the situation as follows:

> …; and that it would be very strange if Antony, who had such great experience in land-fights, did not take the advantage of the force, number, and courage of his legions, but on the contrary put his whole confidence in his fleet.[14]

---

[10] Crevier, *Roman History*, 45.
[11] Crevier, *Roman History*, 45.
[12] Crevier, *Roman History*, 45.
[13] Crevier, *Roman History*, 45.
[14] Crevier, *Roman History*, 46.

Crevier has departed from the discussion of the prearranged plan; this is about the decision to fight at sea. He turns to his explanation of why Antonius decided to abandon the fight on land (at least at first). Instead he focuses on the sea battle:

> Such solid reasons as these would doubtless have made an impression upon Antony, if he had still been capable of judging for himself; but he saw nothing but by Cleopatra's eyes, not determined upon any thing but according to her directions.[15]

Crevier does not understand Antonius' decision to fight at sea (Plutarch *Ant.* 63). Antonius' plan was to try to win the battle of Actium, which most likely would involve a battle on land as well. He goes on to sum up the ship numbers and once again dwells on the question of why Antonius decided to fight a sea battle, quoting Plutarch (*Ant.* 64) and the centurion's plea, trying to reason with his general not to fight an un-Roman sea battle.[16]

Next Crevier describes the actual battle of Actium on 2nd September 31 B.C., where it was decided who should win supremacy over Rome.[17] Antonius offered battle, but this was refused by Octavian, who ordered his ships further away from shore, to give more room for manoeuvre. When fighting began Agrippa tried to sail around the ends of Antonius' line and in doing so created chaos in the opposing line of ships. Crevier stresses that at this point during battle no side had the clear advantage.[18] It was thus very much to the surprise of the ancient and modern writers/historians that Cleopatra's ships, at this exact point in time, hoist their sails and make off for Egypt.

According to Crevier, fear was the likely reason for Cleopatra's flight: 'without doubt fear had seized the princess'.[19] He concludes in wonder:

> There was nothing very surprising in that behaviour of Cleopatra; but Antony's conduct on this occasion is quite inconceivable. It is not possible, says Plutarch, to discover in it either the General, or the man of courage and conduct. He seemed even to have lost the power of following his own

---

[15] Crevier, *Roman History*, 46.
[16] See D. Feeney, *Caesar's Calendar: Ancient Time and the Beginnings of History* (Berkeley, 2007), 120–1 on the Roman idealisation of their land-based self-sufficient pre-expansion days. The Romans were in the own view not very interested in the sea.
[17] Crevier, *Roman History*, 48.
[18] Crevier, *Roman History*, 49–51.
[19] Crevier, *Roman History*, 51.

inclinations, and verified what is commonly said of lovers, *viz.* that their soul dwells entirely in the person whom they love.[20]

Cleopatra thus betrayed Antonius, but he, following her, betrayed his men and himself. The battle is lost and Crevier continues: 'The number of dead did not exceed five thousand; and the whole number of vessels which were taken amount to three hundred'.[21] Plutarch is thus given the final say, stressing that Octavian captured 300 ships in the battle of Actium (*Ant.* 61.1–2; 68.1) and that the number of dead enemies in the battle was no more than 5,000 dead (*Ant.* 68.2).

For modern scholars Crevier's lack of footnotes and secondary scholarship may seem strange at first, but this should not be confused with unprofessional behaviour or lack of methodology; Crevier and his contemporaries knew the ancient evidence. Knowledge of this evidence thus makes it easy to follow Crevier's line of enquiry. He, having interpreted the evidence on the battle of Actium, concludes that Plutarch is more likely than Cassius Dio, who is therefore rejected. There is nothing in the eighteenth-century practice, as exemplified here by Crevier, their use of evidence and the reading of sources, and the assumptions that underlies these practices, that are notably different from the methods of today. This is analytical historical research. It may thus be that we modern historians are too quick to dismiss certain sources, as this article will indeed suggest. Moreover one might ask if the professionalisation of history has prevented us from seeing the 'emotional' as a serious historical factor. The question is, of course, whether Crevier's view on the battle of Actium is typical for the eighteenth century.

## The Standard Eighteenth-Century View on the Battle of Actium

Rollin has Cleopatra suggest, following Plutarch (*Ant.* 63), that it would, if need be, be easier to escape by sea, which Antonius listens to, at the same time ignoring his officers. They advise him not to fight a sea battle and to send Cleopatra home to Egypt.[22] Rollin reaches his conclusion after a thorough investigation of the context of the period of the triumvirate. He continues:

> The contest was doubtful for some time, and seemed as much in favour of Antony as Caesar [i.e. Octavian], till the retreat of Cleopatra. That queen,

[20] Crevier, *Roman History*, 51.
[21] Crevier, *Roman History*, 52.
[22] Rollin, *Roman History*, 403–4.

frightened with the noise of the battle, in which every thing was terrible to a woman, took to flight when she was in no danger, and drew after her the whole Egyptian squadron … Antony, who saw her fly, forgetting even himself, till then, had had exceedingly well disputed. It, however, cost the victor extremely dear. For Antony's ships fought so well after his departure, that, though the battle began before noon, it was not over when night came on; So that Caesar's troops were obliged to pass it on board their ships.[23]

In England the ghost writer of Nathaniel Hooke, perhaps Dr Gilbert Stuart, a noted historian and reviewer, has similar views. Hooke died in 1763 and the fifth edition 1770 of his work *The Roman History. From the Building of Rome, to the Ruin of the Commonwealth. Illustrated with maps and other plates* is the first to comprise all four volumes, thus for the first time including volume IV with comments on Actium.[24] Just like Crevier Hooke/Stuart interprets closely the preliminaries before addressing the actual battle of Actium; again, this is analytical historical research.[25] Agrippa's raids, and the desertions are mentioned[26] and he then carries on describing the grand council:

> …, but Cleopatra biased him the other way, and obliged him, against his will, to hazard his empire and life in a sea-fight, and this only that, in case of a defeat, she might escape with greater ease. Dio pretends that she even advised him to march back to Egypt.[27]

Hooke/Stuart dismisses Cassius Dio as unlikely and instead prefers the account of Plutarch. In a footnote the differences between a defeat on land and on sea are explained: Octavian perhaps had better chances in a sea battle, but the same would have been was the case on land according to Hooke/Stuart. But in case of a defeat on land Antonius would have found it difficult to escape, whereas in a sea fight an escape

---

[23] Rollin, *Roman History*, 404.
[24] I would like to thank Dr Gareth Sampson for his helpful comments on Hooke. See also G. Sampson, I. Macgregor Morris and J. Moore, 'Nathaniel Hooke', in E.J. Jenkins (ed.), *Eighteenth-Century British Historians* (The Dictionary of Literary Biography vol. 336) (New York, 2007), 188–92. The publishers wanted to give the impression that the ghost writer used Hooke's notes, but there is no solid evidence to back this up.
[25] N. Hooke, *The Roman History. From the Building of Rome, to the Ruin of the Commonwealth. Illustrated with maps and other plates*, fifth edition (London, 1770), 430. He also stresses that the decision to fight at sea rested on the idea that it would be easier to escape should they fare badly in battle (1770, 426–31 on the period covered in this article).
[26] Hooke, *Roman History*, 427.
[27] Hooke, *Roman History*, 428.

was possible.[28] This may be wrong after all, but the historian is trying to make sense of the material in front of him (see below). Importantly, Antonius' 'limited' chances for victory do not make the historian accept the prearranged plan to flee. Again, the tale of the centurion's plea is mentioned (Plutarch *Ant.*64), followed by the actual fighting.[29] Hooke/Stuart concludes:

> ..., when Cleopatra, wearied with expectations and overcome with fear, unexpectedly tacked about, and fled towards Peleponnesus with her sixty sail: And, what is still more surprising, Antony himself, now regardless of his honour, fled precipitately after, and abandoned his men who generously exposed their lives for his interest. Having reached Cleopatra's galley, he went into it, and sat a long time in a melancholy posture, without desiring to se the Queen, though he had followed her, says Plutarch, without any apparent reason but the thoughts of her absence.[30]

Montesquieu expresses a similar view:

> The battle of Actium was fought, Cleopatra fled, and drew Antony after her. It evidently appeared by the circumstances of her future conduct, that she afterwards betrayed him; perhaps that incomprehensible spirit of coquetry so dominant in her sex, tempted her to practice all her arts to lay a third sovereign of the world at her feet.
>
> A woman, to whom Antony had sacrificed the whole world, betrayed him.[31]

Even Oliver Goldsmith, in a book for schools and colleges and with no original research or interpretation, agrees, showing that in the case of Actium the difference between the scholars and the popular historians was virtually non-existent:

> But all of a sudden, Cleopatra determined the fortune of the day. She was seen flying from the engagement, attended by sixty sail; struck, perhaps, with the terrors natural to her sex: but what increased the general amazement, was, to behold Antony himself following soon after, and leaving his fleet at the mercy of the conquerors.[32]

---

[28] Hooke, *Roman History*, 428 n. i.
[29] Hooke, *Roman History*, 429–31.
[30] Hooke, *Roman History*, 430.
[31] C.-L. de Secondat Baron de Montesquieu, *Reflexions On the Causes of The Rise and Fall of the Roman Empire* (London, 1759), 183.
[32] O. Goldsmith, *The Roman History from the Foundation of the City of Rome, to the Destruction of the Western Empire*, vol. II, sixth edition (London, 1789), 78f.

The comments on the gender of Cleopatra are typical of the period but should not make us dismiss the theory of betrayal in general.[33] All in all these views are very close to one found in Crevier and in fact the theory of Cleopatra's betrayal does seem to have been completely dominant until the end of the long eighteenth century (see below).[34] Whether 'proper' historians or epitomising historians, they all seem to agree on this particular issue. Even Romantic poets followed these themes developed by historians. This is an interesting feature, showing that the work of these historians were having a genuine impact in forming popular opinion about the battle, and that the poets were responding to the themes they raise; this is very much in tune with the thought of the time. Waller Rodwell Wright, the consul-general of the Ionian Islands during their period as a British protectorate during the early years of the nineteenth century, tells the story of love, the greatest of stories, in his *Horae Ionicae*.[35]

> But whither strays my thought? This classic shore
> Recalls the strain to themes of ancient lore.
> Behold you ruins, sacred to the brave
> That trumph'd on Ambracia's blood-strain'd wave!
> There spreads the op'ning bay in prospect wide,
> And Arta's gulph receives the rushing tide –
> Arta, whose waves beheld the fated hour
> That tore from Anthony the wreath of pow'r –
> Where Actium proudly rears her trophied head,

---

[33] Similar T. Blackwell, *Memoirs of the Court of Augustus. Continued, and Completed, from the Original Papers of the Late Thomas Blackwell, … by John Mills, Esq.*, vol. III (London, 1763), 176; Hooke, *Roman History*, 427–8.

[34] It is amongst others found in A. Adams, *Classical Biography: Exhibiting Alphabetically the Proper Names, with a short Account of the Several Deities, Heroes, and other Persons* (Edinburgh, 1800), 284; J. Adams, *The Flowers of Ancient History. Comprehending, on a New Plan, the most Remarkable and Interesting Events, as well as Characters, of Antiquity*, third edition (London, 1796), 245; J. Aikin, *General Biography; or Lives, Critical and Historical, of the most Eminent Persons of all Ages, Conditions, and Professions, Arranged according to Alphabetical Order. Chiefly Composed by John Aikin, M.D. and the late Rev. William Enfield, LL.D.*, vol. I (London, 1799), 315; L.-P. Anquetil, *A Summary of Universal History; in Nine Volumes. Exhibiting the Rise, Decline, and Revolutions of the different Nations of the World, from the Creation to the Present Time*, vol. III (London, 1800), 444; E. Edward Button, *Rudiments of Ancient History, Sacred and Prophane … By Way of Question and Answer. Designed for the use of Schools*, third edition (London, 1757), 359f; C.J.A. Hereford, *The History of Rome, from the Foundation of the City by Romulus, to the Death of Marcus Antonius. In Three Volumes. By the Author of The History of France …*, vol. II (London, 1792), 467, R. Millar, *The Whole Works of the Reverend Robert Millar … In Eight Volumes*, vol. IV (Paisley, 1789), 328f.

[35] W.R. Wright, *Horae Ionicae. A Poem, Descriptive of the Ionian Islands, and Part of the Adjacent Coast of Greece* (London, 1809), 27–8.

> Octavius triumph'd, and his rival fled.
> He who, unmov'd, the work of death had view'd,
> With eager haste his trembling love pursu'd;
> Resign'd the glorious prize for which he strove;
> For empire fought, and was subdu'd by love.
>
> Now, through the limits of the spacious plain
> That parts her waters from th' Ionian main,
> Nicopolis, majestic in decay,
> Records the triumphs of that fatal day.

Irwin Eyles in his elegy on the occasion of the victory of Admiral Nelson at the Nile writes similarly on this story of passion:[36]

> From Actium thus, the slave of passion fled,
> For Beauty's smile, his life and fame to wave,
> Thus, to his former glories, Pompey dead,
> In Egypt found a dagger and a grave![37]

Lord Byron, the famous English poet, also tells this extraordinary story of love and passion in *Stanzas Written in Passing the Ambracian Gulf*:

> Through cloudless skies, in silvery sheen,
> Full beams the moon on Actium's coast:
> And on these waves for Egypt's queen
> The ancient world was won and lost.
>
> And now upon the scene I look,
> The azure grave of many a Roman;
> Where stern Ambition once forsook
> His wavering crown to follow *Woman*.
>
> Florence! whom I will love as well
> As ever yet was said or sung,
> (Since Orpheus sang his spouse from Hell)
> Whilst thou art fair and I am young;
>
> Sweet Florence! those were pleasant times,
> When worlds were staked for ladies' eyes:
> Had bards as many realms as rhymes,
> Thy charms might raise new Antonies.

---

[36] This idea in fact has a long history. Dante places Cleopatra in the Second Circle of Hell (Canto 5.63) of *The Divine Comedy*, together with other lustful figures. She is thus placed 'higher' than the Seventh Circle, Second Circle, the place of figures who committed suicide. Her sin was that of lust.

[37] I. Eyles, *Nilus; an Elegy. Occasioned by the Victory of Admiral Nelson over the French Fleet on August 1, 1798* (London, 1798), 9.

> Though Fate forbids such things to be,
> Yet, by thine eyes and ringlets curl'd!
> I cannot lose a world for thee,
> But would not lose thee for a World.
> *(November* 14, 1809)[38]

It does not matter if Cleopatra's betrayal or Antonius' flight is stressed by the poets, as this is basically the same story, taken from Plutarch. Importantly, the prearranged plan is not mentioned as an option. Historians and poets alike conclude that Antonius fled the scene of battle, leaving his fleet and army behind, out of love for Cleopatra.[39] This is of course also the line famously taken by Shakespeare. Why has this been dismissed? It is because it is seen as too good a story, or perhaps because it is thought that feelings should not be part of the decisions of generals in war? Is it that unlikely that Antonius might have followed Cleopatra because he loved her, as indeed the ancient evidence suggests?

## Kromayer and the Nineteenth and Twentieth Centuries

As mentioned there has been a general consensus on the central issue on the battle of Actium since Kromayer, which rejects the account given in the ancient evidence, according to which Cleopatra decided to flee and Antonius, much to the surprise of the ancient evidence, to follow her. Instead the modern consensus is that the withdrawal was in accordance with a prearranged plan.[40]

Even though this theory in its modern form dates back to Kromayer, he was in fact articulating what had already been suggested, most notably in the account of the Battle of Actium by Colonel William Martin Leake, an English topographer, in his *Travels in Northern Greece*.[41] Even though today hardly any scholarship before Kromayer is taken into account, it seems wrong, certainly from a historiographical point of view, to leave out the likes of Leake, especially if the commemorations of Octavian after the battle are also considered. The fieldwork of Leake is surely unsurpassed. He 'discovered' Michalitsi when he visited the

---

[38] The text used is that of Lord Byron (edited by J.J. McGann), *Lord Byron, The Complete Poetic Works*, 7 vols. (Oxford, 1980–1993). See also *Don Juan* 4.25–32; *Childe Harold's Pilgrimage* 2.397–402.
[39] Plutarch *Ant.* 66; Velleius 2.85.3; Propertius 2.16.39.
[40] See Kromayer, *Hermes* 34, 33f.; Rice Holmes, *The Architect of the Roman Empire*, 253 on this issue.
[41] W.M. Leake, *Travels in Northern Greece*, vol. IV (London, 1835), 40.

area in 1805; or to be more precise, he was the first modern scholar who understood that Michalitsi had to be the site of Octavian's tent and thus the site of his Victory Monument. His evidence was Cassius Dio, whom he cites:

> The place where his own tent stood he surrounded with squared stones and adorned with captured beaks of ships, and built in it an edifice open to the sky, which he consecrated to Apollo.[42]

Similarly, in volume I of his *Travels in Northern Greece*, as part of his discourse on Nicopolis, Michalitsi is mentioned as the most likely site of Octavian's tent before the Battle of Actium.[43] The conclusion goes back to a thorough reading of ancient texts together with topographical knowledge and understanding. He did not find the Victory Monument and never claimed to have done so.[44] The monument was first discovered in 1913 by Alexander Philadelpheus, but Leake did indeed find the right place:

---

[42] Cassius Dio 51.1.3; Leake, *Travels in Northern Greece*, vol. IV, 40. See also W.M. Leake, *Travels in Northern Greece*, vol. I (London, 1835), especially 180, 193f. For a detailed discussion of Leake's methodology and as a topographer, see M. Wagstaff, 'Colonel Leake and the Historical Geography of Greece', this volume; V.M. Murray and P.M. Petsas, *Octavian's Campsite Memorial for the Actian War* (Philadelphia, 1989), 12–14; I. Macgregor Morris, 'Shrines of the Mighty. Rediscovering the Battlefields of the Persian Wars', in E. Bridges et al. (eds.), *Cultural Responses to the Persian Wars: Antiquity in the Third Millennium* (Oxford, 2007), 249–52; C.L. Witmore and T.V. Buttrey, 'William Martin Leake: a Contemporary of P.O. Brøndsted in Greece and in London', in B. Bundgaard Rasmussen et al. (eds.), *Peter Oluf Brøndsted (1780–1842). A Danish Classicist in his European Context. Acts of the Conference at The Royal Danish Academy of Sciences and Letters* (Copenhagen, 2008), esp. 15, 24. Leake also identified the ruins near Preveza as Nicopolis. In the back of volume I of his *Travels in Northern Greece* there is a map of Nicopolis by T.L. Donaldson. Another visitor to Nicopolis was the Dane Peter Oluf Brøndsted, a contemporary of Leake, who against his will, at least at first, was forced by Ali Pacha to conduct a one day excavation at Nicopolis in 1812. The excavations yielded two local coins, one from the time of Commodus and one from Caracalla. Brøndsted was given the Caracalla coin; Ali Pacha pocketed the other as the latest 'augmentation of his treasury'. See J. Isager, *Peter Oluf Brøndsted. Interviews with Ali Pacha of Joanina in the Autumn of 1812; with some Particulars of Epirus, and the Albanians of the Present Day* (Athens, 1999), 63–74, 74 on the excavations; J. Isager, 'Visitors to Nicopolis in the Reigns of Augustus and Ali Pacha', in K. Zachos (ed.), *Nicopolis B. Proceedings of the Second International Nicopolis Symposium (11–15 September 2002)*, 2 vols. (Preveza, 2007), 34–9.

[43] Leake, *Travels in Northern Greece*, vol. IV, 187 with map of the area.

[44] See Murray and Petsas, *Octavian's Campsite Memorial for the Actian War*, 14 n. 14.

Such a view as Dio here describes, Augustus could not have obtained from the isthmus of Nicopolis, or from any spot in the immediate vicinity, except Mikhalitzi, from whence all the objects stated may be seen.[45]

The theory of the prearranged plan can thus be traced back at least to the end of the long eighteenth century. The unacknowledged source of the theory it seems is the historian John Gillies in 1807, supported by Leake in 1835.[46] In the judgement of Gillies Antonius could not win the Battle of Actium. He writes: From these difficulties a battle only could extricate him.[47] He continues:

> His best officers exhorted him to avoid fighting by sea; but Cleopatra, on the contrary, recommended this measure. She was impatient, it seems, to return to Alexandria; and Antony knew no pleasure equal to that of compliance with her will. He determined to accompany Cleopatra by the readiest way into Egypt, and to fight the enemy if his passage was obstructed. In this design, his fleet was equipped either for a battle or a voyage ….[48]

The 'emotional' is certainly seen as a serious historical factor, but Gillies prefers Cassius Dio and the prearranged plan to flee to the account of Plutarch. He continues:

> In this manner the combat raged for two hours, when Cleopatra, who had viewed it from behind the line, darted through the midst of the combatants, and with crowded sail made all haste to escape from the bay into the open seas … Antony, also, followed her, and though his

---

[45] Leake, *Travels in Northern Greece*, vol. I, 193–4. On the Victory Monument, becoming more and more central to and understanding of the early ideology of the regime of Octavian, see Murray and Petsas, *Octavian's Campsite Memorial for the Actian War*. Since 1995 new excavations have been carried out by Zachos, with remarkable success. See K. Zachos, 'Excavations at the Actian Tropaeum at Nikopolis. A preliminary report', in J. Isager (ed.), *Foundation and Destruction. Nikopolis and Nortwestern Greece. The Archaeological Evidence for the City Destructions, the Foundation of Nikopolis and the Synoecism* (Aarhus, 2001), 29–39; K. Zachos, 'The *Tropaeum* of the Sea-Battle of Actium at Nikopolis: Interim Report', *Journal of Roman Archaeology*, 16 (2003), 65–92; Zachos, *Nicopolis B*.

[46] I would like to thank Dr Andrew Bayliss for bringing my attention to John Gillies' comments on Actium. See J. Gillies, *History of the World, From the Reign of Alexander to that of Augustus, Comprehending the Latter Ages of European Greece, and the History of the Greek Kingdoms in Asia and Africa, from their Foundation to their Destruction*, vol. III (Philadelphia, 1809), 466–8; Leake, *Travels in Northern Greece*, vol. IV, 36.

[47] Gillies, *History of the World*, 466.

[48] Gillies, *History of the World*, 466.

departure was known from both sides, the battle still continued with emulation ....[49]

Given the prevailing eighteenth-century view, this suggests a high level of debate on the subject of Actium in the long eighteenth century and in the nineteenth century. The prearranged plan theory was only accepted after Kromayer and is now deemed the most likely scenario. Thus the prevailing modern view of Actium actually originated in the long eighteenth century.

Kromayer, in a brilliant piece of persuasive scholarship, argues that the position of Antonius had become hopeless and therefore he decided to make a breakout. In what might be described as a typically thorough German academic style, Kromayer dismisses the standard eighteenth-century view on the battle and effectively ends the nineteenth-century discussion on the matter (see below). With Kromayer Cleopatra's betrayal became an unlikely and even unacceptable conclusion and the debate on the battle changed towards the consensus of today.[50] Even though this is a fascinating theory, it must be remembered that this is only a theory. Surely a very good reason is needed if ancient evidence is dismissed and a modern theory, disagreeing with most of the ancient evidence, is accepted instead. As already mentioned Gillies and Leake advocated this theory in the long eighteenth century and Kromayer's theory is in most details similar. Leake writes:

> By the advice of Cleopatra, it was resolved, that after having garrisoned strongly the most important places, she and Antony should return with remaining forces to Egypt: but that avoiding any appearance of a retreat, in order not to discourage their allies, the fleet in moving should advance as if intent on battle.[51]

Their focus is on the statement by Cassius Dio 50.15.1, stressing that Cleopatra was implementing this prearranged plan, rather than betraying Antonius. According to this theory Antonius had in reality lost the battle before it was ever fought, but the account of Cassius Dio is largely rhetorical, and must be contrasted to the much fuller narrative

---

[49] Gillies, *History of the World*, 467.
[50] For a case against Kromayer, supporting Cleopatra's betrayal, see C.H. Lange, *Res Publica Constituta: Actium, Apollo and the Accomplishment of the Triumviral Assignment*, Ph.D. thesis (University of Nottingham, 2008), chapter 4. A revised version of my thesis will be published by Brill in 2009.
[51] Leake, *Travels in Northern Greece*, vol. IV, 36.

of Plutarch, which includes much more factual detail.[52] Importantly, aside from Cassius Dio's narrative, arguing for a decision to withdraw at the council before battle, this prearranged plan is not mentioned in any other ancient evidence.

The twentieth-century alternative view to the prearranged plan is found in William W. Tarn, using Horace *Epode* 9, suggesting that Antonius wanted to fight, but treachery of the fleet forced him in the end to flee.[53] The poem cannot be taken to support the theory of Tarn that the fleet of Antonius deserted him; *Epode* 9 cannot be taken to resolve the matter and lines 19–20 can never be decoded for certain. Ronald Syme, building on Tarn's 1931 article, reaches the conclusion that there was little fighting and few casualties at Actium. He famously called the Battle of Actium a 'Shabby affair'.[54] The idea in fact goes at least back to George Rawlinson, Syme's predecessor as Camden Professor at Oxford:

> These repeated defections reduced the triumvir to a state of despondency, and led him most unhappily to accept Cleopatra's fatal counsels. Under pretence of giving battle to his adversary's fleet, Antony, on the morning of September 2, B.C. 31, put to sea with deliberate intention of deserting his land force and flying with Cleopatra to Egypt. Actium was not a battle in any proper sense of the term.[55]

---

[52] Kromayer, *Hermes* 34, 44 and 48; Leake, *Travels in Northern Greece*, vol. IV, 36. According to W.W. Tarn, 'The Battle of Actium', *Journal of Roman Studies*, 21 (1931), 182; W.W. Tarn, 'Actium: A Note', *Journal of Roman Sstudies*, 28 (1938), 168 Horace is a primary source, whereas Livy, Velleius, Florus, Plutarch, Cassius Dio and Orosius are secondary. He concludes that it is better to rely on Horace because of Cassius Dio's use of rhetoric (rightly criticising Kromayer and the prearranged plan). This seems to be a misconception of history, judging ancient evidence by modern historical standards and furthermore, all writers used rhetoric or literary techniques. See S.A. Oakley, *A Commentary of Livy Books VI–X*. vol. I: *Introduction and Book VI* (Oxford, 1997), 7–10. Tarn's idea is refuted by J. Kromayer, 'Actium. Ein Epilog', *Hermes* 68 (1933), 363–4, suggesting that Plutarch's source can be traced back to the battle and that Cassius Dio used Livy and the autobiography of Augustus. On Cassius Dio, see J.W. Rich, *Cassius Dio. The Augustan Settlement (Roman History 53–55.9)* (Warminster, 1990).

[53] Tarn, *Journal of Roman Studies*, 21, 173; W.W. Tarn, 'The Actium Campaign', in S.A. Cook et al. (eds.), *Cambridge Ancient History, 10: The Augustan Empire, 44 B.C.–A.D. 70* (Cambridge, 1934), 104–5; R. Syme, *The Roman Revolution* (Oxford, 1939 (1952)), 297. Ferrabino, *Rivista de Filologia e di Istruzione Classica*, 52 (1924), 470–1 was the first to use *Epode* 9 and argue that one of Antonius' generals refused to fight and returned to port. The treachery of Sosius decided the battle.

[54] Syme, *The Roman Revolution*, 297. See also Pelling, *The Triumviral Period*, 59, accepting Kromayer's take on the battle, but describing the battle of Actium as a 'lame affair'.

[55] G.A. Rawlinson, *Manual of Ancient History. From the Earliest Times to the Fall of the Sassanian Empire* (Oxford, 1880), 452.

Most scholars since Syme have accepted Kromayer's conclusions over Tarn's.[56] The one important issue where the two combatants Kromayer and Tarn agree, is that the old theory that the battle was lost because of Cleopatra's treachery can safely be dismissed, a point that has been accepted all too willingly by subsequent scholars.[57]

## The Situation Before the Battle

All the evidence suggests that Antonius did not choose Actium as the site for battle. At Rome it was claimed that Antonius and Cleopatra were planning to make war on the Roman state and to invade Italy and Rome.[58] However, in reality there is hardly much truth in that, even though they were surely planning for war. In the end Octavian did not wait until spring, as Antonius probably thought he would. Antonius set up his winter quarters at Patrae, leaving his fleet at Actium about 200 km away.[59] Octavian arrived at Actium first, taking Antonius completely by surprise, as Crevier stressed correctly.[60]

As part of the manoeuvres before battle Antonius made sure the sails were on board, something quite unusual in ancient times.[61] Ancient sea battles were fought close to land and thus sails would not be needed, and while this could be interpreted as showing an intention to flee, it seems more likely that this was a simple matter of Antonius keeping his options open

---

[56] See Murray and Petsas, *Octavian's Campsite Memorial for the Actian War,* 132, n. 6.
[57] See Kromayer, *Hermes* 34, esp. 1, 33f; Kromayer, *Hermes* 68, 377–80; Tarn, *Journal of Roman Studies,* 21, 173 and esp. 196; Murray and Petsas, *Octavian's Campsite Memorial for the Actian War,* 133 summing up the modern view that Cleopatra did not betray Antonius.
[58] Livy *Per.* 132; Velleius 2.82.4; Tacitus *Ann.* 3.18; Plutarch *Ant.* 56.1–2; 58.1–2; 60.2; 62; Pausanias 4.31; Cassius Dio 50.3.2; 50.9.2; 50.12–13; Florus 2.21.1–3. See Kromayer, *Hermes* 34, 9; V. Fadinger, *Die Begründung des Prinzipats. Quellenkritische und staatsrechtliche Untersuchungen zu Cassius Dio und der Parallelüberlieferung* (Berlin, 1969), 189–194; A.J. Woodman, *Velleius Paterculus. The Caesarian and Augustan Narrative (2.41–93)* (Cambridge, 1983), 212. Pelling, *The Triumviral Period,* 48 rightly stresses that the decision of Antonius to bring Cleopatra so close to Italy was a mistake from a political point of view.
[59] Cassius Dio 50.11–13. Kromayer, *Hermes* 34, 9.
[60] Crevier, *Roman History,* 39. See also E. Kraggerud, *Horaz und Actium: Studien zu den politischen Epoden* (Oslo, 1984), 70; Carter, *The Battle of Actium. The Rise and Triumph of Augustus Caesar,* 208 stresses that the plan of Octavian was to avoid battle until at full strength and then drive the enemy back and the fleet, deprived of land support would have to flee. But why make a surprise attack and then wait?
[61] Pluarch *Ant.* 64 and Cassius Dio 50.31.2. See Kromayer, *Hermes* 34, 35; Pelling, *The Triumviral Period,* 58.

in case the battle did not go according to plan.⁶² Crevier rightly stresses this as an assurance.⁶³ The riches of Antonius and Cleopatra were also on board (Cassius Dio 50.15.4) and Antonius even decided to burn part of his fleet.⁶⁴ According to Kromayer all these factors are enough for us to accept Cassius Dio 50.15.1 and the intention of Antonius and Cleopatra to flee.

Kromayer thus asks, as mentioned above, why Antonius accepted a sea battle; he answers that the blockade of Agrippa made his choices limited. Again, he draws the same conclusion reached by Leake.⁶⁵ According to Kromayer's theory the raids and capture of Greek cities by Agrippa meant Antonius was effectively blockaded: the fleet of Octavian was superior before Actium, with Agrippa capturing Methone, Patrae, Leucas and perhaps Corinth, which led to a blockade of the Ambracian Gulf and the fleet of Antonius. According to Kromayer the capture of Leucas effectively completed the blockade.⁶⁶ This also meant that Antonius' supply routes were cut off.⁶⁷ Prior to Kromayer, Crevier and Hooke/Stuart also advocated the idea that Antonius lost Leucas, Patrae and Corinth, both suggesting that Antonius' choices were limited.⁶⁸

The ancient accounts all point to desertion, disease and hunger amongst Antonius' troops.⁶⁹ Ultimately, the attack on Methone gave Octavian

---

⁶² Tarn, *Journal of Roman Studies*, 21, 189; Johnson, *Augustan Propaganda*, 49.
⁶³ Crevier, *Roman History*, 47. This equals the 'Plan B' of Tarn, *Journal of Roman Studies*, 21, 188.
⁶⁴ Cassius Dio 50.15.4; Plutarch *Ant.* 64.1. See C.B.R. Pelling, *Plutarch. Life of Antony* (Cambridge, 1988), 276. See also Horace *Odes* 1.37. See Tarn, *Journal of Roman Studies*, 21, 183–184 and Tarn, *The Actian Campaign*, 105, implying that Octavian burned the ships after the victory, not Antonius. Tarn, *Journal of Roman Studies*, 21, 192 he calls the idea that Antonius burned ships 'The silly perversion'. But this is contrary to all the evidence (Cassius Dio 50.15.4 and Plutarch *Ant.* 64.1). See also Richardson, *Journal of Roman Studies*, 27, 155–156; Pelling, *Plutarch. Life of Antony*, 276.
⁶⁵ Kromayer, *Hermes* 34, 9; Leake, *Travels in Northern Greece*, vol. IV, 34.
⁶⁶ Kromayer, *Hermes* 34, 9–28. See also Richardson, *Journal of Roman Studies*, 27, 159; Johnson, *Augustan Propaganda*, 48; Reinhold, *From Republic to Principate*, 103. On Corinth, see Cassius Dio 50.13.5, who puts the capture of Corinth before Actium, Plutarch *Ant.* 67.7 after. The best account on the build up to the battle is still Kromayer's article from 1899. According to Grant, *Cleopatra*, 205–207 losing Methone meant losing the war, as there would be a blockade of Actium. Against this theory of a blockade, see Lange, *Res Publica Constituta*, chapter 4.
⁶⁷ Velleius 2.84.1, Cassius Dio 50.13.5–6, 14.4; Florus 2.21.4. See Woodman, *Velleius Paterculus*, 221–222. See also Kromayer, *Hermes* 34, 19–20, 25–26; Reinhold, *From Republic to Principate*, 103. Oros. 6.19.6 on Agrippa's interception of supply ships.
⁶⁸ Crevier, *Roman History*, 38–42; Hooke, *Roman History*, 427.
⁶⁹ Orosius 6.19.5ff, Velleius 2.84.1, Cassius Dio 50.11–15, 50.27.8 and Plutarch *Ant.* 63, 68.4. On the desertions, see Woodman, *Velleius Paterculus*, 222 with a list. Rawlinson, *A Manual of Ancient History*, 452 observes that this decided the engagement.

the possibility to cross to Corcyra (Corfu) and then Actium.[70] But did this mean that Antonius did not have a chance of winning? And, more importantly, did he accept that this was the case? And why did he not use his land army? According to Crevier they were spectators, but surely they were there for a reason.[71] Theodor Mommsen, a leading ancient historian of the nineteenth century, is certainly right in stressing that it is most likely that Antonius' legions were present at Actium to be used in a land battle.[72] Of course some of them were fighting at sea, but they could easily have been deployed on land after an unsuccessful sea battle. Surely both generals had grounds to hope for victory.[73] Vitally, while the eighteenth-century scholars accepted that Antonius choices were limited, they were still surprised that a Roman general did not stand and fight.

## The Battle of Actium: Cassius Dio versus Plutarch

According to Cassius Dio the council before the battle saw Cleopatra suggest that they should flee and fight another day, as the battle was lost before it had been fought. This is, as mentioned, supported by the likes of Leake and Kromayer, but perhaps the most extreme example of supporting this idea is found in Josiah Osgood, who very recently concluded that in some ways Antonius had the better of the day, outwitting Octavian by escaping from Actium.[74] This is a very odd approach, as it does not take the consequences of Antonius' actions into account. The battle cannot be isolated from the war, which ended on 1 August 30 B.C. at Alexandria. By escaping Antonius only postponed what his flight made inevitable.

Furthermore, Cassius Dio contradicts himself at 50.33.1–2, apart from being isolated amongst the ancient evidence. Cassius Dio 50.33.1–2 is very close to the information in the rest of the ancient evidence, as it

---

[70] Richardson, *Journal of Roman Studies*, 27, 156 n. 15; J. Osgood, *Caesar's Legacy. Civil War and the Emergence of the Roman Empire* (Cambridge, 2006), 372.
[71] Crevier, *Roman History*, 48.
[72] T. Mommsen, *Römisches Kaisergeschichte. Nach den Vorlesungs-Mitschriften von Sebastian und Paul Hensel 1882/86, Herausgegeben von Alexander Demandt* (Munich, 1992), 85.
[73] Crevier, *Roman History*, 36.
[74] Osgood, *Caesar's Legacy*, 374. See also Kromayer, *Hermes* 34, 44 and 48; Leake, *Travels in Northern Greece*, vol. IV, 36; F. Cairns, 'Horace Epode 9: Some New Interpretations', *Illinois Classical Studies*, 8.1 (1983), 91, stressing that Antonius was not technically defeated. Pelling, *The Triumviral Period*, 59 stresses that 'Cleopatra arguably won it', because they achieved all they could have hoped, thus supporting Cassius Dio and Kromayer.

focuses on Antonius and his disbelief when he learned that Cleopatra was fleeing. According to Plutarch Cleopatra ran away at a time when the battle was yet to be decided; it is at this crucial point that Antonius chose Cleopatra above his men (Plutarch *Ant.* 66). There simply is no reliable method by which we can conclude that Cassius Dio 50.15.1 is the truth, i.e. what actually happened, whereas 50.33.1–2 is the 'propaganda' of Octavian, as some modern scholars do.[75] It may indeed be that both stories are the 'propaganda' of the regime.

The main problem when addressing the notion of Cleopatra's betrayal is, as mentioned, that both sides of the modern twentieth-century debate, Kromayer and Tarn, agreed this never happened.[76] The main evidence for Cleopatra's betrayal is a Late Latin translation of Josephus (Against Apion) *C. Apion.* 2.59, a Jewish historian from the first century A.D.:

> *Sed quid oportet amplius dici, cum illum ipsum in nauali certamine relinquens, id est maritum et parentem communium filiorum, tradere eum exercitum et principatum et se sequi coegit?*

> But what more need be said, when she, deserting even him – her husband and the father of their children – in the naval battle, compelled him to surrender his army and imperial title to follow her?[77]

*Relinquens* is perhaps better translated as 'leaving' not 'deserting', but there surely is no prearranged plan in Josephus. Similarly, Virgil (*Aen.* 8.704ff), the Augustan poet, mentions that Actian Apollo fires the first shot of the battle and as a result Cleopatra flees (*Aen.* 707–8):

> *ipsa videbatur ventis regina vocatis*
> *vela dare et laxos iam iamque immittere funis.*

> The queen herself was seen to woo the winds,
> spread sail, and now, even now, fling loose the slackened sheets.[78]

Velleius, an early first-century Roman historian, agrees and stresses that Cleopatra took the initiative in the flight and that Antonius chose her above his soldiers (2.85.3). In fact this is also found in Plutarch (*Ant.*

---

[75] See Reinhold, *From Republic to Principate*, 114.
[76] See especially Kromayer, *Hermes* 34; Tarn, *Journal of Roman Studies*, 21, 196; Grant, *Cleopatra*, 213; Murray and Petsas, *Octavian's Campsite Memorial for the Actian War*, 133 ignores the evidence, as there is agreement on this matter in the modern debate.
[77] Translation by H.St.J. Thackeray, *Josephus, The Life Against Apion* (Cambridge Mass. and London, 1926). Pelling, *Plutarch. Life of Antony*, 284 suggests that Cleopatra's betrayal is mentioned first by Josephus. This is hardly true.
[78] Translated by H.R. Fairclough, *Virgil Aeneid 7–12, The Minor Poems* (Cambridge Mass. and London, 1934).

66.3), Florus (2.21.8–9), a Roman historian writing during the reign of Hadrian and Cassius Dio (50.33.2). The sources except Cassius Dio are all in agreement: Cleopatra ran away and Antonius followed her.

As mentioned all the ancient evidence on the battle could be dismissed as propaganda of the regime, including Cassius Dio 50.15.1. But the only possibility we have is to work with historical probability and use the evidence at hand. All the evidence suggests that Cleopatra betrayed Antonius, with the exception of Cassius Dio, who contradicts himself. Nothing in the historical context dictates that Cleopatra's betrayal is unlikely or indeed impossible. One possible explanation may be the attitude towards Plutarch in the eighteenth century versus the attitude in nineteenth- and twentieth-century scholarship. In the eighteenth century his reputation was high, but already during the early nineteenth century we witness Plutarch's fall from grace. The problem with that theory is that Cassius Dio is normally not considered a good source either.

## Conclusion: Cleopatra's Betrayal

Even in the nineteenth century the idea of Cleopatra's betrayal was not dismissed by all scholars; Leopold von Ranke, a very influential German historian of the nineteenth century, suggests that Antonius was betrayed by Cleopatra and made after her when she fled:

> Als Cleopatra Gefahr sah, warf sie sich mit ihrem Geschwader in die Flucht, mitten durch die kämpfer. Antonius, schwächer als seine Leidenschaft, eilte ihr nach und liess seine flotte in der hand der Feinde.

> When Cleopatra saw danger, she fled together with her fleet throwing herself through the middle of the combatants. Antonius, weaker than his passions, hurried after her and left his fleet in the hand of the enemies.[79]

On the issue of the battle of Actium Ranke, one of the founding fathers of modern historical research in Germany of the nineteenth century, was a binding link between the eighteenth-century and the nineteenth-century approach to the battle. It seems that the critical method of the nineteenth century did not necessarily create a difference in approach to the battle of Actium.[80]

---

[79] L. von Ranke, *Weltgeschichte, 2.2: Die Römische Republik und Ihre Weltherrschaft* (Leipzig, 1882), 387–8. Translation by Carsten Hjort Lange.

[80] M. Gelzer, 'Caesar als Historiker', in D. Rasmussen (ed.) *Caesar* (Darmstadt, 1967), 438f. sums up a standard nineteenth- and twentieth-century definition of a historian, as a person with a university decree in history, but at the same time he rightly concludes that the critical method, although it goes back to Niebuhr and Ranke, at least in Germany, was also found during the Renaissance and especially during the Enlightenment.

Mommsen rightly observes that the sources are not positive towards Cleopatra. The prearranged plan is mentioned and then dismissed. He neither believes in treachery nor 'petulant' treachery; Cleopatra fled because she thought it best for her and her fleet. He suggests that she wanted to win the naval battle, something the Ptolemies traditionally mastered. In the end it was understandable for Cleopatra to flee, thus saving her fleet, when things went wrong, but completely incomprehensible that Antonius followed her.[81] Mommsen's description of the battle, using mainly Plutarch's conclusion (*Ant.* 66, 68), is closer to Crevier's eighteenth-century views than Kromayer's theory.

Furthermore, it needs to be remembered that Cleopatra was ruler of Egypt, not just the lover of Antonius; this is Mommsen's vital contribution to this discussion. According to Mommsen Cleopatra did not betray Antonius, but she did flee the battle without telling him first. Perhaps she did not flee out of fear after all, but because she tried to save what was hers, at least for the time being. She was after all only a client ruler. Importantly, even Leake, accepting Cassius Dio and the prearranged plan, suggests that Antonius' men were surprised and dismayed 'On beholding this shameful flight of their commander'.[82] To accept the prearranged plan does not necessarily mean to dismiss the idea of betrayal altogether; in this case Antonius' betrayal of his men.

Why should historical probability dictate that Antonius thought it unlikely to win? Most likely he thought he could win, but being the good general he was, he had a 'Plan B'. William Ledyard Rodgers, a Vice Admiral in the US Navy during the early twentieth century believes that Antonius did not merely try to escape, but instead: 'Like every good commander, Antony was ready for the worst while hoping for the best'.[83]

This certainly fits a Roman general better. However, Rodgers also suggests that Antonius' plan was to escape with as many soldiers as possible, if he did not win.[84] The problem is that he did not do so, but simply left his fleet and army behind. It seems that Cleopatra and Antonius left the battle before it was decided, as stressed by Plutarch, the most thorough source on the battle, and thus the answer may lie somewhere else. It

---

[81] Mommsen, *Römisches Kaisergeschichte*, 85–6. Similarly, V.E. Gardthausen, *Augustus und seine Zeit* (Leipzig, 1891/1896), 377–83, who accepts Cleopatra's betrayal.

[82] Leake, *Travels in Northern Greece*, 38.

[83] W.L. Rodgers, *Greek and Roman Naval Warfare. A Study of Strategy, Tactics, and Ship Design from Salamis (480 B.C.) to Actium (31 B.C.)* (Annapolis, 1937), 535.

[84] Rodgers, *Greek and Roman Naval Warfare*, 535. Similarly, Grant, *Cleopatra*, 211, suggesting that that was the plan, but in the end they were not able to achieve this. This is in principle possible, but not what the sources suggest.

is hardly an unlikely scenario that during battle, before it was decided, Cleopatra lost her nerve and fled to Egypt, or alternatively, decided that the battle was lost and fled. She did save her fleet, at least for the time being, but this meant the battle of Actium was lost and Antonius was closer to losing the war altogether.

In conclusion, the debate on the battle of Actium raged all through the nineteenth century, with both sides (the prearranged plan and Cleopatra's betrayal) represented. If we consider the long eighteenth century, Gillies and Leake supported the prearranged plan of Cassius Dio, which seems to have been deemed unlikely by scholars writing before Gillies. This changed with Kromayer and the later modern consensus.

Since Kromayer the theory of Cleopatra's betrayal has been deemed unacceptable, but it is time to take a critical stance towards the theory of the prearranged plan. It is time to dismiss Cassius Dio and accept the prevailing picture presented in the ancient evidence. It is time to re-evaluate the battle of Actium and take into account the standard perception of the battle held in the eighteenth century, which rightly prefers Plutarch over Cassius Dio. Cleopatra wanted to fight at sea, which Antonius accepted. The battle itself was most likely decided because Cleopatra lost her nerve and fled, leaving Antonius behind to decide what to do. This equals Cleopatra's betrayal, even though she might have thought it best for Egypt to save her fleet. Looking at the ancient evidence, first and foremost Plutarch, this seems much more likely than the prearranged plan of Cassius Dio. Importantly, Cleopatra's betrayal caused Antonius to betray his fleet and army at Actium, thus in reality losing him the war against Octavian. It would thus seem that for Antonius at least nothing went according to plan at Actium.

We can choose to stress the differences between the eighteenth-century and modern historical writing, but we should not dismiss secondary material on the grounds that it is it is old. A careful reading of the likes of Crevier clearly demonstrates that the methodology and knowledge of ancient evidence has not changed significantly over time, although the ways historical scholarship is presented have. It is not difficult to follow Crevier's line of enquiry, as he is very close to Plutarch's description of the battle. Having interpreted the ancient evidence before him, Crevier concludes that Plutarch is more likely than Cassius Dio; that it is most likely that Cleopatra fled the scene of battle, leaving Antonius behind. This was not according to a prearranged plan; this was betrayal of Antonius by Cleopatra. He then, out of love for her, betrayed his men, following Cleopatra and leaving them behind. The ancient evidence should not easily be dismissed and neither should the 'emotional' as a serious historical factor.

## 6. History as Theoretical Reconstruction? Baron D'Hancarville and the Exploration of Ancient Mythology in the Eighteenth Century

*James Moore*

The challenge of the enlightenment to traditional structures of religious belief is widely regarded as one of the most important aspects of modern European history.[1] However, the role of eighteenth-century historians in changing scholarly understandings of the *origins* of religious belief has not been widely recognised. Historians who revealed the complexity of pre-Christian religious belief suggested new chronologies for human history and possible new sources for modern civilisation. New comparative methods of historical study revealed some apparent fundamental similarities between ancient societies in key aspects of belief and worship and the appearance of similar images and systems in different societies. This raised intriguing opportunities for the historian. Firstly, it emphasised the importance of comparative method, to trace both the diffusion of belief systems and also to understand why certain societies developed at different rates.[2] Secondly, this new methodology raised intriguing questions about the relationship between history and the natural sciences. The suggestion that all belief systems had fundamentally common features implied that there were common processes at work which a more scientific method of historical analysis may reveal and explain. If history was to understand these processes it would have to engage with broader debates about environment, perception, psychology and human understanding. Thus philosophical issues and controversies popularised by David Hume in

---

[1] For general background on the religious debates of the enlightenment, see M. Hutton and D. Porter (eds.), *Atheism from the Reformation to the Enlightenment* (Oxford, 1992), J. Byrne, *Glory, Jest and Riddle: Religious Thought in the Enlightenment* (London, 1996), B. Young, *Religion and Enlightenment in Eighteenth-Century England: Theological Debate from Locke to Burke* (Oxford, 1998).
[2] For recent discussions of the relationship between comparative method and theory, see R. Segal, *Theorizing about Myth* (Amhurst, 1999).

the mid-eighteenth century were to have a significant impact on the nature of historical enquiry in the field of ancient religion.[3]

Late twentieth-century historiographical trends have seen a re-emergence of debates about the comparative study of myth and cultural diffusion of ancient religion and civilisation. Bernal's *Black Athena* has become both famous and controversial, exploring the alleged 'blindness' of Western scholarship to African influences on European belief systems and cultural practice.[4] The work has helped to stimulate a considerable literature on the methodologies of ancient religion which has again highlighted the importance of cross-cultural comparative research in understanding religious activity.[5] Yet this is nothing new; the first debates about the origin of classical deities in Africa and Asia took place three centuries ago when enlightenment *philosophes* first came into contact with Indian and Oriental belief systems, and sought to make sense of these heathen systems in the context of existing classical scholarship. The responses to the discovery of these religions were complex. Bernal accused eighteenth- and nineteenth-century scholars of fabricating a history which emphasised the Aryan origin of Greek gods and neglecting the influence of 'Black' Egypt. Yet it is important to see that this is not only questionable but also that it is only one aspect of eighteenth-century enlightenment debate about the nature of ancient belief. Throughout this period, many scholars concerned themselves not with the diffusion of specific classical deities, but instead tried to develop theories about why geographically separate prehistoric societies adopted apparently similar religious worship and similar primordial gods. This was part of an attempt not only to provide a universal explanation for mythological systems but also to provide a framework through which all religions could be interpreted. In many respects this debate lies at the heart of the enlightenment project. While some saw all 'heathen' religions as a debased form of Christianity, others

---

[3] D. Hume, *Philosophical Essays Concerning Human Understanding* (London, 1748), *The Natural History of Religion* (London, 1757). Hume was, of course, also a celebrated historian and one strongly influenced by his classical and historical education see: T.M. Olshewsky, 'The Classical Roots of Hume's Skepticism', *Journal of the History of Ideas*, 52 (1991), 269–87. For his religious views, see E. Mossner, 'The Religion of David Hume', *Journal of the History of Ideas*, 39 (1978), 653–63.

[4] M. Bernal, *Black Athena: the Afroasiatic roots of Classical Civilization*, 2 vols. (London, 1987–1991) and M. Bernal, *Black Athena Writes Back* (London, 2001). Also see M. R. Lefkowitz and G.M. Rogers, *Black Athena Revisited* (London, 1996).

[5] See, for example, W. Burkert, *The Orientalizing Revolution* (Cambridge, Mass., 1992), D. Frankfurter, *Religion in Roman Egypt: Assimilation and Resistance* (Princeton, 1998), W. Doniger, *Splitting the Difference: Gender and Myth in Ancient Greece and India* (London, 1999), R. Buxton (ed.), *Greek Religion* (Oxford, 2000).

began to view all belief systems as naturalistic polytheistic phenomena, produced by forces of the environment.⁶ Thus mythology became an important battleground of the anticlerical *philosophes* such as Diderot, who sought to use the emerging methods of comparative religion to undermine the central tenets of Christian teaching.⁷

This article focuses on the historical work of the most ambitious, controversial, yet strangely neglected eighteenth-century historical mythologist, Pierre François Hugues, better known by his self-styled moniker Baron D'Hancarville. D'Hancarville's comparative method and revolutionary theories on the centrality of fertility cults to all mythological systems anticipated James Frazer's *Golden Bough* by more than a century. His attempts to decode the symbolism inherent in ancient art demonstrated how object-centred research could provide new insights into ancient history and go beyond the confines of the philological schools. In short, D'Hancarville aspired to rival Winckelmann by providing a prehistory of art and civilisation, exploring the fundamental origins on which Winckelmann's theories were grounded. Although D'Hancarville never attained the lasting reputation of Winckelmann this should not blind us to his importance in the eighteenth-century study of the ancient world. His work on William Hamilton's collection of Greek vases and Charles Townley's sculpture gallery helped stimulate broader interest in the material culture of the ancient world. Indeed one might say it fundamentally shaped modern tastes for vase and ceramic decoration.⁸ Moreover when the Hamilton and Townley collections became part of the British Museum, D'Hancarville's work provided the basis of British Museum scholarship on classical antiquities for more than half a century. His thesis on the centrality of fertility cults within mythology was republished by one of his patrons, Richard Payne Knight, and was still in print at the end of the nineteenth century.

Yet D'Hancarville has received short shrift from modern scholars. Francis Haskell viewed him almost as a figure of the counter-enlightenment, combining a Romantic attachment to the exotic and a love of the irrational with fanciful and unproven theories.⁹ Two of D'Hancarville's

---

⁶ F. Manuel, *The Changing of the Gods* (Hanover and London, 1983).
⁷ See N. Aston, *Religion and Revolution in France* (Basingstoke, 2000), J. Bradley (ed.), *Religion and Politics in Enlightenment Europe* (Notre Dame Ind., 2001), J. Barker, *Diderot's Treatment of the Christian Religion in the 'Encyclopédie'* (New York, 1941), A. Wilson, *Diderot,* 2 vols. (New York, 1972).
⁸ M. Vickers, 'Value and Simplicity: Eighteenth-Century Taste and the Study of Greek Vases', *Past and Present*, 116 (August, 1987), 98–137.
⁹ F. Haskell, 'The Baron D'Hancarville; An Adventurer and Art Historian in Eighteenth-Century Europe', in F. Haskell (ed), *Past and Present in Art and Taste* (Yale, 1987), 31–45.

four volumes on the Hamilton collection are dismissed as unreliable, credulous, pedantic and badly written although Haskell makes no real attempt to place the work in the context of other eighteenth-century writing on mythology.[10] G.S. Rousseau, in his study of Richard Payne Knight, tends to view D'Hancarville's ideas primarily as part of an assault on organised religion, influenced by homosocial, even homoerotic, interest in the creative force of the phallus.[11] Although the case is powerfully put, some of his assertions about the sexual predilections of the Townley circle are based on remarkably scanty evidence. There is no real evidence of homoerotic desire either for D'Hancarville, or his patrons Charles Townley and Richard Payne Knight. Indeed for a man who, according to Rousseau, 'had never been interested in women', Charles Townley spent a remarkable amount of time visiting London brothels and composing erotic poems to members of the fair sex.[12] Perhaps D'Hancarville's reputation suffered more because of his associations with Payne Knight. Famously 'wrong' about the Elgin marbles, Knight is often depicted as an aloof, erratic figure, isolated from the main intellectual currents of the period. The title of his principal modern biography *Arrogant Connoisseur* sums up current attitudes to this controversial figure – and this from a group of writers who were relatively sympathetic to Payne Knight's importance in the history of taste and scholarship.[13] As D'Hancarville never published his main works in English, Payne Knight was responsible for disseminating his ideas in the British scholarly community. As this article will show, the methods that Payne Knight used to present D'Hancarville's ideas on the worship of creative forces focused heavily on priapic cults – and his choice of graphic illustrations depicting wax representations male genitalia may have been designed to shock as much as to persuade.[14]

It would, however, be unfair to blame D'Hancarville's patrons entirely for his diminished literary reputation. His method of scholarship and personal behaviour did not fit well with the moral standards of later

[10] Haskell, *Past and Present*, 39.
[11] G.S. Rousseau, 'The Sorrows of the Priapus: Anticlericalism, Homosocial Desire, and Richard Payne Knight', in G.S. Rousseau and R. Porter, *Sexual Underworlds of the Enlightenment* (Manchester, 1987), 101–53.
[12] Rousseau, 'Sorrows,' 114. G. Vaughan, 'The Collecting of Classical Antiquities in England in the 18th Century: a Study of Charles Townley (1737–1805) and His Circle', University of Oxford D.Phil. thesis (1988), 176.
[13] M. Clarke and N. Penny, *The Arrogant Connoisseur: Richard Payne Knight 1751–1824* (Manchester, 1982).
[14] P. Funnell, 'The Symbolic Language of Antiquity', in Clark and Penny, *Arrogant Connoisseur*, 50–63, esp. 51–5.

generations, and especially those of the Victorian period. His baronetcy was phoney, Winckelmann viewed him as a thief, he spent various periods of his life in gaol having run up extravagant debts and in his spare time published explicit pornography depicting men enjoying the intimate company of goats. What is remarkable is that despite this eminent British collectors and scholars of the eighteenth century, such as William Hamilton and Charles Townley, were prepared to overlook his indiscretions and continue to finance his scholarly work – something which says much about his acknowledged brilliance as well as his personal charm. During his time working on the Hamilton collection, D'Hancarville was first expelled from Naples, possibly because of his role in pornographic publications, before ending up in a Florentine gaol. Yet Hamilton stood by D'Hancarville, implying that D'Hancarville was simply being persecuted for outshining the *Accademia Ercolanese* in his knowledge of the ancient world.[15] Similarly Townley supported D'Hancarville's studies in London. In his correspondence, Townley reported that D'Hancarville had been 'filling his belly frequently at my house with an occasional loan of 5 guineas'.[16] Yet it seems that his overall level of support was much greater than this. In all Haskell estimates that Townley was supporting D'Hancarville to the tune of £180 per annum and such was the burden on Townley that he had to solicit the support of his friend Richard Payne Knight to help support D'Hancarville's work.[17] Yet their faith in the baron seemed unshakeable.

## Research into Ancient Religion: The Intellectual Background

D'Hancarville's work reflected two contemporaneous movements in eighteenth-century intellectual history. Firstly, there was a new awareness of the importance of material culture to study the past. Secondly, growing interest in the religion of non-Western peoples, stimulated by travel and exploration, began to offer new insights into the origin of religious belief. Scholars increasingly turned their attention to the ways in which physical non-literary remains of antiquity could both corroborate literary accounts and provide a history of periods where known literary accounts were silent. Momigliano, in his well-known *Studies in Historiography,* saw this movement primarily in terms as a response to increasing scepticism

---

[15] I. Jenkins and K. Sloan (eds.), *Vases and Volcanoes Sir William Hamilton and his Collection* (London, 1996).
[16] Cited in Haskell, *Past and Present*, 41.
[17] Haskell, *Past and Present*, 41.

about the reliability, or even authenticity, of ancient literary sources.[18] Some mid eighteenth-century writers took literary scepticism to the extreme, giving absurd primacy to non-literary remains. Père Hardouin, finding contradictions between numismatic sources and ancient sources, concluded that all the ancient texts, with the exception of Cicero, Pliny, Horace and Virgil, were late fourteenth-century Italian forgeries.[19] Yet in most cases non-literary remains were used to supplement, clarify and elucidate ancient texts. Interest in and study of ancient material remains was, of course, not new. The collecting of antiques had a long history and seventeenth-century regal patronage of the antiques market helped stimulate serious scholarly interest in such objects.[20] Moreover the discovery of the Capitoline marbles not only heralded the beginnings of modern archaeology, but also demonstrated how excavation and antiquarian study could provide a substantial amount of additional information about ancient civilisations that went far beyond the writings of ancient historians such as Livy. Such was the importance attached to the Consul lists contained on the marbles that for the next two centuries histories of Rome often reproduced this new discovery *verbatim*. Pighuis' sixteenth-century *Fasti* and Catrou's *Histoire Romaine* of 1725 both published the names in their entirety, and the lists first found their way into an original English-language Roman history through the agency of Nathaniel Hooke little over a decade later.[21] Archaeological discoveries such as these assisted the development of modern historical scholarship by illustrating the need for new interpretations and studies which went beyond the ancient authorities.[22] Many scholars still saw material public documents, such as inscriptions and memorials, as a much more reliable source that the ancient texts. Jacques Spon made his belief in the superiority of archaeological sources clear in his 1679 *Réponse à la critique publiée par M. Guillet*, while eighteen years later Francesco Bianchini took the chroniclers to task for citing only literary evidence, arguing that archaeological evidence provided both 'symbol and proof of what happened'.[23] These new histories did not always depend on high profile

---

[18] A. Momigliano, 'Ancient History and the Antiquarian', in *Studies in Historiography* (London, 1966), first published in the *Journal of the Warburg and Courtauld Institutes*, 13 (1950), 285–315.

[19] Momigliano, *Studies*, 16.

[20] F. Haskell and N. Penny, *Taste and the Antique* (Yale, 1981).

[21] Pighius, *Fasti* (n.d. but 1570s?); F. Catrou and P. Rouillé, *Histoire Romaine* (Paris, 1725–37); N. Hooke, *The Roman History* (London, 1738–71).

[22] Momigliano, *Studies*, 9.

[23] Cited in Momiglaino, *Studies*, 14–15.

archaeological discoveries such as the Capitoline marbles. Ordinary everyday objects were increasingly seen as important. Coins were often a key resource, with numismatics playing a central part in both Bianchini's ecclesiastic histories and Valliant's history of the Ptolemies and Seleucids.[24] These sorts of objects were, of course, to provide important sources for D'Hancarville's research, and his tendency to give such objects primacy over literary accounts simply reflected prevailing eighteenth-century attitudes of sceptical empiricism.

The growing obsession with ancient civilisations, stimulated partly by archaeological discovery, raised some difficult questions about the nature of human origins and belief systems.[25] It coincided with Western discovery of Asian religions, especially Hinduism, and the faith systems of the indigenous people of the Americas.[26] Coming at a time of philosophical scepticism towards religion, the effect was to spawn a whole range of controversial enquiries into the nature of ancient religion and its relationship with other recently rediscovered 'primitive' peoples. Many were quick to spot the apparent relationships and similarities between geographically distant belief systems. In most cases doctrinaire Christians were keen to subsume all forms of ancient belief within a framework of universal Christianity – in this view a primitive form of Christianity was seen as the essence of all religions in all places. Christian scholars trawled ancient religions to rediscover a Christian element. Thus Ralph Cudworth's modestly titled *True Intellectual System of the Universe* argued that ancient Egyptians, despite their obvious polytheistic belief system actually acknowledged one supreme god – and similar conclusions were drawn with other ancient civilisations.[27] Even as late as the 1780s some progressive thinkers, such as Septchenes of the French royal court, still attempted to identify a single supreme god, akin to the Christian god, in polytheistic classical religion.[28] However, by the second decade of the eighteenth century this approach was facing a formidable challenge from those who sought to find a totalising explanation of world-wide

[24] Momigliano, *Studies*, 8.
[25] For example, see S. Marchand, *Down From Olympus: Archaeology and Philhellenism in Germany 1750–1970* (Princeton, 1996).
[26] Anon, *The Agreement of the Customs of the East Indians with Those of the Jews and Other Antient People* (1705), Alexander Hamilton, *A New Account of the East-Indies* (1727), La Croze, *Histoire du Christianisme des Indes* (1758), J. Richardson, *A Dissertation on the Languages, Literature and Manners, of Eastern Nations* (1778).
[27] Manuel, *Changing*.
[28] Le Clerc de Septchenes, *The Religion of the Ancient Greeks Illustrated by an Explanation of Their Mythology* (London, 1787), 21–2.

religious practices without necessarily subordinating their conclusions to existing Christian doctrines. Andrew Ramsay, in his fictional historical romance *The Travel of Cyrus*, argued that all the mythologies of China, Egypt, Greece, Israel and Persia exhibited common features, despite their apparently dissimilar gods and practices of worship. All myths had a fundamentally similar structure, each relating a time of perfection, a period of collapse, a prospect of restoration and a specific deity presiding over human fortunes.[29] Interestingly by this time, because of the growth of general religious scepticism, many were more concerned to try to use comparative study to demonstrate that by nature man was a religious animal, rather than focus on specifically Christian interpretations. Some focused on religion as a universal natural phenomenon, while others tried to find naturalistic explanations of 'heathen' religion. Thus while John Toland's *Letters to Serena* (1704) emphasised the naturalism and 'innate reasonableness' of religious belief, John Trenchard's *The Natural History of Superstition* (1709) focused on the psychology of fear in primitive society and how hallucinations could produce the irrational belief and pagan gods.[30] Trenchard's views on the role of fear in creating myth were widely shared in the mid-eighteenth century and were an important influence on early philological attempts to decode myth. The work of C.G. Heyne seemed to show how primal fears and subsequent psychological reactions, generated mythologies around naturally occurring forces, which then became represented in the forms of symbols, such as rivers, beasts and mountains.[31] Although not the first to discuss the emergence of ancient religious symbols, his attempts to locate this symbolism in the context of a historically grounded theory of natural religion clearly anticipates the approach D'Hancarville adopted little over a decade later.[32]

Although Heyne represented an important precursor of the German philological school, much of the most radical and controversial work on the origin of myth was being produced by Frenchmen. Given D'Hancarville's background and scholarly connections it seems likely that the radical scholarship of de Brosses, Diderot and Holbach was most influential in the general trajectory of his work. De Brosses' *Du culte des diex fétiches* (1760) attempted to demonstrate, using examples from modern west Africa and ancient Egypt, that object worship was

---

[29] A. Ramsay, *The Travels of Cyrus* (London, 1728).
[30] Manuel, *Changing*, 30–3.
[31] B. Feldman and R. Richardson, *The Rise of Modern Mythology* (London, 1972), 216–17.
[32] Heyne's *Quaestio de causis fabularum seu mythorum veterum physicis* appeared in 1764.

the first and universal stage of religious development after the flood.³³ Although his dependence on Christian chronology is not an approach that D'Hancarville shared, de Brosses highlighted the centrality of fetish worship in early religion and the importance of explaining the symbolism associated with it. De Brosses himself rejected allegorical interpretations of object worship, arguing that such interpretations were inconsistent with worship of ugly or obnoxious creatures.³⁴ However his account of how the anthropomorphic Greek took shape out of ancient divine rocks has parallels in the work of D'Hancarville on the emergence of ancient religious art and symbol. De Brosses' explanation of how the names of Greek gods came to be applied to rocks and objects may be unsatisfactory, but it opened the intriguing possibility that Greek religion could in fact be the blend of several elements – one from the north and another introduced from Asia. In short, de Brosses highlighted the direct relevance of Asian sources for the study of the origin of Greek religion almost a generation before Sir William Jones published his comparative works on gods of Greece, Italy and India in *Asiatick Researches*.³⁵

Holbach shared de Brosses' interest both in the possibilities of comparative mythology and in the importance of the decoding of the symbols of that mythology. Famous for his onslaughts on established religions, Holbach also sought to explain the basic uniformity of religious origins through naturalistic phenomena, arguing that certain elements of nature represented the first deities. The worship of these deities was distorted by civilising processes, poetry and storytelling, into a mythology that eventually became of complex mesh of allegories and symbols.³⁶ However, as these allegories and symbols came from essentially common natural phenomena, one might expect them to manifest similar features and meaning.

Alongside this interest in the comparative symbolism of religion came a closer examination of the naturalistic elements that were supposedly the origins of worship. Since the 1720s scholars had been aware of the sexual element within ancient mythology. Lafitau's work on the Canadian Indians, aptly described by Felman and Richardson as 'a sort of eighteenth-century *Golden Bough*', provided a voluminous text on primitive and

---

³³ Feldman and Richardson, *The Rise*, 168–70; C. De Brosses, *Du culte des diex fétiches* (Paris, 1760).
³⁴ F. Manuel, *The Eighteenth Century Confronts the Gods* (Harvard, 1959), 194–5.
³⁵ W. Jones, 'On the Gods of Greece, Italy and India', in *Asiatick Researches*, 1801.
³⁶ Feldman and Richardson, *The Rise*, 177–9.

procreative rites, together with a comparison with ancient practices.[37] De la Croze's work on the history of Christianity in India highlighted sexual elements in Indian worship while Jablonksi's *Pantheon Aegyptiorum* (1750–2) related the orgies and sodomitical religious practices associated with the Nile.[38] Of course the sexual symbolism evident in ancient art went far beyond somewhat dry discussions of human origins towards ongoing debates about the nature of beauty and artistic achievement. In recent years some have read in Winckelmann's works an obsession with sexualised beauty in young men.[39] In many respects this is, however, nothing new. Diderot's *Essai sur la peinture* (1765) argued that the worship of sensual beauty was a key part of Greek cultish practice and that Greek tribute to beauty combined a mixture of the sacred and the profane. Yet it is important to emphasise that interest in the sexual character of myth was not limited to radical and anticlerical opinion. Le Batteux, a French abbé and member of the *Academie des Inscriptions*, saw all religion as a conflict between active and passive forces, reducing the sexual symbolism of myth into this single principle.[40] Universal creative and reproductive forces were thus symbolised through to the active male and passive female. Thus, by the time D'Hancarville was composing his catalogues for the Hamilton collection, many scholars, especially those in France, saw sexual interpretations of imagery and sexual allegories as essential to understanding ancient and primitive societies.

Strangely there is little evidence of this type of work in Britain or from British scholars. Hume was clearly an important influence in the theories of perception and psychology inherent in explaining naturalistic mythic belief, while Wood's scholarship on Homer emphasised the relation between myth creation and Greek appreciation of landscape and natural forces.[41] Yet until D'Hancarville, few British-based scholars appear to have engaged in detail with sexualised interpretations of mythological subjects. Indeed, one might say that D'Hancarville's work was something of a reaction against the conservatism inherent in British mythological circles. This conservatism is typified by Bryant's highly influential *A New System, or Analysis of Ancient Mythology* first published in 1774. Although this work did not come into circulation before D'Hancarville's first

---

[37] Feldman and Richardson, *The Rise*, 42; P.J. Lafitau, *Moeurs des Sauvages Amériquains comparées aux moeurs des premieres temps* (Paris, 1725).
[38] Manuel, *Eighteenth Century*, 259.
[39] A. Potts, *Flesh and the Ideal: Winckelmann and the Origins of Art History* (London, 1994).
[40] Manuel, *Eighteenth Century*, 260–1.
[41] R. Wood, *Essay on the Original Genius of Homer* (London, 1775).

volumes on the Hamilton collection had already appeared, it represented something of a reactionary attempt to return to an older school of research subordinated to biblical studies. For Bryant all ancient myth derived from the period after the flood, when men were disorientated and confused:

> In short we must look upon ancient mythology as being yet in a chaotic state: where the mind of man has been wearied with roaming over the crude consistence without ever finding out one sport, where it could repose in safety.[42]

Largely ignoring the work of French scholars, Bryant proceeded to prove the integrity of his system by demonstrating that the roots of words in ancient languages were the same. Thus the root of all belief was in a sense the spot on Mount Ararat in Armenia, where the Ark came to rest.[43] He also, however, allowed for a complex diffusion of patterns of religious ideas, suggesting, for example, that the term pator in Greek and Roman derived from Egyptian religious terminology, perhaps brought over by priests termed patres.[44] Although serious mythologists may have dismissed Bryant's work as nonsensical sophistry, there can be little doubt that it had widespread appeal to those with orthodox religious viewpoints who resented the apparent anticlericalism of French scholarship. His work attracted the admiration of important contemporaries such as William Blake and John Wesley, as well as influential thinkers of later generations such as G.S. Faber.[45] Moreover it represented a fundamental challenge to the modern rationalist school. While D'Hancarville cannot be read as in any sense a reply to Bryant, D'Hancarville's radicalism can be seen as an attempt to break from Christian chronologies and consolidate existing sexualised views about the origin of myth into a coherent formula.

## D'Hancarville's Career and Scholarly Development

Little is known about D'Hancarville's early career. He was born Pierre François Hugues in 1719 at Nancy, the son of a textile merchant. By the late 1750s he was an associate of Winckelmann, who seemed to have enjoyed a somewhat ambivalent relationship with the eccentric Frenchman. On the one hand Winckelmann seems to have viewed D'Hancarville with

---

[42] J. Bryant, *A New System, or Analysis of Ancient Mythology* (London, 1774), vol. I, xvii.
[43] Bryant, *New System*, vol. II, 3.
[44] Bryant, *New System*, vol. I, 283–4.
[45] Feldman and Richardson, *The Rise*, 242–3.

a considerable degree of distrust. When writing to Muzell-Stosch, the nephew of the great collector, he warned him to be wary of D'Hancarville's avaricious tendencies, advising him that '[w]hen you show him your gems keep a very close look-out to see what he is doing with his hands'.[46] Certainly D'Hancarville's predilection for living on borrowed money and adopting *nom de plumes* hardly inspired universal confidence. However Winckelmann clearly had respect for D'Hancarville's literary ability – or at least enough to install him as librarian to Cardinal Albani. Indeed given Winckelmann's responsibility for the papal collections its seems strange that he would install in Albani's library someone he regarded as untrustworthy. Perhaps, then, his earlier comments were partly tongue in cheek. Certainly D'Hancarville was heavily influenced by Winckelmann – indeed his contact with Winckelmann may have fired his literary and scholarly ambition. Jenkins's recent work on D'Hancarville has highlighted how the Frenchman sought to be compared with the celebrated antiquaries of the period – particularly Caylus and Winckelmann.[47] D'Hancarville's research on the Hamilton collection is littered with references to their scholarship, while making it clear that he intended to better their work. D'Hancarville sought not only to be more insightful but also to demonstrate how visual analysis could provide a history for an earlier period for which there were no literary sources. D'Hancarville would go back beyond Winckelmann, taking up the story several hundred years before Winckelmann began.

Sir William Hamilton's decision to commission D'Hancarville to produce a catalogue of his collection was not especially surprising. Following the death of Winckelmann, D'Hancarville was clearly one of the leading experts on antiquities in Italy and he held a privileged position as librarian to the Albani library. What is, perhaps, surprising is the degree of control Hamilton gave to D'Hancarville over the direction of the project. A whole series of artists and illustrators were employed on the volume and the whole organisation of the work was left in the hands of D'Hancarville.[48] The extensive illustrated catalogue came out in four parts, the first in 1768, the second in 1770, and the final two in 1776. Vickers has argued that the organisation and staggered publication dates of the volumes was essentially a marketing exercise, with the first volumes intended to whet the public appetite for what was to come – much of the

---

[46] See Haskell, *Past and Present*, 32–3.
[47] Jenkins, *Vases*, 45–64.
[48] N.C. Ramage, 'The Initial Letters in Sir William Hamilton's "Collection of Antiquities"', *Burlington Magazine*, 129 (1987), 446–56.

introductory material was held over into volume two.[49] There is certainly good reason to accept this explanation – Hamilton was trying to sell his collection to the British museum and the 8,000 guineas that the Museum paid for the collection in 1772 represented the first major sale of Greek vases and ceramics in any country. However, as Vickers acknowledges, the organisation of the volumes is very curious. D'Hancarville spends much of the first volume discussing the origin of the Etruscans and their letters, together with the remnants of their history, yet the key and valid argument of the whole work was that the pots in the collection were not Etruscan, but Greek.[50] This emphasis on the Etruscans is particularly surprising given that D'Hancarville is keen to stress the originality of his main insights. His preface states

> the nature of our work may be considered absolutely new, for no one, has yet undertaken to search out what system the Ancients followed to give their Vases, that elegance which all the World acknowledge to be in them, to discover rules the observation of which conduct infallibly to their imitation ….[51]

From the outset D'Hancarville is keen to emphasise the inadequacy of other works, including those of Caylus and Montfaulcon, stressing that his catalogue is also to be a textbook in taste, indicating the complete shape and relative proportions of the vases. In a sense, then, the Hamilton collection was intended to be for Greek ceramics what the *Antiquities of Athens* was for Greek architecture.[52]

Yet it is clear that the volumes were more than a marketing tool and a textbook of taste. They represented a serious piece of historical scholarship on an important collection. Almost immediately after becoming British ambassador at the court of Naples in 1764, Hamilton began his purchases, acquiring not just individual items, but complete collections, including the celebrated Porcinari collection and a significant part of the Mastrilli. Within a year of coming to Naples he began to make plans to publish his antiquities.[53] The commission represented a considerable opportunity for D'Hancarville to propound his theories to a large audience and to build

---

[49] Vickers, 'Value and Simplicity', 106. P. D'Hancarville, *Collection of Etruscan, Greek and Roman Antiquities from the Cabinet of the Hon. William Hamilton …* (Naples, 1768–76).

[50] Vickers, 'Value and Simplicity', 106.

[51] D'Hancarville, *Collection*, vol. I, vi.

[52] D'Hancarville, *Collection*, vol. I, vi–viii.

[53] N. Ramage, 'Sir William Hamilton as Collector, Exporter and Dealer: The Acquisition and Dispersal of his collection', *American Journal of Archaeology*, 94 (1990), 469–80.

his reputation as the successor to Winckelmann. At times D'Hancarville seems so determined to propound his theories that he seems almost indifferent to the key object of the commission – to document and explain the items in the Hamilton collection.[54] His celebrated 'theory of signs' is evident and prominent in the Hamilton work and much attention is paid to ancient mythology. D'Hancarville saw art being designed not to express, but instead to symbolise, with post primitive art carrying with it a reminder of its origins. Thus the visual historian could trace the symbols of the past through successive artistic evolutions and illustrate how ancient symbols could survive to the present. D'Hancarville's views on the symbolic nature of art and its reconstitution and survival were not wholly original. Griener has recently alleged that many of D'Hancarville's views were plagiarised from the work of Octavian Guasco, and that by dating all his volumes in 1767 he deliberately tried to make it appear that his work preceded that of Guasco in 1767.[55] This explanation does not, however, seem entirely plausible. D'Hancarville's final volumes came out so much later than the first – nine years in fact – that no one would be fooled by a false imprint. Indeed, if there had been a deliberate ploy to publish the collection in stages and thus tantalise the audience, then one would expect the antiquarian community to be fully aware that the work was published over several years as each instalment would have been eagerly awaited. In any case, many of D'Hancarville's more interesting insights into mythology come in the final two volumes, which all of D'Hancarville's contemporaries would have realised were published several years after the first. D'Hancarville makes it clear on page three of his third volume that many of his views had been revised since the publication of the first two volumes and is modest enough to highlight the inevitable speculative nature of much of the work.[56] This statement alone reveals to the reader that the third and fourth parts of the catalogue were published significantly later.

The third volume highlights both D'Hancarville's theory of signs and the contrasts between his approach to primitive art history and that of Winckelmann. In his discussion of the 'knobby and globular' form of Etruscan gem engraving, D'Hancarville attempts to impart meaning to the primitive shapes. This contrasts sharply with Winckelmann's more mechanistic explanations, which view the shapes as merely the product

---

[54] An observation made by Jenkins, see Jenkins, *Vases*, 48.
[55] P. Greiner, *Le Antichita Etrusche, Greche et Romane 1766–1776 di Pierre Hugues d'Hancarville* (Rome, 1992) 51, cited in Jenkins, *Vases*, 51.
[56] D'Hancarville, *Collection*, vol. III, 3.

of early craftsman coming to terms with new forms of working. This theory of meaning is important for D'Hancarville as he seeks to show, using Pausanias, how worship of rough stones and sealstones represent early forms of symbolic worship. Some of this discussion does appear to have been influenced by Guasco's work, especially that which relates to the way stones take on a divine identity.[57] However the key source for both Guasco and D'Hancarville is Pausanias, and D'Hancarville would clearly have read Pausanias independently of Guasco's account. Indeed Pausanias is the key source for much of his historical interpretation of gem engraving, and thus the origins of Greek art. In some cases he perhaps used Pausanias a little too uncritically – for example, his assertion that gem engraving was already known at the time of the siege of Troy relied on a single reference in Pausanias. On this basis he argued that while the Greeks may have owed their cultural origins to the Orient, they did not owe their art to that source. This represented a key disagreement with Guasco who argued that art was at a more advanced at an earlier state in Egypt and Persia, and indeed other contemporary antiquarian opinion which still saw Egypt as the original home of classical civilisation.[58]

Clearly some of D'Hancarville's conclusions were mistaken, although some which seem the most gross today were common eighteenth-century misapprehensions. The tendency, for example, to read all crude or unelaborated works as primitive or 'early' was one that many art historians displayed – including Winckelmann. What is important about the Hamilton volumes is that they firmly established D'Hancarville's scholarly credentials. Moreover the research pointed to the possibility of being able to decode mythical symbols through careful visual analysis. In his early work D'Hancarville seems to have taken many of the Hamilton vase images at face value, even in some cases reading them as depictions of actual events. In his first volume D'Hancarville interprets the famous Boar Hunt vase as an actual formerly unknown legendary hunt in Campania, either unmentioned in literary sources or lost. By the third volume he focuses instead on the mythical meaning of the objects apparent in the hunt, pointing, for example, to the way in which the birds may signify the divine media of fate and destiny.[59] This change in emphasis in the interpretations offered is illustrative both of D'Hancarville's intellectual growth and his increasing interest in decoding the visual language of

---

[57] Jenkins, *Vases*, 99.
[58] For more details see Jenkins, *Vases*, 99–100.
[59] Jenkins, *Vases*, 157.

antiquity. Indeed there are already hints of D'Hancarville's awareness of the importance of sexual symbolism in divine objects. His discussion of ancient jewellery and the scarab beetle illustrates his awareness of the importance of earth and sun deities in mythological systems – the passive and active forces that regulate reproduction – while also showing a knowledge of comparative mythology and the practices of modern west African tribes on the coast of Guinea.[60] In many respects, therefore, we can already see the main tenets of D'Hancarville's thinking in this work on the Hamilton collection.

Despite the critical success of the volumes, D'Hancarville's interest in all things sexual caused him some difficulties. During the early 1770s he published picture book pornography purporting to be representative of ancient works. *Veneres Et Priapi* was presented as a pocket catalogue of engraved stones, possibly derived from images displayed in the rooms of *Elephantis,* the Greek courtesan famous in the ancient world for writing a notorious sex manual.[61] It was actually a collection of bawdy pictures compiled for erotic effect although, of course, similar sexual images do appear in many forms of Greek art.[62] This particular tour de force was later followed up by *Monumens de la vie Privée des Douze Césars,* which also claimed to be based on ancient sources.[63] These publications included English text and may have been produced under the patronage of an Englishmen less prone to indebtedness than D'Hancarville. It is even possible that Charles Townley supported D'Hancarville in these publications – Townley was certainly fascinated by the priapic imagery evident in the gems and Vaughan, Townley's most important biographer, is convinced that their mutual interest in erotic material was a significant factor in their friendship.[64] If this is the case it undermines previous assumptions that the two men did not meet until introduced by Hamilton when Hamilton returned to England briefly in 1777.[65] It is certainly possible that Townley supported D'Hancarville's later pornographic works on the theme of

---

[60] Jenkins, *Vases*, 99.
[61] P. D'Hancarville, *Veneres Et Priapi* (n.d. but 1770s).
[62] Some, at least, appear to have been inspired by objects in particular private collections, see for example D'Hancarville, *Veneres,* plate LXX, although no references were provided!
[63] P. D'Hancarville, *Monumens de la vie Privée des Douze Césars* (Rome, 1780). This ran to many editions and was probably subject to unauthorised reprinting and recompiling.
[64] Vaughan, thesis, 53.
[65] Rousseau, *Sexual Underworlds*, 114.

the Twelve Caesars which contained a number of images derived from the first.[66] However Townley's friendship with D'Hancarville went far beyond a common interest in the erotic and pornographic. By the end of the 1770s Townley had emerged as perhaps the most important collector of Greco-Roman antiquities in Britain, combining a zeal for collecting with a genuine scholarly interest in the ancient world – and, in particular, ancient mythology. It was this interest that was to be the basis of their most important collaborations.

Townley bought his first important antique work, a Greco-Roman statue of a boy playing a game of tali, in 1768 and over the next twenty years collected a wide range of sculptures, bronzes, gems, pastes and other items of antiquarian interest.[67] Although a number of his acquisitions were purchased from the great palaces and villas of Rome, such as the Barbarini, the Burioni, the Mattei and the D'Este, Townley also supported contemporary excavations in Rome, particularly those of Gavin Hamilton and Thomas Jenkins.[68] By the late 1770s Townley was showing increasing interest in the collecting of antiquities for their documentary and symbolic value, as can be particularly seen in his collecting of antique pastes.[69] By 1779 Townley and D'Hancarville were close associates and spent much of that year touring British country houses. D'Hancarville's influence on the English collector was already apparent and around this time Townley composed a treatise 'The Science of Antiquity' – a work which was never published but which showed his depth of interest in matters of Greek mythology.[70] It not known when D'Hancarville began composing his major work *Recherches sur l'origine, l'esprit et les progrès des arts de la Grèce*, but it is reasonable to suppose most of the work was composed between 1781 and 1785, during which he spent most of his time in London, supported by Townley, assisted later by Richard Payne Knight. However, while it was an original treatise, it clearly built on the work that he had already published for Hamilton.

---

[66] P. D'Hancarville, *Monumens du culte Secret des Dames Romaines; D'Après une suite de Pierres gravees sous leur Regne, pour servir de suite à la Vie des Douze Césars* (Rome: 1787).
[67] For a brief outline, see E. Edwards, *Lives of the Founders of the British Museum* (London, 1870), 369–412.
[68] The major collections in Rome at this time are outlined in A. Clark, 'The Development of the Collections and Museums of 18th-Century Rome', *Art Journal*, 26 (1966–7), 136–43. Also see Haskell and Penny, *Taste*, 62–73.
[69] Vaughan, thesis, 204.
[70] Vaughan, thesis, 392–3.

## D'Hancarville and the Sexual Interpretation of Myth

In many respects D'Hancarville's *Recherches* reflected the growing belief that sexual symbolism was inherent in primitive belief systems and played a central role in all mythology. Mitter argues that these sexual interpretations coincided with the increasing European interest in India in the 1780s.[71] Yet, as this article has illustrated, many prominent scholars were interpreting ancient religion in terms of the worship of sexual and generative powers twenty years earlier. D'Hancarville was clearly influenced by this intellectual environment. His work can certainly be said to have paralleled that of Holbach, Boulanger, de Gebelin and especially that of Dupuis. However it is important to note that the most influential work of the time of sexual symbolism in mythology, Dupuis' *Origine de tous les cultes ou la Religion universalle* was not published until nine years after D'Hancarville's *Recherches*.[72] Dupuis did produce articles on mythological subjects before 1794. Some of his research was published in the *Journal des Scavants* in 1778 and Septchenes refers to a *Memoires sur l'origine des Fables* by Dupuis published before 1787.[73] However these did not represent a fully worked through theory and were not circulated widely.[74] D'Hancarville was probably not aware of it and it seems, giving the timing of the publications, Dupuis was more likely to have drawn on D'Hancarville. Ironically, then, the biggest immediate influence on D'Hancarville was not so much the French mythological school as D'Hancarville's friend the English palaeographer and philologist Thomas Astle. Astle's 1784 publication *The Origin and Progress of Writing* was a landmark work of comparative history and anthropology, illustrating how writing emerged across cultures as imitative or symbolic representation.[75] Although it is not known whether the two men discussed their work in any detail, the similarity of the methodological approach is highly suggestive – both were fascinated by comparative symbolism and the possibility of developing a totalising theory to explain what was perceived to be a naturalistic phenomenon.

---

[71] P. Mitter, *Much Maligned Monsters: The History of the European Reaction to Indian Art* (Oxford 1977), esp. 85–104 cited in Rousseau, *Sexual Underworlds*, 116.
[72] C. Dupuis, *Origine de tous les cultes ou la Religion universalle* (Paris, 1794).
[73] Septchenes, *Religion*, 53.
[74] For example William Cockburn, writing an extensive commentary on French mythological research in 1804, was unable to obtain a copy and references to it were very rare. W. Cockburn, *Remarks on a Publication of M. Volney called 'The Ruins' etc* (Cambridge, 1804), 21.
[75] T. Astle, *The Origin and Progress of Writing* (London, 1784), cited in Vaughan, thesis, 387.

# Baron D'Hancarville and the Exploration of Ancient Mythology

D'Hancarville's *Recherches* was an attempt to describe an ancient and universal system from which all religions were derived through a comparative analysis of symbolism. For D'Hancarville ancient theology took a predominantly intense sexual character, focused on the forces of creation and recreation. Primitive man tended to create symbols to represent these primordial powers, choosing those which best illustrated or communicated these forces. Thus eggs provided a natural symbol of female reproductive power, while similar primordial masculine attributes of strength were provided by the symbol of a bull. Later the features of symbolic animals, such as bull horns, were attributed to anthrophomorhic gods and heroes, thus explaining the appearance of bull-like characteristics on male portraits and mythical figures depicted as half man and half beast. By comparing the pottery, sculpture and coinage of classic and non-classical cultures D'Hancarville attempted to demonstrate that all societies based their religion around the same naturalistic reproductive urge and consequently primitive societies tended to create similar images in their visual art. Thus D'Hancarville was presenting a framework for the comparative analysis of all religions – a framework that would allow patterns of divergence and diffusion across the globe to be understood.

The first two volumes of the *Recherches* appeared in 1785 and it is clear that D'Hancanville intended to develop the thesis further. Unfortunately he was side-tracked by negative reviews, especially that of Henry Maty of the *New Review,* and the only additional volume which appeared was essentially a detailed response to this essay.[76] Interestingly, Maty's review of the work was not as devastatingly critical as one might imagine from D'Hancarville's rather ill-tempered response. Indeed the critical reception of the work and Richard Payne Knight's later interpretation was generally favourable.[77] The *Recherches* were, after all, grounded in genuine empirical research. The first volume begins with a detailed discussion of the origins of Greek coins. It is here where we find the stones that the ancients originally worshipped as emblems of the Gods and ancient temples long since destroyed. This is followed by an explanation of the origins of the arts in Greece, from where, according to D'Hancarville they are carried all over Asia by the Scythians. The third and fourth chapters of the first volume are scholarly but highly complex and somewhat jumbled comparisons of arts in India and Asia. A key feature of the account is the tension that exists between D'Hancarville's desire to represent Greece as

---

[76] Burton Feldman, preface, P. D'Hancarville, *Recherches sur l'origine, l'esprit et les progrès des arts de la Grèce*, vol. 1 (New York edition, 1984), vi.
[77] Funnell, 'Symbolic Language', in Clarke and Penny, *Arrogant Connoisseur*, 54–5.

the originator of art and the naturalistic explanations which see particular symbols as the universal form of religious expression across the cultures studied. Just as with his work on the Hamilton collection, D'Hancarville is prepared to accept that the Greeks may have owed their broad cultural origins to the East, but not their art.[78] The second volume attempts to reconcile this view with recent discoveries about the belief systems of north European nations, and in particular their relationship to Greece. Again similar patterns of symbolism and apparent belief system are discovered and compared with knowledge derived from classical sources.

The main problem with D'Hancarville's study is that it is not presented in a logical and clearly structured way, making the narrative difficult to follow, even for specialist eighteenth-century scholars. Indeed it is difficult to disagree with Maty's basic assessment of the core argument:

> As a medallist, I confess myself entirely incapable of judging what degree of merit are to be given to them [D'Hancarville's views]. Ingenious and plausible they certainly are, and supported by a considerable share of learning, how far it is all solid others will determine. As a reviewer, I must confess I could have wished for less tautology, more order, more clearness, less mixture of old and known things with the new, and a smaller torrent of erudition.[79]

Significantly however Maty also recognises the complexity of the subject, acknowledging the difficulty inherent in drawing conclusions on the basis of image similarity. Indeed Maty clearly believed that decoding the similarities was impossible and that without literary evidence they would remain a mystery. However it is in this that D'Hancarville is at his most innovative. While he uses literary evidence to support his broad historical chronology, D'Hancarville seeks to go beyond the literary evidence to analyse images which are the only sources we have available to decode ancient myth. In doing so he was attempting to apply the latest thinking on the importance of sexual symbolism, while trying to mobilise material from a huge range of cultures in support of his central thesis. It is easy to criticise D'Hancarville for adopting the approach of the Encyclopaedists in trying to find a single totalising explanation for all mythical experience and religious belief, but in fact D'Hancarville is actually remarkably frank about the limitations of his study.[80] As even his arch critic Maty observes, D'Hancarville is very modest about the difficulties inherent in his work and only ever describes his work as 'conjectures'.[81] Only subsequent

---

[78] Jenkins, *Vases*, 99–100.
[79] H. Maty, *A New Review*, January 1785 in D'Hancarville, *Recherches*, III, 57–64.
[80] See the characterisation of D'Hancarville's work by Haskell, *Past and Present*, 45.
[81] Maty, *A New Review*, in D'Hancarville, *Recherches*, III, 58.

scholars, influenced perhaps by the work of Knight, have viewed him as a theorist seeking totalising explanations. Indeed the evolutionary and discursive style of the volumes suggests that much uncertainty remained in D'Hancarville's own mind.

Unfortunately D'Hancarville never had the opportunity to finish his work. The third volume – primarily a response to Maty's review – added little new material and distracted D'Hancarville from further progress. It is impossible to assess just how damaging Maty's review was but the volume was not a commercial success. By March 1787 only 200 of the 313 copies printed had been sold and only 100 of the supplementary third volume. Most, it seems, were sold to Townley's associates. D'Hancarville was keen to produce a second edition and, significantly, to market the volume in France, a country which showed a long and continuing interest in the sexual aspects of mythology. It is not known if, while in Paris, D'Hancanville was in contact with Dupuis, but given their mutual interests this seems not unlikely. Yet no further volumes appeared. However, the critical impact of the *Recherches* was considerable. The philologist Charles Vallencey was particularly warm in his praise. Vallencey's interest is particularly significant as he was one of Britain's leading mythologists and a pioneer of comparative religion. William Lock sent D'Hancarville a note congratulating him on the quality of the work and even David showed interest in D'Hancarville's work on the Townley collection.[82] Indeed it is clear the influence of the *Recherches* went well beyond the Townley circle. Even Heyne's work on the iconography of the Portland vase, published in the *Gottingen Review* of 1786 can be read as a response, or perhaps more precisely an attack, on D'Hancarville.[83]

## Richard Payne Knight's 'Translation' of D'Hancarville

D'Hancarville's return to France did not mark the end of his influence in England. Indeed the most controversial chapter in the life of his ideas was about to begin. Richard Payne Knight had shown a close interest in D'Hancarville's scholarship for some time and had helped support him when Townley's funds ran short. Knight's writings after 1785 show a strong influence of D'Hancarville works – indeed one might view his major work *An Inquiry into the Symbolic Language of Antiquity* as little more than an English version of D'Hancarville. However it was his 1786 privately

---

[82] Vaughan, thesis, 398.
[83] Vaughan, thesis, 396.

circulated *Discourse on the Worship of the Priapus* that showed the immediate influence of D'Hancarville on Knight's thinking. The *Discourse* is now one of the best-known mythological works of the eighteenth century, not least because of its sexually explicit nature and its somewhat salacious language. It has invited widespread speculation about Knight's own sexuality and the homosocial nature of the eighteenth-century scholarly community.[84] Yet its origins lie partly in D'Hancarville's research and partly in the discovery of modern phallic worship in Isernia by men employed by Sir William Hamilton. Knight, adopting Hamilton's reports, concluded that the worship in Isernia was a relic of ancient paganism, a devotion to the divine personification of male fertility, the god Priapus.[85] In other words, the ritual was a living relic of the practices described by D'Hancarville. Knight used this as a starting point to introduce and acknowledge D'Hancarville's theories and to construct an erudite framework of comparative mythology around the worship of the phallus.[86] The treatise was re-written for publication as the introduction to the second volume of *Select Specimens of Ancient Sculpture* planned by the Society of Dilettanti. The first volume, also charged to Knight, was, of course, one of the finest and most influential scholarly catalogues of the period and the proposal to give D'Hancarville's views prominence in the second volume was an indication of the esteem in which he held the views of the Frenchman. However the slow progress of the volume prompted Knight to publish his revised text privately as *An Enquiry into The Symbolic Language of Ancient Art and Mythology* in 1818 and later to serialise it in continuous instalments in the *Classical Journal.*[87]

Knight's approach was similar to D'Hancarville, although his starting point for understanding fertility cults was the phallus. Beginning with Egypt, using Herodotus, he notes how women were said to carry images of Osiris with 'a moveable phallus of disproportionate magnitude', while the Greeks on their art represented the phallus alone as a disembodied symbol.[88] This he compares with the practices of the Iols of Native America, ancient Scandinavians and Hindus. Just as with D'Hancarville, much of the comparative material is drawn from ethnographic sources

[84] A. Ponte, 'Architecture and Phallocentrism in Richard Payne Knight's Theory', in B. Colomina (eds.), *Sexuality and Space* (New York 1992); Rousseau 'Sorrows'; Funnell in Haskell, *Past and Present*, 50–64.
[85] A. Ballantyne, *Architecture, Landscape and Liberty: Richard Payne Knight and the Picturesque* (Cambridge 1997), 89–90.
[86] F. Messman, *Richard Payne Knight The Twilight of Virtuosity* (Paris, 1974), 46.
[87] R.P. Knight, *An Inquiry into the Symbolic Language of Ancient Art and Mythology* (London, 1818).
[88] Knight, *An Inquiry*, 6 [1836 edition].

and travel literature, such as Lafitau's *Moeurs des Sauvages Amériquains* and Maurice's *Indian Antiquities*.[89] Knight moves on to discuss the broader symbolism of early mythology and immediately it is clear that he owes much to D'Hancarville. After discussing the symbolism of the egg and the serpent, he moves on to discuss the bull, again in terms almost identical to D'Hancarville:

> To express the attribute strength, in symbolic writing, the figure of the strongest animal would naturally be adopted … The mystic Bacchus, or generative power, was represented under this form, not only upon the coins, but in the temples of the Greeks: sometimes simply as a bull; at others, with a human face; and, at others, entirely human except the horns or ears.[90]

His conclusions about the geographical origin of mythological symbolism were also similar. Both D'Hancarville and Knight adopted an essentially naturalistic approach, denying that simply because the same symbols could be seen everywhere, all beliefs were derived from a single geographical source. The symbols of strength, fertility, nutrition and reproduction were universal ones because they were derivative of universal natural phenomena, making reference to animal and plants types that were visible across the globe.

Yet despite the serious scholarly pretension of the subject matter, Knight seems to delight in the sexual imagery of his subject. He revelled in his discussion of the feasts of Bacchus which, while historically grounded in the works of Plutarch and others, were given an obviously titillating orientation in Knight's prose:

> Considering the general state of reserve and restraint in which the Grecian women lived, it is astonishing to what an excess of extravagance their religious enthusiasm was carried on certain occasions; particularly in celebrating the orgies of Bacchus. The gravest matrons and proudest princesses suddenly laid aside their decency and their dignity, and ran screaming among the woods and mountains, fantastically dressed or half-naked, with their hair dishevelled and interwoven with ivy or vine, and sometimes with living servants. In this manner they frequently worked themselves up to such a pitch of savage ferocity, as not only to feed upon raw flesh, but even to tear living animals to pieces with their teeth, and eat them warm and palpitating.[91]

---

[89] J. Lafitau, *Moeurs des Sauvages Amériquains comparées aux moeurs des premiers temps* (Paris, 1724), T. Maurice, *Indian Antiquities* (London, 1794–1800).
[90] Knight, *An Inquiry*, 8 [1836 edition].
[91] Knight, *An Inquiry*, 21 [1836 edition].

Similarly, Funnell notes Knight's interest in the obscene aspects of religious practice and his 'raffish delight in the indecency of its subject'.[92] This inclination to go beyond the bounds of ordinary scholarly convention was shared by both D'Hancarville and Knight. Yet it probably damaged Knight more than D'Hancarville, for Knight was a public man, a one time member of parliament and a leading figure in the Society of Dilettanti. Knight's *Discourse* with its sexually-explicit illustrations of priapic idols was only intended for private circulation and the negative reaction of some members of the Society of Dilettanti may explain why Knight later tried to buy back all existing copies of the book. Sir Joseph Banks, for the Society of Dilettanti, who controlled distribution of the work, sent out no review copies and after a clericalist backlash, rumours even spread that the government viewed the publication as seditious.[93] Indeed, the rather ambivalent reaction of Society members to Knight's views may have been a contributory factor in the delay of the second volume of *Select Specimens* and explain why his treatise did not come out in book form again until 1818.

Interestingly, when the *Discourse* was reprinted in the form of the 1818 *Inquiry*, much of the more sexually-explicit material had been removed. After being serialised in the *Classical Journal*, the book went into a second edition and then a third edition in 1836. As late as 1892 the work was being republished in New York as *The Symbolic Language of Art and Mythology*.[94] Despite the passing of years, publishers still feared that the volume would spark controversy and the editor noted that the new 1892 edition had 'been carefully divested of the details and examples, which … were likely to expose it to popular clamor'.[95] Yet what is more remarkable is that the treatise was still regarded as a very important piece of scholarship. The 1892 edition's author Alexander Wilding praised Knight as 'one of the most thorough scholars of the earlier period of the present century' who had analysed 'an invaluable collection of ancient and curious learning'.[96] Indeed, although he recognised some of the assertions might appear fanciful, Wilding noted how many more recent scholars, such as Layard, Bonomi and the Rawlinsons owed a debt to

---

[92] Funnell in Clark and Penny, *Arrogant Connoisseur*, 58; also cited in Rousseau, *Sexual Underworlds*, 119–120.
[93] For more details on the reception of the volume see Rousseau, *Sexual Underworlds*, 120–2.
[94] A. Wilder [ed.], R.P. Knight, *The Symbolic Language of Ancient Art and Mythology* (New York, 1892).
[95] Wilder, *Symbolic*, 7–8.
[96] Wilder, *Symbolic*, 5.

Knight's work – even suggesting that some of their ideas may have been derived directly from it.⁹⁷

In many respects, however, this continuing enthusiasm for the book should not be surprising. D'Hancarville's views, often communicated through the medium of Knight's work, were remarkably influential. Although Knight's reputation was damaged by his criticism of the Elgin marbles, he remained an influential figure in debates about artistic taste.⁹⁸ Similarly although Townley's Greco-Roman collection, acquired by the British Museum in 1805, was eventually displaced by the Elgin marbles as the centrepiece of the Department of Greek and Roman Antiquities, the Townley collection was still recognised as valuable and instructive. Sir Henry Ellis's catalogue of the Townley collection, published in 1846, provided a detailed examination of these works and demonstrated the debt contemporaries owed to D'Hancarville's earlier scholarship.⁹⁹ It was only a generation later that British Museum publications begin to attack D'Hancarville's views directly, starting with Edward Edwards's criticism in his well-known *Lives of the Founders of the British Museum* published in 1870.¹⁰⁰ Yet the fact it was thought necessary to criticise an eighty-year-old French language publication which had enjoyed only very limited circulation illustrates the influence D'Hancarville had enjoyed. One can also see D'Hancarville's influence on German scholars, through Seeman's well-known handbook *The Mythology of Greece and Rome*.¹⁰¹ The English edition, published in 1877, echoes D'Hancarville in identifying the source of religion in 'men's observations of Nature, and her various active and creative forces', although, perhaps understandably his consideration of priapic cults reflected typical Victorian circumspection.¹⁰²

Indeed, one might say that D'Hancarville's influence went far beyond that of historical scholarship and challenged the reluctance of cultural elites to address the sexual aspects of human psychology. In particular his work, and that inspired by him, was part of a movement that helped to encourage a more open debate about sex and nudity in art. Many serious connoisseurs still felt uncomfortable about the nudity inherent in many Greek and Greco-Roman works of art, seeking to modify them to render them less indecent. In contrast radicals opposed this form of mutilation.

---

[97] Wilder, *Symbolic*, 9.
[98] Ballantyne, *Architecture*, 48–58.
[99] H. Ellis, *The Townley Gallery of Classical Sculpture in the British Museum* (London, 1846).
[100] Edwards, *Lives*, 375–6.
[101] O. Seeman, *The Mythology of Greece and Rome, with Special Reference to its Use in Art* (London, 1877).
[102] Seeman, *Mythology*, 12, 113.

George Cumberland, well acquainted with D'Hancarville's theories, was a strong advocate of more openness, issuing a polemical response to those who sought to conceal the phallus in works of Greek art:

> Let us away with this affectation; and let our travelled ladies, who have walked without harm with gentlemen through every Museum in Europe, and beheld all that Grecian Art, even when it was playful, could shew, teach their countrywomen, that true modesty disdains not to examine, with a steady eye, the masculine parts of the antique statues, conscious that they are as chastely represented as those of children by the hand of nature, which innocence may, and does daily, behold unblushing; which nothing which led hypocrisy affects to fear; and which, when mutilated, or destroyed, or clumsily concealed, shews only a disposition to affect a refinement that assuredly betrays, to a close observer, the index of a narrow mind; and has a cruel tendency to depress the hand of Art, which is never more elevated than when describing the human form divine as it came from the hands of the mysterious great first Cause.[103]

D'Hancarville and Knight had helped open a debate about decency in art, and particularly sculpture, that was to continue throughout nineteenth-century Britain.

## D'Hancarville's Historiographical and Theoretical Legacy

Yet perhaps D'Hancarville's most important legacy is to be found in France. Just a few years after D'Hancarville's return to Paris, Dupuis produced his legendary work on the origin of all religious worship, which applied understandings of the sexual symbols of fertility to astrological events and signs of the zodiac. Although it is not known whether Dupuis ever discussed mythology with D'Hancarville, the similarity of their interests and approach suggests that some form of collaboration may have taken place. Dupuis had been working on the origin of myth since the 1770s but his first works, published in the *Journal des Scavants*, did not appear until 1778, well after D'Hancarville's last two volumes of the Hamilton collection. Moreover the work for which he is known, *Origine des tous les cultes ou lat Religion universalle,* the first extensive exposition of his views, did not appear until well after D'Hancarville's *Recherches*. Manuel has argued that the major influences over Dupuis were the obscure French abbé Charles Le Batteux and Boulanger.[104] However, as Manuel

---

[103] G. Cumberland, *Thoughts on Outline, sculpture, and the System that Guided the Ancient Artists in Composing their Figures and Groups* (London 1806), 44–5.
[104] Manuel, *Eighteenth Century*, 264–5.

himself points out, Boulanger argued that primitive religion grew out of the perception and fear of destructive natural forces.[105] Dupuis, like D'Hancarville, emphasised the importance of the creative forces of nature as the originating force in the creation of myth. In this sense, Dupuis' etymology is much closer to that evident in D'Hancarville's *Recherches*. His methodological culling of travel literature about religious cults across the globe reflects both the approach adopted by D'Hancarville as well as D'Hancarville's lively interest in symbolism. Dupuis' discussion of the active and passive forces sexual forces observed in nature, Bacchic and Priapic worship and fertility cults all echo the interests and arguments of D'Hancarville and Knight. What is remarkable is that very few have considered the connection between Dupuis and the scholarship, undertaken a few years previously, over the other side of the English Channel. Feldman and Richardson note the similarity, but assume that Dupuis must have adopted this approach independently.[106] This does, however, seem a little unlikely, given the similarity in methodology, subject matter and theoretical interpretation.

One can see why D'Hancarville and especially Knight would not want to have been associated with Dupuis' work. Dupuis' sympathy with revolutionary theology and political radicalism made him a central figure of revolutionary France and he became honoured as one of the great minds of the Directorate.[107] Dupuis' work was only published in England in the form of extracts at this time and it was Volney who was responsible for the broader dissemination of Dupuis' ideas in England.[108] Yet the work of Dupuis and Volney provoked a violent response from both the Anglican and Nonconformist establishment in England.[109] Joseph Priestley responded with a lengthy rebuttal, while provincial religious leaders felt it necessary to condemn from the pulpit a dangerous French book that had 'excited a considerable degree of attention on the continent'.[110] If we are to believe some sources, Knight was already being

---

[105] Manuel, *Eighteenth Century*, 265–6.
[106] Feldman and Richardson, *The Rise*, 277.
[107] Manuel, *Eighteenth Century*, 265–6.
[108] Anon, *Christianity A Form of The Great Solar Myth From the French of Dupuis* (London, n.d.), C. Volney, *The Ruins, or a Survey of the Revolution of Empires* (London, 1819 edition), see esp. 228–33. In Volney we see much of the comparative symbolic analysis of D'Hancarville, including that of the bull and the egg, see Volney, *Ruins*, 245.
[109] For background on the political and religious turmoil in England during this period, see S. Deane, *The French Revolution and Enlightenment in England, 1789–1832* (London, 1988).
[110] J. Priestley, *A Comparison of the Institutions of Moses with those of the Hindoos and Other Ancient Nations* (Northumberland, 1799), J. Estlin, *The Nature and Causes of Atheism* (Bristol, 1797), 37.

viewed as a political and religious subversive after the publication of his *Discourse* so he may have been reluctant to associate himself with the views of Dupuis. Moreover as Knight's own work was largely derived from that of D'Hancarville, he could hardly object if someone else had refined D'Hancarville's theories in France – particularly if D'Hancarville had met Dupuis while in Paris. What cannot be disputed is the influence that Dupuis' views had on continental opinion. Dupuis' work ran into countless editions and was soon translated into English, German and Spanish.[111] Dulaure and de Tracy helped disseminate his views in continental Europe through their own related publications and his many American readers included John Adams.[112] In 1816 Adams even wrote to Jefferson suggesting the formation of a society to promote the Frenchman's writings.[113] Dupuis' politically radical and anti–religious views may have made him less well read in early nineteenth-century Britain but there can be little doubt that the approach he adopted influenced future historians of historical mythology, including William Cox and the virtual founder of comparative anthropology, E.B. Tyler.[114] What is remarkable is that both Dupuis' approach is essentially that of D'Hancarville. Even if Dupuis did not plagiarise D'Hancarville or directly adopt his ideas, the similarity of views demonstrates that D'Hancarville's views were not absurd, wildly speculative or inconsistent with the intellectual currents of the period. It illustrates that in many respects D'Hancarville was in the radical mainstream of enlightenment philosophy; a philosophy which not only captured figures such as Townley and Knight, but had an international influence on the study of comparative religion. Indeed, it may have been the similarities between the views of D'Hancarville and Dupuis that limited his popularity in Britain. It is significant that Knight's major work did not appear until after the Napoleonic Wars when fears of French radicalism were beginning to ebb. Despite these limitations there can be little doubt that D'Hancarville was a pioneer at the forefront of the science of mythology. By the early twentieth century advances in empirical archaeology inevitably highlighted the somewhat conjectural nature of D'Hancarville's work. However, even critical

---

[111] The most readily available English version is probably C. Dupuis, *The Origin of All Religious Worship* (New Orleans, 1872).

[112] J.A. Dulaure, *Des Cultes qui ont précédé et amené L'idolatrie et l'adoration des figures humaines* (Paris, 1805), D. de Tracy, *Analyse raisonée de l'Origine de Tous les Cultes* (Paris, 1804); see also Feldman and Richardson, *The Rise*, 277–8.

[113] Bernal, *Black Athena*, 251, Manuel, *Eighteenth Century*, 278.

[114] For an early twentieth-century perspective on these issues, see L. Spence, *An Introduction of Mythology* (London, 1921).

publications were forced to acknowledge the importance of the scholarship. Goodland's 1931 *Bibliography of Sex Rites and Customs* described Knight's *Inquiry* as a 'a well-known "classic"', despite highlighting its limitations.[115] Significantly too, some commentators began to see links between the modern psychoanalytical work of Freud and the primitive sexual symbolism in D'Hancarville and Knight. Pevsner saw the psychological insights inherent in Knight's work as direct precursors of Freud, viewing them as 'expeditions into the subconscious amazing for their date'.[116] D'Hancarville may never have matched Winckelman's fame as an art historian but D'Hancarville's status as a pioneering scholar is difficult to refute.

## Scholarly Reputations and the Study of Myth

Ackerman's recent biography of Frazer notes how he has become something of an embarrassment to modern professional anthropologists. The speculative nature of the work and its use of unreliable secondary ethnographic reports mean that Frazer is rarely noted in any of the professional lineages acknowledged today. Yet he remains an important figure in the history of religion and his comprehensive comparative method has never been entirely eclipsed.[117] Much the same may be said of D'Hancarville. In some respects, however, D'Hancarville was much more of a pioneer than Frazer. He developed a sexual theory of the origins of mythology that was to be influential for much of the following century. He inspired the work of perhaps Britain's leading artistic opinion-former of the early nineteenth century, Richard Payne Knight, and anticipated the work of France's greatest mythologist, Charles Dupuis, by almost a decade. Equally importantly, he helped open up debate about the role of sex in art that would continue through to the Victorian period and beyond. Moreover, unlike Frazer, he was careful to emphasise that his sexual theory and sexual interpretation of ancient iconography was speculative and evolving. While the work of Knight might have a somewhat prescriptive feel to it, D'Hancarville's does not. Instead D'Hancarville shows an awareness of the difficulties of interpreting non-literary sources, while still attempting a formidable comparative project in primitive art.

---

[115] R. Goodland, *Bibliography of Sex Rites and Customs* (London, 1931), 328, cited in Messman, *Knight*, 51.
[116] N. Pevsner, 'Richard Payne Knight', *Art Bulletin*, 31 (1949), 293–309, esp. 298.
[117] R. Ackerman, *J.G. Frazer, His Life and Work* (Cambridge, 1990 edition), 1–3, 102–3.

Yet there is little doubt that, in some respects, D'Hancarville, like Frazer, is something of an embarrassment to modern scholarship. His penchant for producing pornography, 'removing' antiques without permission, living off the wealth of others and spending time in gaol inevitably make some suspicious about his scholarly integrity. His main work, the *Recherches*, was badly organised, highly complex and inaccessible to all but the specialist. It was, as D'Hancarville admitted, a speculative work, in an age when rigorous empiricism was a central historical and philological canon. He was also something of a lone wolf, operating independently outside the established academies of England, Italy and France, working for gentleman collectors and sometimes, as in the case of Hamilton, compromising his academic integrity in order to enhance the value of particular collections. D'Hancarville's attempts to rival Winckelmann were, of course, unsuccessful and while voluminous literature has been dedicated to Winckelmann, D'Hancarville has been marginalised. Yet the importance of sexual imagery in interpreting the ancient world is universally recognised and has stimulated some of the most important works of feminist classical scholarship of the last two decades.[118] Similarly the 'Black Athena' debates of recent years only serve to highlight how sophisticated late eighteenth-century scholarship on the origin of myth was – and the important contribution D'Hancarville's made to this debate. In some respects he was, of course, somewhat myopic and perhaps too influenced by contemporary philhellenism's determination to maintain Greece's cultural centrality. Yet despite D'Hancarville's desire to emphasise the role of Greece as the originator of the visual arts, he maintained a naturalistic theory of mythical development – where all primitive religions derive from a common naturalistic impressions – and appreciated the importance of understanding newly discovered cultures of Asia. He was one of the first to adopt a sexual theory of myth through a complex comparative framework that engaged with new discoveries about Hinduism, Native Americans and west Africans. His works on Hinduism anticipated the growing interest in the East over the following century, from that of Sir William Jones in England to F. Max Muller and the philological school in Germany. Even E.B. Tyler's path-breaking anthropological work *Primitive Culture* of 1871 shared not only

---

[118] For example, E. Keuls, *The Reign of the Phallus* (California, 1993), esp. the additional bibliography, 435–9, D. Lyons, *Gender and Immortality: Heroines in Ancient Greek Myth and Cult* (Princeton, 1996), Doniger, *Splitting the Difference,* S. Deacy and A. Villing (eds.), *Athena in the Classical World* (Boston, 2001). For recent literary interpretations of Priapus, see M. O'Connor, *Symbolum Salacitatis: a Study of the God Priapus as a Literary Character* (New York, 1989).

D'Hancarville's belief in naturalistic approach but also the importance Non-western belief systems in exploring the source of myths.[119] While D'Hancarville himself did little to disseminate his own ideas, the works of Knight and Dupuis ensured that his basic views remained influential for over a century. He illustrates the humanistic preoccupations of the period, the search for religious origins outside Christian chronologies and the role of antiquity in the reinterpretation of the present. D'Hancarville was relatively unusual in looking to Asian sources for classical religion. Dupuis, Septchenes, Volney and most other French mythologists all looked to Africa to find the immediate predecessors of Greek gods.[120] Yet, in practice, there was little interest in trying to link religious origins to a single geographical origin. Their real interest was trying to understand the natural processes whereby geographically separate societies came to develop apparently similar religious practices and believe in similar deities. The work of D'Hancarville and his contemporaries demonstrates that far from being Aryan or Euro-centric, the eighteenth-century search for the origins of 'Black Athena' was rooted in a universal naturalistic philosophy.

---

[119] E. Tyler, *Primitive Culture* (London, 1871).
[120] For example, see the work of Bergier and Pluche; *L'Abbé Bergier, L'Origine des dieux du Paganisme* (Paris, 1774), L'Abbé Pluche, *Histoire du Ciel*, 2 vols. (Paris, 1748).

## 7. Colonel Leake and the Historical Geography of Greece

*Malcolm Wagstaff*

William Martin Leake's career represents a vital chapter both in the 'rediscovery' of classical Greece and in the development of historical geography as a scholarly discipline. He was not only a keen supporter of the Hellenic style in art and architecture but also widely travelled in Classical lands. Moreover, as Henry Fanshaw Tozer put it in 1872, he made 'an epoch in the study of Greek geography',[1] and his high reputation has endured to the present day.[2] Leake's reputation rests primarily on his researches on the geography and topography of ancient Greece.[3] Leake's major publications, however, also contain much material about early nineteenth-century Greece. This chapter is devoted to both aspects of Leake's contribution to the historical geography of Greece. But, first of all, who was he?

His family name is Martin Leake, and William Martin Leake (1777–1860) was an officer in the Royal Regiment of Artillery. His career began as a cadet (1792–4) at the Royal Military Academy, Woolwich, which then provided the only military education available in Britain, and he served throughout the Revolutionary and Napoleonic Wars (1793–1815). On being commissioned he was posted to the West Indies (1795–8) before being appointed to the British Military Mission to Turkey (1799–1802). In 1804 he was sent by the Foreign Office as military adviser to the local Ottoman authorities in Greece and Albania, where a French attack was expected. He was there for almost three years and travelled widely before being put under house arrest in February, 1807. After his release, the British Plenipotentiary in the region sent him to discover if Ali Pasha, the most powerful Ottoman governor in Greece at the time, would support the French, should they invade or remain loyal to the Sultan and favour the British. Leake returned to Greece in 1809 with a

---

[1] H.F. Tozer, *Lectures on the Geography of Greece* (London, 1873), 32–4.
[2] H. Angelomatis-Tsougarakis, *The Eve of the Greek Revival: British Travellers' Perception of Early Nineteenth-Century Greece* (London, 1990), 14, 20.
[3] I draw a basic distinction between the two terms: 'geography' is concerned with the regional scale, 'topography' with the local scale or place.

cargo of ordnance and munitions for Ali Pasha and remained as British resident at the Vezir's court for about a year. During this time he travelled in Epirus and Thessaly.

Back in Britain Leake was given the brevet rank of lieutenant-colonel (1813). He became a member of the African Association (1813); later he was its secretary. Leake also joined the Society of Dilettanti (1814) and was elected a fellow of the Royal Society (1815). His first book, *Researches on Greece*, appeared in 1814. When Napoleon escaped from Elba in 1815 and began his 'Hundred Days', Leake was sent as British observer to the army of the Swiss Cantons. On his return in 1816, Leake remained in the army for another eight years, reaching the full rank of lieutenant colonel in the Royal Artillery in 1821. Although never on half-pay, implying active service, he seems to have been able to devote his time, and indeed the rest of his long life, to scholarly activity. A steady stream of articles and books resulted. Finally, Leake helped to establish the Royal Society of Literature (1821) and the Royal Geographical Society (1830), as well as the Travellers' Club (1819), and he was an early member of the Athenaeum (1824). Leake died at Hove in January, 1860, a little before his eighty-third birthday.

Leake's contribution to the historical geography of ancient Greece was a by-product of his professional work. His study of the geography of Asia Minor arose from a journey across the peninsula in January and February, 1801 when a member of the British Military Mission to Turkey and his subsequent return to Istanbul after convalescing at Alanya on the south coast following at attack of jaundice.[4] However, much of the historical geography in the book was compiled from ancient sources and modern travel writing. By contrast, Leake's research on the Peloponnese,[5] Epirus, Thessaly and Macedonia[6] was based on personal observations made during his two independent missions, 1804–7 and 1809–10. This work is the focus of the present chapter.

For his first independent mission Leake was instructed to gather military and political intelligence, as well as to advise the Ottoman authorities about improving the coastal fortresses. His second mission had a much more diplomatic character, but he was also instructed to collect intelligence about political changes in Albania. Both missions, but the first in particular, required Leake to visit many parts of Greece. On his journeys he collected information about local social and economic conditions, the political

---

[4] W.M. Leake, *Journal of a Tour in Asia Minor with Comparative Remarks on the Ancient and Modern Geography of that Country* (London, 1824; reprinted Hildesheim and New York, 1976).
[5] W.M. Leake, *Travels in the Morea*, 3 vols. (London, 1830).
[6] W.M. Leake, *Travels in Northern Greece*, 4 vols. (London, 1835).

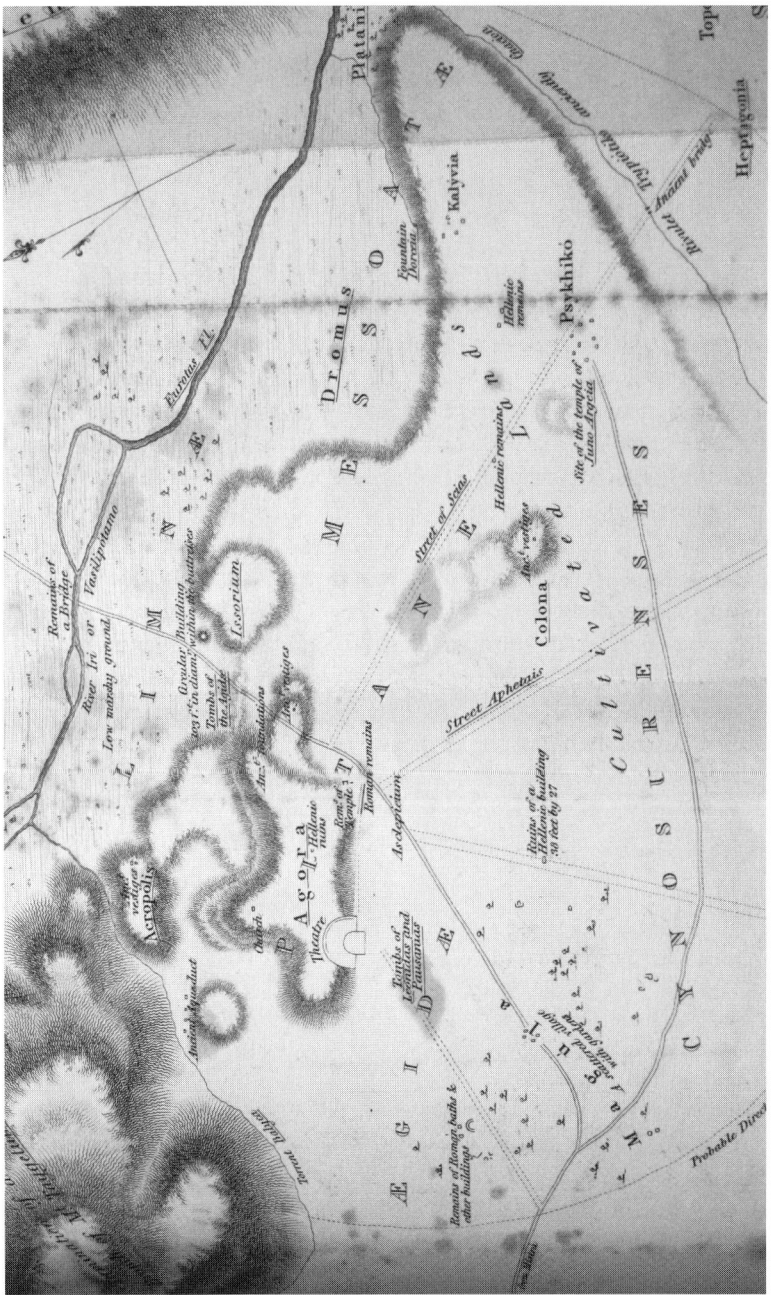

Fig. 5. Plan of Sparta [detail] illustrating William Martin Leake's cartographical style (W.M. Leake, *Travels in the Morea* (London, 1830), courtesy of the Joint Library of the Hellenic and Roman Societies)

situation and administrative arrangements, as well as the landing places on the west coast, the routes into the interior, the fortresses and other aspects of what he called the military geography of the regions traversed. I will come back to this later. Leake also used his travels to pursue an interest in ancient geography. He was not unique in this, of course. Other western travellers in Greece at the time shared Leake's interest, the outcome of an education based on the ancient Latin and Greek authors.

**Ancient Greece**

Leake's observations provided the basic raw materials for his research on the geography of ancient Greece. They were supplemented, partly in the field and partly in his London study, by an amazing command of the ancient literary sources, a characteristic especially commended by Tozer.[7] A major source was Pausanias, especially for the topography of ancient Athens and the geography of the Peloponnese and part of central Greece. The sources are more fragmentary for other parts of the country but include the major Greek and Roman historians. Occasionally, Leake was frustrated by a lack of sources, notably for Epirus: '… it is a mortifying disappointment to the geographer', he wrote, 'to be unable to apply a single name with absolute certainty, so scanty are the notices of Epirus in ancient history …'.[8]

The publications, which resulted from Leake's fieldwork and literary exegesis, can be divided into two sets. The first and largest set consists of two major works, his *Topography of Athens*[9] and his *Numismata Hellenica*,[10] but also includes papers on the 'Trojan controversy',[11] the price Edict of Diocletian,[12] ' the stade, as a linear measure',[13] Cos,[14] ancient Syracuse,[15]

---

[7] See Tozer, *Lectures on the Geography of Greece*, 33.
[8] See Leake, *Travels in Northern Greece*, vol. IV, 73.
[9] London, 1821; second edition, London, 1841.
[10] London 1856; second edition, 1859.
[11] W.M. Leake, 'Remarks on the Trojan Controversy', *The Classical Journal*, 18 (1818), 141–50.
[12] W.M. Leake, 'On an Edict of Diocletian, Fixing a Maximum of Prices Throughout the Roman Empire, A.D., 303', *Transactions of the Royal Society of Literature*, 1 (1829), 181–204.
[13] W.M. Leake, 'On the Stade, as a Linear Measure', *Journal of the Royal Geographical Society*, 1838.
[14] W.M. Leake, 'Memoir on the Island of Cos. Inscriptions from the Island of Cos', *Transactions of the Royal Society of Literature*, second series, 1 (1843), 1–19.
[15] W.M. Leake, 'Topographical and Historical Notes on Syracuse: with Two Plans', *Transactions of the Royal Society of Literature*, second series, 3 (1850), 237–76.

Caesar's campaign in Greece,[16] Kythera,[17] and, following the publication of Dr. Smith's *Dictionary of Ancient Geography*, on 'some disputed questions of ancient geography',[18] as well as numerous shorter articles and letters on ancient Greek inscriptions. The second set of publications contains Leake's major travel works, *Travels in the Morea* (1830, with a supplement, *Peloponnesiaca* 1846) and *Travels in Northern Greece* (1835). There is no space to write about Leake's papers and articles in the first set. *Numismata Hellenica* is a catalogue of Leake's coin collection, but he published it 'to make these monuments of ancient Greece as conducive as possible to the illustration of its geography, art, mythology, and history'.[19] It need detain us no further. The *Topography of Athens* is an attempt to reconstruct the townscape of Athens at the time of Pausanias, the antiquarian traveller of the second half of the first century A.D. I have dealt with this elsewhere.[20] However, it is worth mentioning that the second volume of the second edition (1841) incorporates the *Demi of Attica*, an essay published originally in 1829.[21] It deals, first, with the geography of ancient Attica (natural divisions, mountains, plains, rivers), ancient political divisions and then the location of the ancient *demi*, together with anything else which was then known about them. Appendices include discussions of the battles of Marathon and Salamis. On Marathon, just to take one example,[22] Leake summarises Herodotus' account of the battle, but then tries to sort out the topography of the Graeco-Persian encounter, comparing the 'narrative of Herodotus with the map of Attica, and with the topographical plan of the district of Marathon which is annexed to these remarks.'[23] Leake and John Squire, an officer in the Royal Engineers, investigated and mapped the plain in 1802, when they were on their way home from Egypt, but Leake visited it again briefly on 29 January, 1806.[24]

[16] W.M. Leake, 'On the Military Operations of Caesar in Greece, Ending with the Battle of Pharsalia', *Transactions of the Royal Society of Literature*, 2nd series, 4 (1851), 68–87.
[17] W.M. Leake, 'Some Remarks on the Island of Cerigo, Anciently Cythera', *Transactions of the Royal Society of Literature*, second series, 4 (1851), 255–60.
[18] W.M. Leake, *On Some Disputed Questions of Ancient Geography* (London, 1857).
[19] See W.M. Leake, *Numismata Hellenica*, vii.
[20] J.M. Wagstaff, 'Pausanias and the Topographers: the Case of Colonel Leake', in S.E. Alcock, J.F. Cherry and J. Elsner (eds.), *Pausanias: Travel and Memory in Roman Greece* (Oxford, 2001), 190–206.
[21] W.M. Leake, 'On the Demi of Athens', *Transactions of the Royal Society of Literature*, 1 (1829), 114–283.
[22] W.M. Leake, *The Topography of Athens*, second edition, vol. II (London, 1841), 203–8.
[23] Leake, *The Topography of Athens*, vol. II, 209.
[24] W.M. Leake, *Travels in Northern Greece*, vol. II (London, 1835), 431–2.

From their titles, Leake's travel works seem to be representative of a literary genre popular at the time. They are more than that. In fact, Leake used the classic daily travel journal as a framework on which to hang comments on ancient geography and contemporary conditions. As far as ancient geography is concerned, examination of his texts reveals that he had four tasks:

1) to locate the topographical names mentioned in the ancient sources in the early nineteenth-century landscape;

2) to allocate an ancient name, dedication or function to the ruins which he either simply saw or visited;

3) to describe what he saw on the ancient sites visited, explored or even, on occasion, planned;

4) to provide an outline of the regional geography of ancient Greece and, occasionally, to locate ancient battlefields such as Pharsalia and Thermopylae.

His method was essentially straightforward. Leake carefully collated the topographical information in the ancient authors and then compared it with the land as he had seen it himself.

As an example of Leake's approach to the problem of locating an ancient place name, I should like to outline possibly his greatest failure. This is his solution to one of the intellectual problems of the time,[25] namely the location of Dodona, the site in Epirus of an oracle of Zeus. Although Leake was proved wrong, we can see how he worked. Leake recognised immediately that he could offer 'nothing more than an opinion' on its location, as 'Dodona has neither been described by any ancient author, so as to be recognised by such description, nor have any remains or monuments been yet discovered tending to supply the deficiency. Hence, Dodona is now the only Greek city of great celebrity, the situation of which is not exactly known by means of a comparison of ancient history with actual appearances: and hence an opinion upon the question of its site, cannot have any better basis than the negative argument, that there is no other situation in which *Dodona* can be placed so as to accord with the mention made of it in history, or as to allow of

---

[25] Lord Byron, 'Childe Harold's Pilgrimage', Second Canto, 53:
   Oh! where, Dodona is thine aged grove,
   Prophetic fount, and oracle divine?
Originally published in 1812. W.M. Rossetti (ed.), *The Poetical Works of Lord Byron* (London and New York, n.d.), 31. J. Hawkins, 'On the Vale of Tempe', in R. Walpole (ed.), *Memoirs Relating to European and Asiatic Turkey* (London, 1817), 517–27.

a consistent adjustment to the several tribes of Epirus to the modern map' than the one selected.[26] Coins and inscriptions were not available to confirm the identification. Leake was totally dependent upon the available literary and topographical evidence. He reviewed this in just over 31 pages of printed text, concluding that Dodona must be identified with 'the extensive remains' at Kastritza, a steep-sided and craggy outcrop of limestone towards the southern end of the lake of Ioannina.[27] In the course of his review Leake produced an overview of the geography of ancient Epirus, which is fairly typical of his work.

> ... commercial republics, colonized or augmented, and supported by the wealth and alliance of some of the principal states of southern Greece, occupied the entire coast of Epirus. Towards the Ambracic gulf, the descendents of Molossus were confined to the mountains by Ambracia, this noble position having attracted settlers from the Peloponnesus at a very early period, and having received, in the eighth century B.C., a second colony consisting of Corinthians, which people about the same time occupied several places in Acarnania. In the Peloponnesian war, all the maritime part of Epirus, including Thesprotia and Chaonia, was republican, while the mountainous districts of the interior, inhabited by warriors, pastors, and cultivators of the soil, still preserved the monarchical form of government ... [He cites Thucydides here].

> The extent and situation of the proper Molossia are clearly described by Scylax. After having stated that the coasts of Thesprotia and of Cassopaea were each half a day's sail in length, that the Cassopaei extended to the Anactoric, meaning the Ambracic gulf, that the gulf was a little less than half a day's sail in length from the στόμα, or strait of Prévyza, to the μυχὸς, or eastern extremity; he adds that the Molossi bordered on the Cassopaei, that their sea-coast was 50 stades in length, and that next to it was the shore of Ambracia, extending 120 stades to that of Amphilochi. The latter distance is confirmed by Dicaearchus; and as the entire length of the northern coast of the gulf from the shore of Lámari, which was the eastern boundary of the *Cassopaei*, to Makinóro, which was the frontier of *Ambracia*, and *Amphilochia*, agrees sufficiently with the total of 170 stades, we can have no hesitation in assigning about three miles of the shore on either side of the mouth of the river of St. George as the position and extent of the *Molossic* sea coast.[28]

In fact, Leake had visited, described and planned what turned out to be the actual site of Dodona. This was a place known, 'as usual', as

---

[26] Leake, *Travels in Northern Greece*, vol. IV, 168.
[27] The ruins have been identified as those of ancient Tekmona, R. Barber (ed.), *Blue Guide: Greece*, sixth edition (London, 1995), 446.
[28] Leake, *Travels in Northern Greece*, vol. IV, 177–9.

Paleokastro and it was located in the valley below Alepukhori and near Dhramisius.[29] However, Leake reasoned that this could not be the site of Dodona: the lack of defensive walls, the situation in a narrow valley and the deficient water supply meant that the site was not that of the expected town; though the 'nature of the buildings' suggested that it might have been an Ἱερὸν and place of public assembly for the country of the *Molossi*.[30] Leake offered no alternative identification for the site.

As an example of the reverse process, assigning a name to an ancient site, we can take the case of the remains at Neokhori. Ali Pasha had recently established this particular new village a little inland from the Gulf of Arta, the Ambracic Gulf of Antiquity. Nearby, 'on the last fall of the mountains', Leake found the 'ruins of an ancient city'. The site was largely overgrown with trees, but traces of defensive walls and the remains of a possible temple could be seen. Leake was disappointed at not being able to find any 'fragment of sculpture'. No inscription seemed to survive either on the site or in the two neighbouring churches, the type of building where such material had often been reused. Leake makes no reference to any coin finds.[31] The paucity of archaeological data again forced Leake to reason his way to an identification on the basis of topographical information in Strabo, Thuydides, Polybius and Livy, supplemented by his identification of other places in the region and some information on other extensive remains in the area provided by Captain Mitji Kondoianni, who commanded 200 *armatoli* based nearby.[32] He concluded that the site was that of *Argos Amphilochium* and Hammond subsequently proved him right.[33]

Descriptions of ancient sites are numerous in Leake's *Travels*. They are often brief, but they become quite long where there was much to document. A short example, to give some of the favour, is an 1805 description of Gythium, a site situated near a small port then called Marathonisi.

'The remains of *Gythium*, called Palèopoli, are situated in a valley terminating in the sea …'. Ninety yards inland from the shore were 'the remains of a theatre, constructed of a semi-translucent kind of white marble, of a very coarse grain, and marked with broad parallel streaks of brown'. The diameter was about 150 feet. Behind the theatre, on the eastern

---

[29] Leake, *Travels in Northern Greece*, vol. I, 264.
[30] Leake, *Travels in Northern Greece*, vol. I, 268.
[31] Leake, *Travels in Northern Greece*, vol. IV, 238–9.
[32] Leake, *Travels in Northern Greece*, vol. IV, 239–52.
[33] N.G.L. Hammond, *Epirus: The Geography, the Ancient Remains, the History and the Topography of Epirus and Adjacent Areas* (Oxford, 1967), 239–40.

side of the principal height, Leake observed 'several remains of buildings, in the Roman style, with tiles and mortar, and some courses of rough stones between layers of mortar'. These included 'a long building divided longitudinally into two, each division having an arched roof, which has fallen', and the 'remains of some baths'. 'Other masses of Roman buildings' were located towards the sea. 'Some foundations of large buildings' projected into the water and could be traced below sea level. Coins and fragments of architecture were often brought to light by the peasants in the cornfields of the plain. The ruined structures were being plundered to build nearby Marathonisi, a comparatively recent foundation.[34]

The site of Gythium is recognisable today, though the plundering of the site continued for over a hundred years and when I lived in Yithion, as Marathonisi was re-named, some forty years ago an army camp blocked much exploration. Like the accounts of ancient sites by other travellers of the eighteenth and nineteenth centuries, Leake's descriptions are valuable because they indicate what was still extant at the time of his visit. Most of his identifications have stood the test of time, despite his failure over Dodona. For example, in 44 cases of identifications made in volumes 1 and 2 of his *Travels in Northern Greece* where I have been able to check his identifications reasonably easily, I found that he was correct in all but 6 cases, a success rate of 86 per cent. Moreover, Leake's command of the ancient literary sources and his detailed knowledge of the topography, as well as his 'sound judgement and great sagacity',[35] mean that his views still command respect. The result of his efforts, much approved in his own time, was a type of historical geography where the prime objective was the location of places, both in absolute terms and also in relation to each other. Leake was not concerned to reconstruct total regional syntheses of the sort commended by Gilbert as the objective of historical geography,[36] though post-modernists might be able to read his texts for his imaginative geographies of ancient Greece.[37] Although he had something to say about the spatial organisation of ancient society and economy, this does not amount to an attempt at human regional geography. Materials for such a project are there, nonetheless, in the Leake's data about early nineteenth-century Greece.

---

[34] W.M. Leake, *Travels in the Morea* (London, 1830), 244–6.

[35] W. Smith (ed.), *A Dictionary of Greek and Roman Geography*, second edition (London, 1873), 1017.

[36] E.W. Gilbert, 'What is Historical Geography?', *Scottish Geographical Magazine*, 48 (1932), 129–36.

[37] R.A. Butlin, *Historical Geography: Through the Gates of Space and Time* (London, 1993), 62–8.

## Early Nineteenth-Century Greece

'Among the travellers he [Leake] is without doubt the most trustworthy as an historical source, richer in all kinds of information, and remarkably consistent', wrote Helen Angelomatis-Tsougarakis,[38] echoing the view of other contemporary scholars. Some of Leake's information is clearly geographical in character, such as his regional-scale descriptions of landscape or his weather observations and his comments on climate, while his concern with military geography led him to attempt to understand the relative disposition of different kinds of terrain and the location of the various natural route ways. Much of his other data, however, also has geographical potential in that they are spatially referenced, that is: they are spatially located and have spatial form and spatial extent. Leake describes the administrative organisation of the different regions visited, notes the principal settlements, indicates the size of population and its composition (Muslim/Christian, Greek/Albanian/Vlach), produces figures on taxation, and sketches the patterns of social relations and the types of local economy (including manufacturing and trade, as well as farming). Some of the data occur as sporadic observations in the daily journal, for example on land use. Other data are found in extended descriptions of places and areas. All the texts, however, must be read carefully to extract the geographical information, preferably using the procedures formalised as *content analysis*.[39] Attempts should always be made to map Leake's data, for this exercise reveals both its potential and also its limitations.

As an example of Leake's data we can consider his descriptions of the *Kaza* of Ioannina and the district of Ágrafa.

'The kazá of Yénya (as the Turks call Ioánnina) is divided into four nahiyé', Leake tells us. He goes on to provide the names of the *nahiyés* and to locate each of them. He notes that there is a total of 184 settlements and gives the names of the principal places, with an indication of their population size in terms of the number of houses. This looks fine, until one tries to map the settlement data and thereby turn them into geographical information about the settlement patterns of the *kaza*. Problems then emerge. First, it is difficult to locate all the names on modern topographical maps, partly because names have changed since the Ottoman occupation ended in 1913 and partly because Leake's own

---

[38] H. Angelomatis-Tsougarakis, *The Eve of the Greek Revival: British Travellers' Perception of Early Nineteenth-Century Greece* (London, 1990), 20.

[39] K. Krippendorf, *Content Analysis: An Introduction to its Methodology* (Beverly Hills and London, 1980); D.W. Moodie, 'Content Analysis: a Method for Historical Geography', *Area*, 3 (1970), 146–9.

map of Northern Greece is on too small a scale to be really useful in the exercise. Secondly, some places may have lost relative status over time and are now difficult to find anyway. Third, it is clear that in focusing upon what he named as the principal places (31 out of a total of 184, or 16.8 per cent), Leake has not only omitted the majority of the settlements but also tended to give a distorted impression of the Ioannina district.

Leake's account of Τὰ Ἄγραφα is fuller since it includes information not only on settlements but also on the economy.[40] Ágrafa is '... the largest of the traditional districts of the Píndhos' and '... one of the most difficult areas to penetrate in Greece'.[41] Leake writes in 1810, Ágrafa 'may be described as comprehending the mountains bordering on *Thessaly* which connect *Pindus* with *Othrys* as well as with *Oeta* ...'.[42] He goes on to define its borders and to give its dimensions – about 50 English miles south-east to north-west and about 35 miles across. He says there are 85 villages and 7,685 houses in which, fifteen years before (*c*.1795), there were more than 50,000 inhabitants but the number – in 1810 – is 'supposed to be somewhat reduced'. Leake knows of 15 large and many smaller monasteries. He names, however, only 13 villages (15.3 per cent of the total) and 5 monasteries. Even these are difficult to locate on the modern topographical map. Leake also knew of the remains of 18 Hellenic cities and fortresses.

'Although Ágrafa consists of mountains and narrow rocky valleys' Leake continues, 'industry, security, and in some parts a fertile soil' enable the people to export 'several kinds of agricultural produce to the rich but desolate districts around them' and he gives figures for the export of wine, butter, cheese, wool, silk, sheep and goats, oxen and cows, together with the prices per unit. Local corn production, he notes, was about a sixth short of requirements.[43] Leake goes on,

> the villages which are least favoured in respect of soil have resources in the manufacture of various articles of cotton and wool, such as coarse cloths, shawls for the head and girdle, and towels. It is reckoned that one-third of the inhabitants of Ágrafa gain a livelihood by weaving. There are also many workers in gold and silver; and at Skalátina is a fabric of sword-blades, gun-barrels, and locks of pistols, which last are sold at 15 piastres each. A large proportion of the Agrafiótes, like other mountaineers of Greece,

---

[40] Leake, *Travels in Northern Greece*, vol. IV, 266–79.
[41] Naval Intelligence Division, *Geographical Handbook Series: Greece* (London, 1942), vol. 3, 17 and 18. Leake's *Travels* were major sources for volumes 1 and 3.
[42] Leake, *Travels in Northern Greece*, vol. IV, 268.
[43] Leake, *Travels in Northern Greece*, vol. IV, 272–8.

gain a livelihood abroad as shopkeepers or artisans, or as carriers in the neighbouring districts.[44]

Now, Leake never went to Ágrafa. His account, therefore, raises in acute form the questions of his sources and their reliability. The most obvious sources are the local officials to whom Leake had privileged access because of his official status and, in Central Greece, the support of Ali Pasha. He had meetings with them; he sometimes stayed in their houses. But did they open their records? Other informants were village headmen, doctors, schoolmasters and his escorts and guides. Leake admits, however, that he consulted local literary works. For example, he copied 'a poetical description of Mani' which he was shown at Mistra. About a third of it consists of a catalogue of 117 villages, each with a brief description.[45] He also possessed printed copies of the eighteenth-century geographies of Meletios, Bishop of Athens, and the priest-academic, Daniel Philippedos, from Melies in Pelion. Although he found mistakes in their ancient geography, he nonetheless used their information about modern conditions, as for example in discussing climate. The problem of reliability remains, though. It needs to be tested. Considerable critical work is required, using the accounts of contemporary travellers such as Dodwell and Gell, as well Greek and Ottoman administrative and legal sources.

Leake noted the geographical outcomes of several socio-economic processes. These include labour migration (as mentioned in the case of Ágrafa), settlement desertion, transhumance between the Pindhos and the plains of Thessaly and what has been called *çiftlikisation*.[46] Çiftlikisation was widespread in the Balkans and it has been a topic of considerable interest to modern scholars. It is the process by which a community of independent farmers, collectively responsible for their tax obligations, was transformed into a community of sharecroppers where the taxes were paid on its behalf from the major share of the harvest taken by the landowner. On several occasions Leake described how pauperisation and communal debt led to the establishment of *çiftliks*. Thus, he selected the village of Siúrpi, near Armyro (Almiro), as an example of what he called 'the ordinary process' by which Greek villages were reduced in a few years from a comparatively flourishing state and

---

[44] Leake, *Travels in Northern Greece*, vol. IV, 273.
[45] W.M. Leake, *Travels in the Morea* (London, 1830), vol. I, 332–9.
[46] S. Faroqhi, *Approaching Ottoman History: an Introduction to the Sources* (Cambridge, 1999), 101–3.

often to complete desertion or conversion from an *eliftherokhorio* into a *tjiftlik* (*çiftlik*):⁴⁷

- the community became unable to pay the tax and borrowed at 12 per cent interest from urban-based Albanians or Turks
- the creditors came to receive their annual interest and quartered upon the village until the money was forthcoming; since it was seldom ready, they consumed the villagers' produce, making them still poorer
- some families left, leaving the remainder to carry an increased burden of repayment
- eventually the community became unable to pay in cash and so agreed to pay in kind
- the final step would be for Ali Pasha, or one of his sons, to take over the village's debt on condition of its becoming his *çiftlik*, that is the villagers give up their land in return for sharecropping contracts
- Ali, or his son, would then compound with the creditors to pay the interest at an easy rate from his share of the harvest.

Leake also observed how long-abandoned, overgrown land was brought into production again with labour imported from outside as sharecroppers and, in so doing, he provided perhaps the earliest description of the distinctive form of *çiftlik* village recognised later by the Serbian geographer, Jovan Cvijić.⁴⁸

At 4.35 on 21 December 1806, Leake arrived at a *çiftlik* on the site of ancient Dion in Macedonia.⁴⁹ It had been 'lately established' by Veli Pasha, Ali Pasha's son. Greek labourers had been sent, together with an Albanian manager. A small tract of arable had been cleared by burning the scrub of *paliúri* (Jerusalem Thorn, *Paliurus spina-christi* Miller). 'The houses are built on three sides of a quadrangle with a fountain in the centre', Leake wrote in his journal. 'One of the rows of houses has been occupied by strangers since the place fell into Vely P.'s hands, since it is the policy of the Vizir and his sons to attract Christians to cultivate their farms by giving them some advantage which they have not elsewhere, the principal of which is that of not being subject to konaks [free board and lodging for officials, soldiers and their mounts]. Vely has allowed them to build a church here, an indulgence which Ali also never refuses'.

---

⁴⁷ Leake, *Travels in Northern Greece,* vol. IV, 339–40.
⁴⁸ J. Cvijić, *La Péninsule Balkanique: Géographie humaine* (Paris, 1918), 222–4.
⁴⁹ Leake, Manuscript Journal No. 1 (Cambridge University, Library of the Faculty of Classical Studies); Leake, *Travels in Northern Greece,* vol. III, 408.

Leake was not unique among western travellers of the eighteenth-nineteenth century in providing spatially referenced material, which can be used to reconstruct the historical geography of the period. His significance lies in his spatial coverage, together with the amount and consistency of the detail provided. He travelled in the Mani at the southern tip of the mainland, as well as in the Strimonas valley in the north. Attica, Epirus, the Peloponnese and Thessaly were familiar to him, and he visited a number of the Ionian and Aegean islands. He lived for months in Ioannina and Salonica, then the principal cities of the territories which later became the Greek state, but he knew provincial centres like Tripolitsa (Tripolis), Larissa and Athens as well, and he had passed through and stayed in numerous obscure villages, both in the mountains and the plains. The data he collected were wide-ranging and carefully presented. His major deficiencies as a writer are a plain, sparse style and a general lack – though not a total absence – of evocative descriptions of landscape. His books contain maps and plans, but no landscape drawings, and the scholar must look elsewhere for such material.

## Conclusion

Colonel Leake was not really ahead of his time as a scholar. Like many of his contemporaries, his prime interest was in recreating a framework of known and located places as a basis for understanding the history of ancient Greece. It was a geography largely of towns, but also of military and political events. As far as I am aware, he never defined a period of study, but wrote frequently about 'Hellenic' settlements and remains, distinguishing Roman from earlier and later building techniques, but he also gave Homeric references where appropriate. In other words, Leake worked in a long-established tradition of Classical and Biblical scholarship. His geography of ancient Greece was the geography behind a certain kind of history.[50] It depended ultimately upon the techniques of literary criticism developed earlier in the Enlightenment.

By contrast, Leake's accounts of the contemporary scene suggest that his thinking may have been moving in a new direction. He remained interested in the location and naming of places; he carefully recorded his travel times, took compass bearings and made geodesic observations

---

[50] See Gilbert, 'What is Historical Geography?'. He cites A. E. Zimmern, *The Greek Commonwealth: Politics and Economics in Fifth-Century Athens* (Oxford, 1911). See also Butlin, *Historical Geography*, 2–12.

so that he could construct maps. What we might recognise as 'terrain analysis' was fundamental to his military geography. But Leake was also concerned to publish factual data about other aspects of Greece, which he had collected during his official missions and which give a picture of the country as he found it before the Uprising of 1821. In the course of this work, he set out what he thought were the relationships between different phenomena and described the causal processes, which he believed were at work. Labour migration, for example, he recognised as the result of harsh living conditions, whether environmental (as in the mountains, where resources were limited) or generated by the exploitation and oppression of the Muslim ruling class. Transhumance was similarly described as a response to the winter cold and snow of the high mountains, on the one hand, and the availability of milder weather and under-used land in the plains and coastal areas, on the other. Leake realised that *çiftlikisation* was an economic, social and political process. But his data show, what he did not point out himself, that it was characteristic of the low-lying areas of central and northern Greece, though not absent elsewhere. In other words, Leake was feeling towards the 'richer view of geography' set out by Thomas Arnold (1795–1842) somewhat later than the publication of his travels.[51] Best known now as the reforming headmaster of Rugby School, Arnold had found time to produce an edition of Thucydides (1830–35), especially valuable for its geographical notes.[52] In the third of his *Introductory Lectures on Modern History* as the Regius Professor in 1842, Arnold stressed both the importance of a 'plan-like knowledge of geography' – 'a knowledge of the relative position and distance of places from one another' – and also of 'the real geography of a country, its organic structure if I may so call it: the form of its skeleton, that is, of its hills: the magnitude and course of its veins and arteries, that is of its steams and rivers: let me conceive of it as of a whole made up of connected parts; and then the position of man's dwellings, viewed in reference to those parts …'. 'A real and lively knowledge of geography brings the whole character of a country before our eyes and enables us to understand its influence upon the social and political condition of its inhabitants'.[53] Thomas Arnold has been credited with founding the study of historical geography in Britain.[54] Perhaps Leake has a prior claim!

[51] T. Arnold, *Introductory Lectures on Modern History* (Oxford, London, 1842), 163.
[52] *Dictionary of National Biography*, vol. 1, 585–9.
[53] See Arnold, *Introductory Lectures on Modern History*, 158–9, 167.
[54] J.N.L. Baker, 'The Development of Historical Geography in Britain during the Last Hundred Years', *Advancement of Science*, 8 (1951–2), 406–12; J.N.L. Baker, 'The History of Geography in Oxford', in his *The History of Geography* (Oxford, 1963), 119–29.

# PART THREE

# The Politics of Historiographical Development

# 8. The Rise and Fall of the Roman Historian: The Eighteenth Century in the Roman Historical Tradition

*Gareth Sampson*

For students and scholars of the Roman Republic, modern scholarship on the subject starts with the various works of Mommsen in the late nineteenth century.[1] Any scholarship before Mommsen is ignored, or dismissed as not worthy of consideration, and lies neglected and unread in the special collections of our great libraries. If any scholars from the period before Theodor Mommsen are known, then it would be Edward Gibbon and Barthold Niebuhr. Yet this view automatically dismisses some three hundred years of scholarship on the subject and has resulted in two serious side effects. Firstly, the vast majority of Roman historians have no knowledge of the works that preceded Mommsen and therefore are completely unaware whether they are replicating material and approaches that have already been examined.[2] Secondly, this scholarship has been allowed to be classified as fodder for classical traditionalists or those who work in the oddly-named field of 'reception'. By their very nature these classifications have served to cut off this scholarship from the mainstream field of historical study. This paper will trace the development of the genre of Roman historical scholarship in the eighteenth century and argue that it formed the bedrock of the modern discipline. Furthermore, it will act as a guide for the modern Roman historian to the various works that exist in this field and attempt to introduce them in terms of subject matter and give some indication of the overall value and usefulness of the works.

Before we can begin this process, we must return to the two figures that do more to obscure this subject than any other; namely Edward Gibbon and Barthold Niebuhr. In terms of the areas of eighteenth-century scholarship and Rome, Edward Gibbon's name is usually the first one that

---

[1] Most notably T. Mommsen, *Römische Geschichte* (Berlin, 1854–6).
[2] A notable exceptions to this trend was Arnoldo Momigliano. Currently Ronald Ridley and John Rich are also working in this field.

is most celebrated and most frequently cited.[3] To say that this is unhelpful would be an understatement. Gibbon's famous work *The Decline and Fall of the Roman Empire* is completely atypical of the scholarship on Roman history from the eighteenth century.[4] For a start, it came at the end of nearly a century's worth of Roman scholarship and at a time when the mainstream research was waning, through death and intellectual subject exhaustion. Secondly, the subject matter was the Roman Empire, when the vast majority of work in this century was conducted on the Roman Republic (far outweighing any of the other fields of ancient history). Thirdly, the very style of his work, the grand sweeping narrative and the choosing of a time period that had few remaining ancient sources (especially in considering those of the Roman Republic), were atypical of the rest of the century's output.[5] It was this new style which elevated Gibbon's work out of the field of Roman history and into that of a literary classic, where it remains today. Regardless of the work itself, we need to realise that there is far more to eighteenth-century Roman scholarship than Gibbon.

Next, we have the figure of the renowned scholar Barthold Niebuhr, who is widely, and perhaps wrongly, acknowledged as the first great Roman historian. Niebuhr's volumes of Roman history certainly started a new phase of scholarship on Rome,[6] but they did not create the discipline, as the 'myth' of the man and his works apparently now suggests.[7] Niebuhr's status as the first 'serious' and 'professional' historian of the period owes more to his university position than it does to anything else. The myth that has built up around Niebuhr was more the product of the university historians who followed him than the man himself. As anyone who reads his lectures soon discovers, Niebuhr was more than aware of the corpus of historians who preceded him, from the sixteenth century onwards, and his debt to them.[8]

---

[3] Even Professor Momigliano entitled one of his articles as 'An Eighteenth-Century Prelude to Mr Gibbon', *Sesto Contributo alla storia degli studi classici e del mondo antico* (Rome, 1980), 251–60.

[4] E. Gibbon, *The History of the Decline and Fall of the Roman Empire* (London, 1776–88).

[5] The only comparable works are the four volumes of Echard's Roman History, which covered the period from the foundation of Rome to the fall of Constantinople (c.753 B.C.–A.D. 1453). This project was not conceived as one piece of work, but a Roman history and three sequels (1695–1705), as detailed below. The series of works by Rollin, Crevier and Le Beau also covered the same period (again as detailed below).

[6] B. Niebuhr, *Römische Geschichte* (Berlin, 1811).

[7] An excellent example of this mythologising of Niebuhr can be found in A. Momigliano, 'Niebuhr and the Agrarian Problems of Rome', *History and Theory*, 21 (1982), 3–15.

[8] B. Niebuhr, *Lectures on the History of Rome,* trans. L. Schmitz (London, 1849), lecture x.

If we free our minds from the shackles of thinking that Niebuhr was the first professional Roman historian then we can analyse the eighteenth-century works and judge them on their own merit, rather than on the basis of an arbitrary chronological cut-off point. It can be argued that it was the eighteenth century that saw the creation of the discipline of Roman history and furthermore it was in this century that Roman history was at the centre of the political debates that raged across Northern Europe and were central to Enlightenment thought. From the House of Commons to the political philosophies of Voltaire, Rousseau and Montesquieu and ultimately through the French and American Revolutions, we find the use and misuse of Roman history.

Central to this process was a core of rigorous historical analysis, centred on several different, but interconnected schools of study, which transcended matters of nationality and religion and was powered by the scholars of Britain and France. Whilst their countries may have spent the majority of the eighteenth century at war, these two communities united to produce scores of historical works, either on specific periods or topics, or on a broader scale. A glance at the bibliography shows the number of works produced, all of which now lie sadly neglected, collecting dust in the special collections of our great libraries. Then, as today, there were a number of works produced whose substance (in terms of source use and clarity of analysis) were open to question, but the majority form an impressive collection of historical analysis.

The first question that must be considered is how and why this new wave of historiography came about. From the Renaissance onwards, learned men had produced tracts on various aspects of Roman history and culture.[9] One of the earliest of these was produced by Niccolo Machiavelli who, although more famous these days for his work *The Prince*, produced a treatise entitled *Discourses on the First Ten Books of Titus Livius*, which despite its title, offered the author's thoughts on the whole of the history of the Republic.[10] The work is an interesting one and a useful complement to Machiavelli's more famous political treatise, but remains more political analysis than history. Nevertheless, the mid to late sixteenth century saw the rise of a number of Italian scholars producing works on aspects of Roman history. Central to this process was the discovery of the remains of the Consular Fasti, the so-called 'Capitoline Marbles', in the Roman Forum in 1546. In terms of Roman political history, such a find outstrips even that of Pompeii and Herculaneum two centuries later.

---

[9] Though we must not forget the work done prior to the Renaissance by pioneering scholars such as Petrarch.
[10] N. Machiavelli, *Discorsi sopra la prima deca di Tito Livio* (Florence, 1531).

Table 1: Roman History before 1650 (in chronological order)

| Author | Title | Published |
|---|---|---|
| Machiavelli, N. | *Discorsi sopra la prima deca di Tito Livio* | Florence, 1531 |
| Machiavelli, N. | *Discourses on the First Ten Books of Titus Livius*, trans. H. Neville | London, 1531 |
| Mexia, P. | *Istoria Imperial y Cesarea* | Seville, 1547 |
| Sigonio, C. | *Regum, consultum, dictatorum ac censorum Romanorum Fasti* | Modena, 1550, 1555 |
| De Grouchy, N. | *De comitiis Romanorum libri tres* | Paris, 1555 |
| Sigonio, C. | *Fasti consulares ac triumphi acti* | Venice, 1556 |
| Panvinio, O. | *Fasti et triumphi Romani* | Venice, 1557 |
| Sigonio, C. | *De antiquo iure civium Romanorum* | Venice, 1560 |
| Pighius, S. | *Annales Magistratuum et Provinciarum* | Antwerp, 1599 |
| Mexia, P. | *The Historie of all the Roman Emperors beginning with Caius Iulius Caesar, and successiuely ending with Rodulph the second now raigning* | London, 1604 |
| Bellenden, W. | *Ciceronis Princeps* | Paris, 1608 |
| Bellenden, W. | *Ciceronis Consul, Senator, Senatusque Romanus* | Paris, 1612 |
| Raleigh, W. | *The Historie of the World in Five Books* | London, 1614 |
| Pighius, S. | *Annales Romanorum 1–3*, ed. A. Schottus | Antwerp, 1615 |
| Coeffeteau, N. | *Histoire Romaine depuis le Commencement de l'Empire d'auguste, jusqu'a Licinius* | Paris, 1621 |
| Cluverius, P. | *Italia Antiqua* | Leiden, 1624 |
| Bellenden, P. | *De Tribus Luminibus Romanorum* | Paris, 1633 |
| Mexia, P. | *The Imperiall historie: or The Lives of the Emperours, from Iulius Caesar, the first founder of the Roman Monarchy, unto this present yeere* | London, 1623 |

The most famous of these works were the editions of the Consular Fasti published by Carlo Sigonio, starting in 1550, which analysed the find and attempted to co-ordinate the names on the Fasti with the histories of Livy, with mixed results.[11] Sigonio stands out as the leading sixteenth-century Roman scholar, with dozens of works on various aspects of Roman constitutional history (as well as scores of other subjects) published between 1550 and his death in 1584.[12] Other scholars included Sigonio's principal rival Nicholas de Grouchy, and Onofrio Panvinio.[13] Special

---

[11] C. Sigonio, *Regum, consultum, dictatorum ac censorum Romanorum Fasti* (Modena, 1550, 1555) and *Fasti consulares ac triumphi acti* (Venice, 1556).

[12] See W. McCuaig, *Carlo Sigonio* (Princeton, 1989), 345–56 for a complete listing. This is an invaluable one volume work on Sigonio and his contemporaries.

[13] N. De Grouchy, *De comitiis Romanorum libri tres* (Paris, 1555), O. Panvinio, *Fasti et triumphi Romani* (Venice, 1557).

mention must be made of the Dutch scholar Stephanus Pighius who continued the work on the Consular Fasti to its logical conclusion by producing a comprehensive work on all known Republican magistrates, which was not bettered until Thomas Broughton in the 1950s.[14]

Yet despite all this activity, the scope of these works was limited, as, it must be said, was their impact. Primarily, these works were restricted to questions surrounding the Roman magistracies and in particular the Consulate itself. Although much more work needs to be done on their transmission, it does appear the impact of these Renaissance works on later Roman scholarship remained minimal. One notable exception was Stephanus Pighius, whose work on Roman magistrates continued to be used throughout the seventeenth, eighteenth and nineteenth centuries.[15]

From the end of the sixteenth until the late seventeenth century there appears to have been a change of emphasis in terms of the scholarship of the ancient world. This is best summed up by the reasons given by Laurence Echard, who in 1695 wrote what has long been believed to be the first 'modern' work on Roman history.[16] He gave two principal explanations for why he wrote a history of Rome. Firstly, there was the problem that none of the surviving ancient sources covered the period as a whole and that if one wanted to gain an understanding of the whole of the Roman period then they would have to combine a large number of disparate sources: 'But how extraordinary soever they are, they are either all Fragments, or else so unfinished, that a compleat Body of Roman History, for six or seven hundred Years, can never be gotten out of any one of 'em'.[17] The second reason he gave was that all modern scholars before him had produced works that either only dealt with Roman history as part of a wider history of the ancient world or had inadvertently mirrored the surviving ancient sources and only produced works on part of Roman history:

---

[14] S. Pighius, *Annales Magistratuum et Provinciarum* (Antwerp, 1599) and *Annales Romanorum* (Antwerp, 1615). For it's modern counterpart see T. Broughton, *Magistrates of the Roman Republic* (New York, 1952).

[15] The Pighius Fasti was reprinted in J. Graevius, *Thesaurus Antiquitatum Romanarum* II (Utrecht, 1694), as well as the appendices of the Roman histories of Catrou, Ozell, Bundy and Hooke. The latter meant that it was still in print into the 1830s.

[16] *The Roman History from the Building of the City to the Perfect Settlement of the Empire by Augustus* (London, 1695). *Eighteenth-Century British Historians* (New York, 2007), 95–103, has an up to date biography on Echard.

[17] L. Echard, *Roman History Preface*, quoting the seventeenth-century English, transliterated into the modern alphabet, but keeping the same spelling and capitalisations.

There never was any thing of this kind in our language before, nor any thing relating to the Roman Affairs, but either what has been intermix'd with much more other History, or what has contain'd but a few years of this Part. Of these I find none of any Note besides Raleigh, Ross, Howel, the Author of the History of the two Triumvirates, and Pedro Mexia, Author of the Imperial History; the last two of which are translations.[18]

Here, we have a clear statement detailing the works that proceeded Echard, which, at first glance, allows us to see how the historiographical process evolved. Of the five authors which Echard mentions, the three English authors are all 'universal histories' of the ancient world, which included sections on the Roman period. Of the three, the first, and by far the most famous, was *The Historie of the World in Five Books* by Sir Walter Raleigh, completed during a lengthy stay in the Tower of London between 1603 and 1616.[19] The book was one of the first early modern works of universal history, with the first two books focusing on biblical history and the final three on the history of Greece and Rome. His final book took Roman history down to the fall of Macedon in 167 B.C. Any further volumes were prevented by an unfortunate encounter with an executioner's axe in 1618. Raleigh's work long remained a key analysis of the ancient world; especially his insight into the Punic Wars, and was in print until the early twentieth century.

The two other names cited by Echard; those of Alexander Ross and William Howell were both in a similar vein. Ross' was a direct continuation of Raleigh's, picking up in 167 B.C., whilst Howell's was in the same mould.[20] Two other works mentioned by Echard – Pedro Mexia and the author of the Triumvirates work – are both of interest. Pedro Mexia was a Spaniard who wrote a history of the Roman Emperors in 1547, translated into English in 1604 and 1623, which provides us with a direct link to the Renaissance works.[21] The other work was a *History of the Triumvirates* by Samuel Broë, also known as Citry de la Guette, published

---

[18] Echard, *Roman History Preface*.
[19] W. Raleigh, *The Historie of the World in five books* (London, 1614).
[20] A. Ross, *The History of the World the Second Part in Six Books, being a Continuation of Famous History of Sir Walter Raleigh, Knight* (London, 1652), W. Howell, *The Elements of History from the Creation of the World, to the Reign of Constantine the Great* (London, 1670).
[21] P. Mexia, *Istoria Imperial y Cesárea* (Sevilla, 1545). There were two seventeenth-century English translations: *The Historie of all the Roman Emperors beginning with Caius Iulius Caesar, and successiuely ending with Rodulph the second now raigning* (London, 1604) and *The Imperial Historie: or The Lives of the Emperours, from Iulius Caesar, the First Founder of the Roman Monarchy, unto this present yeere* (London, 1623).

in French in 1681 and translated into English in 1686.[22] The latter is especially fascinating as it is one of the earliest modern specialised works on Roman history, yet has largely been ignored by modern scholarship.

With these works in mind, we can clearly see how Echard's history developed and the overall general trend concerning the scholarship of Rome. The sixteenth-century Renaissance scholars produced works on aspects of constitutional history. The seventeenth-century scholars developed the historiography of Rome in a fuller fashion and related it as part of a wider world history. Clearly Echard saw that to study Rome in detail, one needed to gain a fuller picture of the history of Rome as a whole.

Arnaldo Momigliano went further and labelled these early Roman histories (both Echard's and later that of the Abbé de Vertot),[23] as histories of revolution.[24] There is some truth in the matter, and he is quite right to pair up these early attempts at Roman history. Neither author was focused exclusively on Roman history or even the ancient world in general. Echard is more noted for his history of England,[25] whilst Vertot wrote a number of 'revolution' books.[26] Momigliano also acknowledged that strictly speaking Echard's work was not chronologically the first one on Roman history of the early modern 'pre-Niebuhrian' era. As he commented:

> When many years ago I tried to find which had been the first histories of Greece and Rome I ran into trouble. There seems to have been no Roman history before those by L. Echard (about 1695) and R.-A. Vertot (1719). In any case, the first really important work on the Roman Empire was *L'Histoire des Empéreurs* by S. de Tillemont, and this was only a critical collection of sources.[27]

---

[22] S. De Broé, *Histoire de Triumvirates* (Paris, 1681), published in English as *The History of the Triumvirates,* trans. T. Otway. (London, 1686).

[23] He makes no mention of William Wotton's *Roman History* (see below).

[24] A. Momigliano, 'Ancient History and the Antiquarian', *Journal of the Warburg and Courtauld Institutes*, 13 (1950), 294; Echard (about 1695) and Vertot (1719) introduced into Roman history the popular notion of history by revolution.

[25] L. Echard, *The History of England. From the First Entrance of Julius Caesar and the Romans, to the Conclusion of the Reign of King James the First* (London, 1707-17). Though there is a good recent work on his contribution to Roman history; R. Ridley, 'The Forgotten Historian, Laurence Echard and the First History of the Roman Republic', *Ancient Society*, 27 (1996), 277–315.

[26] He published works on the Revolutions in Sweden and Portugal as well as a work on the Knights Hospitallers.

[27] A. Momigliano, 'An Eighteenth-Century Prelude to Mr Gibbon', *Sesto Contributo alla storia degli studi classici e del mondo antico* (Rome, 1980), 254.

Louis-Sébastien de Tillemont did indeed write a history of the Roman Emperors, begun in 1690.[28] That Echard was not aware of this work is not strange in itself, as he had restricted himself to works in English only and de Tillemeont's was never translated. In fact de Tillemont's work was predated by a similar work by Nicolas Coeffeteau and both bring to mind the much earlier work of Pedro Mexia, although again little work has been done on the connections between these studies.[29]

However, of what Momigliano was unaware (like most scholars of this period), is that there is in an earlier history of Rome, which predates Echard, Tillemont and Broé. In 1675 a French scholar, Pierre Moret de la Fayolle, released a two volume history of Rome.[30] The work takes an annalistic form and details Roman history, in a reign by reign format, from the Alban kings down through the Republic until the Dictatorship of Caesar. Moret apparently took a similar line of reasoning to Echard in that his desire was to analyse the whole of Roman history and have all the ancient sources in one place. To say the work is obscure would not be to do it justice. Not only was Echard not aware of it, presumably due to its publication in French (there are no records of a translation), but the work was not consulted by any of the scholars that followed Echard. In fact, references to the work can only be found in eighteenth-century book catalogues, which apparently reveal a second edition in 1682, and encyclopaedias.[31] Momigliano is not alone in not knowing of this work as no other modern scholar who works in this field has yet acknowledged it in print.[32]

However, though Moret was the first scholar to produce a specific work on Roman history as a whole, it was Echard who had the greatest impact. In terms of historical scholarship the work suffers from being little more than a collection of all the relevant sources in one place, combined to produce a clear and unambiguous narrative. In fact, that is the work's key flaw: namely the uncritical manner in which he treats his sources, which, when combined in this way, should reveal a number of glaring discrepancies between the various individuals accounts. Nevertheless,

---

[28] L-S, de Tillemont, *Histoire des empereurs et autres princes qui ont régné pendant les six premiers siècles de l'Église* (1690–8).

[29] N. Coeffeteau, *Histoire Romaine depuis le Commencement de l'Empire d'auguste, jusqu'a Licinius* (Paris, 1621).

[30] P. Moret de la Fayolle, *Histoire de la République Romaine* (Paris, 1675).

[31] P. Bayle, *A General Dictionary, Historical and Critical: in which a new and accurate translation of that of the celebrated Mr. Bayle IV* (London, 1736), 202.

[32] I am indebted to Dr Ian Macgregor Morris for bringing these volumes to my attention and am grateful for the loan of them from his private collection.

this innovative new form of historical work, the grand Roman narrative, was a significant commercial success. It was this factor, combined with what his intellectual peers perceived to the work's poor scholarship that appears to have sparked off the revolution in ancient historical writing, particularly in the field of Roman history.[33] In short, a new genre had been established which attracted scholars on both an intellectual and commercial level.

Echard's history of the Republic was soon followed by three volumes on the Roman Empire with both series receiving a number of new editions.[34] Echard also returned to Raleigh's universal history and published a new abridged edition himself.[35] It is clear that Echard's works helped to create a new field of ancient history; the grand narrative covering the whole of the period and written for a mass market. Whilst it collected all the surviving sources in one place and wove them into a cohesive narrative, his scholarship lacked a critical cutting edge, with the sources themselves remaining unchallenged.

However, at the time of its publication, it must be pointed out that it was far from clear that Echard's work had created a whole new field. Certainly, his work had a far greater readership than that of Moret's, including a French edition, but there were still other competing genres of ancient history.[36] The most obvious one was the use of ancient history, again particularly the Roman Republic, in political treatises. Once again the origins of this practise are obscure, and it is always difficult to draw a dividing line between a political tract which uses ancient history and an ancient history which makes political points. Nevertheless, by the

---

[33] A good example of this can be found in the preface to Nathaniel Hooke's first volume of Roman history: 'the Author had an especial regard to those persons, who, wishing to be acquainted with the Roman history by reading it in English, found Mr Echard too brief to satisfy their curiosity'. N. Hooke, *The Roman History From the Building of Rome to the Ruin of the Commonwealth*, vol. I (London, 1738), i.

[34] L. Echard, *The Roman History from the Settlement of the Empire by Augustus Caesar, to the Removal of the Imperial Seat by Constantine the Great* (London, 1698), *The Roman History from the Removal of the Imperial Seat by Constantine the Great, to the Taking of Rome by Odacer and the Ruin of the Empire in the West & from the Ruin of the Western Empire to its Restitution by Charlemagne* (London, 1704), *The Roman History from the Restitution of the Western Empire by Charlemagne, to the taking of Constantinople by the Turks* (London, 1705).

[35] L. Echard, *An Abridgement of Sir Walter Raleigh's History of the World* (London, 1698).

[36] L. Echard, *Histoire Romaine Depuis La Fondation de Rome jusqu'a la translation de l'empire par Constantin 1–16*, trans. D. de Larroque and P. Desfontaines (Amsterdam, 1730–42).

seventeenth century, at least in British scholarship, we can see the rise of the political tract making use of ancient history.

This process was dramatically given a boost by the clashes between the crown and commons during the period of the civil wars in Britain, the Protectorate and Restoration. The best known examples of this process can be found in the works of James Harrington and John Milton.[37] Both the *Commonwealth of Oceana* and the two essays on the *Defence of the People of England* are full of references to Roman historical events and precede many common themes found throughout the eighteenth-century histories. The most obvious ones being the references to the overthrow of the king and the creation of the Republic, as well as the slaying of the 'tyrant', Caesar.[38] There are also references to numerous popular tribunes, as well as more obscure events from the early and middle Republic.

The growth of parliamentary power soon saw the growth of this type of historiographical-political history. One of the best examples of this being Jonathan Swift's pamphlet *A Discourse on the Contests and Dissensions between the nobles and commons in Athens and Rome*, where he argues that the Gracchi prove the dangers of populist politics and thus justify the system of rotten boroughs that were currently in place in England.[39] As a work of historical analysis it is obscured by the author's prejudicial views on the characters and events of Greece and Rome, but remains a classic example of how to misuse history for political purposes, and if nothing is an entertaining read. Given the clashes between crown and commons and the within the commons themselves between Whig and Tory, this genre of historical writing also flourished throughout the eighteenth century.

However, there is an inherent danger in assuming that all works on Roman history produced in the eighteenth century are nothing more than political works, rather than histories in their own right. The best example of this oversimplification is Addison Ward's 1960s article 'The Tory View of Roman History' where every eighteenth-century Roman historian has to be either a Whig or a Tory.[40] Certainly there was a far

---

[37] J. Harrington, *The Commonwealth of Oceana* (London, 1656). J. Milton, *A Defence of the People of England* (London, 1651) and *A Second Defence of the People of England* (London, 1654).

[38] Milton, *First Defence*, chapter 5.

[39] J. Swift, *A Discourse on the Contests and Dissensions between the nobles and commons in Athens and Rome with the consequences they had upon both those States* (London, 1701), 60–2.

[40] A. Ward, 'The Tory View of Roman History', *Studies in English Literature 1500–1900*, 4 (1964), 413–56. However, aside from this desire to fit all Roman historians into a framework of being either a Whig or a Tory, it presents a good overview of many of the important works.

closer connection between the politicians and historians of the period, but that reflected the greater status that men of education possessed and the circles that they moved in. The political tract utilising ancient history was merely one of the genres in this century, and it is the contention of this paper to argue that it was one that actually became less dominant as the century progressed. Aside from the main two genres of Roman historical writing this century (the long standing historiographical-political and the newer grand history), there are a sub category of works which appear to reflect the Renaissance concept of antiquarian works, which continued to collect information on Roman society or produce treaties on specific constitutional offices. Good examples of this can be seen with Kennet's popular work, the *Romae Antiquae Notitia* (first published in 1703) and then throughout the century and more obscure works, such as Nicholas Brunell's treatise on the Tribunate of the Plebs and Carolus Skunk's work on Consular Tribunate.[41]

Thus, at the start of the eighteenth century, Echard's work and the grand history of Rome, was merely the newest of three competing genres. However as the century progressed, it was the one that came to dominate the field. Following Echard, another English scholar, William Wooten, released another populist history of Rome, this time focussing on the mid-imperial era.[42] Wotton is remembered today, more for his involvement in the English arm of intellectual argument between the so-called 'Ancients and Moderns', over whether ancient or moderns society was the intellectual superior, than his Roman history.[43] More importantly, Wotton's Roman History, though limited in its timescale, from the Antonine to the Severan dynasty (A.D. 96–235), was an early attempt at critical analysis and did raise some questions over the sources for the period, though the work was preceded by that of de Tillemont.[44]

The next major work on Roman history came from a Frenchman, the Abbé René-Aubert Vertot, who produced a series of works on the various revolutions which affected the nations of Europe. In 1719, he produced the *Révolutions Romaine*, which focused on the theme of the

---

[41] B. Kennet, *Romae Antiquae Notitia* (London, 1703), N. Brunell, *De Tribunis Romanae Plebis* (Holmiae, 1698) and C. Skunk, *Tribuni Militum Consulari Potestate* (Upsala, 1697).

[42] W. Wotton, *A History of Rome, from the Death of Antoninus Pius, to the Death of Alexander Severus* (London, 1701).

[43] For an overview of this debate, see J. Levine, *The Battle of the Books: History and Literature in the Augustan Age* (Ithaca, 1991).

[44] There is a very useful modern work which comments upon both Echard's and Wotton's Roman History; Levine, *The Battle of the Books*, 344–6.

collapse of the Republic (a theme repeated throughout the works that followed).[45] As we have seen, Momigliano grouped Echard and Vertot together as historians of revolution and there is a great deal of truth in that. Nevertheless, both helped to forge a market for the grand Roman history and both inspired their peers. Vertot's work received its English translation in 1722 by a talented translator named John Ozell.[46] As yet these first two works (Echard and Vertot) were both written in isolation from each other and had been over twenty years apart. However, two developments in the 1720s saw this change and saw the foundation of the discipline of ancient history, focused on this Anglo-French axis (another new feature of this period). Both of these developments originated in France. The first was the publication of the first volumes of the twenty-volume *Histoire Romaine*, by the French priest François Catrou and his writing partner Pierre Rouille.[47] Their work began 1725 and produced volumes of Roman history from the time of the Kings to the end of the Republic and their books became the first of the great Roman histories. They were noted for its analysis of the various problems thrown up by the evidence, both in the text and in footnotes and the detailed referencing of the sources.

Not only was their work significant in itself, but it acted as a stimulus for further publications, which continued this sophisticated new level of historical analysis. However, this would not have been immediately apparent, as the initial response from England was far from encouraging. Two English scholars who both specialised in translating French works got themselves into a heated and highly public spat over who was going to translate this new work. Naturally Ozell assumed that the honour would be his, due to his work on the Vertot translation and was outraged to learn that another scholar, Richard Bundy, had also decided to publish a translation.[48] This led to Ozell publishing two polemical pamphlets on the shortcomings of his rival's work, including this cutting description of Bundy's work:[49] 'whoever buys this translation [Bundy's] will buy a pig in a poke and stones instead of bread to eat with'.[50] Ironically Ozell

---

[45] R.-A. Vertot, *Histoire des révolutions de la République Romaine* (Paris, 1719).
[46] R.-A. Vertot, *The History of the Revolutions that Happened in the Government of the Roman Republic*, trans. J. Ozell (London, 1722).
[47] F. Catrou and J. Rouille, *Histoire Romaine*, 20 vols. (Paris, 1725–37).
[48] F. Catrou and J. Rouille, *The Roman History*, 6 vols., trans. R. Bundy (London, 1728–37).
[49] J. Ozell, *Mr. Ozell's Defence Against the Remarks Publish'd by Peele and Woodward, under the name of the translators, on his translation of the Roman history* (London, 1725) and *No I. of the Herculean Labour: or, the Augæan Stable Cleansed of its Heaps of Historical, Philological and Geographical Trumpery* (London, 1729).
[50] Ozell, *No. 1. of the Herculean Labour*, 58.

is more remembered for these pamphlets than any of his other work. In many ways Ozell was proved right as the Bundy translation rendered the subtleties of Catrou's scholarship into dull narrative and fortunately disappeared without a trace within the literary community. Strangely, there is little mention of Ozell ever having published his translation despite the very fact that his first pamphlet was a defence of his own translation. This would not be surprising given the reputation he earned for being more concerned with Bundy's work than his own. However, at least four volumes of Ozell's Roman History saw print in 1725, covering Rome from its foundation to the dissolution of the Latin League.[51] It is not clear whether Ozell's Roman History ran to more than these four volumes.

However, it was the publication of Catrou's work and the controversy over the English translation that led to a further development; namely the entry into the field of Nathaniel Hooke. At the time Hooke was a minor scholar who had produced several translations of French quasi-religious works and was more known for his background; being the Catholic nephew of the more famous Nathaniel Hooke Snr, who was the chief agent of James II in exile and an author of the Jacobite rebellion of 1715.[52] Hooke not only believed that he could do a better job of translating Catrou's work into English than either Ozell or Bundy, but soon came to the conclusion that he could write a better Roman history than Catrou himself.[53] This led to his two volume work; *The Roman History From the Building of Rome to the Ruin of the Commonwealth,* which charted the history of Rome from the kings to the death of Gaius Gracchus, at which point he considered the Republic to have begun its inexorable slide into collapse.[54] This work represented the highpoint of Roman scholarship in the eighteenth century and was the standard text on Republican history in Britain until the 1830s, when it was supplanted only by the translations of Niebuhr.

His work was, and still is a fine example of historical analysis and set the standard for Roman histories in a number of ways. Firstly, he followed Catrou's lead in taking a highly critical analysis of the ancient sources, comparing the various inconstancies that occurred in the

---

[51] F. Catrou and J. Rouille, *The Roman History*, 4 vols., trans. J. Ozell. (London, 1725).

[52] The most recent biography of Hooke is G. Sampson, I. Macgregor Morris and J. Moore, 'Nathaniel Hooke', in E. Jenkins (ed.), *Eighteenth-Century British Historians* (New York, 2007), 188–92.

[53] N. Hooke, *The Roman History From the Building of Rome to the Ruin of the Commonwealth*, vol. I (London, 1738), i–ii.

[54] N. Hooke, *The Roman History From the Building of Rome to the Ruin of the Commonwealth*, vol. II (London, 1745).

differing versions of events. Secondly, going beyond Catrou, Hooke made extensive use of previous works in the field, ranging from Raleigh to Pighius, from previous centuries and the various contemporary publications by his peers, on both history and sources and from both sides of the channel. He made extensive comments on the works of Echard, Vertot, Catrou (original and translation), Rollin, de Beaufort and various political tracts and translations. His work contains extensive footnotes and digressions on a number of key issues, ranging from source survival through to working on the original sources available to the ancient Roman historians.[55] More than anyone else, Hooke embodied the cross channel community of Roman scholars that was developing, happily utilising works of both English and French. This latter fact stood him above many of his contemporaries on both sides of the channel; namely that he was a bi-lingual scholar and could read the original work and not the translation. Hooke's achievement was to unify this stream of intellectual thought; the grand narrative history, along with a long running sub-genre of Roman historical research; exploring the origins of the Roman civilisation.

Erasmus provides an excellent analysis of this process which had been ongoing since the early Renaissance.[56] The key questions centred on the various ancient theories for the origins of Rome; either a colony of Trojan exiles or a native city and the chronology involved, along with how trustworthy the surviving sources were (notably Livy and Dionysius). Additional questions centred on the transition from the Kingdom to the Republic and the establishment of the Roman law codes. By the late seventeenth and early eighteenth century, two scholars in particular had released important works on this issue, Jakob Gronovius and Perizonius, along with a third smaller work, by Henry Dodwell.[57] Of these works it was Perizonius' which made the greater impact, both in terms of depth of analysis and longevity of transmission. In particular it was he who pioneered the banquet-song theory for explaining the authenticity of early Roman history. The argument centred on the references to ancient

---

[55] The best assessment of this can be found in his Preface to 'Remarks on the History of the Seven Roman Kings', *Roman History*, vol. I, second edition (London, 1751), i–xxxvii.

[56] H. Erasmus, *The Origins of Rome in Historiography from Petrarch to Perizonius* (Assen, 1962).

[57] J. Gronovius, *Dissertatio de Origini Romuli* (Leiden, 1684), J. Perizonius, *Animaadversiones Historicae* (Amsterdam, 1685) and *Dissertatio de Historia Romuli et Romanae Urbis Origine* (Leiden, 1709), and H. Dodwell, 'Dissertatio de Antiques Romanorum Cyclis', in *De Veteribus Graecorum Romanorumque Cyclis* (Oxford, 1701).

banqueting songs (*carmina*) which celebrated heroes and stories from early Roman history. Although the ancient references we have for them, notably from Cato and Cicero stated that by their day, these songs had vanished;[58] Perizonius speculated that they might have been used by the early Roman historians as the basis for their histories and transmitted into the later, surviving, sources. This theory was revived by Niebuhr in the nineteenth century, who is regarded as its strongest advocate; though it is widely dismissed today.[59]

By the early eighteenth century research into this field had waned, but was revived in the 1720s by a collection of French scholars at the Académie Royal, who published their work in the *Histoire et Mémoirs de l'Académie Royale des Inscriptions et Belles-Lettres*. Central to this work were the scholars Louis-Jean de Pouilly and Claude Sallier, who had a running debate over the origins of Rome. Most notable was the 1722 Académie volume where both men published their respective cases.[60] At first this was a purely French development, with additional work being done by a number of scholars.[61] Saxius and Terasson in particular are also to be noted for introducing the controversial work by Giambatista Vico, the so called 'New Science'; 'Principii di una scienza nuova', into mainstream Roman academic debates, specifically around the issue of the creation of the Twelve Tables and whether it was an imported or a native lawcode.[62] The general assumption being that Vico's work was not widely utilised in this period. In addition, the theories of Gronovius and Perizonius were also revived and updated.

---

[58] Cicero, *Brut.* 19.75, *Tus. Disp.* 4.2.3.

[59] See A. Momigliano, 'Perizonius, Niebuhr and the Character of Early Roman Tradition', *Journal of Roman Studies*, 47 (1957), 104–14 and R. Bridenthal, 'Was There a Roman Homer? Niebuhr's Thesis and Its Critics', *History and Theory*, 11 (1972), 193–213.

[60] L.-J. de Pouilly, 'Dissertation sur l'incertitude de l'histoire des quatre premiers siecles de Rome', *Histoire et Mémoirs de l'Académie Royale des Inscriptions et Belles-Lettres*, 6 (1722), 14–29. C. Sallier, 'Discours sur les premiers monuments historiques des romains', *Histoire et Mémoirs de l'Académie Royale des Inscriptions et Belles-Lettres*, 6 (1722), 30–51, 52–70 and 115–34.

[61] P.-N. Bonamy, 'Dissertation sur l'Origine des Loix des XII Tables', *Histoire et Mémoirs de l'Académie Royale des Inscriptions et Belles-Lettres*, 12 (1740), 27–99. L. de Beaufort, *Dissertation sur l'incertitude de l'histoire des cinq premiers siècles de l'histoire Romaine* (Utrecht, 1738). C. Saxius, *Miscellanea Lipsiensia Nova*, vol. I (1742), 40–79. *Miscellanea Lipsiensia Nova*, vol. II (1743), 409–95. *Miscellanea Lipsiensia Nova*, vol. III (1744), 620–712 and 743–9. A. Terrasson, *Histoire de la Jurisprudence Romaine* (Paris, 1750).

[62] G. Vico, *Principii di una scienza nuova d'interno alla natura delle nazioni* (Naples, 1725).

Despite the clear quality of this research into the origins of Rome, these works for the most part, remained an obscure specialism, limited to the narrow circles of French scholars. Of all these scholars involved, only the work of de Beaufort was notable for its wide circulation.[63] Yet this changed thanks to the work of Nathaniel Hooke, who brought these works into the wider academic consciousness, through both utilising them in general in his Roman history and through his two specialist essays, on the origins of Rome. In 1738 and 1745, as introductory essays to his first and second volumes respectively, Hooke wrote two specialist essays; 'Remarks on the History of the Seven Roman Kings' and 'Dissertation on the Credibility of the first 500 years of Rome'.[64] In addition to these essays, the preface to each volume of history also contained extensive arguments on the reliability of ancient Roman evidence and utilised a number of the works of these French scholars, along with a number of others, in his opening remarks. Thanks to Hooke these views were brought to the attention of British scholars and united with other works, such as that of Sir Isaac Newton, and gave them a far wider audience.

Although he is not noted for his historical contributions, Newton had written a work on the problems of historical chronology, which covered the ancient world from the earliest times onwards.[65] The original document was completed at the request of the Queen and had a limited court circulation. Given his reputation however, this unusual work, which combined astronomy with ancient history found its way to the Continent, where a number of Newton's rivals attacked it in print. This gives us the unusual state of affairs, where we have criticisms of the work being published before the work itself. At some point prior to his death in 1728, Newton wrote a revised version of the work for print, but died before it had been published. *The Chronology of Ancient Kingdoms Amended* was the only one of his works to be published posthumously.[66]

The work disputed the traditional chronology of the seven kings of Rome, as stated by the ancient sources. Hooke worked these arguments into his introductory essays, combined them with those of the French school and thus thrust them into the centre of the historical debate.

---

[63] There is a good modern examination of de Beaufort's work; R. Ridley, *Gibbon's Complement: Louis de Beaufort* (Venice, 1986).

[64] N. Hooke, 'Remarks on the History of the Seven Roman Kings', *Roman History*, vol. I, i–xl and 'Dissertation on the Credibility of the First 500 Years of Rome', *Roman History*, vol. II, i–xxxiii.

[65] Known variously as *The Original Monarchies* or *The Short Chronology of Ancient Kingdoms*, written c.1701–2 and remained unpublished.

[66] I. Newton, *The Chronology of Ancient Kingdoms Amended* (London, 1728).

Hooke's essays and the French works of the 1740s led de Beaufort to produce a second edition of his dissertation in 1750,[67] which in turn was worked into the updated Prefaces and introductory essays in the second and third editions of Hooke's two volumes of Roman history.[68] Thus we can see the vigorous nature of the debate and the health of the academic Anglo-French community, centred primarily on Hooke and de Beaufort. A lively academic debate raged across the Channel with a number of different aspects being brought to bear. Crucial to this debate was the scepticism with which the later Roman Republican sources were treated, especially the works of Livy and Dionysius. What marks these works out is the quality of the arguments not only over what source material survived on the Regal period, but also what sources would have been available to later Republican writers. Many of their arguments and analysis replicate those of today's scholars and preceded the work done by Niebuhr on early Roman history by over half a century. By and large the consensus was that, although there were a number of sources available to later republican writers concerning the Kingdom, much of what they wrote was concerned with the mythical past. One notable feature of these works was the absence of contemporary political comment, which can be found throughout the rest of the eighteenth-century Roman historical works.

If the debate on the origins of Rome was one clear specialist field of research in the eighteenth century, then the other was the Roman Senate, and this was one topic that would never be free from contemporary politics and that was dominated, perhaps unsurprisingly, by British scholars. Early impetus came from the House of Commons itself, when in 1719 Earl Stanhope, Secretary of State, wrote to the Abbé de Vertot, upon the publication of his Roman history, asking him a number of questions on the composition and methods of entry for the Roman Senate, with an eye to being better informed for reforming the House of Commons. His questions, along with Vertot's reply, were then printed.[69] With the British parliament flourishing in its elevated position under the Hanoverians, it is little wonder that many compared them to the Senate of Rome, as Swift had done in 1701. Thus interest in the Roman Senate began to grow, with the 1720s seeing the first

---

[67] L. de Beaufort, *Dissertation sur l'incertitude de l'histoire des cinq premiers siecles de l'histoire Romaine, nouvelle edition, revue, corrigee et augmentee* (The Hague, 1750).

[68] Produced in 1751 and 1757 respectively.

[69] J. Stanhope, *A Memorial sent from London by the late Earl Stanhope, to the Abbot Vertot at Paris. Containing the following questions, relating to the constitution of the Roman Senate* (London, 1721).

tentative works released on this subject.⁷⁰ In many ways this was an English re-invention of the Renaissance tradition of specialist works on the Roman constitution, allied to the English tradition of using Roman history for political purposes. As with the early histories of Rome, the main flaw in these works was their lack of critical analysis, of both the source material and the various workings of the Senate. Statements from the sources, even when contradictory were taken at face value and not examined further.

Nevertheless, this process picked up pace, and the 1740s and 1750s saw four new works published on the Roman Senate. The first three were stand alone works, but the fourth was the culmination of this process and was a work produced by Hooke, which analysed these three previous works and the explanations given by Vertot.⁷¹ Hooke's own work, which at times is as overcomplicated as the title suggests, is nevertheless a excellent treatment of the workings and evolution of the Roman Senate. By analysing the best and worse of his peers' work, combined with his own insight, Hooke produced a textbook one volume history of the Roman Senate, which is unsurpassed until at least the work of Hofmann in 1847.⁷²

This work was again marked by Hooke's usual close analysis of the sources and especially his championing of Livy over the previously more trusted Dionysius of Halicarnassus. In particular, Hooke took exception to the work produced by Conyers Middleton in 1747, both on a personal and professional level. It would be fair to say that the two men disliked each other, which given their differing backgrounds was not surprising. Middleton was a devote Anglican cleric who lived a bookish existence,⁷³ whilst Hooke was a Catholic convert who moved amongst the elite literary circle of Pope, Cibber and later Johnson, and

---

⁷⁰ W. Moyle, *An Essay upon the Constitution of the Roman Government* (London, 1726) and D. Burges, *A Short Account of the Roman Senate* (London, 1729).

⁷¹ Anon. *A Dissertation upon the Constitution of the Roman Senate, by a Gentleman* (London, 1743), C. Middleton, *A Treatise on the Roman Senate* (London, 1747), T. Chapman, *An Essay on the Roman Senate* (London, 1750). N. Hooke, *Observations on 1. The Answer of M. L'Abbé de Vertot to the late Earl Stanhope's Inquiry, concerning the Senate of Ancient Rome, Dated December 1719. II. A Dissertation upon the Constitution of the Roman Senate, by a Gentleman, Published in 1743. III. A Treatise on The Roman Senate, by Dr. Conyers Middleton, Published in 1747. IV. An Essay on the Roman Senate, by Dr Thomas Chapman, Published in 1750* (London, 1758).

⁷² F. Hofmann, *Der römische Senat zur Zeit der Republik* (Berlin, 1847).

⁷³ Again for a recent biography of Middleton, see *Eighteenth-Century British Historians* (New York, 2007), 228–33.

had friends amongst the political and aristocratic elites, as well as many enemies.[74]

In terms of their contemporary reputations, Hooke was lauded for his analysis of Roman History, whilst Middleton had achieved fame for his three volume biography of Cicero which was a commercial if not critical success.[75] Middleton's academic style was the opposite of Hooke's, through its bias in favour of Cicero, which made him the clear 'hero' of the late Republic.[76] To date, Hooke had strenuously avoided working on the last century of the Roman Republic for this very reason of bias towards or against the 'great' figures of the late Republic. Aside from the personal rancour, Hooke attacked Middleton's analysis on the basis of his slavish devotion to Dionysius of Halicarnassus and exclusion of all other, often contradictory, sources. Though at times Hooke's criticisms go too far, his work remains the best single volume on the Roman Senate produced in the eighteenth century. Unsurprisingly, this work provoked a number of later eighteenth-century works, which critiqued and attacked Hooke's own observations.[77]

Aside from these major areas of research, the other area of focus and of most contention centred on the late Republic and it's more controversial figures, from the Gracchi to Caesar. It was this area that was the most politically charged. Although, for the vast majority of his career, Hooke limited himself to commenting on the Gracchi and avoiding the first century B.C. altogether, that did not stop his contemporaries from indulging themselves. As we have already noted, Middleton produced

---

[74] Horace Walpole wrote several letters to his friends (such as 23 February, 1756) accusing Hooke of being a French agent. Given Hooke's Catholicism, his uncle being the notorious Catholic agent Colonel Nathaniel Hooke, and his youngest son being a French churchman, the Abbé Luke Hooke, it was a charge that usually accompanied him.

[75] C. Middleton, *The History of the Life of M. Tullius Cicero* (London, 1741).

[76] Middleton's work on Cicero later came under intense attack when, in 1787, Samuel Parr released a new collective edition of the works of the early seventeenth-century Scottish Renaissance scholar, William Bellenden. In the preface he accused Middleton of the barefaced plagiarism of Bellenden's obscure work; '*that Middleton is not only indebted to Bellenden for many useful and splendid materials, but that, wherever it answered his purpose, he has made a mere transcript of his work*'. See S. Parr, *A Free Translation of the Preface to Bellendenus; containing animated strictures on the great political characters of the present time* (London, 1788), 7.

[77] M. Spelman, *A Short Review of Mr. Hooke's Observations concerning the Roman Senate and the Character of Dionysius of Halicarnassus* (London, 1758), W. Hamilton, *A Short Review of Mr Hooke's Observations concerning the Roman Senate, and the character of Dionysius of Halicarnassus* (London, 1758), M. Bowyer, *An Apology for some of Mr Hooke's Observations concerning the Roman Senate* (London, 1782).

an extensive three volume eulogy to Cicero which lamented the fall of the Republic into the hands of dangerous radicals. Across a wide range of histories, pamphlets and polemics, figures such as the Gracchi, Sulla, Pompey, Caesar, Cato, Cicero and Brutus all rose and fell, hailed as heroes one moment and villains the next, depending on the writer's own point of view or political persuasion. However, through all of these works, a number of clear themes can be seen. The first centred on the Gracchi and concerned the debate centred upon political reform. To many the Gracchi were dangerous demagogues who pandered to the populace and brought about the chaos that befell the late Republic. The fact that these men were insiders, from the very heart of the political elite, made them all the more alarming.

One the one hand, we have the view as best espoused by Swift who determined that the Gracchi showed that any reform was to be avoided. On the other we have Hooke who argued that the Gracchi showed the danger of letting individuals take up the cause of reform rather than the central government taking a firm grip of the process.[78] In all cases historical detail vied for space alongside political comment, but that did not mean that all of these accounts ignored the detail, and this in particular brings us to the crucial subject of agrarian reform.

Not only was agrarian reform the key reform proposed by the Gracchi, especially Tiberius, but the issue of land distribution had a central role in any pre-industrial country, where the aristocracy's wealth and power was based upon land ownership. Central to this issue is the question of how clearly the eighteenth-century scholars understood the details of this process. Again, here we are faced with an orthodox academic view. It has long been an article of faith that it was Niebuhr who was the first scholar to realise that the Gracchan land reforms were targeted at public land, the *ager publicus*, rather than being a wholesale redistribution of privately owned land. We even have the stories that this realisation was the result of his travels to India, which still had a system of public land ownership.[79] More recently it has been acknowledged that the German scholar Christian Heyne, had already made clear this distinction between public and private land in the Gracchan agrarian reforms, prior to Niebuhr. This has been explained away by the champions of Niebuhr, by the claim that he was the first to fully develop this theory to its logical

---

[78] Swift, *A Discourse on the Contests and Dissensions*, 28–40, Hooke, *Roman History*, II, 520–60.

[79] The best example of this is A. Momigliano, 'Niebuhr and the Agrarian Problems of Rome', *History and Theory*, 21 (1982), 11.

conclusion.⁸⁰ If nothing else it allows the German university scholars, and their champions, to maintain their pride of place.

The problem with this is that the majority of the eighteenth-century scholars who commented on the Gracchi, such as Hooke and de Beaufort are perfectly comfortable with the distinction between public and private land and that fact that the Gracchan reforms were only aimed at the *ager publicus*. Every time Hooke mentions land distribution laws of the Gracchi, he is clear to make the distinction between private and '*publick land*'.⁸¹ Thus 'they were allowed no share of the publick land and the usurpers, to cultivate them, chose rather to employ foreigners and slaves, than citizens of Rome'.⁸² However, this distinction was not limited to the most analytical historians. Even in the early work of Echard, this point is clearly made: 'he [Tiberius Gracchus] preferr'd a Law, forbidding any Man to possess above 500 Acres of the Publick Lands, and ordering the Overplus to be divided among the Poor'.⁸³

Therefore, it is abundantly clear that the majority of the scholars of the eighteenth century had clearly understood that the Gracchan land laws were aimed solely at public land, which had been usurped by the aristocrats, and they had done this long before Niebuhr and his supposed revelation. Niebuhr's relationship with his eighteenth-century predecessors is far from clear. In his lectures he states that he was not familiar with the works of Hooke,⁸⁴ but in his histories, in the very chapters on land laws he states that he has clearly read the works of de Beaufort and Hooke and found them wanting.⁸⁵ Ridley has recently addressed this very issue and comes to the same conclusion, namely that the eighteenth-century Roman historians did understand that the Roman agrarian distributions utilised the *ager publicus* and not private land.⁸⁶

We are left with the burning question of how Niebuhr came to believe that he was the first historian to understand this difference and why until recently modern scholarship has believed this falsehood? The second of these questions is far easier to answer than the first, and is centred on modern scholarship's ignorance of these eighteenth-century works. Up until recently scholars have believed what Niebuhr stated, as it tallies

---

[80] Momigliano, 'Niebuhr and the Agrarian Problems of Rome', 10.
[81] Other terms used are usurped land or conquered land.
[82] Hooke, *Roman History*, II, 523.
[83] Echard, *Roman History*, I, 237.
[84] Niebuhr, *Lectures*, I, lxxxvii–lxxxviii.
[85] Niebuhr, *Römische Geschichte*, II, 131.
[86] R. Ridley, 'Leges Agrariae: Myths Ancient and Modern', *Classical Philology*, 95 (2000), 459–67.

with their own preconceptions about the non-institutional scholarship, of the eighteenth century and before. This, more than anything else, re-emphasises the need for these works to be read first hand, or risk becoming reliant on other scholars' (mis)perceptions. The question of how Niebuhr came to his conclusion is more difficult. Of his statements about Hooke, the following one rings more true:

> Somewhat later than Rollin, Hooke, an Englishman, wrote a Roman history with which I am but little acquainted. This book is not much known in Germany, and does not even exist in our university-library. All I can say about him is that he followed the view of de Beaufort, and wrote a history of those times only in which he believed it to deserve credit. He does not enter into any of the deeper questions.[87]

Thus we have one of the foremost scholars of Rome, showing his ignorance of one of the foremost works on Roman history. Niebuhr appears to misrepresent the scope of the book stating that it covered 'only of those times in which he believed it to deserve credit', whereas in fact the work covered the whole Regal period and the Republic up until Caesar. He then dismisses the quality of his scholarship, noting that Hooke 'followed de Beaufort' and that he 'does not enter into any of the deeper questions'; this view ignores Hooke's two introductory essays and his work on the Senate, not to mention the overall sophisticated source criticism and analysis. It seems that there are certain key words and phrases which sum up Niebuhr's attitude to much of the scholarship that went before him; 'Englishman, not much known in Germany' and 'university library'. Thus a whole era of Anglo-French scholarship is dismissed as being of minor interest and not up to university quality. This allows for monumental errors such as not noticing that the Anglo-French school clearly understood the difference between public and private land in Rome.

There is a further factor. We do need to acknowledge that there were a number of works written in the eighteenth century that did not make this distinction clear, but these are on the whole not produced by the historians of the period. In fact this very issue is an excellent litmus test of the quality of any particular work on Roman history from the period. All the leading historians of the period show their awareness of this distinction; whilst inferior works by men such as Oliver Goldsmith do not make this crucial distinction. However, it is clear that if we move away from the historians of the period and look at the more politically

---

[87] Niebuhr, *Lectures*, I, lxxxvii–lxxxviii.

based works, this distinction between public and private land was an easy one to omit. For the existing political elites it benefited them to neglect to mention that the Gracchi only wanted to redistribute public land, and play up the image that they enacted a wholescale distribution of private land, in order to make the proposals seem more radical. Yet the same argument was used by those writers who were advocating reform and overturning the old regime. If they could reach back into the past and show that an advanced civilisation such as Rome had enacted wholescale land reform, then it bolstered the case for modern day reform. In these ways, the more political the topic, the more that it was open to manipulation. For the pre and post-revolutionary writers that Niebuhr was acquainted with, this distinction would not have been made. Niebuhr it seems was an early victim of later scholars' inability to separate the ancient histories from the political works.

Only one other figure vied with the Gracchan reforms for such scholarly attention, and that was Julius Caesar. Whilst a figure such as Sulla was universally condemned by commentators from all political persuasions, Caesar attracted a large degree of uncertainty. A superb general certainly, but was he a megalomaniac who plunged his state into civil war and became a tyrant, or was he a soldier statesman who stabilised his country and was then treacherously murdered? Throughout the works of the eighteenth century there was no overall view, but we can see some clear trends. When Sir Walter Raleigh was writing his history, Caesar was the epitome of the great commander and a man to be lauded. His political activities were discretely ignored. By the mid-seventeenth century and John Milton, however, Caesar had become a byword for tyranny, and Oliver Cromwell was lauded as a new Brutus.[88] For the majority of the eighteenth-century writers, Caesar's military genius could not outweigh his political tyranny. Thus we see more works lauding Cato, Cicero and Brutus than Caesar. Britain had already seen the dangers of a military dictatorship and throughout these works one has the clear sense that the danger was an ever present one. Nevertheless, both the Roman historians of the periods, like wider British educated society, was split on how to view Caesar; tyrant or statesman. There exist several good modern studies on the various views of Caesar in the eighteenth century.[89] Ironically, Hooke, who had spent so long avoiding the contentious last century

---

[88] By the eighteenth century Cromwell himself had been transformed from a new Brutus to a new Caesar.

[89] A. Ward, 'The Tory View of Roman History', *Studies in English Literature 1500–1900*, 4 (1964), 413–56 and F. Turner, 'British Politics and the Demise of the Roman Republic; 1700–1939', *Historical Journal*, 29 (1986), 577–99.

of the Republic, has been dragged into this debate, being lauded as an example of a highly balanced analysis of Caesar and his achievements, in contrast to many of his peers.[90] Ward even goes as far as saying: 'Hooke's appraisal of Cato, for example, is in essence that of Ronald Syme in his definitive study The Roman Revolution'.[91] These plaudits, whilst welcome, are problematic, due to the fact that it is unlikely that Hooke ever wrote them, given that he had died eight years before the volume was published. Nevertheless, they are a good indicator that a balanced analysis of Caesar could be reached, even in such a highly politicised atmosphere, again showing the quality of the history of the period.

As can be seen, the apogee of this wave of historical scholarship came in the 1730s–1750s when numerous works were published. Furthermore these publications were not completed in isolation, but formed part of a wider academic community which interacted and generated fresh works. At the same time as Hooke's Roman history was published (beginning in 1738), another monumental Roman history began its release. This was by the French scholar Charles Rollin, who had spent the years 1730–8 working on a general history of the ancient world, which was the most popular and widely reprinted general history of the period.[92] In 1738 he began a nine-volume history of Rome.[93] We can only speculate over the reasons for such a venture. Not only was it a natural successor to his universal history of the ancient world, but the first venture had been such a commercial success. This, coupled with the market for Roman history, gave the project a certain inevitability. Thus France saw the publication of a nine-volume work on Roman history, growing to sixteen in the English translation, barely one year after the twentieth and final volume of Catrou's Roman history.

If we examine the three histories, Catrou's, Rollin's and Hooke's which were all available in this short period, we find some interesting comparisons. Both the French scholars undertook monumental works (twenty volumes and nine volumes respectively) whereas Hooke contented himself with merely the two. In terms of scope Catrou took his history down until the reign of the Emperor Tiberius, whereas Rollin choose the Battle of Actium. Although the Battle of Actium in 31 B.C. is taken as the most standard cut-off point for popular works on the Republic, in the eighteenth century, this was not usually the case. In

---

[90] Ward, 'Tory View', 449–51, Turner, 'British Politics', 582–4.
[91] Ward, 'Tory View', 454.
[92] C. Rollin, *Histoire Ancienne des Egyptiens, des Carthgaginois, des Assyriens, des Babyloniens, des Medes et des Perses, des Macédoniens, des Grecs* (Paris, 1730–8).
[93] C. Rollin and J.-B. Crevier, *Histoire Romaine* (Paris, 1739–50).

fact, the Battle of Pharsalus, in 48 B.C. was the more common choice for the point the Republic ended. In reality, Rollin never actually reached this point, as he died in 1741 at the age of 80. However this did not stop the publication of his history. His publishers, determined not to lose sales, hit on a novel, and soon to be repeated tactic; they commissioned another scholar to continue the project, whilst keeping the name of the series as Rollin's Roman History, a tactic later repeated for Hooke. Thus we have the odd situation that volumes one to five of Rollin's history was written by himself, whereas volumes six to nine were written by another scholar, Jean-Baptiste Crevier, but still named Rollin's Roman history. Upon completion, Crevier began a fresh twelve volume work on the Roman Emperors, down to the Emperor Constantine.[94] This process continued when Charles Le Beau added another twenty-two volumes from the history of Constantine onwards, well into the Byzantine period. Upon his death in 1778, a further five volumes were added, which took the whole project down to the fall of Constantinople in 1453.[95] Thus these scholars completed a Roman history from the foundation of the city down to the fall of Constantinople in a monumental forty-eight volumes.

Although more work needs to be undertaken on the differences between the scholarship of Rollin and that of Crevier, the work as a whole is more of a narrative account and less critical in its use of ancient sources. That said, both Catrou's and Hooke's works suffer from the opposite problem, notably extensive footnotes and asides which the general reader may not have appreciated. Certainly in France, Rollin's work became the standard text on Roman history, soon replacing Catrou, and, as we have seen, was popular in Germany also. In Britain however, Hooke's volumes remained the most popular, though the sixteen volumes of Rollin in translation saw a number of reprints.

Catrou was responsible for re-introducing the magisterial fasti of Stephanus Pighius (1599 and 1615) to an eighteenth-century audience. He included Pighius' list of magistrates as appendices in volumes four, eight, nine and sixteen, but removed all the differentiation between the categories of attested, partially attested and speculative.[96] This altered version was incorporated into the works of Ozell, Bundy and Hooke,

---

[94] J.-B. Crevier, *Histoire des Empereurs Romains, depuis Auguste jusqu'a Constantin* (Paris 1749–55).

[95] C. Le Beau and H.-P. Ameilhon, *Histoire du Bas-Empire, en commençant a Constantine le Grand* (Paris, 1756–1811).

[96] This indicates that he used Graevius' reprint of Pighius rather than the original; J. Graevius, *Thesaurus Antiquitatum Romanarum*, vol. II (Utrecht, 1694).

all of whom further remove any references to Pighius. In Hooke's case this is curious as he uses Pighius in his main text. Thus Pighius' work was transmitted (or mis-transmitted) throughout the eighteenth century and into the nineteenth (along with each individual Hooke reprint, up to 1830).[97]

As well as the historians, a number of other scholars produced works on Rome that fall under the categories of political tracts utilising ancient history. The most famous of these were Thomas Gordon's *Political Discourses,* on both Sallust and Tacitus, which, despite the titles, had less to do with each ancient author's work and was focused on political analysis.[98] In a similar vein came Thomas Blackwell's *Memoirs of the Court of Augustus*, which, again, had less to do with Augustus and more to do with the British court and contemporary politics.[99] Despite the polemical nature of both these works, and the genre they represented, nevertheless they remained a popular and profitable literary genre and helped to augment the works of the histories in keeping Rome at the forefront of the intellectual and political life in this period.

However, by the 1760s, it is apparent that this particular genre of works was coming to an end. Old scholars died out and new scholars took the study of Rome into two different directions. Firstly came a new generation of British scholars who took the process of studying Roman history into a terminal decline. The main wave of Roman Republican history had been so successful that later writers cashed in on a ready made market without wanting to put in the research and analysis. The best example of this is Oliver Goldsmith, who produced a totally unnecessary populist Roman history.[100] A recent biography of Goldsmith used the following telling phrase: '[h]is historiographical contribution was to synthesize and popularize the work of other historians, often borrowing extensively from their words'.[101] The work most copied was that of Hooke, from which Goldsmith removed all the detailed analysis and simply returned to the earlier practise of doing nothing more than telling an exciting story. This ensured that he this work was constantly used by schools of the time, but added nothing to the intellectual progress of studying Roman history.

---

[97] This being the last reprinted edition of Hooke.
[98] T. Gordon, *Political Discourses in the Works of Tacitus* (London, 1728) and *Political Discourses in The Works of Sallust* (London, 1744). Gordon also has a fresh biographical entry in volume 336 of the *Dictionary of Literary Biography*, 153–9.
[99] T. Blackwell, *Memoirs of the Court of Augustus* (London, 1753–63).
[100] O. Goldsmith, *The Roman History from the Foundation of the City of Rome, to the Destruction of The Western Empire*, 2 vols. (London, 1769).
[101] Again see *Eighteenth-Century British Historians*, 144.

Hooke, in his final years, was persuaded to take his Roman history down to the end of the Republic. Throughout the 1750s he had constantly refused to do so, preferring to work on a second and third edition of his first two volumes, and his work on the Roman Senate. When he died in 1763 he was in the process of finishing this new third volume, which took his history down to the outbreak of the civil war between Caesar and Pompey. His publishers rushed the volume out the following year, but it was far from a finished version.[102] Worse was to happen when, seven year later, Hooke's publishers (echoing Rollin's twenty years earlier) produced, in his name, a fourth volume covering the period of Caesar.[103] Nevertheless, it was a great commercial success.[104] In terms of the academic quality, whilst the volume was not up to Hooke's normal standard is still a good piece of research and does take a unusual (for the time) line on Caesar; namely that he was the inevitable consequence of the failure of reform. How much of this volume Hooke had planned we will never know, but it does bear some of his hallmarks. The 'Hooke industry' saw another nine editions released between his death and the translation of Niebuhr into English in the 1830s. His younger son (the Abbé Luke Hooke) even released a French translation version of Hooke's history, thus completing the circle.[105]

In the midst of this cycle of reprint and derivation, a few important works were produced. The two most notable ones being Louis de Beaufort producing his long awaited two volume history of the Roman Republic and a two volume work on the tribunate of the plebs, echoing the Renaissance vein of scholarship, written by the Abbé Seran de la Tour.[106] However, these were the last gasps of the process and the Anglo-French scholarship on Roman history collapsed into a trough that it was not to emerge from until the mid-nineteenth century, to be supplanted by German university

---

[102] N. Hooke, *The Roman History From the Building of Rome to the Ruin of the Commonwealth*, vol. III (London, 1764).

[103] Until recently, no-one who has commented on Hooke's views on Caesar has noted that he had been dead for eight years when the work as written and there is no evidence that he left any notes. This has been corrected in the most recent biographical essay, see E. Jenkins (ed.), *Eighteenth-Century British Historians*, 192.

[104] N. Hooke, *The Roman History From the Building of Rome to the Ruin of the Commonwealth*, vol. IV (London, 1771).

[105] N. Hooke, *Discours et reflexions critique sur l'histoire et le gouvernement de l'ancienne Rome*, 3 vols., trans. L. Hooke (1770–84). See T. O' Connor, *An Irish Theologian in Enlightenment Europe: Luke Joseph Hooke 1714–96* (Dublin, 1995).

[106] L. de Beaufort, *La Republique Romaine*, 2 vols. (Hague, 1766). Seran de la Tour, *Histoire du tribunat de Rome, depuis sa creation jusqua la reunion de sa puissance a celle de l'empereur Auguste* (Amsterdam, 1774).

scholarship. Although this scholarly tradition went into decline, at the same time new generations of Anglo-French scholars took the study of Roman history in fresh directions and in the process gave the subject a far higher profile than ever before. These can best be described as the 'philosopher historians', men such as Montesquieu, Voltaire and Rousseau along with Edward Montagu, Adam Ferguson and Edward Gibbon. To this group of men, the study of Roman history was not an end in its own right but merely a method used to understand, or to construct, political and philosophical systems with which to understand or change contemporary civilisations. The level of the historical analysis varies drastically not only between the various writers, but also between their own works.

The best example of this variety occurs with Montesquieu, whose early work on the *Reflections on the Causes of the Rise and Fall of the Roman Empire* was a brief narrative of the Republic and the Empire with only a cursory analysis or understanding of the individual events.[107] However his later work, *The Spirit of the Laws* is a far more impressive work of historical scholarship.[108] This took the form of a close analysis of the origins and evolution of the Roman offices and institutions, echoing the work and focus of the Renaissance scholars and displayed a valuable analysis of Rome's political and social intuitions. Similar works can be found in Rousseau's *The Social Contract* and Voltaire's *Philosophy of History*.[109]

A number of the key pre-revolutionary thinkers in France contributed works on Roman history, many of which are notable historical works in their own right. These include a number of works by Gabriel Bonnot de Mably; notably his *Observations sur les Romains* and *De la legislation*.[110] At the same time, several British scholars were producing similar works. In the 1750s came Edward Montagu's *Reflections on the Rise and Fall of the Antient Republicks*.[111] The 1770s and 1780s saw two notable works produced by British authors. Firstly there was Adam Ferguson's *Progress and Termination of the Roman Republic*, which in itself is an unusual work.[112] As an analysis of

---

[107] Montesquieu, *Considérations sur les causes de la grandeur des Romains et de leur decadence* (Paris, 1734).
[108] Montesquieu, *De l'esprit des lois* (Paris, 1748).
[109] J. Rousseau, *Du contrat social* (Paris, 1762), book IV. Voltaire, *Essai sur les moeurs et l'esprit des nations* (Paris, 1756).
[110] G. de Mably, *Observations sur les Romains* (Paris, 1751) and *De la legislation* (Paris, 1789).
[111] E. Montagu, *Reflections on the Rise and Fall of the Antient Republicks* (London, 1759).
[112] A. Ferguson, *The History of the Progress and Termination of the Roman Republic* (London, 1783). Again, see *Eighteenth-Century British Historians*, 104–9.

the rise and fall of a civilisation it makes a notable contribution to political philosophy, but does not stand up to scrutiny as a history of Rome. His three volumes breeze through the early history of Rome in an almost indecent haste to reach the last century B.C. Considering the wealth of material available to any Roman scholar by this point, there is little excuse for such brevity in a work of such size. Secondly there was Edward Gibbon's legendary *The History of the Decline and Fall of the Roman Empire*, whose contribution to western literature far outweighs his contribution to Roman history.[113]

Thus, the late eighteenth century saw a shift away from the study of Roman history as an end in itself to the study of Rome as a means of understanding the political development of western civilisation. In many ways this was the logical development of the whole pre-Niebuhrian process. It began with works on the sources themselves, then treatises on aspects of Roman history. Next came the major histories and their political counterparts and finally came the political philosophies. The latter two categories differ through one's use of Roman history as an allegory for contemporary politics and the other using Roman history to construct theories of political systems and evolution and ultimately create a new blueprint for political and social development. Although much work has been done on the role of the classics in the works of the 'philosopher historians', little has been done on the role of the histories and their influence on these men.

The final evolution of this process came towards the end of the eighteenth century when these theories had a chance of being put into practice, during the American and French Revolutions, when new political systems were being sought. As already noted a number of the key French revolutionary thinkers had underpinned their philosophies with an analysis of Roman history and many of these works were consulted by the leaders of the French revolution, notably Jean Mounier, who turned to Montesquieu and Mably when grappling with the problem of how to turn France's unwritten constitution into a written one. Although the French Revolution re-introduced the trappings of the Roman Republic, such as the offices of Consul and Tribune, the effect of Roman history on the revolution is hard to assess given the revolution's collapse into the Terror and then the First Empire. Much has been written on the classical influences on the French revolution, but more work needs to be done on the role of the ancient histories.

[113] Gibbon, *Decline and Fall*.

Table 2: Records of the 1787 Federal Convention (Selection)

| Ref | Constitutional Issue | Ancient Reference | Who By |
|---|---|---|---|
| 1.74 | Multiple Executive power | 30 Tyrants or Decemvirs. | Wilson |
| 1.135 | Dangers of Rich vs. Poor | Patrician vs. Plebeians | Madison |
| 1.151 | Multiple representatives | Increasing number of Tribunes | Madison |
| 1.157 | State vs. Federal | Despotic Roman Emperors | Wilson |
| 1.158 | Representatives | Tribunes of Plebs. | Madison |
| 1.159 | Representatives | Tribunes of Plebs | Dickerson |
| 1.254 | Division of Executive Power | The First Triumvirate | Wilson |
| 1.285 | Federal Structure | The Failure of Amphyctionic Council | Hamilton |
| 1.290 | Dangers of Tyranny | Roman Emperors elected by the Army | Hamilton |
| 1.323 | Federalism | Roman Proconsuls & Persian Satraps | Hamilton |
| 1.326 | Weaknesses of Federal Structure | Persian and Macedonian Dominance | Hamilton |
| 1.329 | Division of Executive Power | The Roman Dictators | Hamilton |
| 1.424 | Dangers of Rich vs. Poor | Patrician & Plebeians intermingling | Hamilton |
| 1.448 | Neighbours at War | Punic Wars | Madison |
| 1.459 | Use of Ancient Historians | Rollin's *Ancient History* | Madison |
| 1.465 | Benefits of an External Threat | Roman Warfare to divert revolts | Madison |
| 2.300 | Benefits of a Dual Executive | Roman King to Two Consuls | Morris |
| 2.371 | Pro Slavery | Greco-Roman social order | Pinckney |
| 2.372 | Anti Slavery | Flaws in the Greco-Roman systems | Dickinson |

Across the Atlantic however, in the aftermath of the American Revolution, we can see that these ideas had a far greater impact. Unlike their later French counterparts, the American founding fathers found themselves with a blank slate on which to create a new constitution. Furthermore, we know that several of the central figures involved in drawing up the American constitution had already published works that touched on ancient history.[114] In the deliberations that took place in the Constitutional Convention of 1787, we can find numerous references, both positive and negative, taken from Roman history. Table 2 is a list of the occasions when aspects of Roman history occurred and in relation to what topic, though the list is by no means exhaustive. As can be seen the founding fathers frequently referred back to Roman examples to propose, support and oppose the various forms of government. This large number of examples is supplemented by the number of ancient

---

[114] For a good overview of this, see C. Richard, *The Founders and the Classics, Greece, Rome, and the American Enlightenment* (Harvard, 1995).

sources which appear. Far from just the obvious ones, namely Polybius and Cicero, we find references to Livy, Dionysius, Dio Cassius, Tacitus, Sallust and Plutarch. Modern histories mentioned in the debate include Ferguson's *Progress and Termination of the Roman Republic*, Rollin's *Roman History* and even Swift's infamous pamphlet. As with the French revolution, a large amount of work has been conducted on the classical influences on the American constitution.[115] Once again, however, more work needs to be done on the uses of the ancient histories in these processes.

Regrettably, this marked the high point of the influence of the ancient world upon modern political life. In America's case, all too soon the teaching of ancient history was downgraded to such a point that by the 1840s de Tocqueville stated in his work on the American people that they 'cared but little for what occurred at Rome and Athens'.[116] Just as the study of ancient history took an apparent downward spiral towards the end of the eighteenth century so the influence of the subject upon the political life of Europe also took a downturn, from which it has not yet recovered. It is therefore not perhaps a coincidence that the post-revolutionary nineteenth century saw a decline in the study and use of Roman history. From its central position in the field of ancient history and political philosophy, the study of Rome, and in particular the Anglo-French movement, collapsed. New works were not commissioned and the mass market saw endless reprints of Hooke, Rollin and unfortunately Goldsmith. In terms of fresh works, Greek history appears to emerge from the shadows and eclipse that of Rome.

Today scholars tend to see the work of Niebuhr as marking the beginning of modern historiographical studies, with the groundbreaking works of the eighteenth century forgotten, or dismissed as unprofessional; merely the works of amateur scholars. However, this need not be the case; these works should be judged in their own right and the eighteenth-century cannon of historical works needs to be acknowledged as a turning point in Roman historiography. Works on chronologies, antiquities and

---

[115] Richard, *The Founders and the Classics*, also see R. Ames and H. Montgomery, 'The Influence of Rome on the American Constitution', *Classical Journal*, 30 (1934), 19–27, G. Chinard, 'Polybius and the American Constitution', *Journal of the History of Ideas*, 1 (1940), 38–58, J. Euben (ed.), *Athenian Political Thought and the Reconstruction of American Democracy* (Cornell, 1994), R. Gummere 'The Classical Ancestry of the United States Constitution', *American Quarterly*, 14 (1962), 3–18 and *The American Colonial Mind and the Classical Tradition* (Harvard, 1963), P. Rahe, *Republics Ancient and Modern* (Chapel Hill, 1992).

[116] A. de Tocqueville, *De la démocratie en Amerique*, vol. II (Paris, 1840), 80.

universal histories were overtaken by detailed analytical scholarship on the origins of the Republic, its institutions, its political evolution and ultimate collapse. They represent the foundation of modern knowledge about ancient Rome and key landmarks in the development of critical historical method. If nothing else, then today's scholars need to read these works and make their own judgments on their quality and contribution. If not then we are doomed to repeat the mistakes of past scholars, such as Niebuhr, and run the risk of ignoring work that has already been done. Perhaps there is no better statement on the subject than that of Montesquieu's: 'It is impossible ever to be tired with so agreeable a subject as ancient Rome'.[117]

---

[117] Montesquieu, *De l'esprit des lois*, book xi, chapter 8.

# 9. Greek, but not Grecian? Macedonians in Enlightenment Histories*

*Andrew J. Bayliss*

Modern practitioners of ancient history are all products of an education system that prioritises certain historical periods over others. In the field of 'Greek History', this prioritisation is most evident in the designation of the period from *c.*500–322 B.C. as 'Classical'. In comparison, the titles given to other periods in Greek History can only seem less 'mainstream' titles e.g. 'Archaic', 'Hellenistic', or 'Byzantine'. Such nomenclature seems to suggest that the periods in question have not yet achieved, or have since lost, 'Classical' status. This is particularly the case for the so-called Hellenistic period, a period when much of western Asia and the eastern Mediterranean seaboard was divided between several Graeco-Macedonian kingdoms. This chapter will be examining the place of Macedonian and Hellenistic History in modern scholarship, and be seeking to explain how and why these important strands of history stand not only outside mainstream Greek History, but also outside traditional Ancient History as a whole.

Macedonian and Hellenistic History by their very names are separated from mainstream 'Greek History'. By definition, 'Macedonian' history cannot be 'Greek' history, and the use of the term 'Hellenistic' clearly differentiates this period from Hellenic i.e. Greek History, suggesting that the period is Greek-like rather than actually Greek.[1] The term 'Hellenistic' is ultimately derived from the German term 'Hellenismus' (i.e. Hellenism), which was itself derived from the Greek verb Ἑλληνίζω – 'to speak Greek'.[2] The precise

---

\* This paper was largely written while I was a post-doctoral Research Fellow on Professor Alan Sommerstein's Leverhulme-funded project 'The Oath in Archaic and Classical Greece' at the University of Nottingham. Aside from thanking Alan for his support during my time at Nottingham, I would like to thank Dr Ian Macgregor Morris, Dr Carsten Lange and Dr Vicky Jackson for their assistance in writing this article. None are responsible for any of the opinions expressed in this article, and any errors are entirely my own.

[1] G.R. Bugh, 'Introduction', to G.R. Bugh (ed.), *The Cambridge Companion to the Hellenistic World* (Cambridge, 2006), 3.

[2] The term 'Hellenism/Hellenismus' is ultimately derived from the Acts of the Apostles 6.1, where the Ἑλληνισταί (Hellenising jews) are opposed to the Ἑβραῖοι (jews). Cf. A. Momigliano, 'J.G. Droysen Between Greeks and Jews', *History and Theory*, 9 (1970), 142.

meaning of this 'unhappy title'³ derives from J.G. Droysen's employment of the term Hellenismus in his seminal multi-volume work *Geschichte des Hellenismus* (1836–1843) to designate the spreading of Greek culture over the non-Greek lands conquered by Alexander the Great. His usage of the term Hellenismus went well beyond the simple meaning Hellenism. Droysen's extension of Hellenismus to mean 'not just "correct Greek", but a "fusion of Greek and non-Greek"',⁴ makes it difficult to translate adequately. François Chamoux argues that there is no exact equivalent in English or French for the term,⁵ while Simon Hornblower argues that 'the German is best not translated'.⁶ It is lamentable that the term has been clumsily rendered as 'Hellenistic' in English and 'Hellénistique' in French, for 'Hellenistic History' and 'histoire Hellénistique' imply that the period is 'Greekish' and therefore inferior to actual Greek History.⁷

In current historical practice, Macedonian and Hellenistic History sit uncomfortably between the two pillars we know as 'Greek History' and 'Roman History'. Despite numerous overlaps – in all aspects of historical inquiry – they fit into neither Greek nor Roman History, holding a place akin to an illegitimate child of one or the other. Cartledge observes, 'The Hellenistic entity tends to be something of a stepchild, a Cinderella, in ancient Graeco-Roman studies'.⁸ A better analogy would perhaps be the Ugly Sisters, for whereas Cinderella goes on to charm the handsome prince and live happily ever after with him, Macedonian and Hellenistic history are still unable to charm mainstream scholars. A brief visit to any academic library will confirm the marginal place of Macedonian and Hellenistic History; fewer books are published, fewer articles are written,⁹ and Macedonian History is catalogued separately from Greek and Roman History or Archaeology, sometimes even in the same section as histories of the modern nation states of Bulgaria, Romania, and the former Yugoslav republics.

Typically, the rise and fall of the Macedonian empire is seen by modern scholars in negative terms, as a period of inevitable decline and stagnation,

---

³ P. Cartledge, 'Introduction' to P. Cartledge, P. Garnsey and E. Gruen (eds.), *Hellenistic Constructs: Essays in Culture, History, and Historiography* (Berkeley, 1997), 2.
⁴ *Oxford Classical Dictionary*, 678. Hornblower argues that Droysen 'gave "Hellenismus" a powerful and extended sense'.
⁵ F. Chamoux, *Hellenistic Civilization*, translated by M. Roussel (Oxford, 2003), 1.
⁶ *Oxford Classical Dictionary*, third edition (Oxford, 1996), 678.
⁷ The first use of the term hellénistique certainly had negative connotations. J.J. Bossuet used the term in 1681 as a means of describing the Greek of the Septuagint, the 'Hellenized' version of the Old Testament.
⁸ Cartledge, 'Introduction', 3.
⁹ G. Shipley, 'Recent Trends and New Directions', in G.R. Bugh (ed.), *The Cambridge Companion to the Hellenistic World* (Cambridge, 2006), 318.

and little more than an 'untidy, unwieldy and confusing interregnum between Greek and Roman history'.[10] The period has typically been so little valued that even Droysen felt the need to apologise for writing his doctoral dissertation on Ptolemaic Egypt.[11] Glenn Bugh recently wrote:

> Scholarly books on Greece continue to be published with little or no serious discussion of the Hellenistic period and with no shame attached to rounding out surveys of Greek history with the battle of Chaironeia in 338 or the death of Alexander in 323, as if Greek history had ended and nearly 1,500 documented *poleis* sprinkled throughout the Mediterranean, Black Sea and Asia had mysteriously vanished.[12]

The recent appearance of several modern discussions lamenting this marginalisation has served to underline the tendency in modern scholarship on Greek History to revere Classical Athens above all else.[13] Other poleis (with the possible exception of Sparta) and other epochs tend to be seen as tangential, and are relegated to the fringes (none more so than the history of Macedon and the Hellenistic period). Because the prioritisation of Classical Greece within the field of Ancient History is so ingrained today, it is easy to take it for granted that the other periods of Greek History – e.g. the Archaic, Hellenistic, Roman, and Byzantine – have always sat outside mainstream scholarship, and that they have always been overlooked, marginalised, and disparaged. However, this is by no means the case. Even a cursory reading of the pioneering works of 'Greek History' by eighteenth-century writers such as Jacques de Tourreil, John Gast, William Mitford, John Gillies, and Gabriel Bonnot de Mably will show that the founders of our discipline were by no means fixated on the so-called 'Classical Period', and in fact endeavoured to tell the story of Greece from all periods of antiquity – from mythical times to the Roman conquest, and that Macedonian and Hellenistic History were regularly discussed, and often considered crucial parts of *Greek* History.

---

[10] S.E. Alcock, 'Breaking up the Hellenistic World: Survey and Society', in I. Morris (ed.), *Classical Greece: Ancient Histories and Modern Archaeologies* (Cambridge, 1994), 173.

[11] J.G. Droysen, *De Lagidarum regno Ptolemaeo rege* (1831), reprinted in *Kleine Schriften zur Alten Geschichte* (Leipzig, 1894), vol. II, 351. Cf. A. Momigliano 'J.G. Droysen Between Greeks and Jews', 141.

[12] G.R. Bugh, 'Introduction', 2.

[13] Apart from Bugh, 'Introduction', see also Shipley, 'Recent Trends and New Directions' and S.M. Burstein, 'New Ways of Being Greek in the Hellenistic Period', in W. Heckel and L.A. Tritle (eds.), *Crossroads of History: The Age of Alexander* (Clairemont, 2003), 217–42.

But why did the situation change? How did we end up in a system that sees the Macedonians as tangential to Greek History and not worthy of study or interest? It is certainly not due to a dearth of activity or a lack of longevity. The achievements of Philip of Macedon, Alexander the Great, and their Successors cannot be underestimated. Philip raised a hitherto inconsequential kingdom on the fringes of the Greek world to the status of a superpower in the ancient Mediterranean world. Alexander's conquests established a Graeco-Macedonian empire that stretched from the Danube to the Indus. The fortunes of the separate kingdoms that grew out of his conquests admittedly ebbed and flowed as they squabbled amongst themselves, but more importantly, they *endured*. Despite the absorption of the Macedonian homeland by the Romans in 168 B.C., the Attalids ruled in Asia Minor until 133 B.C., the Seleucids ruled a vast kingdom in Asia until 63 B.C., there was a Graeco-Macedonian kingdom in Bactria until at least 53 B.C.,[14] and the Ptolemies lasted until 30 B.C., even managing a stab at complete world domination by way of Cleopatra's liaison with Marcus Antonius (Mark Antony).

Furthermore, even when viewed through the distorted lens of Classical Greece and Rome, the Hellenistic period was by no means without distinction. Great works of literature, history and philosophy were produced. This was the period of Polybius, Theophrastus and Apollonius of Rhodes, and the time of the development of Stoic, Epicurean, and Utopian philosophies. There were great advances in natural sciences. Ptolemy Soter founded the first library and the first museum at Alexandria, both of which remained centres of learning and research for centuries afterwards. The significance of the advances made in the Hellenistic period cannot be underestimated. Shipley observes, 'the advances in mathematics, astronomy, physics, and engineering that were made in the period still underlie modern science', while the scholarship and libraries, art and architecture were 'explicitly taken as models until the twentieth century',[15] a fact which has been recognised even by the harshest of critics.[16]

---

[14] Shipley, 'Recent Trends and New Directions', 403.

[15] Shipley, 'Recent Trends and New Directions', 318.

[16] While the nineteenth-century historian George Rawlinson deplores the degenerate nature of the Hellenistic kingdoms caused by their exposure to 'Asiatic ideas', he nonetheless acknowledges the great advances in mathematics, astronomy, geography, ethnology and natural history during the Hellenistic period that were brought about 'partly through this opening up of Oriental stores'. See G. Rawlinson, *Manual of Ancient History, From the Earliest Times to the Fall of the Sassanian Empire*, second edition (Oxford, 1880), 217.

# Greek, but not Grecian? Macedonians in Enlightenment Histories 223

Macedonian and Hellenistic History is a crucial part of many eighteenth-century Greek histories. Indeed, epochs that are now on the periphery such as Archaic and Hellenistic Greece were seen to be as important for study as Classical Greece, with the search for political models going well beyond the scholarly debate over Classical Athens and Sparta. Leading Macedonians – especially Philip – are clearly seen in these eighteenth-century works as admirable and talented statesmen who are very much part of the Greek world. Furthermore, the decline of the Graeco-Macedonian empire is seen as lamentable rather than contemptible. In nineteenth-century histories we see a sharp contrast from the eighteenth-century works. Macedonians are no longer admirable, talented, or even Greek – they are barbarians who stand apart from Greeks – while the Hellenistic Period is dismissed out of hand as a period of abject misery and failure, a time when degenerate Greeks inevitably squander the glorious achievements of their ancestors and grovel at the feet of their barbarous Macedonian masters. To a considerable extent, twentieth- and twenty-first-century scholarship implicitly follows this line of thought.

The reasons for this change in attitude in the nineteenth century are many and diverse. Some are more understandable and justifiable (both intellectually and morally) than others. There are several key factors which overlap and combine to explain why Macedonian history and the Hellenistic period hold marginal places in scholarship today: firstly, modern (and ancient) views of race and geography; secondly, modern attitudes to the concept of 'Liberty'. A comparison between the works of the pioneers of Greek History who were writing in the eighteenth century – in particular Gast, Mably, Robertson, and Gillies – and the views to those of more recent pioneers in the field – especially George Grote, J.G. Droysen and B.G. Niebuhr will demonstrate a marked difference in attitude regarding each of these issues.

## Part 1: Geography and Race

For pioneering eighteenth-century writers such as Tourreil, Mably, Robertson, Gast, and Gillies, Macedonian and what is now known as 'Hellenistic' history, were an integral part of Greek History. Many even go so far as to suggest that Macedonia was part of Greece, and that Macedonians were Greek.

Philip of Macedon was central to what was arguably the first modern work of Greek History, Jacques de Tourreil's 1691 'Historical Preface' to the speeches of Demosthenes (translated into English in 1702). This work necessarily focuses heavily on Macedon in order to place the Athenian orator's speeches in their proper context. It is interesting to note that the first versions of Temple Stanyan's *Grecian History* (1707–39) is very similar in focus, as is John Gillies' first foray in Greek History in *The Orations of Isocrates, and A Discourse on the History, Manners, and Character of the Greeks, from the Conclusion of the Peloponnesian War to the Battle of Chæronea* (1778).[17]

Gabriel Bonnot de Mably's *Observations sur l'histoire de la Grèce* (1766, translated 1784) covers Greek history down to the defeat of Perseus by the Romans in 168 B.C. and the final absorption of Greece by the Romans in 146 B.C. Philip of Macedon, Alexander the Great and their Successors all play leading roles in Mably's discussion of Greek affairs. According to Johnson Wright, Mably saw the struggles of the Hellenistic monarchs against the might of Rome as a lesson he could use to educate the people of his day. For Wright,

> the most vivid and interesting passages in the two *Observations* are those which treat Hellenistic Greece, where Mably could gauge the attempts of various Greek leaders to preserve or recover their "liberty" in an age of general corruption – clearly the classical epoch that was most relevant to, and has the most to teach his European contemporaries, in Mably's eyes.[18]

John Gast's *History of Greece from the Accession of Alexander of Macedon till its Final Subjection to the Roman Power* (1782) was published as a follow up to his 1753 *The Rudiments of the Grecian History, from the First Establishment of the States of Greece, to the Overthrow of their Liberties in the Days of Philip the Macedonian*, a work composed as a dialogue between three Greeks by the names of Palaemon, Eudoxus and Cleanthes. Gast covered what we now know as the Hellenistic period in a straight forward narrative under the title *History of Greece from the Accession of Alexander of Macedon till its Final Subjection to the Roman Power*. He began this work by announcing that 'The annals of Greece include, perhaps, the most interesting and instructive portion of the History of Man',[19] thus from the outset emphasising the importance of this latter period of Greek History to the story of Greece as a whole. For Gast, there is no question

---

[17] This seems to suggest that 'Greek History' in the modern sense begins when writers seek to place orators such as Demosthenes, Isocrates and Lysias in their context, a task made necessary by the fact that aside from Diodorus, there is no extant ancient narrative covering these periods.

[18] J.K. Wright, 'Conversations with Phocion: The Political Thought of Mably', *History of Political Thought*, 13 (1992), 394.

[19] J. Gast, *History of Greece from the Accession of Alexander of Macedon till its Final Subjection to the Roman Power* (London, 1782), v.

that Philip of Macedon, Alexander the Great, and their Successors are Greek. He even goes so far as to suggest that 'The history of Alexander ... is the history of Greece'.[20] This represents quite a volte-face on the part of Gast whose first foray into Greek History ended with the death of Philip, and the observation that 'for the Grecians, after the battle of Chaeronea, every year seems to have added to their meanness and abjectness, until what Philip had begun, Alexander and his successors, and at last wide-wasting Rome, completed'.[21] The change from 'Grecian History' to the 'History of Greece' is marked. In 1793 both volumes were republished posthumously with the title *History of Greece: Properly so called*, thus further emphasising that the Hellenistic period was in fact Greek.

William Robertson, whose popular *History of Greece* was first published in 1768 and reached a ninth edition by 1829 despite being little more than a plagiarised translation of a French history by Pons Augustin Alletz,[22] covers Greek History from mythical times to the Roman conquest. In his 'Preface', Robertson explicitly states that his work should not be compared to those of Stanyan and Goldsmith because they stop at the deaths of Philip and Alexander respectively.[23] Robertson justifies extending his Greek History to the Roman conquest by observing that for other writers, 'the end of the history of Greece is ... extended to the period of the extinction of the government of the Seleucidae in Asia by Pompey the Great ... and, by some authors ... to the time that the race of the Lagidae failed in Egypt'.[24]

Moreover, Robertson explicitly states that Macedon is part of Greece, and that Macedonians are Greek. In his Preface he writes: 'For Philip, king of Macedon, *one of the districts of Greece*, profited by those dissensions of *the other Greeks*' [italics added].[25] Unlike many of his predecessors and those who would follow, Robertson even goes so far as to include the kingdom of Epirus in Greece. He claims that 'Greece was distinguished into six principal divisions, Macedonia, Thessaly, Epirus, Achaia, or Greece properly so called, Peloponnesus, and the Islands'.[26]

---

[20] Gast, *History of Greece*, 11.
[21] J. Gast, *The Rudiments of the Grecian History, from the First Establishment of the States of Greece, to the Overthrow of their Liberties in the Days of Philip the Macedonian* (Dublin, 1753), 537.
[22] G. Ceserani 'Narrative, Interpretation, and Plagiarism in Mr. Robertson's 1778 *History of Ancient Greece*', *Journal of the History of Ideas*, 66 (2005), 419ff.
[23] W. Robertson, *History of Ancient Greece* (Edinburgh, 1793), xii.
[24] Robertson, *History of Ancient Greece*, 36.
[25] Robertson, *History of Ancient Greece*, x.
[26] Robertson, *History of Ancient Greece*, 17–18.

William Mitford in his *History of Greece* (1784–1810) also sees Macedon as a part of Greece, describing the Macedonian people as 'a people of Grecian race' located 'on the northern border'.[27] He observes,

> in the heat of party contest among the republics, the foul language of democratical debate would sometimes stigmatise the Macedonians with the name of barbarians. But this is not found from any others. Among the Greek historians their Grecian blood has been universally acknowledged. Their speech was certainly Grecian, their manners were Grecian, their religion was Grecian; with differences, as far as they are reported to us, not greater than existed among the different republics.[28]

In his *Philosophical Dissertations on the Greeks* (1788, translated 1793), Cornelius de Pauw explicitly includes Macedonia as part of Greece, which he describes as comprising everything 'from the extremity of Peloponnesus to the confines of Macedonia'.[29] Moreover, he refers to the Macedonians as 'Greeks'. When discussing what he perceives as the limited importance of the gymnasia to Greek military prowess, de Pauw writes,

> The Macedonians, who were constantly styled barbarians by Demosthenes, possessed strong nerves, joined to a certain degree of good sense; and without practising such exercises [as at the gymnasia], they defeated *the other Greeks* almost in every battle [italics added].[30]

Even Oliver Goldsmith – a writer who has been cited as evidence that British historians perceived that the Macedonians 'did not deserve the name Greek'[31] – explicitly includes the kingdom of Macedon in Greece. Thus, he writes '[a] spirit of liberty prevailed all over Greece, and a general change of government was effected in every part of the country except in Macedonia'.[32] Although Goldsmith believes that the Macedonians are 'in a manner barbarous',[33] they are nonetheless resident in Greece.[34]

---

[27] W. Mitford, *The History of Greece*, vol. V (London, 1818), 192.
[28] Mitford, *History of Greece*, vol. V, 195.
[29] C. de Pauw, *Philosophical Dissertations on the Greeks*, vol. I (London, 1793), 85.
[30] de Pauw, *Philosophical Dissertations*, vol. I, 104.
[31] K.N. Demetriou, 'Historians on Macedonian Imperialism and Alexander the Great', *Journal of Modern Greek Studies*, 19 (2001), 27.
[32] O. Goldsmith, *The Grecian History, from the Earliest State to the Death of Alexander the Great, By Dr. Goldsmith*, vol. I (London, 1785), 9.
[33] Goldsmith, *The Grecian History*, vol. I, 429–30.
[34] Thus, Goldsmith, vol. 1, 429, begins the very sentence that Demetriou 'Historians on Macedonian Imperialism', 27, cites as evidence that Goldsmith considers the Macedonians as not being Greek with the words, 'During these transactions, a power was growing up in Greece, hitherto unobserved, but now too conspicuous and formidable to be overlooked …'.

Rather than not deserving the designation Greeks, the Macedonians do not deserve to be known as 'Grecians'.³⁵ This distinction will be discussed in more detail below.

Perhaps the most emphatically 'Greek' of the 'long eighteenth-century histories' covering the Hellenistic period was published in 1807. After completing his 1786 work, *The History of Ancient Greece*, John Gillies commenced researching and writing his two-volume sequel entitled *History of the World*. It took two decades to produce, not least because there was a hiatus towards the beginning of his research while he wrote his *View of the Reign of Frederick the Great with a Parallel between that Prince and Philip II of Macedon* (1789). Any doubts that *The History of the World* is in fact a Greek History should be dismissed at once. Gillies gives the work the subtitle *Comprehending the Latter Ages of European Greece, and the History of the Greek Kingdoms in Asia and Africa, from their Foundation to their Destruction*. Thus, for Gillies, the kingdoms of the Antigonids, Seleucids, and Ptolemies are Greek, and belong rightly in Greek History. Moreover, Gillies models his writing on the first Greek Historian, Herodotus, claiming that '[a]fter the example of the *first* of Historians, in point not only of time but of merit, I have inquired, as he does on nearly a similar occasion, who they were, those ancient and once illustrious nations subdued and long governed by the Greeks and Macedonians'³⁶ – thus again stressing the Greek orientation of his work.

Gillies consciously links his *History of the World* to his earlier *The History of Ancient Greece*, observing that it 'continued and completed' the earlier work.³⁷ In his *Preface* he refers to the work as the second part of his Greek History, with the title, *History of Ancient Greece, its Colonies and Conquests*, and claims that it 'necessarily rises above the first in greatness and novelty of design' – thus stressing his belief in the importance of his task.³⁸ It is clear that he saw his *History of the World* as an extension or expansion of his earlier work. He observes:

> Through my respectful adherence to a model, the nearest of any to perfection, my readers will proceed easily from the known to the unknown; and the history of Greece, the country to which we are indebted for our general acquaintance with antiquity, will naturally expand into the history of the Eastern world, and of those remote regions of the South and West

---

³⁵ Goldsmith, *Grecian History*, vol. I, 447.
³⁶ J. Gillies, *History of the World: Comprehending the Latter Ages of European Greece, and the History of the Greek Kingdoms in Asia and Africa, From their Foundation to their Destruction*, vol. I (London, 1807), iii.
³⁷ Gillies, *History of the World*, vol. II, 823.
³⁸ Gillies, *History of the World*, vol. I, vii.

which gradually fell into the sphere either of its military exertion or of its commercial intercourse.[39]

Gillies ends his *Preface* with a plea – 'I anxiously crave for the present work the same indulgence which its precursor continues to experience'.[40] It is to be much lamented that it did not.

Like Gast, Gillies' attitude to the Macedonians evolves over the course of his writings. In his early works he seems to view Macedon as separate from Greece.[41] Yet while his *History of Ancient Greece* ends with the death of Alexander the Great, he nonetheless claims that 'Alexander was himself a Greek', and goes so far as to state that 'his kingdom was founded by a Grecian colony'.[42] By the time of the publication of the *History of the World*, Gillies describes the Hellenistic kingdoms as Greek,[43] and he describes his history of what we know as the Hellenistic period as effectively 'Part 2' of his *History of Ancient Greece*.

Yet for nineteenth-century historians (with the obvious exception of Connop Thirlwall, who nonetheless does not see Macedonians as Greek),[44] Macedonian and Hellenistic history is not worthy of inclusion in Greek History. This is best illustrated by George Grote, arguably the most influential Greek historian of the nineteenth century. When discussing the military campaigns of Eumenes of Cardia – the Greek general and former secretary of Philip of Macedon and Alexander the Great to whom Plutarch devoted a Greek *Life* – Grote argues that they have no place in his Greek history:

> His [Eumenes of Cardia] gallant struggles, first in Kilikia and Phenicia, next (when driven from the coast), in Susiana, Persis, Media, and Parætakênê – continued for two years against the greatly preponderant forces of Ptolemy, Antigonus, and Seleukos, and against the never ceasing treachery of his own

---

[39] Gillies, *History of the World*, vol. I, iii–iv.
[40] Gillies, *History of the World*, vol. I, viii.
[41] Gillies, *View of the Reign of Frederick the Great with a Parallel between that Prince and Philip II of Macedon* (London, 1789), 5, when comparing the courts of Philip and Frederick observes that they were at 'Macedon, towards the north of Greece, and Brandenburgh in the north of Germany'.
[42] Gillies, *The History of Ancient Greece*, vol. II (London, 1786), 635.
[43] As noted above, Gillies describes the Hellenistic monarchies as 'the Greek kingdoms in Asia and Africa', and consciously links the *History of the World* to his earlier *History of Greece*.
[44] C. Thirlwall, *The History of Greece*, vol. V (London, 1835–44), 154ff. draws a clear distinction between 'the state of Macedonia' and 'the Greeks'. Cf. K.N. Demetriou, 'Historians on Macedonian Imperialism', 30.

officers and troops – do not belong to Grecian history. They are however, amongst the most memorable exploits of antiquity.[45]

Despite the fact that these events are 'amongst the most memorable exploits of antiquity', Grote can find no place for them in his 'Grecian History'. This is not merely a matter of geography, for Grote was quite content to devote large sections of his work to the Greeks of Sicily and Asia Minor. It is as much to do with the fact that Eumenes was fighting against Macedonians, and in the eyes of Grote, Macedonians are not Greek. If we are in any doubt as the Grote's opinions on Macedonians, we need only look to his views on Alexander the Great:

> Alexander … like his father Philip, was not a Greek, but a Macedonian and Epirot, partially imbued with Grecian sentiment and intelligence … The basis of Philip's character was Macedonian, not Greek: it was the self-will of a barbarian prince, not *ingenium civile*, or sense of reciprocal obligation and right in society with others, which marked more or less even the most powerful members of a Grecian city, whether oligarchical or democratical. If this was true of Philip, it was still more true of Alexander, who inherited the violent temperament and headstrong will of his furious Epirotic mother Olympias.[46]

This sentiment is certainly present in other nineteenth-century works, for example B.G. Niebuhr's *Lectures on Ancient History*, in which he argues that Philip 'spoke Greek from his infancy, but he did not acquire the sentiments of a Greek',[47] and George Rawlinson, who clearly distinguished between Hellenic, Macedonian and Asiatic peoples in his *Manual of Ancient History*. For Rawlinson, Macedonians are clearly inferior to Greeks. When discussing Alexander's plan to bring about a 'racial fusion' between the European and Asiatic peoples of his empire, Rawlinson argues that 'the integration of races would have improved the lower types of humanity', but that the new race 'would have fallen far below the Hellenic, *perhaps even the Macedonian type*' [italics added].[48] Interestingly (and not that surprisingly), Rawlinson regularly cites the work of Niebuhr in the Macedonian section of his history.

---

[45] G. Grote, *History of Greece*, reprinted from the second London edition, vol. XII (New York, 1900), vol. XII, 342.
[46] Grote, *History of Greece*, vol. 12, 2.
[47] B.G. Niebuhr, *Lectures on Ancient History, From the Earliest Times to the Taking of Alexandria, Comprising the History of the Asiatic Nations, the Egyptians, Greeks, Macedonians and Carthaginians*, L. Schmitz (ed.), translated by Dr Marcus Neibuhr, vol. II (London, 1852), 255–6.
[48] Rawlinson, *Manual of Ancient History*, 209.

It may be that the nineteenth-century historians were influenced by the foundation of the modern kingdom of Greece in 1832. When Britain, France and Russia set the boundaries of Otto's new kingdom they limited his territory to little more than Athens, the Morea (i.e. the Peloponnese) and the nearby Aegean islands then known as the Archipelago. The northern border of Greece was set roughly in line with the town of Lamia, thus cutting off the Greeks in Thessaly, Epirus and Macedonia from their southern brethren. Thessaly would not become part of the Greek kingdom until 1881, whilst Macedonia and Epirus (along with Crete and the islands off Asia Minor) were not incorporated into Greece until 1913. With Niebuhr delivering his lectures in the late 1820s, Grote writing in the 1840s, and Rawlinson writing in the 1880s, it is by no means inconceivable that the exclusion of Macedon and Epirus from the modern kingdom of Greece influenced these historians who were writing many decades before these territories became part of Greece and therefore 'Greek' in a modern sense.

It is worth pointing out that the boundaries of Greece set in 1832 accorded with what the early nineteenth-century travellers had already perceived as representing Greece. For the most part the travellers were not interested in the north of Greece, and concentrated their activities in the Morea, Athens, and the Archipelago.[49] They typically entered Greek territories from the west through the Ionian Islands (usually Zante) or from the east via Smyrna. Few ventured into Macedonia or Thrace, except for a somewhat obligatory short visit to the city of Salonica.[50] The only obvious exception was William Martin Leake, who travelled extensively in both southern and northern Greece, and was the only Briton to visit both eastern and western Macedonia.[51] His *Travels in the Morea* (1830) and *Travels in Northern Greece* (1835) proved popular and can still provide useful information for the modern archaeologist or ancient historian (see C.H. Lange, 'The Battle of Actium and the "slave of passion"', pp. 115–36, above). For Leake who was writing just after the foundation of the kingdom of Greece,[52] Macedonia and Epirus are naturally not part of

---

[49] Most trips included an almost obligatory visit to the court of Ali Pasha at Ioannina.
[50] H. Angelomatis-Tsougarakis, *The Eve of the Greek Revival: British Travellers' Perceptions of Early Nineteenth-Century Greece* (London, 1990), 11–12. Even Henry Holland, who published his travel notes under the title *Travels in the Ionian Islands, Albania, Thessaly, and Macedonia, &c* (London, 1815), really only saw Salonica when he travelled to what he called 'Macedonia'.
[51] Angelomatis-Tsougarakis, *The Eve of Greek Revival*, 13.
[52] Although his work was not published until the 1830s, Leake had in fact conducted his travels to what would later become Greece in the first decade of the nineteenth century. For a detailed discussion of Leake's travels and publications, see M. Wagstaff, 'Colonel Leake and the Historical Geography of Greece', 169–83, above.

the then new nation known as Greece, but at the same time there is no question that he views the northern lands and peoples as Greek.[53] But while the Greeks themselves would have agreed with Leake, his opinions regarding the northern Greeks are not representative of his British, French or German contemporaries.[54]

A prime example is F.S.N. Douglas, whose 1813 work, *An Essay on Certain Points of Resemblance between the Ancient and Modern Greeks* makes little mention of the north of Greece. Douglas claimed to have embarked on his journey to Greece in order 'to discover the countrymen of Pericles in the inhabitants of modern Athens, or to compare the sturdy mountaineer of Maina with the disciple of Lycurgus'.[55] At no time does Douglas suggest that he would like to find the countrymen of Alexander the Great or Philip of Macedon in the wilds of northern Greece. In fact, apart from a brief visit to 'Saloniki' Douglas does not put even a toe into the north of Greece. From the outset, he makes it clear that for him Greece equates to 'the Morea and Archipelago'.[56] Douglas argues that the Greeks of the mainland have degenerated in habits, language and culture, due to interbreeding with 'Wallachians' and other members of 'the Sclavonian race'. Even the Athenians of his day have little claim to be Greek. He suggests that 'the pure Greek blood is more likely to be found in the islands of the Archipelago'.[57] Douglas seeks to solve the tricky question of what constitutes Greece

---

[53] W. M. Leake, *Travels in Northern Greece* (London, 1835), consistently refers to the inhabitants of these regions as 'Greek'.

[54] The views of the great European powers did not accord with those of the Greeks themselves. In his famous 1844 speech outlining the 'Megali Idea' that Greece should encompass all the ethnic Greeks, the Greek Prime Minister Ioannis Koletti argued, 'The Kingdom of Greece is not Greece. [Greece] constitutes only one part, the smallest, poorest. A Greek is not only a man who lives within this kingdom but also one who lives in Jannina, in Salonica, in Serres, in Adrianople, in Constantinople, in Smyrna, in Trebizond, in Crete, in Samos and in any land associated with Greek history or the Greek race'. Cf. R. Clogg, *A Short History of Modern Greece* (Cambridge, 1986), 76. The question of what territory is Greek and what is not is still a contentious issue in the region today, with the modern state of Greece at odds with the former Yugoslav Republic of Macedonia (FYROM) over the very name Macedonia after almost two decades of wrangling over the issue. The Greek Prime Minister Kostas Karamanlis recently observed in a speech, 'I myself am a Macedonian, and another two and half million Greeks are Macedonians'.

[55] F.S.N. Douglas, *An Essay on Certain Points of Resemblance Between the Ancient and Modern Greeks* (London, 1813), 1–2.

[56] Douglas, *Essay*, 30.

[57] Douglas, *Essay*, 42–3.

and Greek in his own day by going back to the ancient evidence. He argues,

> Some confusion has been occasioned by the different ideas attached by various writers to the denominations Greece and Greeks. When they are exclusively restricted to those commonwealths that took part in the Peloponnesian war, or those that sent deputies to the council of the Amphictyons, Macedonia, Epirus and Constantinople will lie without their limits; and if a wider range be taken, besides these βαρβαροι [barbarians], which I have already mentioned, there will be a danger of confounding with the descendants of the Hellenes, many nations of perfectly different origins, but whose religion and habitual language have embodied them with the Greeks.[58]

For Douglas there is no doubt that Macedonians are barbarians who do not deserve to be described as Greek or to be known as part of Greece – his use of the Greek term βάρβαροι (barbarians) emphasises his denial of their Greek identity. Few nineteenth-century historians or travellers would have disagreed. The nineteenth-century attitude to northern Greeks and Macedonians is perhaps best summed up by the *Encyclopaedia Britannica* entry for Thessaly from 1888. Here, the perception of a racial distinction between Macedonians and Greeks could not be more clear: 'In race, as in geographical position, the Thessalians held an intermediate place between the non-Hellenic Macedonians and the Greeks of pure blood'.[59] The idea of a racial distinction between Ancient Greeks and Macedonians has proved persistent. Often a lone voice in a sea of disbelief, N.G.L. Hammond regularly stressed that the Macedonian royal house was Greek. According to Hammond: 'In the early fifth century the royal house of the Temenidae was recognized as Greek by the presidents of the Olympic games. Their verdict was and is decisive; for modern critics adduce no evidence'.[60] A clear example of the modern prejudice that Hammond criticises here comes from Loeb edition of Isocrates, *Philip*. Where Isocrates writes that Heracles was 'progenitor' of the Macedonian race,[61] the Loeb editor George Norlin helpfully notes that this 'was precluded because of his divinity'.[62] Even Hammond himself is not immune to the notion that Macedonians differ racially from Greeks. While he regularly championed the Greek cause of the Macedonian royal house, Hammond was not so ready to describe the Macedonian populace as

---

[58] Douglas, *Essay*, 40.
[59] *Encyclopaedia Britannica* (1888), xxiii.
[60] Hammond, *History of Greece*, 534–5.
[61] Isocrates, *Philip*, 105.
[62] Cf. *Isocrates* I, George Norlin (ed.) (Harvard 1928, reprinted 1991).

Greek. Hammond often argued that the population of Macedon was not Greek, and twice described Macedon as 'a fusion of Greek and barbarian element' in the *Oxford Classical Dictionary*.[63]

It is worth pointing out that objections to Macedonians being Greek appear in the eighteenth-century works of de Tourreil and Rollin. Both maintain that 'the kings of Macedon pretended to descend from Hercules by Caranus, and consequently to have been Greeks originally'.[64] All this is in spite of the ancient evidence such as Plutarch, who began his *Life* of Alexander by observing that 'he [Alexander] was a descendant of Heracles through Caranus on his father's side, and a descendant of Aeacus through Neoptolemus on his mother's: this is accepted without any question'.[65]

The idea of a racial distinction between Macedonians and Greeks owes much to the manner in which post-Classical Greeks tried to distance themselves from their Macedonian neighbours. This move saw ancient writers favour genealogies that racially separated the Macedonians from the Greeks. Classical Greek writers provided genealogies that make the eponymous hero Makedon the son of Zeus and Thyia, the daughter of Deucalion,[66] or the son of Aeolus,[67] and thus the grandson of Hellen.[68] Such genealogies stress the 'Greekness' of Makedon by making him the nephew of Hellen, or a direct descendant of Aeolus.[69] However, Hellenistic Greek writers often made Makedon the son of Lycaon,[70] the King of Emathia – thus making Makedon Pelasgian by race, i.e. not Hellenic.

---

[63] *Oxford Classical Dictionary* (Oxford, 1949), 526; *Oxford Classical Dictionary*, second edition (Oxford, 1970), 634. Hammond does not make this distinction in the *Oxford Classical Dictionary*, 904–5. Here Hammond observes that 'from Philip onwards the Macedonian court was a leading centre of Greek culture'. Nonetheless, Hammond still manages to suggest that there is a distinction between Greek and Hellenistic Greek culture, arguing that 'the policies of Alexander spread the *Greek-based* "Hellenistic" culture to the east' [italics added].

[64] C. Rollin, *The Ancient History of the Egyptians, Carthaginians, Assyrians, Babylonians, Medes and Persians, Macedonians, and Grecians*, translated 1738, second edition, vol. IV (London, 1738–1740), 251. Cf. J. de Tourreil, 'Historical Preface' to *Several Orations of Demosthenes* (London, 1702), 5.

[65] Plutarch, *Alexander*, 2.

[66] Hesiod, *Eoeae*, f. 7.

[67] Hellenicus, f. 74.

[68] N.G.L. Hammond, *A History of Macedonia*, vol. 1 (Oxford, 1972), 276; Burstein, 'New Ways of Being Greek in the Hellenistic Period', 228.

[69] Curiously J. Hall, *Hellenicity: Between Ethnicity and Culture* (Chicago, 2002), 165 argues that Hesiod's genealogy separates Makedon 'from the ranks of the Hellenes'. Although Hesiod does not make Makedon a direct descendant of Hellen, he is nonetheless closely related to Hellen, since his mother is Hellen's sister.

[70] Aelian, *On the Characteristics of Animals* 10.48; Apollodorus 3.81.

The distinction between Greeks and Macedonians in the nineteenth century is also reflected in the usage of the terms 'Greek' and 'Grecian'. For eighteenth-century writers such as Gast, Gillies, Robertson, Goldsmith and the English translators of Mably and de Pauw, 'Grecian' and 'Greek' are not synonyms. Grecians are always Greek, but not all Greeks are Grecian. Thus, Demosthenes is both a Grecian and a Greek, whereas Philip of Macedon is a Macedonian and a Greek, but most certainly not Grecian. Most remarkably, Mitford explicitly describes the Macedonians as 'a people of Grecian race'.[71] Temple Stanyan and Thomas Leland refer to Macedonians and Grecians and do not use the term 'Greek' as a noun.[72] However, for nineteenth-century writers such as Grote, Thirlwall and Rawlinson, 'Grecian' and 'Greek' are synonyms. Thus, Philip and the Macedonians can never be Greek.

The distinction between Macedonians and Grecians but not between Macedonia and Greece is particularly clear in Temple Stanyan's *Grecian History* (1707–39, revised in 1751). Stanyan states that he will not include Greek affairs after the accession of Alexander the Great in his work on the grounds that, 'the Affairs of Alexander … are not, strictly speaking, to be look'd upon as a Continuation of the *Grecian* Story, since they relate almost entirely to *Macedonia* and *Persia*'.[73] Yet later in his work (when discussing the geography of Greece) Stanyan makes it clear that Macedonia is – at times – a part of Greece, and therefore what later writers would term 'Greek'. He places Macedonia 'on the North' of Greece along with Illyricum and Epirus, yet distinguishes the latter two locales from Greece and Macedonia as lands with 'a mixt Dependence on the Grecians and Barbarians'. He goes on to say of Macedonia,

> [a]s for *Macedonia* in general, we are not yet to consider it as part of *Greece*, 'till by a large Accession of Territory it grew formidable to the most remote and powerful states of *Greece*; and from thence laid the Foundation of that Sovereignty it soon after assum'd under the Title of the Third Monarchy.[74]

Thus for Stanyan, the Macedonia of Philip (and Alexander) comes to be a part of Greece,[75] yet its inhabitants cannot be seen as Grecian. Therefore the

---

[71] Mitford, *History of Greece*, vol. IV, 192.
[72] T. Stanyan, *The Grecian History* (London, 1751); T. Leland, *History of Philip, King of Macedon, Now Corrected* (London, 1806).
[73] Stanyan, *Grecian History*, 'Preface'.
[74] Stanyan, *Grecian History*, vol. I, 9.
[75] Gast makes a similar distinction between the Macedonia of Philip and that of his ancestors in his 1753 *Rudiments of Grecian History*. When describing the confines of Greece, Gast (p. 2) places the northern boundary at 'the *Macedonian* Mountains'. His primary speaker Palaemon later clarifies matters by explaining (pp. 215–16) that '*Macedonia* and the Countries adjacent received the Name of *Grecian* only in later days'.

history of Macedonia has no place in his *Grecian History*. Stanyan's decision to take his history no further forward than the Battle of Chaeronea is not at all surprising when one considers that his work is entitled *Grecian History*, rather than 'History of Greece' like those of Gillies, Mitford, Thirlwall or even Grote.[76] Had he been writing a 'Greek History' rather than a 'Grecian History', its format may have been rather different.

The central place of Macedonia within Greece and the eighteenth-century historical accounts of Greece is perhaps best illustrated by the map included in the 1739 edition of Stanyan's *Grecian History* (see figure 6). This map, entitled 'Mapp of *Ancient Greece*', depicts the Greek peninsula, the Aegean Sea, the Asia Minor coast, as well as the eastern part of Sicily in an inset. Macedonia is particularly prominent, and is labelled in a way that suggests that kingdom incorporated not only lower and upper Macedonia, but also Epirus and much of Thessaly. An almost identical map (differing only in fonts and labels) was included in Robertson's 1778 and 1786 editions under the title 'A Map of *Ancient Greece*'. Another similar map (this time printed over two pages) appears in the 1793 edition of Gast's *History of Greece*. The importance of Macedon to the history of Greece, and its relative lack of importance in the eighteenth century can be seen in the maps accompanying the 1793 English translation of de Pauw's *Philosophical Dissertations on the Greeks*. The publishers included two maps, both depicting the Greek peninsula, the Aegean Sea, and western Asia Minor, with the titles 'Ancient Greece' and 'Modern Greece'. Both are virtually devoid of geographical features or labels north of Thermopylae. The former has a label for 'Macedonia' in the largest font used, thus indicating the importance of Macedonia in ancient Greece and its importance to the work itself. But the label which is squeezed in at the top sits so awkwardly that one suspects that it was an afterthought, rather than an integral part of the cartographical plan.[77]

The eighteenth-century historians differ markedly from their nineteenth-century successors also in their views of Philip of Macedon.

---

[76] It is worth reiterating that Gast ended his *Rudiments of Grecian History* at the battle of Chaeronea, and continued the story of the Greeks and Macedonians under the title *History of Greece*.

[77] Maps are by no means an integral part of the Greek histories from the long eighteenth century. There were no maps included in the early editions of Gast, no maps accompanied Mably's *Observations on the Greeks*, and Mitford's mammoth work contained only a map of Thermopylae. Mitford, *History of Greece*, vol. II, 88, directs his readers to 'the map' when describing the Greek landscape, but this is an imaginary 'good map' (p. 306) that his readers are consulting rather than any map included amongst his volumes.

For Leland, Mably, Gast, Mitford and Gillies, Philip is first and foremost a figure to be admired, a statesman to be emulated. Leland and Gillies both explicitly compared Philip to Frederick the Great. This was not a comparison intended to be an insult to either monarch. Frederick himself consciously sought comparison with Philip and Alexander. He is said to have been inspired to reform the Prussian army after reading about Philip's reorganisation of the Macedonian phalanx. Frederick also reputedly responded to Voltaire's suggestion that he should heed Cato's philosophy on politics by mimicking Alexander's response to Parmenion when the latter advised Alexander to accept the Persian king Darius' offer of all the territory west of the Euphrates. Just as Alexander retorted 'I would if I were Parmenion',[78] Frederick responded to Voltaire's suggestion with the words, 'Glaubt mir, wennich Voltaire wär'.[79] Even the British Ambassador to Prussia drew the parallel between Philip and Frederick, observing,

> Here one frequently draws comparisons between the Prussian army and that of the Macedonians. If Alexander the Great with just a handful of well-drilled soldiers was able to achieve wondrous things, what will the Prussian army not be capable of undertaking, since their army is without doubt the best and most select in all Europe?[80]

Frederick's conscious emulation of the Macedonian kings no doubt inspired Gillies to write his *View of the Reign of Frederick the Great with a Parallel between that Prince and Philip II of Macedon* (1789), when he spent a considerable sojourn at the Prussian court.

Gillies admired Philip as much as he admired Frederick. He admires what he calls 'the liberal spirit of the Macedonian government',[81] and even went so far as to suggest that 'it should come as no surprise that Isocrates should regard the battle of Chaeronea, by which Greece became subject to a Philip, not as their misfortune, but as their deliverance'.[82]

Mably saw Philip as 'a politician superior to all events, and formed to govern mankind'.[83] Mably also noted that 'There is no precept of Policy,

[78] Plutarch, *Alexander*, 29.4.
[79] F.M.C. Wailes-Fairbairn, *Alexander the Great: A Case Study in German Attitudes to Greatness between Napoleon & Hitler*, unpublished D.Phil. thesis (Oxford, 1992), 421.
[80] Reinhold Koser, *Geschichte Friedrichs des Grosse,* vol. I (Stuttgart, 1893), 161, cited by Wailes-Fairbairn, 422.
[81] Gillies, *History of Ancient Greece*, 'Preface'.
[82] J. Gillies, *The Orations of Isocrates, and A Discourse on the History, Manners, and Character of the Greeks, from the Conclusion of the Peloponnesian War to the Battle of Chaeronea* (London, 1778), Preface.
[83] Gabriel Bonnot de Mably, *Observations on the Manners, Government, and Policy of the Greeks, translated from the French of the learned Abbé Mably* (Oxford, 1784), 196.

but can be found in the life of the Macedonian Monarch; and whoever acts on the same principles, will never fail to have success'.[84]

William Mitford was also an ardent admirer of the Macedonian monarchy, paying it the ultimate compliment of a comparison with the British constitution, a compliment only matched by Homeric Phaeacia.[85] For Mitford, 'the king was supreme, but not despotic. The chief object of his office, as in the English constitution, was to be conservator of peace of his kingdom'.[86] Mitford even went so far as to suggest that Demosthenes was a traitor to his country for favouring Persia over Philip.[87] Mitford was convinced that Demosthenes should have used his oratorical prowess to convince the Athenians to support Philip rather than oppose him, and marvels that some of the 'ancients' were able to put the Persian connection out of sight, and that the 'moderns', most notably Rollin, were able to maintain that Demosthenes was 'a pure Grecian patriot'.[88] Macaulay would later savagely criticise Mitford for this, but would nonetheless maintain, 'I hold the same opinion with Mr Mitford respecting the character and views of that great and accomplished Prince'.[89] It would be nearly two hundred years before any serious historian would suggest that Demosthenes used his rhetorical powers for anything other than the most glorious cause, that is freedom, or that his opposition to Philip might have been a mistake.

For the nineteenth-century writers, Philip and his Successors are nothing but barbarian despots. Whereas eighteenth-century writers such as Stanyan, Mably, Robertson, saw Philip as having become a brilliant, if not ideal statesman as a result of his time spent as a hostage at Thebes,[90] Niebuhr argued that Philip was too barbarous to have been able to learn from Epaminondas:

> … it must not be forgotten that Alexander had the invaluable advantage of an excellent education at the hands of Aristotle; the blessed effects of which

---

[84] Mably, *Observations on the Greeks*, 154.
[85] M.L. Clarke, *Greek Studies in England, 1700–1830* (Cambridge, 1945), 108. Cf. Mitford, *History of Greece*, vol. I, 84.
[86] Mitford, *History of Greece*, vol. V, 192.
[87] Mitford, *History of Greece*, vol. V, 77.
[88] Mitford, *History of Greece*, vol. V, 77 n. 15.
[89] T.B. Macaulay, 'On Mitford's History of Greece', *Knight's Quarterly Magazine*, November 1824.
[90] Stanyan, *Grecian History*, 212; J. Gast, *The Rudiments of the Grecian History, from the First Establishment of the States of Greece, to the Overthrow of their Liberties in the Days of Philip the Macedonian* (Dublin, 1753), 628; Mably, *Observations on the Greeks*, 153–4; Robertson, *History of Greece*, 356.

were never completely obliterated, although he emancipated himself from its influence. Philip had not received such an education, in which the mind was directed to what was truly good and noble. He spent his early youth at a half barbarous court, where indulgence in vice was part of the ordinary life. There can be no doubt that he spoke Greek from his infancy, but he did not acquire the sentiments of a Greek. He had, it is true, been at Thebes; but the story that he was educated in the house of Epaminondas, must certainly be taken with the greatest limitation; and who can say, whether the unpretending and modest virtue of an Epaminondas was understood by the young prince?[91]

Grote saw the Macedonians as ignorant barbarians who could barely communicate with the outside world:

> The Macedonians, though speaking a language of their own, had neither language for communicating with others, nor literature, nor philosophy, except Grecian and derived from Greeks. Philip, while causing himself to be chosen chief of Hellas, was himself not only partially hellenized, but an eager candidate for Hellenic admiration.[92]

Remarkable words indeed, although one does wonder how any society or culture develops a language specifically for communicating with others!

The nineteenth-century view of Macedonians as barbarians comes through clearly in Niebuhr's description of Antipater, the close friend of Philip, and a man of letters who ensured that his son was educated by Aristotle. According to Niebuhr:

> Antipater was in his way a respectable man; he possessed a kind of barbarian honesty, he was a distinguished general, and Macedonia was immensely indebted to him; but he was as rude and cruel as a Turk or an Algerian. Every attempt of the Greeks appeared to him as a rebellion of slaves, just as many an otherwise honest man, cannot understand that his Negroes are anything else but brutes.

It is hard to imagine Gast, Mitford, Gillies, Mably or even Goldsmith making such a claim. Such a negative, racial-based comparison would have been completely out of place in an eighteenth-century Greek History.

## Part 2: Modern attitudes to 'Liberty'

The underlying causes of the modern aversion to Macedonian and Hellenistic History are not limited to concerns about race or geography.

---

[91] Niebuhr, *Lectures on Ancient History*, vol. II, 265–6.
[92] Grote, *History of Greece*, vol. XII, 2.

Equally fundamental is the issue of 'Liberty'. The first modern works of Greek History are not merely concerned with retelling the past; they are equally a search for political models, a search for the ideal state.

In the eighteenth century, the ancient world was the focus of debate amongst those who sought to comment on modern politics and thought through a study of antiquity. The best example of this debate is the so-called 'Athens-Sparta debate', a key part of the so-called 'Quarrel of the Ancients and Moderns' or the 'Battle of the Books', which arose when radicals and reformers turned to antiquity for political models to counter the *ancien régime* of modern Europe.[93] This debate saw the 'Spartophiles' on one side – Mably, Rousseau, Adam Ferguson and Claude Helvetius pitted against the 'Athenophiles' – Voltaire, David Hume, Adam Smith and Cornelius de Pauw – on the other.[94] This debate extends to the first Greek Histories, perhaps partly due to the fact that the fledgling field of enquiry was the province of amateurs.[95] Gillies and Mitford have been seen to 'contrast the peaceful permanence of the Spartan constitution with the ever-recurring *stasis* which marked the evolution and decay of Athenian democracy'.[96] But the debate goes well beyond Athens and Sparta. Other ancient societies, most notably Rome, and the Macedonian monarchy of Philip are also discussed as political models. Philip seems particularly popular with Greek historians such as Gillies and Robertson, who dedicated their works to King George III. Given his open admiration for both Philip and Frederick the Great, it is not surprising to find that Gillies spent time at the Prussian court.

---

[93] I. Macgregor Morris, 'The Refutation of Democracy? Socrates in the Enlightenment', in M.B. Trapp (ed.), *Socrates from Antiquity to the Enlightenment* (Aldershot, 2006), 210.

[94] I. Macgregor Morris, 'The Paradigm of Democracy: Sparta in Enlightenment Thought', in T.J. Figueira (ed.), *Spartan Society* (Swansea, 2004), 347.

[95] Stanyan adds Esq. to his name, while Gibbon and Mitford were both Hampshire squires and officers in the militia. In the eighteenth century, Classicists studied Classical texts, and 'History' was not an issue for them. Greek History as a field would remain the preserve of amateurs for some time to come. When George Grote published his famed *History of Greece*, the response of the Cambridge Classicists was a spirited defence of the merits of Thucydides in the form of Richard Shilleto's, *Thucydides or Grote?* (Cambridge and London, 1851). Cf. Clarke, *Greek Studies in England*, 103.

[96] Cartledge, 'Introduction', xxvii. This is, however, a somewhat simplified view, for Gillies does see positives at Athens, and Mitford is often highly critical of Sparta. Cf. Macgregor Morris, 'The Refutation of Democracy', 217.

The fundamental issue in these debates is 'Liberty', a term that was in flux and open to numerous interpretations. The focus on liberty means that Hellenistic History holds an awkward place in the search for political models. Firstly, Philip, Alexander, and their Successors can be seen as actively depriving the Greeks of their liberty. Secondly, the takers of liberty ultimately lose their own liberty to the Romans. Thus, the Hellenistic period can be viewed as a period which begins with the Greeks' failure to maintain their liberty against opposition from Macedon, and ends with Alexander's Successors failing to maintain their liberty in the face of opposition from Rome. For these reasons some eighteenth-century thinkers were dismissive of what we now know as the Hellenistic period.

Although many eighteenth-century historians (e.g. Mitford, Gillies and Mably) admired Philip and saw him as the ideal statesman, some, like Stanyan and de Pauw, saw Philip and the Macedonians as takers of liberty. Thus, whereas Gillies could agree with Isocrates that Philip's victory over the Athenians at Chaeronea was their deliverance, de Pauw condemned Philip as 'the destroyer of liberty',[97] and Stanyan saw Philip and Alexander as the enemies of liberty.[98] Gast likewise criticises Philip and Alexander for taking away the liberty of the 'Grecians'.[99] On the other hand, because he viewed Philip and the Macedonians as Grecians, Mitford could never have seen things this way.

Some writers also dismiss the Hellenistic period as a period bereft of liberty. With the Greeks being defeated by the Macedonians, who in turn met defeat at the hands of the Romans, the Greeks and Macedonians of the Hellenistic period are sometimes portrayed as squanderers of liberty. This sees the Hellenistic kings cast in the role of barbarian or Asiatic despots, and even drawing direct comparison with modern royal courts. According to de Pauw, when citing Livy, the Macedonian courts were places where,

> Never … did slaves appear more cringing than in the presence of kings; but in all other places their insolence was beyond measure. Immediately attached to the court, they wore its livery like other servants, and ate in a particular apartment of the palace. Some among them were indeed very

---

[97] de Pauw, *Philosophical Dissertations*, vol. II, 129.
[98] Stanyan, *Grecian History*, 340 says of Philip: 'By a mixture of some good qualities, with a great many bad ones, he [Philip] accomplished his ends, so far at least, that he had thoroughly opened the way to the destruction of the liberties of Greece'.
[99] See J. Gast, *History of Greece: Properly so called* (Dublin, 1793), vol. I, 563ff. on Philip and vol. II, 112 on Alexander. Gast states that Alexander 'forgot that he was their king [and] attempted to become their tyrant'.

rich, and others, only pretenders to fortune, incurred debts in proportion to their expenditure. From being so accustomed to such degrading subjection, they could neither endure liberty, nor support the restraint of civil laws, which are the choicest benefits that ever philosophy conferred on a human race.[100]

Furthermore, de Pauw observes with no small irony,

> Philip ... instituted this class of nobility, whose functions corresponded exactly with the great offices of modern courts; for pantlers, cupbearers, chamberlains, and train-bearers, indicate sufficiently, by their very names, the origin of such honorable employments.[101]

This line of thought was common in antiquity, where the courts of the Antigonids, Seleucids and Ptolemies were often portrayed by Greek and Roman writers as filled with parasites and flatterers prostrating themselves before decadent kings. This went hand in glove with the idea that liberty ended in Greece with the Macedonian victory of the Greeks in the Lamian War (324–322 B.C.). According to Momigliano,

> A tradition which goes back to antiquity makes the decline of Greece coincide with the death of Alexander the Great – or rather with the death of Demosthenes. This is a deserved tribute to the role of Athens in Greek civilisation. In literary terms it means Classicism. To cite Plutarch only, both Demosthenes and Cicero ended their lives as soon as their countrymen ceased to be free (Plutarch, *Demosthenes*. 3).[102]

Symptomatic of this attitude is the fact that the great Greek uprising against the Macedonians after the death of Alexander the Great which was known initially as the 'Hellenic War' (*IG* II$^2$ 448, 505, 506) is recast as the 'Lamian War' by later Greek writers (partly for political reasons), thus seemingly downgrading a united war for the liberation of Greece to the status of a squabble over an insignificant Malian town.[103]

Nonetheless, despite the critical tone, eighteenth-century writers still saw the Hellenistic period as relevant, with the loss of liberty and collapse of empire in the period being seen as a lesson to be learned for the modern world. Unlike their nineteenth-century successors, the eighteenth-century historians see the collapse of the Macedonian empire before the might of Rome as lamentable rather than contemptible. Rather than seeing the

---

[100] de Pauw, *Philosophical Dissertations*, vol. I, 178.
[101] de Pauw, *Philosophical Dissertations*, vol. I, 178.
[102] Momigliano, 'J.G. Droysen Between Greeks and Jews', 140.
[103] See N.G. Ashton, 'The Lamian War – *stat magni nominis umbra*', *Journal of Hellenic Studies*, 104 (1984), 152–7.

decline as a result of human degeneracy or ineptitude, Mably and Gillies saw the decline as a result of lamentable political disunity.

Instead of blaming Alexander's successors for squandering his conquests, Mably blames Alexander himself for pushing too far, and going beyond the sensible plans of his father.[104] He even dares to belittle Alexander by describing him as having 'entered Asia with as little precaution as Agesilaus'! Rather than seeing the decline of Macedon as a result of degeneracy or incompetence, Mably even goes so far as to suggest that the Macedonians could have defeated the Romans under more favourable circumstances. He explicitly blames the Aetolians for bringing about the downfall of the Antigonid king Philip V by 'favouring the Roman arms',[105] and preventing Philip from producing 'an army capable of astonishing the Roman legions'.[106] Ironically, that is what Philip's son Perseus did. The Roman general Aemilius Paulus would later describe the Macedonian phalanx at the battle of Pydna in 168 B.C. as the most terrifying thing he ever encountered.[107] For Mably, things might have been different for the Macedonians with a little luck on their side.

The underlying theme of Mably's work seems to be 'what might have been had the Macedonians united the Greeks under their leadership?', or 'if only they had been able to unite the Greeks'. Indeed as noted above, Wright has argued that Mably saw the Roman triumph over Macedonia as a valuable lesson for his own time.[108] This was not so much because he thought the Romans should be admired for their success, but rather because his contemporaries could learn from the mistakes of the Macedonians in failing to unify the Greeks against the Romans. Had the Greeks been unified, then the Romans might not 'ever have emerged

---

[104] Mably, *Observations on the Greeks*, 195–6. Robertson, *History of Greece*, 482, likewise blames Alexander for the downfall of his empire, arguing that 'Alexander, by pushing his conquests to so immense an extent, was the occasion of the utter ruin of his own family, and of the total extirpation of his relations; that murder and destruction were the fruits of his conquests, about which his generals slaughter one another with the most shocking cruelty; and that the states of Greece were victims of their quarrels'. de Pauw, *Philosophical Dissertations*, vol. I, 166, is also highly critical of Alexander, describing him as 'destined … to remain an assassin and a drunkard'.
[105] Mably, *Observations on the Greeks*, 258.
[106] Mably, *Observations on the Greeks*, 250–1.
[107] According to Plutarch, *Aemilius Paulus*, 19, 'when he [Paulus] saw the strength of the interlocked shields and the fierceness of their onset, amazement and fear took possession of him, and he felt he had never seen a sight more fearful'.
[108] Wright, 'Conversations with Phocion', 394.

from their primitive obscurity'.[109] Perhaps it was important for Mably to perceive that the Greeks could have recovered their liberty as he grew increasingly despondent about 'the prospects for the recovery of French "liberty"'.[110]

Gillies also portrayed the Greek world after Alexander as much more than a pitiful decline into obscurity and defeat at the hands of the Romans. He began his *History of the World* by indicating that, while he had adopted such a view when writing his *The History of Ancient Greece*, he was consciously rejecting it in the later work. He writes that Alexander's short reign,

> may be viewed under two different aspects: either as the termination of republican Greece, thereby drained of her strength, and thenceforth eclipsed of her splendour; or as the commencement of a Grecian dynasty in the East ... In treating the subject under the former point of view, I endeavoured in a preceding work, to unfold the plan of Alexander's campaigns, and accurately to describe his battles and sieges. But, in contemplating his reign under its second and still more important aspect, as the foundation of a new empire, destined speedily to dissolve into many separate monarchies, it becomes necessary to advert, not only to the exploits which he atchieved, but to the extraordinary undertakings which he meditated, and which verging as they certainly did on romantic heroism, were nevertheless, the boldest of them, confined within strict practicable limits.[111]

Significantly, Gillies explicitly states that Alexander's foundation of 'a Grecian dynasty in the East' is the 'still more important aspect' of his reign than the ending of the liberty of 'republican Greece'. Throughout the work he focuses on the dissolution of Alexander's empires into separate kingdoms. Like Mably, Gillies seems to have seen the fall of the 'Grecian dynasty' as a useful lesson rather than a sorry tale of degeneracy, and was perhaps inspired by contemporary events, with Napoleon trampling across Europe just as the Romans had trampled over the Greek world.[112]

---

[109] Mably, *Observations on the Greeks*, 270–1, goes so far as to suggest that the Romans triumphed over the Greek world due to the brilliance of their 'Republick' rather than the brilliance of their leaders. For Mably, it is the sheer number of brilliant leaders amongst the Greeks that prevented unity and led to their subjection to Rome. Thus, he argues, 'had extraordinary talents and merit been less diffused among the Grecians, the part they acted might have been more considerable'. Mably raises doubts as to whether the Romans would 'ever have emerged from their primitive obscurity, if, at their beginning, they had met such opponents as Athens or Sparta'.
[110] Wright, 'Conversations with Phocion', 407.
[111] Gillies, *History of the World*, vol. I, 1.
[112] A. Momigliano, 'George Grote and the Study of Greek History', in *Studies in Historiography* (London, 1966), 59.

For Grote, Niebuhr and other nineteenth-century writers, however, the Hellenistic period is nothing but a tedious slide into mediocrity. There are no lessons to be learned from their degeneracy. In his preface Grote states that Greek history falls into six 'compartments' from 776 B.C. until the end of the generation of Alexander. These compartments 'exhaust the free life of collective Hellas'.[113] The period after Alexander has no place in his Grecian history because not only do too many events take place outside of Grote's vision of the Greek world, but also because the Greeks in the post-Alexander world do not have political liberty. Grote writes in his preface:

> After the generation of Alexander, the political action of Greece becomes cramped and degraded, – no longer interesting to the reader, or operative on the destinies of the future world ... as a whole, the period, between 300 B.C. and the absorption of Greece by the Romans, is of no interest in itself, and is only so far of value as it helps us to understand the preceding centuries.[114]

Unlike Mably and Gillies, the nineteenth-century writers such as Grote were unable to feel any kinship with Philip, Alexander and their Successors. As Richard Jenkyns has argued, 'Englishmen wanted to see themselves as modern Athenians. They felt virtually no temptation to compare their empire with that of Macedon'.[115]

The contrast between the attitudes of the writers of the nineteenth century and their eighteenth-century predecessors is most marked in the descriptions of Perdiccas, Alexander's friend and the regent of the vast Macedonian empire upon his death. Whereas Mably sees Perdiccas as doomed to fail for no reason other than 'the defect of having been the equal of all the Captains who had been trusted with the government of the Provinces',[116] Niebuhr sees Perdiccas the worst of the barbarians:

> Perdiccas was the worst of all. He seems to have been a Macedonian noble. Although we read little of a nobility and the like among the Macedonians, yet he appears in all circumstances as a person of great pretensions. He was guilty of every licence, even the greatest cruelties, without being bloodthirsty like Antipater, who was another Duke of Alba. Perdiccas was a purely Oriental and unprincipled character: a man of very moderate talents, to whom nothing was sacred.[117]

---

[113] Grote, *History of Greece*, vol. I, ix.
[114] Grote, *History of Greece*, vol. I, x.
[115] R. Jenkyns, *The Victorians and Ancient Greece* (Oxford, 1980), 334.
[116] Mably, *Observations on the Greeks*, 207.
[117] Niebuhr, *Lectures on Ancient History*, vol. III, 43–4.

# Greek, but not Grecian? Macedonians in Enlightenment Histories 245

This is markedly different from Mably's view of Perdiccas. Mably argued that even if Perdiccas had all the qualities and talents of Philip he could not possible have maintained order in the vast Macedonian empire:

> Had Perdiccas, who was appointed to the Regency, possessed all the qualities and all the talents of Philip, he could not possibly have maintained order and subordination. Nothing could repair him from the defect of having been the equal of all the Captains who had been trusted with the government of the Provinces.[118]

Perhaps the best example of the nineteenth-century view of Macedonian and Hellenistic History comes from Niebuhr:

> In the earlier history of Greece we like to follow the great men step by step; but all these Macedonians leave us perfectly indifferent; we feel no interest whether one is defeated or the other; not even the tragic fall of Lysimachus can make an impression on us; I look upon it with greater indifference than I should feel at a bull-fight, in which a noble animal defends itself against the dogs that are set at it. I could wish that the earth had opened and swallowed up all the Macedonians. Every one intimately acquainted with ancient history will share this feeling of indifference with me. And when we are under the influence of such a feeling, it is not easy to dwell upon a history like this: it does not impress itself upon our mind.[119]

It should be clear by now how Leland, Gast, Robertson, Gillies and Mably would have responded to this statement, and what prejudices prompted Niebuhr to view the Macedonians in this way.

The term 'Grotean' is sometimes used as a means to single out a work of Greek History for praise. Thus Cartledge recently wrote in connection with an essay on Classical Athens 'the highest compliment I could pay to it would be to call it Grotean (rather than "Grote-esque")'.[120] To make comparison with Grote 'the highest compliment' for a modern historian elevates Grote's work above that of his eighteenth-century predecessors and places him on an equal footing with modern scholars. It is a distinction he does not deserve. Grote's racially charged message and outdated notion of Greek identity continues to haunt us today in the current overemphasis of Classical Athens in the discipline of Greek History and the marginal place of Macedonian and Hellenistic History in the modern discipline of Ancient History as a whole. The emulation of Grote would be better termed 'Grotesque' in the sense of 'grotesque distortion'. For by following his example, we run the risk of missing out

---

[118] Mably, *Observations on the Greeks*, 207.
[119] Niebuhr, *Lectures on Ancient History*, vol. III, 50.
[120] Cartledge, 'Introduction', xvii.

Fig. 6. Detail of Macedonia and the Greek mainland
(T. Stanyan, *The Grecian History* (2nd edn., London, 1739),
courtesy of Ian Macgregor Morris)

on some of the richest periods of Greek History. Greek History did not end in 322. Grote may have thought so, but Gast, Mably, Robertson, and Gillies knew otherwise, well before Grote had ever dreamed of writing a Greek History. To conclude, it is worth noting that it is two hundred years since John Gillies published his *History of the World*. Momigliano once described his work as 'a feat for which nobody has yet given him credit'.[121] After two hundred years it is perhaps time we gave Gillies the credit he is due, by treating Macedonian and Hellenistic History as legitimate and mainstream parts of Greek History, as did the founders of the discipline of Greek History.

[121] Momigliano, 'George Grote and the Study of Greek History', 59.

10. Navigating the *Grotesque*; or, Rethinking Greek Historiography
===

*Ian Macgregor Morris*

In the fields of Greek and Roman History the earliest historians still consulted today are George Grote and Barthold Niebuhr. The discipline of Ancient History, in the academic imagination, was founded in the nineteenth century. However, the contributors to this volume have shown the breadth, variety and enduring relevance of the historiography of antiquity produced in the long eighteenth century. Thus the question must be considered as to why this historiography has been so written out of the modern historical consciousness. It cannot merely be the case that, with the professionalisation of the discipline, earlier works simply became irrelevant: not only is there much of interest in these works, but as the basis of the modern discipline they remain crucial to understand its mechanisms and assumptions.

The question of earlier historians is rarely asked and quickly dismissed.[1] Commentators remain trapped in nineteenth-century constructs of eighteenth-century historiography. Indeed, not only are the historians of the eighteenth century not consulted by practicing ancient historians, but they are even rarely read by students of historiography. Laird Okie argued that the 'tendency of scholars to focus on a few big names has produced an incomplete and somewhat distorted picture of eighteenth-century historiography'.[2] While Hume and Ferguson receive some notice from students of political philosophy, Gibbon alone is still considered as an historian.[3] Other writers are primarily known, if at all, through Victorian paraphrase and criticism, resulting in an

---

[1] One of the few exceptions to this is Giovanna Ceserani, who has dared to undertake a re-assessment of some of this historiography. See 'Narrative, Interpretation, and Plagiarism in Mr. Robertson's 1778 History of Ancient Greece', *Journal of the History of Ideas*, 66 (2005), 413–36; and 'Modern Histories of Ancient Greece: genealogies, contexts and eighteenth-century narrative historiography' (Version 1.0) Princeton/Stanford Working Papers in Classics (2008).
[2] L. Okie, *Augustan Historical Writing* (Boston, 1991), 1.
[3] See J.G.A. Pocock's masterful series of studies, *Barbarism and Religion* (Cambridge, 1999–2005).

almost entirely dismissive attitude to their works. Modern scholars are so hampered by the assumptions enshrined by the Victorians, that they can but repeat them. Thus, for example, Kyriacos Demetriou, the leading authority on Grote, having stated that Grote was heavily influenced by German Romantic classicism – which he certainly was – goes on to claim that German '*historismus* affirmed more freely than the Enlightenment historiographers the significance of emotional and irrational factors'.[4] Yet, as Carsten Lange has shown in his case-study, not only were Enlightenment historians often more willing to credit emotional factors than their modern counterparts, but also their readings of antiquity informed and even determined the Romantic understandings of historical events. Similarly, various commentators refer to Niebuhr's 'discovery' of the true nature of the *ager publicus*;[5] but, as Gareth Sampson has shown in his article, this was understood long before Niebuhr, and his greatest achievements included, perhaps, the presentation of so much of his work as being original.

There also remains an assumption that the histories of the Enlightenment do not really qualify as 'scholarship', that they are the idle products of 'Gentlemen amateurs'. But it is an unconsidered assumption, and few modern practitioners of Ancient History are even aware of these works. Paul Cartledge summarises twenty-first century perceptions:

> The writing of history was then only barely emerging from the shadow of *belles lettres* to claim the status of a nascent discipline, although it was not to be codified and routinised as such – involving a university degree and the appropriate apparatus of scholarly journals and so forth – for almost a century more.[6]

Cartledge's definition of proper academic practice is problematic. It shows a lack of awareness of the periodic and pamphlet literature of the period, or the complex scholarly networks and discourses which Sampson has amply illustrated in the case of Roman history. Moreover, it could be taken to imply the anachronistic notion that these writers could not be classed as 'historians' simply because they lacked a system of regulation – indeed, the term 'routinised' suggests intellectual

---

[4] K.N. Demetriou, *George Grote on Athenian Democracy* (Frankfurt, 1999), 70–1. To be fair to Demetriou, he does prefix his statement with the words 'On the whole …', thus allowing that the polarity is not absolute, but he is still operating under the same assumptions.

[5] Demetriou, *Grote*, 74; K. Vlassopoulos, *Unthinking the Greek Polis* (Cambridge, 2007), 31.

[6] P. Cartledge, 'Introduction', in G. Grote, *A History of Greece*, ed. J. Mitchell and M. Caspari (London, 2001), ix.

restriction and control – and the socio-cultural codes and etiquette which define the modern discipline.

In an attempt to answer this question, I will consider the case of Greek history, which perhaps offers a more clear-cut and absolute example than that of Roman history, although similar patterns can be detected in both. In order to do this, we must consider a wide range of issues, which for convenience have been divided into five sections. The first will present a brief survey of eighteenth-century Greek historiography and modern attitudes to it. The second section, 'Politics of the Grotesque', will turn to the political context of the nineteenth-century critics, and then consider the Enlightenment discourses which spawned this context. It will be shown that some of the radical ideas of these critics were in fact developments of the very eighteenth-century histories they sought to shun. The third section, 'Establishing the Grotesque', will examine the ways in which these critics systematically deconstructed that eighteenth-century historiography with the intention of rendering it both intellectually and politically suspect. The fourth part takes the discussion into the sphere of modern scholarship, to consider the ways in which the ideas enshrined by the nineteenth-century critics continue to influence scholarly opinion on both ancient history and eighteenth-century historians. In the fifth and final section, 'Navigating the Grotesque', it will be suggested that many of the assumptions upon which the modern discipline is based derive from the politicised concerns of nineteenth-century scholarship. The origins of attitudes such as Athenocentrism and Hellenocentrism lie in the racialised discourse of nineteenth-century historiography, and it will be suggested that the key to challenging these assumptions lies in re-examining the very eighteenth-century histories the nineteenth-century critics attacked. The very different prejudices of the eighteenth century can serve to highlight those of the modern discipline.

Yet first we must turn to the eighteenth-century histories themselves. To identify a point at which the serious study of Greek history began is fraught with difficulties, and risks falling into the very assumptions which surround the notion of Grote as the 'first' historian of Greece. However a new development can be detected in the late seventeenth century in the work of the translator Jacques de Tourreil.[7] Although drawing on a range of traditions and inspired by the growing interest in Greek literature, Tourreil appears to have conceived of the relevance of Greek history in a

---

[7] On Tourreil, see G. Duhain, *Jacques de Tourreil: Traducteur de Demosthéne* (Paris, 1910); Ceserani, 'Modern Histories of Ancient Greece', 13–14.

new way. Earlier writers had considered the nature of ancient institutions, while antiquarians had considered material culture.[8] Yet Tourreil envisioned something quite different in the preface to his 1691 edition of Demosthenes. Classical texts, he suggested, did not exist merely as works of art above time and place, but were the product of a particular context.[9] A text would be 'mere Greek to those who are unacquainted with the Country ... They will be apt to stumble every step they take, like those who are travelling in the dark'.[10] In effect, a text cannot be understood without a knowledge of its context. Tourreil displayed a sophisticated understanding of the historicity of texts, and the necessity of context. To this end he prefaced his translation with an analytical narrative of Greek history from the earliest times to the days of Demosthenes.[11] This can rightly be regarded as the earliest modern history of Greece, inspired by a desire to appreciate fully the texts which were already the subject of philological and aesthetic considerations and were taking centre-stage in European cultural life in the 'Quarrel of Ancients and Moderns'. These developments were situated in more general trends in which interest was developing from textual criticism to the material culture and geography of the past.[12] It was a remarkably fertile period in European thought, and for the first time, the *history* of ancient Greece mattered.

Tourreil's work as widely read well into the eighteenth century, serving as a point of reference for the authors of the *Encyclopédie*. Temple Stanyan and Charles Rollin both cite him as an important precursor, and as representing a quite new phenomenon. Stanyan's *Grecian History* (1707–39) sought to develop Tourreil's narratological framework, and greatly

---

[8] Debates over institutions date to the middle ages: see G.C. Furr '*Jhesu Nichil Est Commune Ligurgo*: A French Humanist Debate of c.1405', in *Medievalia et Humanistica*, 12 (1984), 187–200; on later discussions, see K. Vlassopoulos, 'Sparta and Rome in Early Modern Political Thought', in S. Hodkinson and I. Macgregor Morris (eds.), *Sparta: Classical Tradition* (Swansea, forthcoming).

[9] Pocock consider's the late-seventeenth-century realisation of the *context* of classical texts (J.G.A. Pocock, 'Classical and Civil History: The Transformation of Humanism', *Cromohs*, 1 (1996), 1–34).

[10] 'Historical Preface', in *Several Orations of Demosthenes* (London, 1702), 1.

[11] The Preface has been all but overlooked, and is even underplayed by Tourreil's biographer. See Duhain, *Tourreil*, 236–53. Only Ceserani recognises its importance ('Modern Histories of Ancient Greece').

[12] The growth of antiquarian collectors could not but fuel a curiosity concerning the societies which produced ancient artifacts. Meanwhile, the publications of the 'first' archaeological travellers to Greece, Jacob Spon and George Wheler, inspired both debate and controversy. John Potter's magisterial *Archaeologia Graeca* (1698) reflects many of these varied interests.

popularised Greek history in Britain.[13] Rollin, whose *Histoire ancienne* (1730–8) would become the standard for the rest of the century, sought to take the subject further.[14] In emphasising the role of Providence as the key causal factor in historical change, Rollin dissolved the dissonance between sacred and secular history, and helped to make pagan history a suitable subject for Christian modernity.[15] Moreover, through his careful balance of eulogy and criticism, he hoped to settle the 'Quarrel' in favour of the Moderns but with due respect to the Ancients. His comparative approach and all-inclusive understanding would set the tone for Greek History for the rest of the eighteenth century.

Once thus established, the discipline of Greek history developed into a context for numerous Enlightenment discourses. Writers such as Gabriel Bonnot de Mably, Montesquieu, Adam Ferguson, David Hume, Claude Helvetius and Rousseau generated a series of debates which both featured, and contributed to, re-evaluations of many aspects of Greek history and culture. While some of these works only discussed Greece within larger contexts, both ancient and modern, this reflected the inherently comparative nature of history-writing; and a significant number were exclusively devoted to ancient Greece.[16] While modern commentators may not consider these works as 'History' in the accepted sense, these works certainly played a central role in the growing interest in, and understanding of, the history of Greece.

These histories were situated within a wider context of engagement with Greek history and culture, which included developments of the literary interests which had inspired Tourreil, the aesthetic concerns of Winckelmann, and the proto-archaeology of the travellers.[17] The division between these genres was fluid. Moreover, they precipitated a second wave of narrative histories which sought to supplant the works of Stanyan and Rollin, such

---

[13] Thomas Hind's *History of Greece* appeared the same year as Stanyan's first volume, but appears to have had much less of an impact. Stanyan, however, impressed Diderot to the point that the Frenchman undertook a translation in 1743. On Hind and Stanyan, see Ceserani, 'Modern Histories of Ancient Greece', 10–11.

[14] Ceserani considers the *Histoire ancienne* to be, in effect, a contextualised history of Greece ('Modern Histories of Ancient Greece', 8; on Rollin, see 7–10). On the various continuations and relevance of Rollin's project, see Sampson and Lange's contributions to this volume.

[15] Pocock discusses the fundamental problems facing definitions the secular and sacred in history in the early eighteenth century ('Classical and Civil History').

[16] Key here are Mably's *Observations sur les Grecs* (1749); Abbé de Gourcy, *Histoire philosophique et politique des loix de Lycurgue* (1768); W. Young, *The Spirit of Athens* (1777); Cornelius de Pauw, *Recherches Philosophiques sur les Grecs* (1788); F. Schiller, *Die Gesetzgebung des Lykurgus und Solon* (1790).

[17] On these issues, see the Introduction to this volume.

as those by John Gast and Claude Millot. These in turn were followed by the two works which later generations would take to represent the Greek historiography of the eighteenth century as a whole: the Histories of John Gillies and William Mitford. These later works involved a development of the narrative approach of the early eighteenth-century writers, engaging with the discourses of the philosopher-historians, resulting in sweeping and sophisticated histories. These were the works, especially that of Mitford, which the nineteenth-century critics would seek to demolish. Before Grote, however, another school of scholarship emerged based around the German universities; yet while much is made of their impact upon him, it was the works of Gillies and Mitford against which his work was defined. They stood at the end of a century of scholarship which had been both self-aware and sharply critical of its own practice, and would serve as the context which produced the works of the nineteenth century.

The process of the decline of the status of the great ancient historians of the eighteenth century is not simply one of supercedence, of better histories replacing poorer ones. The obscuring of the former is much too absolute for that. Rather, in the case of Greek history at least, a new school of thought, politically motivated, consciously and purposefully destroyed the reputations of their predecessors. They announced themselves as the founders of a new discipline, born fully-formed from their own genius. The primary reasons for the disappearance of the ancient histories of the eighteenth century were political, not scholarly. The historians of the nineteenth century did not merely replace those of the previous generation: they quite literally wrote them out of history.

In the case of Greek history, the point of departure is the *History of Greece* of George Grote. It remains the earliest history of Greece still consulted by historians.[18] Cartledge humourously refers to Greek history before Grote as 'B.G.',[19] but the humour reveals an underlying truth: the role of Grote within the development of Greek historiography is perceived as that of a saviour. He supercedes all that came before, to the extent that, to some, he even surpasses the ancients themselves.[20] Cartledge goes on to state that

---

[18] Ceserani, 'Modern Histories of Ancient Greece', 2.

[19] P. Cartledge, 'Introduction', xi.

[20] Thus Alexandra Lianeri in her discussion of Orientalism, suggests that 'conceptually' Grote can be seen to precede Herodotus. See 'The Persian Wars as the 'Origin' of Historiography: Ancient and Modern Orientalism in George Grote's *History of Greece*', in E. Bridges, E. Hall and P.J. Rhodes (eds.), *Cultural Responses to the Persian Wars* (Oxford, 2007), 337. While Lianeri is clearly considering levels of meaning within the texts, the ways in which she prioritises Grote's reading is an example of the centrality of his work in the modern discipline.

the role call of his predecessors is not long, nor is it especially distinguished; their achievement on the whole amounting to little more than paraphrase of Herodotus and Thucydides.[21]

Cartledge refers to only four Greek historians of the eighteenth century, all of them British. Demetriou includes a few more, again British.[22] As this volume has shown, this is hardly a representative sample. And the vigorous debates which formed the basis of eighteenth-century historiography reveal a highly critical treatment of sources, far surpassing 'paraphrase'. The suggestion that much of their work qualifies only as 'party' histories also does not stand up to scrutiny.[23]

Moreover, considering these writers in isolation instantly prevents any recognition of the complex pan-European nature of the history-writing community of the Enlightenment. Recently Jonathon Israel has convincingly argued that the national focus of much modern scholarship has prevented scholars from seeing the pan-European interactions which define and form the most crucial aspects of Enlightenment thought.[24] To remove them from these contexts is to see only one piece of a much larger and more complex discourse. Yet this remains quite unexplored by scholars on this issue, with only Jennifer Roberts recognising the relevance of the continental debates. More typical is Arnaldo Momigliano, who went so far as to assert that there was no Greek history written on the continent before the nineteenth century.[25] To fail to recognise the close interaction between writers of different nationalities is to fail to understand the development of historiography in the eighteenth century.[26]

Morever, this failure hampers any understanding of the origins of the modern discipline, or any fair assessment of Grote's achievement. As we shall see, modern scholarship on these writers is strewn with error, misunderstanding, and based on assumptions quite alien to the

---

[21] P. Cartledge, 'Introduction', xi.
[22] Cartledge considers Stanyan, Goldsmith, Gillies and Mitford; Demetriou wisely relegates Goldsmith to his footnotes, considers Montagu, and also briefly William Young and William Drummond, but does not consider them historians ('In Defense of the British Constitution: The theoretical implications of the debate over the Athenian Democracy in Britain, 1770–1850', *History of Political Thought*, 17 (1996), 289). However, the paucity of these samples remain.
[23] Demetriou, *Grote*, 48, 271. The party-history model, as Peter Liddel shows in his discussion of William Young, is anachronistic and misunderstands the nature of history writing in the period.
[24] J. Israel, *Radical Enlightenment* (Oxford, 2001).
[25] Momigliano, 'George Grote and the Study of Greek History', in G.W. Bowersock and T.J. Cornell (eds.), *Studies on Modern Scholarship* (Berkeley, 1994), 22.
[26] On the networks in Roman history, see G. Sampson, this volume.

writers in question. Scholars feel obliged to insist upon the superiority of Grote and to place the eighteenth-century writers in a context of intellectual inferiority.[27] This superiority is a feature which originates in the writings of Grote and his champions in the mid-nineteenth century. Every historian, of course, purports to write a superior history to his predecessors – otherwise there would be little point in putting pen to paper – and Grote is typical in doing this. However, more unusual is the level of invective in his dismissal of earlier writers,[28] and, more pertinent perhaps, the way in which scholars of the twentieth century have accepted his judgements. This is not to deny Grote's achievement. His history is undoubtedly a work of the greatest importance in the tradition of Greek historiography. But the continued insistence on Grote's supposed impartiality – or 'acceptable' prejudices[29] – is contrasted with a vision of partisan and unobjective predecessors. This must be bought into question. Grote, as did his predecessors, read his prejudices into his work. That his prejudices *appear* to be more palatable to modern academics than those of, say, William Mitford, does not preclude the possibility that they colour his understanding of the ancient world. An uncritical acceptance of his work, moreover, means that his prejudices also colour *our* understanding – prejudices of which we are all but unaware. The judgements Grote passed upon his predecessors need no verification, for the simple reason that Grote himself made them. We need not return to Mitford to discover the accuracy of these criticisms, or even to consider the possibility that Mitford's works include merits quite forgotten. The very act of Grote's critique is enough. As the forefather of our discipline, we need not – indeed must not – think beyond Grote.

Criticisms of the prioritising of Grote have gone no further than attempting to reveal earlier writers who shared some of his opinions, and thus recent works have appeared championing the cause of Connop Thirlwall and Edward Bulwer-Lytton.[30] In effect, they seek to do nothing

---

[27] For example, A. Ataç, 'Imperial Lessons from Athens and Sparta: Eighteenth-Century British Histories of Ancient Greece', *History of Political Thought*, 27 (2006), 642.

[28] Although, it should be noted, certain eighteenth-century writers did the same. Most notably, see Cornelius de Pauw's savage attacks on Rousseau, among others (*Philosophical Dissertations on the Greeks*, vol. II (London, 1793), 117–18, 184). It is a noteworthy point that it is the apologists of Athens who most often descend to such invective. The spirit of Demosthenes lives on.

[29] That is to say, prejudices that match our own. Demetriou rightly observes that a key feature of the modern admiration of Grote is the 'substantial concurrence with him on matters of liberal ideology' (*Grote*, 270; see also 273).

[30] P. Liddel (ed.), *Bishop Thirlwall's History of Greece* (Exeter, 2007); E. Bulwer Lytton, *Athens: Its Rise and Fall*, ed. O. Murray (London, 2004).

more than relocate the legend of Grote, not to question it. There has been no attempt to examine the foundations of the Grotean myth, to understand the origins of his reputation and reconsider his position in the history of Greek historiography. None have sought to navigate the 'Grotesque'.

Paul Cartledge, in the introduction to the recent republication of the abridged edition of Grote's *History*, suggests that the influence of Grote should be termed 'Grotean', not 'Grotesque'. Andrew Bayliss, in his contribution to this volume, rightly suggests that the reverse may be more suitable. Grote's influence on the modern discipline is absolute, and any influence so absolute, however laudable the principles upon which it is based, must be malign; for it does not allow for reassessment. Grote remains important to the modern discipline because his legacy, for good and ill, all but defines it. Moreover, this involves not only the vision of Athens he created, but also the dismissal of all earlier writers which than vision engendered.

## Politics of the Grotesque: Utilitarianism and the Rise of Athens

Grote was closely associated with the 'Philosophical Radicals', a group of political and intellectual figures, inspired by the Utilitarian philosophy of Jeremy Bentham and James Mill.[31] During the 1820s and 1830s, the years during which Grote was working on his *History*, the 'Radicals' were seeking to precipitate wholesale political reform. They had hoped to align with the more moderate, reform-minded Whigs; and thus, despite differences over the extent and nature of the reform they proposed, it is not surprising to find in the realm of Greek historiography a Whig such as Lord Macaulay in close agreement with Grote. Their vision of Athens, and venom towards her eighteenth-century critics, were primarily determined by their various political concerns. In addition, there were others sympathetic to what Momigliano described as the 'liberalization of English political and intellectual habits', such as Connop Thirlwall, who would make their own contribution to the coming developments.[32]

The political element of Grote's approach are acknowledged even by his admirers, accepting that he was motivated by his own concerns and

---

[31] See J. Hamburger, *Intellectuals in Politics: John Stuart Mill and the Philosophical Radicals* (Yale, 1965); W. Thomas, *The Philosophical Radicals* (Oxford, 1979). The term 'Radical' is, of course, a relative one. In comparison with the radical thinkers of the Revolution, Grote's circle were distinctly moderate; but usually it is used in comparison with the Whigs and Tories.

[32] Momigliano, 'Grote', 20.

saw contemporary political uses to his history.³³ The fundamental issue at stake was that the Utilitarians needed an Athens which could, very loosely, be taken as a political model.³⁴ However, the context of the Utilitarian vision of Athens lay in a longstanding debate over constitutional forms, combining what scholars have termed the 'classical republican tradition' – the discourse surrounding a political system based on civic and political participation – and the 'Quarrel of Ancient and Moderns', the ongoing series of debates which pitted antiquity against modernity. Yet scholars have presented a vision of Grote single handedly re-establishing Athens against a tide of rampant Spartomania.³⁵ This myth, for a myth it is, was itself a creation of the Utilitarians.³⁶ It was a very necessary myth to create, for they needed to present Athens as a *new* model: they could not admit that their vision of Athens was directly based on ideas formulated generations before. Yet although Grote's vision of Athens was not original, the all-sweeping success of his *History* ensured that he was seen as the one who placed Athens centre-stage in the pageant of Greek history. And so fundamental is this to the structure of the modern discipline that it bears further investigation. To appreciate the significance of Grote's attitude to Athens, we must locate it within the Athens-Sparta debate of the eighteenth century; a debate the very existence of which undermines modern scholarly attitudes to Enlightenment histories of Greece.³⁷

Integral to this question is a further assumption which underlies not only analyses of eighteenth-century historiography, but continues to plague the modern discipline of Greek history: the notion that Sparta was a 'conservative' or 'reactionary' state, while Athens was 'progressive'

---

³³ Vaio, 'George Grote and James Mill: How to Write History', in Calder and Trzaskoma (eds), *George Grote Reconsidered* (Hildesheim, 1996) 64, 74; Roberts, *Athens on Trial: the Anti-democratic Tradition in Western Thought* (Princeton, 1994), 241; Demetriou, *Grote*, 126, see also 125. Turner, *The Greek Heritage in Victorian Britain* (London, 1981), 208.

³⁴ Vaio, 'George Grote', 69, 70. Demetriou *Grote*, 61. Frederick Rosen comments on the idea that those active in politics have more need to appeal to practical models, because 'deriving plans of reform from something so abstract as the greatest happiness principle is so improbable as to strike most readers as absurd' (*Bentham, Byron, and Greece* (Oxford, 1992), 16).

³⁵ There are many examples of this argument. See Demetriou, *Grote*, 119, 130; F. Rosen, 'Forward', in Demetriou, *Grote*, vii; M. Chambers, 'Grote's *History of Greece*', in Calder et. al., *Grote Reconsidered*, 11; Cartledge, 'Introduction', xii. Nadia Urbinati attributes this to Mill (*Mill on Democracy* (Chicago, 2002), 2).

³⁶ See J.S. Mill, 'Grote's *History of Greece*', *The Spectator*, 4 April 1846.

³⁷ For details of this debate, see I. Macgregor Morris, 'The Paradigm of Democracy: Sparta in Enlightenment Thought', in *Spartan Society*, ed. T. Figueira (Swansea, 2004), 339–62; Roberts, *Athens on Trial*, 157–74.

and 'liberal'.[38] Any criticism of Athens constitutes a critique of the values of a free society; while any praise of Sparta constitutes a tacit approval of authoritarianism.[39] But the notion that hostility to Athens was a conservative or monarchist stance is a product of the nineteenth-century critiques which still pervade modern scholarship.[40] The idea that to be critical of classical Athens is to be anti-democratic simply does not follow, any more than the equally false notion, that to eulogise Athens is to be pro-democratic.[41] The history of the concept of democracy is a highly complex one;[42] in the light of philosophical concepts such as the 'general will' and the 'social contract', some in the eighteenth century developed the idea that true democracy must consist in the fair implementation of the will of the people, and that this *may* not be best realised in the open voting of the Athenian model. These thinkers criticised Athens not for being a democracy, but for *failing* to be truly democratic. Many of the most radical thinkers of the eighteenth century preferred Sparta, not as a conservative model, but as the closest approximation to true democracy – that is, in its fair representation of the general will.[43] To modern readers these thinkers may have been wrong about

---

[38] Grote portrayed Athens as 'liberal and progressive' (Demetriou, *Grote*, 130; see also 94, 245). Within this Athens, and Athens alone, came to stand for 'democracy'. Indeed Mill specifically excludes other Greek city-states which were democratic, fearing that they might detract from the lustre of the Athenian example (Roberts, *Athens on Trial*, 247).

[39] See for example Michael Whitby's fear that 'the glorification of Sparta ... [can lead] perhaps to toleration of authoritarian practices, whether they be those of Nazi Germany or apartheid South Africa at a national level or of an English public school at a more parochial' ('Images of Spartans and Helots', in A. Powell and S. Hodkinson (eds.), *The Shadow of Sparta* (London, 1994), 89).

[40] For nineteenth-century casting of Sparta, see Mill, 'Grote's *History of Greece* 1'; and Bulwer-Lytton (quoted in Demetriou, *Grote* 50). Modern scholars follow these definitions: thus Jennifer Roberts' account of the Athenian tradition, for example, reveals its assumptions in the title: *Athens on Trial, the Anti-democratic Tradition in Western Thought*. Similarly, Paul Cartledge expresses surprise that Rousseau could be both 'proto-democratic' and 'pro-Spartan' ('The Socratics' Sparta and Rousseau's', in *Sparta: New Perspectives*, ed. S. Hodkinson and A. Powell (Swansea, 1999), 311).

[41] Roberts casts William Young as being anti-democratic for his comments concerning Athens (*Athens on Trial*, 201–2). But Young's comments are presented as constructive criticism. It is clearly the case that Young is criticising 'bad' democracy, rather than democracy per se. See P. Liddel, this volume; and Macgregor Morris, 'The Paradigm of Democracy', 353–5.

[42] E.M. Wood, 'Democracy, an idea of dubious ancestry', in J.P. Euben, et. al. eds. *Athenian Political Thought and the Reconstruction of American Democracy* (Ithaca, 1994), 59–80; R. Palmer, 'Notes on the use of the word Democracy', *Political Science Quarterly*, 68 (1953), 203–26.

[43] See Macgregor Morris, 'The Paradigm of Democracy', 343–4. Urbinati also recognises the existence of Sparta as a model for the far left in nineteenth-century France (*Mill*, 5).

Sparta, but to label them as anti-democratic is to misunderstand both their thought and the complex history of 'democracy'.

These constructs of Sparta existed within the framework of debates over social and political organisation, within which classical models – principally Rome, Sparta and Athens – were considered comparatively.[44] The rising primacy of Athens within the Athens-Sparta debate occurred in the late eighteenth century, predating Grote considerably, and many of the arguments he would use were foreshadowed by the eighteenth-century critics of Sparta. Most fervent amongst them was the Dutch thinker Cornelius de Pauw. De Pauw may be forgotten today: so total has been the marginalisation of pre-Grotean historians, that even those with whom he may have agreed have been discarded from the canon of historiography – a necessary measure if the legend of Grote's originality is to remain unquestioned. Yet his impact at the time was considerable: he succeeding in convincing Horace Walpole for one – never an easy task – and earned the lasting respect of Napoleon.[45] While De Pauw represented an extreme panegyric of Athens, there were many more moderate reassessments of the city which sought to dismiss its negative reputation. William Young's *Spirit of Athens* (1777), while accepting many of the standard critiques of Athenian democracy, sought to present the fundamental tenets of the system as both praiseworthy and realisable, while Jean-Jacques Barthélemy strove to find a middle ground, elucidating the virtues and vices of both Athens and Sparta in a pseudo-Socratic dialogue. As the eighteenth century drew to a close the contrast between Athens and Sparta became increasingly difficult to discern, especially in the atmosphere of philhellenism which called for an appreciation of all things Greek. It was quite possible to admire both Athens and Sparta, and thus in 1806 Chateaubriand could remark that he wished to have lived with Pericles, and died with Leonidas.[46]

Yet the association of Sparta with the aspirations of the Jacobins – a trope realised as early as 1797 by Chateaubriand[47] – dealt a serious blow

---

[44] On the comparative nature of the understandings of ancient constitutions, see: K. Vlassopoulos, 'Sparta and Rome'; and S. Hodkinson, *Comparing Spartan Militarism* (forthcoming).

[45] See Horace Walpole, Letter to Lady Ossory, 24 February 1789 (*Correspondence of Horace Walpole*, ed. W. Lewis, vol. 34 (Yale, 1937–83), 42). Napoleon had an obelisk erected in De Pauw's honour in the German city of Xanten.

[46] *Itinéraire de Paris à Jérusalem* (Paris, 1811).

[47] *Essai historique sur les révolutions* (London, 1797). Roberts (*Athens on Trial*, 222) is missing the point to suggest that Chateaubriand was criticising the Revolutionaries for imitating Sparta rather than Athens. Rather, he critiqued the Jacobins for imitating Sparta in a piecemeal fashion. See I. Macgregor Morris, '*From Ancient Dreams to Modern Nightmares*: Classical Revolutions in Enlightenment Thought', in T. Coignard, P. Davis and A. Montoya et. al. (eds.), *Lumières et histoire* (Paris, forthcoming).

to the reputation of Sparta. In the early years of the nineteenth century the city became the target of an increasing number of scathing critiques, some of which insisted on a marked preference for Athens.[48] It was in the thought of Benjamin Constant, however, that Athens could be said to have finally triumphed.

Key to Constant's thought is not so much – as some have argued – that he rejected classical models altogether, but in his recognition that the terms of the debate had changed.[49] In his essay *The Spirit of Conquest and Usurpation* he remarked that he considered it

> rather odd that it should be precisely Athens that our modern reformers have avoided taking as a model. The reason is that Athens was too similar to us, and they wanted greater difference to have greater merit.[50]

Constant, of course, full well knew that any reforming model needed to be different from the status quo in order to be a model for change. But his comment implies an ignorance on the part of these 'reformers' – and it is clear he is referring here to the admirers of Sparta. They had failed, he suggests, to recognise the absolute difference between antiquity and modernity, and thus proposed impossible visions for the future. It suited Constant's purpose – the promotion of a liberal commercial society – to emphasise the misguided nature of the veneration of Sparta, and thus by implication the entire tradition of classical republicanism. Modern scholars have tended to see this as an outright rejection of classical models, but Constant was more sophisticated than such a conclusion allows.[51] In his famous speech *The Liberty of the Ancients Compared with that of the Moderns*, Constant took a slightly different stance:

> We shall see why, of all the ancient states, Athens was the one which most resembles the modern ones ... Athens, as I have already pointed out, was of all the Greek republics the most closely engaged in trade, thus it allowed to its citizens an infinitely greater individual liberty than Sparta or Rome. If I could enter into historical details, I would show you that, among the Athenians, commerce had removed several of the differences which distinguished the

---

[48] See, for example, François Pouqueville, *Travels in the Morea* (1813), 81–2; William Haygarth, *Greece: A Poem* (London, 1814), 3.505–21, and p. 266.

[49] Vlassopoulos suggests that the *Idéologues* argued that antiquity had no 'relevance for modernity' (*Unthinking the Greek Polis*, 30); but for Constant, and Volney, who is also cited, their rejection centred on *emulation*, and they still saw didactic uses of antiquity. On Volney in this context, see Macgregor Morris, 'From Ancient Dreams to Modern Nightmare'.

[50] *Constant: Political Writings*, ed. B. Fontana (Cambridge, 2002), 105.

[51] For example, Roberts, *Athens on Trial*, 222. The rejection of classical models hardly represented a novel standpoint, having characterised responses to antiquity since the Middle Ages.

ancient from the modern peoples. The spirit of the Athenian merchants was similar to that of the merchants of our days.[52]

His insistence on the similarity between Athens and modern Europe is not a call to emulate the Athenians, for to do so would be falling into the very practice he condemns in others. Rather, his vision of Athens is a way of legitimising what has already occurred: the rise of commercial society in modern Europe. He accepts arguments of the Moderns in the 'Quarrel' which favoured the progress of modernity over classical idealisations, but does so using the main weapon of the radical reformers: classical precedent. Unlike the Athenophiles of the eighteenth century, his Athens is a reality, not an aspiration.

The rise of commerce and the industrial revolution helped to establish an ideal of 'progress' quite at odds with the stability the Spartophiles so admired.[53] Moreover, this coincided with ideas generally attributed to German Romantic Hellenism, which sought to prioritise the aesthetic over the political, and thus venerated the Athenian artistic achievement over all else.[54] Thus Herder could assert that the excesses of the Athenian democrats were justified by their artistic achievements – an attitude which could not be more directly opposed to the eighteenth-century concern with the corruptive effects of the arts.[55] These ideas reveal the great extent to which the very terms of the debate had changed.

The works of Constant could be said to represent the 'triumph' of Athens over Sparta, bringing together the growing emphasis on the commercial on the one hand and the aesthetic on the other, both of which found an echo in Athens, and were diametrically opposed to the frugal, supposedly artistically barren Sparta. Moreover, these developments were situated in a post-revolutionary atmosphere tired of visionary utopianism and the violence which accompanies it. The Athens-Sparta debate was, to all intents and purposes, consigned to the antiquarian volumes whence it had sprung.

---

[52] *Constant: Political Writings*, ed. B. Fontana (Cambridge, 2002), 315.

[53] Urbinati discusses how Mitford presents a sophisticated argument against 'progress' (*Mill*, 37).

[54] On this see Roberts, *Athens on Trial*, 209–20. Although it should be noted that German engagement with Greece at this time was far more complex and subtle than such a reference can allow. See Marylin Butler, *The Tyranny of Greece over Germany* (Cambridge, 1935), and Constanze Güthenke, *Placing Modern Greece: The Dynamics of Romantic Hellenism* (Oxford, 2008). For an account of a very different German response to Hellenism in this period, see Uta Degner, *Bilder im Wechsel der Töne: Hölderlins Elegien und 'Nachtgesänge'* (Heidelberg, 2008), 171–9.

[55] J.G. Herder, *Ideen zur Philosophie der Geschichte der Menschheit* (Riga, 1784–92), Book 13, Part 3.

The mechanisms of Constant's thought would be crucial to Grote's project, although, as Momigliano so generously remarks, Grote 'overlooked' his predecessor.[56] And thus modern discussions of Grote still operate under the assumption that he was battling a tide of Spartomania, which had in reality long receded. By the time of the publication of the *History of Greece*, a tradition of pro-Athenian and anti-Spartan scholarship was well established by the likes of Macaulay, Bulwer-Lytton, Connop Thirlwall and Thomas Arnold, among others. Grote's initial critique of Mitford came in an atmosphere which had largely accepted Athens over Sparta. His originality was to apply this new atmosphere to Mitford's account of that city with a particular venom, and in so doing establish Athens as the model the Utilitarians desired.

Demetriou notes that Grote was not defending the democracy of Athens, but an 'idealised democracy – the model of democracy the utilitarians sought to establish'.[57] In this he is right, and supports the notion that constructs of democracy were in continual flux. It is pertinent that Grote did not propose a model of democracy based on the Athenian. He saw in Athenian democracy virtues which could be realised for the modern world by *representative* democracy. In this he was repeating an argument of eighteenth-century Athenophiles such as William Young and De Pauw. Yet in saying this Grote was, as were his predecessors, ignoring one of the defining features of the Athenian system. Athens without direct democracy would be like Sparta without patriotism; the very concept of representation must be the antithesis of the Athenian system. Indeed, some reformers had taken representation as a measure to *prevent* democracy; Rousseau had argued that it was tantamount to relinquishing freedom.[58] The Utilitarians, of course, were well aware of this. Bentham was less prone to the use of classical precedent than his followers, possibly because he was of a generation in which such recourse to antiquity was the preserve of the radicals who, as we have seen, were prone to eulogise Sparta.[59] His was a programme of more moderate

---

[56] Momigliano, 'Grote', 27.

[57] *Grote,* 127.

[58] Most famously, Madison and Hamilton present representation in this way in the *Federalist* (Nos. 9 and 10). Urbanati suggests Constant envisioned representation as 'an alternative to democracy' (*Mill*, 15, 20). For an interesting discussion of ideas of representation, see Hartog, 'The French Revolution and Antiquity', in R.-P. Droit (ed.), *Greeks and Romans in the Modern World* (New York, 1998), 107–9.

[59] Mogens Hansen remarks that if 'Bentham was inspired by ancient Greek democracy he concealed it remarkably well' (*The Tradition of Ancient Greek Democracy and its Importance for Modern Democracy* (Copenhagen, 2005), 25). Bentham was more concerned with the philosophy, while the 'Radicals' were concerned with political action and thus had greater need of concrete models – see footnote 34.

reform,[60] and he was more concerned with defending his ideology – in essence a constitutional democracy – against those who sought to associate it with the anarchic visions of democracy.[61] The younger Utilitarians, operating in an atmosphere which increasingly saw Athens in a positive light, realised the opportunity to legitimise their vision with classical precedent.[62] And they would not allow the dissonance between their 'democracy' and that of Athens to prevent them: Grote thus argued that representation preserved the 'spirit' – a concept taken from Montesquieu – of Athenian democracy;[63] while John Stuart Mill, developing Grote's thesis, quite ingeniously sought to answer the problem by identifying deliberation as the defining feature of democracy.[64]

Yet the principles which underlay this 'reform' – or development – of the Athenian system are remarkably similar to the arguments used to *discredit* the concept of democracy throughout the eighteenth century, because it relies on the tenet that *direct* democracy is unworkable, or at the very least

---

[60] Frederick Rosen notes that Bentham's 'strategy of reform looks for a middle way between support for the status quo and advocacy of revolution' (*Jeremy Bentham and Representative Democracy* (Oxford, 1983), 221).

[61] Bentham's constitutional democracy was laden with measures to prevent what Mill would later term the 'Tyranny of the Majority'. See F. Rosen, *Classical Utilitarianism from Hume to Mill* (London, 2003), 232–41.

[62] It must be remembered here that although the Philosophical Radicals were followers of Bentham, important differences did exist between their respective ideologies. See F. Rosen, *Bentham and Representative Democracy*, 168–82.

[63] The application of Montesquieu's notion of spirit to Greek history was a well established tradition, and once again shows Grote's debt to his predecessors. See Peter Liddel's contribution to this volume.

[64] Mill identified the 'deliberative style of the Athenian assembly and *dikasteria* over the direct participation of the Athenian demos' as the key component of his model (Urbanati, *Mill*, 61; see also 43–7, 59–61, 70–2). See also J. Riley, who argues at length that Mill shows that representative democracy in the 'Athenian spirit' – once again Montesquieu's vague term – is possible ('Mill's Neo-Athenian Model of Liberal Democracy', in N. Urbinati and A. Zakaras (eds.), *J.S. Mill's Political Thought* (Cambridge, 2007), 221–49). This is not the place to consider the validity of Mill's conflating of Athenian and representative democracy, but it should be stated that although his argument has proved hugely influential, it rests on certain assumptions about the defining features, nature, and purpose of 'democracy'. Throughout this discussion, it must also be remembered that, as Rosen observed, there is no necessary connection between utilitarianism and democracy (*Bentham and Representative Government*, 200). Indeed, the identification of liberalism with democracy is also problematic, and some scholars have questioned the extent of Mill's liberalism: see J. Hamburger, *How Liberal Was John Stuart Mill* (Austin, 1991); M. Cowling, *Mill and Liberalism* (Cambridge, 1963). Urbinati is at pains to challenge these readings. For an insightful discussion of direct democracy and its modern application, see Hansen, *Tradition of Ancient Greek Democracy*, 45–64.

impractical.⁶⁵ Moreover, the notion that a system of 'democracy' based on representation would promote equality and better reflect the general will is reminiscent of another political model drawn from antiquity: Mably's Sparta.⁶⁶ Strikingly, the virtues Grote identifies in Athens – such as individual liberty, equality, and participation in the political process – are the very virtues Mably saw in Sparta. The difference lies not in the virtues of either system, but the principles upon which each was thought to be based. This returns us to one of the key debates of the eighteenth and nineteenth centuries: that of the commercial trading republic versus the agricultural republic; luxury versus virtue. *This* is the Athens-Sparta debate.⁶⁷ When Constant finally settled the argument in favour of Athens, he did so with the insistence that the Athenians were fundamentally 'similar to us' – a commercial, maritime people.

When viewed comparatively, the Spartophiles' vision of Sparta is remarkably similar to the Athenophiles' vision of Athens; and the Spartophiles' critiques of Athens are remarkably similar to the Athenophiles' critiques of Sparta. Both sides of the debate claimed that any injustice or atrocity committed by their preferred city as 'deviation' from the constitution,⁶⁸ while insisting that injustice characterised the very essence of the other. One begins to suspect that eighteenth-century visions of Athens and Sparta were, perhaps, not quite as different as their respective apologists would have us believe.⁶⁹

The difference lies in the point that eighteenth-century thinkers were searching antiquity for alternatives to the status quo; while those in the nineteenth century sought models to legitimise it. Athens did not

---

⁶⁵ Thus Young suggests a democracy 'regulated' by law (*The History of Athens* (London, 1786), 60) while De Pauw suggests that representation would erase 'laocracy' (*Philosophical Dissertations*, vol. II, 120–1). Compare these with the vision of representation suggested by Hamilton and Madison in the *Federalist*, nos. 9, 10, and 55.

⁶⁶ Constant by contrast argued that the Spartan system was not, in reality, representative (Hartog, 'French Revolution and Antiquity', 108); but then, he had a political reason to say so.

⁶⁷ The classic study of this is P. Vidal-Naquet, *Politics Ancient and Modern* (Cambridge, 1995), 82–140. See also Urbinati, *Mill*, 35.

⁶⁸ Thus Mably cites the excesses of Sparta to the time 'her laws were no longer obeyed', and even suggests that helotry was only introduced *after* the time of Lycurgus ('Observations on the Greeks', in *Translations from the French by D.Y.* (Lynn, 1770) 47n.); Grote similarly characterises Athenian injustices to deviations from the Athenian spirit, thus suggesting that the execution of Socrates and the generals after Arginusae, were due superstition and ignorance, which were the remnants of the pre-democratic culture (*History of Greece*, vol. VIII, 271ff.).

⁶⁹ For a recent challenge to the notion of Spartan exceptionalism, see Hodkinson, *Comparing Spartan Militarism*.

represent a radical alternative to the existing social and political structure, because the one feature of the Athenian system which would have overturned modernity itself – indeed the defining feature of the Athenian system, direct political participation – was not part of the programme of the reformers. Rather, Athens was the model of the proto-capitalist, commercial, state. It was a model of moderate reform, leaving the established foundations of society, especially that of property, largely untouched. Rather than a redistribution of wealth, this model suggested the generation of new wealth through commerce. It sought to challenge the power of the landed ruling classes by creating an alternative source of wealth, and thus power. This, in effect, was what was already taking place.

The model of Sparta, on the other hand, was one of radical reform and revolution. Ever since James Harrington suggested Sparta as one of the models for restructuring society, the image of Sparta was one of total change. Both Rollin and Mably singled out Lycurgus' greatest accomplishment as being the reform of the 'manners' of the Spartans – that is to say, he changed the way people thought.[70] This, of course, is one of the charges laid against the Jacobins in their supposed emulation of Sparta. At the heart of Sparta lay such antitheses to the modern world as the redistribution of property and the disestablishment of the family. And this is why no reformers – even the visionary Saint-Just – dared to seriously dream of recreating Sparta.[71] But then, none of the Athenophiles ever wished to recreate Athens. In both cases, they served as models not of political reform, but of the principles with which to undertake reform. They represented two contrasting ways in which to challenge the power of the ruling elites. The Spartan model certainly dominated in the eighteenth century, when the only way to challenge the landed classes appeared – perhaps in France especially – to be by undermining the very basis of their claims to rule. Yet with the burgeoning spheres of industry and commerce came the realisation that the power of these classes need not be directly assaulted, but could be gradually subsumed, as the wealth created by commerce would lead to the development of alternative centres of power. The old aristocracies need not be overthrown; they could simply be ignored. Yet such a transfer of power demanded a change in 'manners' as dramatic as any Lycurgus enacted on his people; for the formerly despised professions of trade and industry needed to acquire a respectability. And, just as the radical reformers did with Sparta, so the moderates turned to antiquity to present a model which would give their aspirations and their principles

---

[70] Macgregor Morris, 'Paradigm of Democracy', 340–1, 344–6.
[71] Even Chateaubriand, having established an image of Jacobins hankering after the laws of Lycurgus, admitted that they did not, literally, attempt to recreate Sparta.

a legitimacy, and a noble heritage. It was for *this* reason they sought to establish Athens as the height of classical excellence.

Thus, the relative reputations of Sparta and Athens were entwined, and representative of some of the defining discourses of the eighteenth and nineteenth centuries. The ascendancy of Athens in part owes to the effects of the Revolution; but its main cause was the general acceptance of the idea of moderate commercially-based reform as opposed to the radical ideologies represented by the Revolution. It was in this atmosphere that the pro-Athenian histories of Greece appeared. Grote did not prompt these developments; he was a product of them.

Of course, in outlining the decline of Sparta and the rise of Athens, it needs to be remembered that these issues are not absolutes, but part of an ongoing series of debates in which the very definitions were in permanent flux. As has been mentioned, there were pro-Athenian histories long before the Revolution. And there would be pro-Spartan accounts throughout the nineteenth and into the twentieth centuries. Moreover, the debates during the eighteenth century were never as clear-cut as such a discussion would suggest. Many, indeed the majority of those sympathetic to reform saw much to admire in a variety of ancient models, and did not necessarily see the qualities of Sparta and Athens as being mutually exclusive.[72] This is not a paradox, but reveals that the patterns of these debates and discourses was complex. Beyond the polemics of Mably, De Pauw, and Grote, most drew upon – or criticised – both Sparta and Athens.

Grote hoped to establish Athens as a model both reflecting and legitimising Utilitarian philosophy. His purpose was more overtly political than that of Constant, his vision more absolute. In Grote's hands, the comparative approach of eighteenth-century historians became one of contrast. Using James Mill's concept of the hierarchy of civilisations, Grote was able to justify the formulation of a set of criteria which would enable an absolute judgement of societies. This both reflected and developed an increasingly 'scientific' approach to history, informed by philosophy and new categories of knowledge.[73] Mill's emphasis on 'intellectual philosophy'

---

[72] Thus Richard Glover is best remembered for his epic poem *Leonidas* (1737), which became a defining feature of the legend of Sparta in the eighteenth century. Yet he was also an active politician and merchant, several times representing the commercial interest in the House of Commons, and wrote a lengthy poetical eulogy of commerce, *London; Or the Progress of Commerce* (1739), while his later writings also eulogise Athens.

[73] Richard Jenkyns remarks that the 'nineteenth century was an age of universal histories; sometimes with heroic enthusiasm, often with fatal superficiality, the Victorians tried to impose laws and systems upon the infinite complexity of human existence' (*The Victorians and Ancient Greece* (Oxford, 1980), 74).

as a mark of civilisation could be brought together with the surge of interest in the aesthetic achievements of the ancients, creating criteria under which Athens achieved a level of excellence with which no other city could compete. Of course, such a portrait of Athens as a centre of philosophical and artistic excellence is in actuality a development of Voltaire's vision of Athens as a society which allowed an individual 'to think and to write'.[74] But when couched in the scientific terminology inferred by the concept of a hierarchy of civilisations, the notion takes on an altogether more absolute nature. For Grote, an essential part of the historian's duty was to determine the 'rank which they [a society] occupy in the scale of human achievement'.[75] Eighteenth-century writers had compared various states on a range of issues, from the cultural to the political, serving to illustrate and delineate the features of those societies by highlighting similarities and differences. But the creation of such criteria, combined with the nineteenth-century notion of progress, made the establishment of a pseudoscientific hierarchy all but inevitable. Grote's Athens, by these criteria, was quite literally beyond compare.

Yet also integral to such a vision was the complete subsumation of alternatives. That Athens was by this time generally preferred to Sparta was not in itself enough, for to succeed as the model the Utilitarians desired would require an absolute contrast with the failure of other Greek states. The Utilitarian writers could not allow the eighteenth-century critiques to go unanswered, lest those criticisms should undermine their own political vision; and even the eighteenth-century advocates of Athens proved problematic, for they not only tarnished the veneer of originality, but also highlighted aspects of Athens which did not suit the Utilitarian project.[76] Thus they launched a string of attacks upon the earlier writers which targeted not only the principle critics of Athens, but the entire intellectual milieu of eighteenth-century historiography. Indeed, they sought to write their predecessors out from the very canon of history.

---

[74] See Vidal-Naquet, *Politics Ancient and Modern* (Cambridge, 1995), 72.
[75] 'Institutions', 281; see Vaio, 'George Grote and James Mill', 71.
[76] A prime example is Cornelius de Pauw. Both Grote and De Pauw sought to exonerate the Athenians for killing Socrates. But while Grote sought to dissociate the democracy from the execution altogether by somewhat unconvincingly attributing it to 'pre-democratic' superstitions (*History* vol 8, 271), De Pauw claimed it was the result of a righteous anger in the wake of the Tyranny of the Thirty, and thus an expression of, rather than inimical to, Athenian passion for liberty. See I. Macgregor Morris, 'The Refutation of Democracy? Socrates in the Enlightenment', in *Socrates from Antiquity to the Enlightenment* (Aldershot, 2007), 220–1. The Utilitarians, so conscious of their philosophy, could not allow what verges on the condoning of the execution; on the Utilitarian admiration for Socrates, see Jenkyns, *Victorians*, 231–3. Macaulay, in his private correspondence, comes to a more intriguing conclusion when he remarks: 'The more I read of Socrates, the less I wonder that they executed him'.

## Establishing the Grotesque: the Marginalisation of Eighteenth-Century Historiography

The reformers thus needed to discredit the historians of the eighteenth century, and this was a task to which they rose with eloquence and wit. To conceal their own political use of the past, they adopted the tactic of making the very same accusation against their predecessors. Thus arose the idea that the historians of the eighteenth century *misused* ancient history. It was not merely that their histories were overtly political; even Grote himself confessed the political usefulness of Greek history. Rather, it was that they used it for 'bad' politics. This interpretation of Mitford characterised both moderate reformers such as Macaulay, and 'radicals' such as Grote. Their critique echoes Benjamin Constant's dismissal of Mably, in that it sought to establish the presence of an illiberal prejudice which hampered any historical understanding.[77] Yet they expanded this into two, contradictory, charges laid upon the historians of the eighteenth century.

Firstly we have the conservatives who deny the achievements of Athens in order to protect their own selfish interests from encroaching revolution and reform. These appear as frightened dullards, partial and partisan, blindly grasping at clichés to defend that which cannot be defended. Chief amongst them is Mitford, but the implications would tarnish all eighteenth-century historians:

> There is a strong tendency in the human mind to worship power ... Everything in an English education tends to nourish, to strengthen, and to perpetuate this tendency; and in the mind of Mr. Mitford, a mind priding itself on adherence to every thing English, it has become absolute idolatry ... He is devoted to kingly government, and to kings, not only with preference, but even with passion and bigotry.[78]

---

[77] 'Mably, whom people nicknamed the Spartan, was a pure-hearted man who cherished morality and thought he loved freedom, but was possessed assuredly of the falsest mind and the most despotic outlook ever to exist. As soon as he happened upon a vexatious measure, in any country, he thought he had made a discovery and proposed it as a model. He detested most of all individual freedom, and when he came upon a nation which was completely deprived of this, he could not stop himself admiring it, even when it had absolutely no political freedom' (*Principles of Politics Applicable to all Governments*, trans. D. O'Keeffe, ed. E. Hofmann (Indianapolis, 2003), 438–9). Constant's critique, of course, is part of the general nineteenth-century assault of eighteenth-century interpretations of Greece, and thus closely related to Grote's project. Once again, Grote had 'overlooked' his debt to Constant (Momigliano, 'Grote', 27).

[78] Grote, 'Institutions of Ancient Greece', *Westminster Review*, 5 (1826), 282.

He is, Grote infers, opposed to any form of individual freedom, for that would undermine the royal power:

> To create a powerful [ruling] one ... [which is] the grand object of Mr. Mitford's admiration, a community thoroughly subject and prostrate is necessary; and it is in this state only that he can tolerate a community.[79]

Therefore, 'the community should be in a state of constant submission'.[80] Not only are his politics despicable, but Grote also insists that the 'moral and political biases of his mind do indeed so strongly pervade every chapter of his work' that '[they] have dictated his general reflections, to pervert and discolour his facts to an inexcusable degree'.[81] Historical truth is less important than his prejudices, hence his 'habit of overstepping his authorities, and exalting his own unwarranted conjectures to the rank of authentic facts'.[82] This would become a standard critique of Mitford: so Macaulay asserted that 'his [Mitford's] passion ... led him to substantially violate the truth on every page',[83] while Mill claimed that Mitford 'always believed his prejudices above his eyes'.[84] Moreover, Mitford's prejudices were presented as being malicious: so Macaulay described him as exhibiting 'a perfect hatred',[85] and Grote remarked that his prejudices appeared 'more copiously on the side of his hatred than on the side of his love'.[86] Mitford thus appears as the most biased of historians,[87] whose prejudices determine his work, and whose vision is one of absolute submission before the king. Grote supports his allegations with carefully chosen examples to highlight Mitford's supposed deficiencies; but the focus of the attack lies in the political prejudice which Grote and Macaulay insist is the driving force behind Mitford's methodology. An extreme monarchism, a distrust and disrespect for the 'community', driven by 'hatred'. He is, in Grote's account, a bitter reactionary, bearing a loathing towards the people; and, what is worse, this made him a bad historian.

This then is one category of eighteenth-century historians. On the other extreme we have the radicals, who dangerously misunderstood

---

[79] Grote, 'Institutions', 283.
[80] Grote, 'Institutions', 284.
[81] Grote, 'Institutions', 282, 307.
[82] Grote, 'Institutions', 314–15.
[83] 'On History', *The Edinburgh Review*, May 1828.
[84] 'The Spirit of the Age, IV', *The Examiner*, 3 April 1831, 210–11.
[85] 'On Mitford's History of Greece', *Knight's Quarterly Magazine* (1824).
[86] Grote, 'Institutions', 284.
[87] 'There have been authors as much and as truly under the influence of bias as Mr. Mitford; but we do not remember any one who has ever manifested its influence in a manner so thoroughly conspicuous' ('Institutions', 284).

antiquity, seeking to impose ancient forms on the modern world. Bearing a naivety that would be fatal, they appear as hopelessly immature and credulous. Macaulay described them:

> The foundations of our constitution were laid by men who knew nothing of the Greeks but that they denied the orthodox procession and cheated the Crusaders; and nothing of Rome, but that the Pope lived there … But, when enlightened men on the Continent began to think about political reformation, having no patterns before their eyes in their domestic history, they naturally had recourse to those remains of antiquity, the study of which is considered throughout Europe as an important part of education ….
>
> How powerfully these books impressed these speculative reformers, is well known to all who have paid any attention to the French literature of the last century … It was not strange that the blind, thus led by the blind, should stumble. The transactions of the French Revolution, in some measure, took their character from these works. Without the assistance of these works, indeed, a revolution would have taken place … but it would not have been exactly such a revolution … The government of a great and polished nation would not have rendered itself ridiculous by attempting to revive the usages of a world which had long passed away, or rather of a world which had never existed except in the description of a fantastic school of writers ….
>
> The spirit excited by these writers produced more serious effects. The greater part of the crimes which disgraced the revolution sprung indeed from the relaxation of law, from popular ignorance … But many atrocious proceedings must, doubtless, be ascribed to heated imagination, to perverted principle … This evil, we believe, is to be directly ascribed to the influence of the historians whom we have mentioned [i.e. Plutarch], and their modern imitators.[88]

Thus were established two stereotypes as the poles of eighteenth-century historiography. Both are extremes and their vices are diametrically opposed. Moreover, Macaulay suggested that there were none who could be placed in between:

> His [Mitford's] occasional remarks on the affairs of ancient Rome and of modern Europe are full of errors: but he writes of times with respect to which almost every other writer has been in the wrong; and, therefore, by resolutely deviating from his predecessors, he is often in the right … [idealisations of antiquity] are the principal errors into which the predecessors of Mr Mitford have fallen; and from most of these he is free. His faults are of a completely different description. It is to be hoped that the students of history may now

---

[88] 'On History', *The Edinburgh Review*, May 1828. The motif of reckless emulation of antiquity as being at the heart of the excesses of the Revolution is one first, and most persuasively, realised by Chateaubriand. See Macgregor Morris, 'From Ancient Dreams to Modern Nightmare'.

be saved, like Dorax in Dryden's play, by swallowing two conflicting poisons, each of which may serve as an antidote to the other.[89]

In effect, there were no moderate histories of Greece in the eighteenth century. All are cast as extreme, and thus both politically and intellectually suspect. In presenting eighteenth-century histories in this way, he discredited existing scholarship and therefore legitimised the 'liberal' histories being written.

Macaulay's division of the eighteenth-century historians was an effective way to dismiss their scholarly credentials. In drawing a link between the idealising view of antiquity and the excesses of the Revolution, he was consciously echoing sentiments and beliefs which had first been suggested by Chateaubriand and then canonised by Constant, so that by the 1820s the association between utopian visions of antiquity and the Revolution had become a powerful tool to discredit many a *philosophe*. In post-Revolutionary Europe, still fixated and mystified by the events of the previous generation, such explanations were plausible and welcome, an easy answer to difficult and disturbing questions. Thus saw the confirmation in intellectual history of what Johnson Wright so aptly described as the 'distorting lens of the French Revolution', through which no eighteenth-century writer could ever be seen in quite the same way.[90] The notion that Mitford's prejudices were a response to the Revolution has become a commonplace in modern scholarship. Yet while it is obvious that his later volumes were indeed effected by the events in France – a trite observation, as there was no aspect of European culture which was *not* effected by the Revolution – to declare it the sole purpose of his work is untenable. Yet the 'distorting lens' could serve to discredit not only the admirers, but also the critics of the Revolution; so Mill could tarnish Mitford further by stating that his history was composed 'during the wildest height of Antijacobin phrensy'.[91]

Having established such a framework of criticism, the reformers next turned to the detail. The key target here once again was Mitford, who was identified, incorrectly, as embodying the worst of the 'conservative' aspects of eighteenth-century historiography.[92] Mitford's history had become the standard work on Greek history, the work with which nearly all the Utilitarians first encountered ancient Greek politics. His reputation remained considerable, and even

---

[89] 'On Mitford's History of Greece', *Knight's Quarterly Magazine* (1824).
[90] Wright made the comment with specific reference to Mably (*A Classical Republican in Eighteenth-Century France* (Stanford, 1997), 7), but it applies equally well to many others.
[91] 'Grote's *History of Greece* I', in *The Spectator*, 4 April 1846, 327–8. See also 'Sedgewick's Discourse', *Collected Works*, vol. 10).
[92] Mitford was taken to represent conservative tendencies by several among the Utilitarians. 'Mill's true opponents,' claims Urbanati, 'were in Mitford's camp' (*Mill*, 15).

those who preferred Athens over Sparta, such as Thomas Arnold, saw much to admire in his pages.[93] As the established standard, it could but bear the brunt of their assault. And thus began a systematic critique of Mitford by Macaulay, Grote and the younger Mill. Byron had famously remarked that Mitford's main qualities lay in 'praising tyrants, abusing Plutarch, spelling oddly and writing quaintly', but also noting that Mitford was 'perhaps the best of all modern historians whatsoever'.[94] Yet while Byron had mingled his critique with praise, the Utilitarians could do no such thing. In the light of such a vibrant reputation, Mitford required special attention.

The attack, when it came, was vicious. In 1824 Macaulay published a review of Mitford's history in the short-lived *Knight's Quarterly Magazine*; two years later, in the Benthamite journal, *The Westminster Review*, Grote wrote what was nominally a review of Henry Clinton's *Fasti Hellenici*, but in fact was a thinly veiled polemic against Mitford. There soon followed further salvoes, delivered in Macaulay's 1828 essay 'On History', repeatedly in the pages of Grote's *History*,[95] and subsequently in the partisan reviews which helped establish the myth of Grote.[96] Mortimer Chambers suggests that, in the wake of Grote's 1826 article, there was 'nothing left of Mitford ... with one clearing blast Grote demolished this multi-volume work'.[97] Such a conclusion may overstate the effect, but it does reflect the savagery of the combined assault on Mitford's reputation, and more crucially reveals the underlying purpose of these pieces: the total destruction of Mitford's legacy.[98]

To this end, the Victorian writers chose the features to critique with great care.[99] Mitford's distrust of Plutarch receives little mention,

---

[93] Arnold considered Mitford, along with Niebuhr, as the 'giants who first cut through the rock and penetrated the tangled thickets of the forest [of ancient history]' ('Early Roman History', *Quarterly Review*, 32 (1825), 72). The pairing with Niebuhr is an interesting one, as it stands in stark contrast to the present day pairing of Niebuhr with Grote. To Arnold's sharply critical eye, Mitford clearly represented a quite new phenomenon in Greek historiography, bearing the very qualities which later generations would bestow upon Grote alone.

[94] Notes to *Don Juan*, 12.19.

[95] Urbinati describes Grote's history with the epithet 'anti-Mitford' (*Mill*, 33).

[96] Charles Austin also penned an anti-Mitford piece for the *Westminster Review* in 1827.

[97] Chambers, 'Grote's *History of Greece*', 11.

[98] Jenkyns notes that Grote wrote his history 'in part with a polemical intention, to destroy Mitford's legacy' (*Victorians*, 14).

[99] Momigliano's comment on Gillies – 'Gillies was not the fool that an isolated quotation can make him look' ('Grote', 17) – shows he full well knew the dangers, and indeed uses, of quoting these historians out of context. Yet standard practice, both in the nineteenth century and today, has been to do exactly that.

being something with which Macaulay whole-heartedly agreed. Yet his admiration for the Greek Tyrants – which could be seen as a radical and highly thoughtful re-interpretation of the sources, very much in the manner Grote was to do for the demagogues and the sophists – would be portrayed as signs of an authoritarian and reactionary writer.[100] Here we see a key feature of their method. As Frank Turner has shown, the nineteenth-century writers 'deliberately distorted' the contents of Mitford's volumes in presenting him as an admirer of Sparta and a champion of oligarchy, while in fact Mitford was highly critical of the Spartan system and repeatedly advocated a mixed constitutional system.[101] Roberts, somewhat generously, claims Macaulay 'misread' Mitford, glossing over the crucial detail that this 'misreading' was deliberate,[102] but concludes that Macaulay's 'true goal appears to have been to purloin the Athenian example for the reformers'.[103] This is a significant admission on Roberts' part, for it accepts that Macaulay's aim in his review was primarily political and based upon error, deliberate or otherwise.[104] Moreover, it was crucial to the reformer's cause – for in attributing pro-Spartan sympathies to their 'Tory' opponents, they sought to validate their own endorsement of Athens as the opposite of Tory ideology.[105]

Although Grote too was writing a highly politicised history, he was quick to lay such a charge upon Mitford. He characterised Mitford as a 'worshipper of power', an apologist for aristocratic rule.[106] Grote himself shared James Mill's 'positive fanatacism' against the ruling classes.[107] Such an accusation of bias on the part of Mitford must take on a new light when we consider the prejudices of the accuser. Now, of course, it can well be argued that the fact

---

[100] See Turner, *Greek Heritage*, 200.
[101] Turner, *Greek Heritage*, 205. Turner does, somewhat unconvincingly, also consider that Macaulay might not have read Mitford 'with care'.
[102] Roberts, *Athens on Trial*, 236. She even goes onto cast Macaulay's reading as a 'misperception'!
[103] Roberts, *Athens on Trial*, 237.
[104] Turner suggests that Macaulay's aims were less overtly political, and that he merely sought to 'remove the subject from current political discourse' (*Greek Heritage*, 206).
[105] Urbinati claims that the 'fact that the Tories endorsed that model [Sparta] to oppose the Athenian confirmed the radical implications of Mill's and Grote's historical and political revision' (*Mill*, 18). That the opponent in question – principally Mitford – was not necessarily 'Tory', and that he did not endorse Sparta, or indeed the crucial detail that those who did endorse Sparta against Athens did so long before the Utilitarians promoted Athens, are all points deliberately concealed in the rhetoric of the reformers.
[106] Vaio, 'George Grote and James Mill', 71.
[107] Vaio, 'George Grote and James Mill', 72.

that Grote despised the principle of aristocracy does not necessarily mean that his judgements upon the subject are invalid; but then, it must also be conceded that the fact that Mitford disliked democracy does not invalidate his judgements upon that subject. Moreover, for us, as students of either modern political thought, or the realities of ancient Athens, it is the discourse between these two extremes which proves most revealing.

There are many other points at which such double standards appear. Grote attacked Mitford's use of modern analogies, which in much modern scholarship has become a general critique of eighteenth-century practice. Yet Roberts alone remarks that this criticism blithely ignores Grote's own enthusiastic use of such comparisons.[108] In both authors, such analogies are used to make political points. As with the discussion of the Athens-Sparta debate above, a close comparison of the Histories of Mitford and Grote reveals much more in the way of similarities than Grote's critique would allow.[109] Grote attacked Mitford for confusing modern politics with ancient, and thus fundamentally misunderstanding the Greek city-states;[110] yet Grote's own use of such comparisons, in the eyes of one of his most enthusiastic reviewers, John Stuart Mill, bestowed an 'ethical import' on Greek history.[111] Thus one Utilitarian glossed over the other's contradictions, transforming them into virtues. The underlying current, once again, is that Grote used his analogies to present 'truths' reflective of Utilitarian philosophy, while Mitford's undermined the very models they sought to promote. The latter must be suppressed even as the former is vaunted. Thus we see the workings of the subtly co-ordinated assault upon Mitford and his contemporaries.

The result of these distortions and misreadings has been fatal to the lasting reputation of Mitford, whose work is now judged only through the judgements of others. Why should a modern historian undertake the daunting task presented by the volumes of Mitford, when such great – and liberal! – names insist that no such effort is necessary. Moreover, with such a dismissal of these earlier historians of Greece, we inevitably

---

[108] 'In the deployment of modern analogies, Grote plainly had set one set of rules for himself and another for Mitford'. Roberts, *Athens on Trial*, 243.

[109] See Turner, *Heritage*, 215. Indeed, the similarity between the authors extends even to their orthography. In his first edition Mitford had adopted a radical English spelling – the origin of Byron's critique of 'spelling oddly' – as part of his theory of the English language. Grote also adopted a 'radical orthography' (Jenkyns, *Victorians*, 160) in his spelling of Greek names. Both men, it seems, took pleasure in flouting such conventions.

[110] Demetriou, *Grote*, 65.

[111] Demetriou, *Grote*, 77.

dismiss their approaches and methods.[112] In accepting the judgements of the Victorians we are bound to accept the assumptions and prejudices which underlie these judgements, and their entire approach to the history of Greece.

The nineteenth-century dismissal of eighteenth-century historiography of ancient Greece was, therefore, based on political grounds. In order to legitimise their own politicised readings of Greek history, and the political programmes they favoured, nineteenth-century writers needed to discredit not only the politics, but also the scholarly credentials of the eighteenth-century historians. To fail to do this would allow critics to seize on earlier readings of Greek history; but once they had cast their predecessors as either hopelessly conservative or dangerously naive, such labels would quickly be associated with any who dared defend them.[113] In order to do this, however, they had to grossly simplify – at times even distort – the views of these eighteenth-century writers, conflating their debates into uncritical monologues, and their differences into uniformity. Only then would readers deem it unnecessary to revisit the eighteenth-century writers, where they might find reasons critique the readings of the new generation. It was a bold and daring stoke, one which sought to sweep away the existing body of scholarship and, in effect, start afresh. And, what is most astounding of all, is the degree to which they succeeded.

## Maintaining the Grotesque: Modern Scholarship and the Dismissal of Eighteenth-Century Historiography

If the likes of Macaulay and Grote sought to distort the reputations of their predecessors, they did so with a firm political conviction, and a thorough knowledge of those they critiqued. Grote, much like Mitford had done before, politicised his readings for what he believed was a greater good. Yet within the current discipline of ancient history the works of the eighteenth-century historians of ancient Greece are dismissed without either the political principle, or the understanding, epitomised by Grote.

The later nineteenth century saw the establishment of a vision of Athens which owed much to Grote: a commercial, imperial power,

---

[112] Vlassopoulos discusses the notion of the 'silencing' of alternatives in the development of Greek historiography (*Unthinking the Greek Polis*, 4–7).

[113] Thus Shiletto, in his critique of Grote's *History*, felt obliged to state that he was a man who was 'proud to call himself a Tory' (*Thucydides or Grote* (London, 1851)). In doing so, he was hoping to pre-empt the obvious response he would receive, and negate the criticism by presenting it as a virtue. In this, perhaps, he failed; but the attempt itself is revealing.

democratic in a very nineteenth-century way.[114] There developed a limited political acceptance of democracy, as seen, for example, in the passing of the Municipal Corporation Act in 1835, which sought to establish urban democracy on what virtually amounted to a city-state model.[115] Even conservatives turned to Athens, reconciling their views with the coming of mass democracy by establishing a construct of elite leadership based upon aesthetic appreciation.[116] The relationship between Britain and Athens became a defining feature of nineteenth-century political culture, legitimising Grote's vision and thereby enshrining his judgements upon the historians of the eighteenth century. The triumph of Athens was the total negation of her critics.

The politics of scholarship too, were changing. In the late nineteenth century the institutionalisation of knowledge developed with the professionalisation of scholarship. A new class of historian arose, very different from the landed gentry and aristocratic patronage which was thought to have characterised the previous century. These historians could identify with the liberal aspirations of Grote, but not his predecessors, whom they believed, by reading the pages of Grote and Mill, to be conservative. These founders of the university discipline looked upon Grote as their predecessor, both academically and politically.

It is little wonder, then, that modern scholarly accounts of the eighteenth-century writers are based primarily on a reading of Grote and Macaulay.[117] They are usually brief and littered with misunderstandings, and in some cases direct error. What is seen as a virtue in the work of Grote is condemned as a vice in his predecessors.[118] Moreover, modern scholars fall into the very basic generalisations and stereotypes concerning the historiography of the eighteenth century created by Macaulay. The notion persists that eighteenth-century historiography of Greece was partisan and uncritical.[119] These historians are judged to show little, if any, variance throughout the course of the century, with the supposed

---

[114] Jenkyns suggests that the imperial element of Athens became increasingly dominant in the later nineteenth century, making it a 'rather different' Athens from the one the 'whigs and utilitarians had admired' (*Victorians*, 334).

[115] J. Moore, 'Periclean Preston – public art and the classical tradition in nineteenth-century Lancashire', *Northern History*, 40 (2003).

[116] Moore, 'Periclean Preston'.

[117] Richard Jenkyns summary of the attitudes of Mitford, for example, consists of a quotation from Macaulay (*The Victorians and Ancient Greece* (Oxford, 1980), 14).

[118] Thus Grote's Utilitarian concerns are cast as positive (Demetriou, 'Defense', 280, 290), while the eighteenth-century writers' contemporary concerns appear as negative or limiting (Demetriou, 'Defense', 280, 281, 282, 283, 289).

[119] Demetriou, *Grote*, 33.

motives of the later historians, such as Mitford, attributed to them all, as if the entire historical corpus of the period constitutes one uncritical and undeliberative mass, devoid of any chronological developments or internal debates.[120] As a result, modern accounts are strewn with errors as the context of these writers is conflated, and thus misunderstood.[121] Conclusions based on only one or two writers, which are often questionable in their own right, are then applied to the period as a whole.[122]

Amidst these generalisations, appear a series of errors and misunderstandings which owe much more to the rhetoric of Macaulay and Grote than to any reading of the eighteenth-century writers themselves, casting them as uncritical and conservative.[123] The negative stereotype of these historians persists, and they were 'amateurs … or retired officials',[124] a description which could, in light of Cartledge's definition of scholarship, be interpreted as negative. The entire Greek tradition of the period is dismissed, with the assertion that 'the history of ancient Greece had no appeal to the interest of the general public',[125] a claim which happily ignores the plethora of histories, poems, plays and paintings, the radical developments in art and architecture, and the traditions which spawned philhellenism; traditions and developments which were deeply rooted in

---

[120] For example: '*Historians commonly started* [my emphasis] their narratives with references to the problems of the day'; '*Almost unanimously* [my emphasis], historians saw in the Spartan model … [a] copy of the British constitution' (Demetriou, *Grote*, 33, 40). Both of these claims are open to question.

[121] Thus Demetriou claims Stanyan and Montagu's works were in part a reaction to the political manoeuvres of George III, apparently unaware that Montagu's work appeared a year before the ascent of that monarch, while Stanyan had died eight years previously ('Defense' 282–3, 286). Similarly, he suggests that John Gillies and Mitford combined Montesquieu and Burke, as a part of 'the reaction against the French Revolution and its intellectual background' (*Grote*, 42), in spite of the minor detail that Gillies had completed his history in 1786.

[122] Demetriou concludes that The likes of Stanyan and Montagu 'were devoid of any illuminating or original comments on political history' (*Grote*, 35). This, of course leads onto his conclusion that 'nothing of importance' was published on ancient politics in the eighteenth century ('Defense', 297).

[123] Thus Demetriou asserts that these 'historians were content simply to reaffirm the verdict of ancient thinkers'; that they 'described approvingly' the Spartan system and 'contrasted it with democracy'; and there was an 'unqualified assertion that political misbehaviour was peculiar to democracy' ('Defense', 282, 284, 293). But many of these writers were highly scathing of ancient thinkers; the Spartophiles were the most fervent critics of modernity; and finally, the 'political misbehaviour' of Sparta too, received sharp critique, especially from Rollin and De Pauw.

[124] Demetriou, 'Defense', 281.

[125] Demetriou, 'Defense', 281.

the history of, and popular fascination with, ancient Greece.[126] Indeed, so irrelevant are these writers, that Demetriou can assert that before the nineteenth century there had been 'nothing of importance [published] on the history of ancient politics'.[127] One wonders, important for whom, or for what? The answers, one suspects, lie in the comfortably unquestioned assumptions of the modern discipline.

Having dismissed the historians of the eighteenth century, scholars can eulogise Grote as the founder of the discipline. His achievement is total. The portrait of a lone genius struggling against a prejudiced establishment is certainly an attractive one for an intellectual hero.[128] But, as we have seen, it is not a wholly accurate one. Grote did not overturn the received opinions on Athens and Sparta, nor write amidst an atmosphere of fervent Spartophilia. Many of the developments attributed to him occurred before he wrote, and he owed much to the writers he so denigrated. And, perhaps most significant of all, there are aspects of his legacy which have had a negative impact upon the discipline.

A few scholars have attempted to re-examine his work, but they still operate under his legacy. The problem lies in that the political prejudices of modern scholarship, which partly derive from nineteenth-century liberalism, power preconceptions both about Grote and about eighteenth-century historiography. Commentators often seem to assume that we must admire and agree with Grote, and condemn the critics of Athens, as if any other conclusion is quite simply perverse.[129] 'We cannot be unsympathetic to his [Grote's] defense of the democratic Athenians', insists Demetriou.[130] The notion that Grote's politics make his scholarship, by definition, superior to his predecessors was enshrined by Momigliano's insistence that Grote 'possessed the all-redeeming virtue of the liberal mind'.[131] These modern preconceptions all but insist on a preference for Grote over his anti-Athenian predecessors. Even a commentator such as Roberts, who remains one of the few scholars to display a detailed and sensitive understanding of the debates of eighteenth-century historiography, strives to find inconsistencies or contradictions in anti-Athenian arguments – something

---

[126] On the development of hellenism in the eighteenth century, see T. Spencer, *Fair Greece, Sad Relic* (Bath, 1974).
[127] Demetriou, 'Defense', 297.
[128] Charles Kahn thus describes Grote's 'immense scholarship and broad intelligence' and 'his heroic conception of history' ('Plato and the Companions of Sokrates', in Calder and Trzaskoma (eds.), *George Grote Reconsidered*, 43).
[129] This, of course, is the term Grote and Mill use to describe Mitford's approach.
[130] Demetriou, *Grote*, xiv.
[131] Demetriou, *Grote*, 28.

she fails to do for the eighteenth-century defenders of Athens – even if those contradictions are not really there.[132]

One cannot escape the conclusion that much of the hostility to Mitford and his contemporaries stems not from what they wrote, but the political stance attributed to them. The term 'Tory' remains a term of abuse to many among the academic profession who, being in the main centre-left or liberal, associate the term with the defence of privilege and opposition to social progress, issues which they often pride themselves in challenging. Yet not only is this definition problematic in an eighteenth-century context,[133] but it remains unclear where Mitford's political loyalties lay.[134] Yet the labelling of Mitford as 'Tory' or conservative appear in almost every modern reference, becoming virtually an epithet.[135] The attribution of Toryism originates, of

---

[132] For example, Roberts claims that Mably is being inconsistent when he cites different points at which Sparta falls into decline due to deviating from the laws of Lycurgus (*Athens on Trial*, 164); but these points are cumulative in Mably's thought, and thus examples of an accelerating process of decline. Similarly, she accuses Rousseau of being 'unconvincing' because he fails to recognise that a 'serious investigation of Athens' would 'inevitably lead to dissonance between the decadence he despises and the egalitarianism he admires' (164); yet he she fails to consider that, for Rousseau, Athens failed to be truly egalitarian, because the effects of commerce and luxury inevitably create inequality. Thus, for Rousseau, there would be no such 'dissonance'. Finally, in her discussion of the prolific essayist the Abbé Jacourt, she alleges that 'nowhere are the inconsistencies of the *Encyclopédie* plainer', citing his admiration of Sparta and his aversion to war as being incompatible (169); however, here she has failed to consider that the vision of Sparta as a militarist state is primarily a creation of nineteenth-century writers, and that to many in the eighteenth-century Sparta was no more aggressive – indeed less warlike – than other poleis, and thus they would see no such contradiction. On the issues of the construct of Spartan militarism, see S. Hodkinson, *Comparing Spartan Militarism* (forthcoming).

[133] It needs to be remembered that within the context of late eighteenth-century politics, 'Tory' and 'conservative' do not necessarily mean the same thing. See F. O'Gorman, *The Emergence of the British Two-Party System, 1760–1832* (1982), L. Namier, *The Structure of Politics at the Accession of George III*, second edition (1957).

[134] Turner is the only modern scholar to attempt to address this question, concluding that Mitford drew his ideology – if we can call it such – from the philosophy of the Country Party. See *Greek Heritage*, 194ff.

[135] J. Ober, *Athenian Legacies* (Princeton, 2005), 29; Demetriou, *Grote*, 39, 46, 52, 65, 97, 245; B. Rapple, 'A Tory history of Ancient Greece', *Contemporary Review*, 266 (1995), and 'History and Ideology', *Papers on Language and Literature*, 37 (2001), 375; Vaio, 'George Grote and James Mill', 60. Vaio's full phrase is the 'right-wing defamation of Athens'; the rather loaded term 'defamation' suggests that such criticism of Athens is libelous, a further critique of any 'anti-Athenian' point of view. Vaio later refers to Mitford's 'notorious right-wing anti-democratic bias' (64–5), thereby conflating the notions of being conservative and being anti-democratic, two features which are not necessarily compatible.

course, among the Utilitarians, whose casting of Mitford as a 'Tory' very much suited their own purposes.[136] As with so many other claims, this too remains all but unquestioned by modern scholars.[137]

Those who criticised Grote are dismissed in the most peculiar of fashions. Thus Demetriou somewhat curiously claims that Richard Shilleto's 1851 attack on Grote 'lacked liberal sense', a statement which seems to imply that Shilleto's scholarly opinions are discredited by his politics.[138] Demetriou continues by insisting that Shiletto 'overlooked' the developments in historiographical practice inspired by Utilitarianism, apparently without considering the possibility that it was these very developments to which Shileto objected. Following John Grote, George Grote's brother, both Cartledge and Demetriou are quick to point out that Shiletto appeared to resent that fact that Grote was not University educated.[139] This they cite as an example of establishment prejudice against Grote, a curious allegation considering Cartledge's own definition of a scholar. Moreover, while they refer to Shiletto's championing of Mitford over Grote, they both fail to consider the fact that Mitford had not held a university post, and although attending Oxford, did not take a degree. Thus, although Shiletto was supposedly attacking Grote's *History* because its author was not a university scholar, in its stead he recommended another history written by a non-university writer.[140]

A sympathy for Grote's politics should not blind us to his prejudices, even if they match our own. The continued references to the eighteenth-century writers as being 'anti-democratic' reinforce the idea that to sympathise with or defend the likes of Mitford is, within the environment of modern academia, politically suspect. Yet, as we have seen, such labels ignore the fluid nature of the term 'democracy', assuming that the versions practiced in Athens are – as the Utilitarians claimed – analogous to our own; and,

---

[136] For example, John Stuart Mill relates how his father warned him against Mitford's 'Tory prejudices' (*Collected Works*, 33 vols., ed. J. Robson (Toronto 1963–91), vol. I, 15), and in his article on the *Phaedro* enigmatically refers to the 'Tory perverters of Grecian history' (*Collected Works*, vol. II, 79n).

[137] Irwin, 'Mill and the Classical World', in *The Cambridge Companion to Mill*, ed. J. Skorupski (Cambridge, 1998), 426.

[138] Demetriou, 'Defense', 280. Demetriou is also careful to include Shilleto's self-confessed Toryism, a detail which he no doubt feels discredits Shilleto academic judgements. See Shiletto, *Thucydides or Grote*.

[139] Cartledge, 'Introduction', xi–xii; Demetriou, 'Defense', 280.

[140] Similar dismissals are made of other nineteenth-century critics of Grote. See Huxley's on Eduard Meyer and William Martin Leake ('Grote on Early Greece', in Calder et. al. *Reconsidered*, 24, 26–7); Cartledge on the objections of the editors of the abridged edition of Grote's *History* ('Introduction', xiii).

more crucially, that the term 'democracy' carried the same connotations and definitions to the writers of the eighteenth century as it does today.[141]

Mitford was not, as Grote would have us believe, opposed to the principle of individual freedom: indeed, his critique of both Athens and Sparta suggest otherwise. Rather, he believed that the direct democratic system of fifth-century Athens was inimical *to* such freedom. Grote's preference for *representative* democracy suggests he, too, was not convinced that direct democracy was a desirable system for the modern world. Yet Mitford's distrust of the Athenian system has become, in the eyes of modern scholars, an opposition to the very principles of modern liberal democracies. Scholars follow Grote in conflating Athenian democracy with the principles of modern liberalism, and thereby further denigrate the writers of the eighteenth century. There is a tendency to use the highly politicised term 'liberal' to describe the both the ancient Athenians and their modern apologists.[142] Thus Roberts describes the pro-Athenian tradition of the eighteenth century – one which most modern commentators do not even recognise – as the 'liberal tradition', and even pairs De Pauw with Voltaire as 'exponents of the liberal view of Athens'.[143] In so doing, she implies that the critics of Athens are illiberal, the antithesis of modern principles, thereby discrediting their judgements. The apologists of Athens are therefore 'like us', the critics are alien. Yet the label is both anachronistic – modern notions of liberalism being nineteenth-century political constructs – and dangerously misleading.[144] To label a radical thinker such as De Pauw as 'liberal' is, quite simply, absurd.[145]

---

[141] Thus Demetriou can claim that 'what might have appeared to Mitford as anarchy' was, for Grote, 'the fundamental laws of political existence which safeguarded individual participation in public affairs' ('Defense', 293). But this statement misses the key point: which is, that the features which Mitford criticised were quite different from those Grote praised. Both writers condemned the execution of Socrates and the trial of the generals; the difference lay in how they believed these events came about.

[142] Demetriou refers to 'Athenian liberalism' ('Defense', 296). This, of course, is something he takes from Grote.

[143] Roberts, *Athens on Trial*, 168, 173. She later combines De Pauw with Constant as the 'liberal predecessors' of Grote (239).

[144] While 'liberal' was a current political term in the eighteenth century, the definitions familiar today are very much nineteenth century.

[145] Roberts also describes De Pauw as displaying a 'striking open-mindedness', *Athens on Trial* (171). He is, indeed, a difficult individual to judge, but has been critiqued for the racialised elements in his work. This is not particularly fair to De Pauw: he was not so much a racist, but rather hated everyone in equal measure. In fairness, De Pauw was a thinker whose originality bordered on both eccentricity and genius, and displayed a fervent desire to challenge every received opinion and fashionable movement. His promotion of democracy must be seen alongside his passionate opposition to philhellenism, which was so extreme that Byron cited De Pauw as one of the writers who framed the discourses over the issues of Greek independence. See the notes to *Childe Harold's Pilgrimage*, in G.G. Byron, *Complete Poetical Works* (1970), 882–3, and Macgregor Morris, *The Age of Leonidas* (forthcoming).

The critics of Athens cannot be allowed any credit, and even arguments they presented which may seem reasonable to modern readers are ignored, passed over without comment, or dismissed on the most innocuous of grounds.[146] Indeed, their very categories of analysis are dismissed.[147] The vision we find in modern scholarship is therefore one of an objective and erudite Grote in sharp contrast to his prejudiced predecessors. Grote's political preferences are unquestioned, his account 'neither mythological nor eulogistic',[148] and his prejudices, where they are admitted, presented as a virtue.[149] Indeed, commentators struggle to attribute virtues to him which even they admit are not in his text.[150] His predecessors, however, display 'bias', 'deliberate inconsistencies', and a 'narrow ideological outlook'.[151] In this way scholars reproduce the politicised judgements of Macaulay and Grote, whilst failing to recognise the political nature of these judgements; and, moreover, remain highly selective in the evidence

---

[146] Thus Roberts mentions Hume's observation that the 'so-called' democracy excluded women and slaves, yet does not consider the legitimacy or otherwise of the critique – yet she is most prepared to counter anti-Athenian judgements elsewhere (*Athens on Trial*, 159). Similarly, Rapple dismisses Mitford's complaint that ninety percent of the Athenian population was disenfranchised, with the comment that Mitford eulogised an English system which also had a large disenfranchised population ('Ideology and History', 373). Rather than considering the legitimacy of Mitford's critique, Rapple prefers to discredit his politics; a tactic, of course, which originated with Grote.

[147] Roberts dismisses Mably's vision of Sparta, claiming he venerated the 'pseudoegalitarian' Spartans, and that he praised the Spartans for avoiding 'real democracy' (*Athens on Trial*, 163). Such a claim implies that Mably considered Athenian democracy as 'real' – which he did not – and that he was praising avoidance of democracy, while in fact he was suggesting that Spartans had *perfected* democracy. On Mably's vision of Spartan democracy, see I. Macgregor Morris, 'Paradigm of Democracy', 343–4; H. Mason, 'Sparta in the French Enlightenment', in Hodkinson, *Sparta: Classical Tradition*. The entire tone of Roberts' account of Mably appears to discredit his ideas, denying him 'democratic' credentials and thus – to modern readers – invalidating his judgements. A similar approach can be seen, for example, in her treatment of Gillies (*Athens on Trial*, 200).

[148] Urbanati, *Mill*, 15.

[149] In his biography of Grote, Clarke insists that while political partisanship can 'distort judgement', it can also 'give an insight to the past which the scrupulously neutral and unpolitical historian may lack' (*Grote*, 126). See also Irwin, 'Mill and the Classical World', 430–1; Gooch *History and Historians in the Nineteenth Century* (London, 1920), 318. This argument, of course, is not applied to Mitford, whose prejudices, in contrast to Grote, 'hampered a proper understanding of Greek history' (Demetriou, *Grote*, 245). Mill is also cast as showing an 'unbiased understanding' of antiquity (Urbanati, *Mill*, 11).

[150] For example, Kahn's attempt to attribute a belief in equal rights for women to Grote ('Plato', 50).

[151] Demetriou, 'Defense', 288, 290, 291.

upon which they base their opinions. In short, there is no attempt, no desire, to question the legacy of Grote.

## Navigating the Grotesque: Reassessing Eighteenth-Century Historiography

It is one thing to argue that a certain school of writers have been marginalised for political reasons, and quite another to show that they are worthy of reconsideration. The mere fact that the nineteenth-century writers obscured and distorted Mitford does not mean, *ipso facto*, that his history is worth reading. However, as the contributors to the volume have persuasively shown, there is much of value to be found within eighteenth-century historiography, both for students of the Enlightenment and of the ancient world itself. Moreover, independent of any consideration of 'quality', there lies a relevance within these works which makes at the very least a cursory understanding of them indispensable to the ancient historian. The modern discipline is based on certain assumptions, and certain approaches, which all too often remain unquestioned. Indeed, most are quite unaware of them. As we have seen in the case of Greek historiography, some of these assumptions were politically generated within a very specific intellectual context. This does not necessarily invalidate them, but an awareness of these contexts is essential to recognise them and thus understand what we do as historians of the ancient world.

In the Greek historians of the eighteenth century, and in their nineteenth-century detractors, we can find these contexts. Moreover, in the former we can also find alternatives, different approaches and ways of thinking. These very differences can serve to highlight the assumptions and deficiencies of our approaches, and, perhaps, on occasion even to correct them. The legacy of Grote, both in terms of his dismissal of these historians and the prejudices which underlay that dismissal, have long been the barrier to a reconsideration. Yet to do so cannot but be beneficial to a Greek historian. At the very least it could validate our assumptions; it might even expose and overturn them. *This* is to navigate the Grotesque.

One of the most remarkable, and most unrecognised, features of eighteenth-century historiography is the diversity of opinion: one of its defining features was its essentially dialogic nature.[152] Yet Macaulay's simple

---

[152] Pocock observes that it was a 'complex world of opposing and interacting values, where history could not be written as a one-way song' (*Barbarism and Religion*, vol. 1, 120).

polarity between Mitford and 'every other writer' helped to cement the belief that there was a lack of debate, and served to isolate Mitford as the bitter reactionary he never was. In doing this, Macaulay did not allow for the many eighteenth-century historians, such as Rollin, who sought to find a balance between emulation and condemnation of antiquity; or for the dialogic approach to ancient themes and history used by writers from Fénelon to Mably and Barthélemy.[153] As we have seen in the case of the Athens-Sparta debate, there were passionate and vitriolic debates, which involved careful reconsideration of the sources. Scholars, desperate to counter the arguments of their opponents, turned to increasingly ingenious ways of using their sources. While many of these bordered on the bizarre, they usually necessitated the most erudite scholarship, for careless work would quickly be deconstructed in the periodic and pamphlet literature. Thus, for example, issues such as the nature of the redistribution of land – or otherwise – at Sparta received the most thorough investigations in the intellectual battles between Mably and the Physiocrats.[154] Within these debates there are many ways in which the eighteenth-century approaches to Greece are so remarkably different to our own, that the very dissonance of understanding can prove illustrating. The eighteenth-century dismissal of luxury and commerce, for example, may appear naive to the modern imagination, but it evinces are quite different view of the role these factors play in any historical society, and thus may help to highlight what we have overlooked, or over prioritised.[155]

Related to this is what we, as practicing ancient historians, understand to constitute 'Ancient History'. Scholars delight in referring to the Spartan 'mirage' – a term coined in the 1930s by François Ollier – or 'myth'. The process of 'debunking' the Spartan myth began, Roberts suggests, in the eighteenth century, although, as we have seen, the majority of scholars consider this to have been the unique achievement of Grote. The vision with which he replaced the Spartan 'mirage' was that of a shining

---

[153] Fénelon, *Dialogues des morts et fables* (1712); Mably, *Entretiens de Phocion* (1763); J.J. Barthélemy, *Voyage du jeune Anacharsis en Grèce* (1787).

[154] On this, see S. Hodkinson, 'Five Words that Shook the World: Plutarch, Lykourgos 16 and Appropriations of Spartan Communal Property Ownership in Eighteenth-Century France', in N. Birgalias, et. al. (eds.), *The Contribution of Ancient Sparta to Political Thought and Practice* (Athens, 2007), 417–31; and P. Christesen, 'Land Tenure and French Socialism', in Hodkinson and Macgregor Morris (eds.), *Sparta: Classical Tradition* (Swansea, forthcoming).

[155] Vlassopoulos discusses the idea of 'silencing', the 'process of the forming of modern orthodoxy, and the exclusion of alternatives' (*Unthinking the Greek Polis*, 4–7). An appreciation of this notion, which he applies to the study of Greek history, challenges the belief that the histories of the eighteenth century were simply superceded.

Athens.[156] Yet this is every bit as fictional as the Sparta of Mably, perhaps even more so: for Mably tried to justify and explain what others saw as the shortcomings of Sparta, while Grote's Athens was quite devoid of such faults.[157] Modern scholarship, however, still operates under a framework of Athenocentrism.[158] While to a degree this is driven by the sources, as Bayliss shows it also owes much to Grote's legacy, with the source-rich Athens of the third century outside the canon of Greek history. Other poleis, too, stand outside the realm of proper Greek history.[159] And while some scholarship has challenged the alluring vision of Classical Athens painted by Grote, it still operates and defines the framework within which we approach the study of Greece.[160] Perhaps it is time that we begin to think also of the Athenian 'mirage'. As the Victorians struggled to be free of the weight of the eighteenth-century vision of Sparta, so we must now re-address Grote's vision of Athens. And here the histories of the eighteenth century can provide useful starting points.

The ancient world beyond the Athenian democrats lies on the periphery of modern classical studies,[161] and eighteenth-century interest in such subjects is cast as bizarre. The rather selective manner in which

[156] It should also be added that this change also saw the rise of what could be called the 'second' Spartan mirage: the image of the strict militaristic state, an exceptional and unique polis, now firmly entrenched in the academic imagination, which no more accords with reality than does the utopia of Mably. This 'mirage' is, at long last, also being debunked. See S. Hodkinson, *Comparing Spartan Militarism* (forthcoming).

[157] In Roberts' words, Grote 'chose not to know that many, many working people in Athens were slaves' (*Athens on Trial*, 255). The unfree of Athens are quite conspicuous by their absence. This was, perhaps, easier to do for Athens than for Sparta. The slaves of the Spartans were in the open, for all to see, working the fields of their masters. But the slaves of the Athenians were concealed, buried forever in Tartarus of Laurium, while their women were safely ensconced behind walls. The unfree of Athens were – metaphorically and literally – conveniently hidden from view, and any imaginary vista of that city showed only the *isonomia* of Pericles.

[158] Arlene Saxonhouse provides a fair description of the vision of Athens in the modern imagination (*Athenian Democracy: Modern Mythmakers and Ancient Theorists* (Notre Dame, 1996), 28).

[159] So that modern commentators on political science can claim that Athens was 'the only democracy in Western history' (Urbinati, *Mill*, 5; see also 16), a claim which happily ignores the many other democratic poleis which even Grote – although not Mill – recognised.

[160] 'Athens must remain the center of a Greek history', proclaimed Momigliano ('Grote', 27) even as he described the need to examine other periods and places. Despite further interests, Athens remains the focus.

[161] Jenkyns comments that, after the death of Demosthenes, 'Athens survived, but not the Athens that Grote admired, and at this point he drew his story to a close' (*Victorians*, 74). It seems later scholarship has tended to do the same.

scholars cite the eighteenth-century writers appears to have the intention of discrediting them by the sheer preposterousness of their views. Mitford's account of Philip of Macedon and Demosthenes are reported with surprise, as if the likes of Demosthenes are, for some reason, beyond critique, while the likes of Philip are beyond reproach.[162] Yet, as Bayliss argues in this volume, encomiums to Philip were far from unusual, and that to some his government, far from being autocratic, was imbued with, a 'liberal spirit'.[163] Even more astounding, however, was Mitford's proposal to write an 'apology' of the Persian type of government, which would, claims Demetriou, 'have astonished even conservative readers'.[164] Yet the anti-Persian attitude which still permeates the study of Greek history is another feature which only appeared in the nineteenth century. The desperate need for the likes of Grote to prove the superiority of Athenian democracy led to a denigration and dismissal of her adversaries, partaking in the increasingly racialised view of the past.[165] Macaulay, among his many criticisms of Mitford, bemoans his 'predilection for Persians, Carthaginians, Thracians', as if such a cosmopolitan reading of the past is in some way distasteful;[166] Mill criticises Mitford's sympathy for what he describes as 'a vulgar Asiatic Sultan like Xerxes'.[167] By the nineteenth century, as Bayliss shows, race had become an issue for

---

[162] Roberts, *Athens on Trial*, 204; Gooch, *History and Historians,* 308.

[163] In the words of Gillies. See Bayliss, this volume, and *Life After Demosthenes*. See also Momigliano 'Grote', 17–18; Turner, *Greek Heritage*, 202. Macaulay, although critical of Mitford's attitude to Demosthenes, admitted that he held 'the same opinion' on Philip as Mitford ('On Mitford')

[164] Demetriou, *Grote*, 39. Roberts also seems to think that such a defense of Persia unusual, *Athens on Trial*, 204.

[165] The rise of racial issues in the understanding of the ancient world is clear from the new histories being published in the early nineteenth century. For example, Müller's *Dorians* prioritises the ethnicity of the Spartans in a way quite alien to the thought of the previous century, which regarded the qualities of the Spartans – for good or ill – as the result of their constitutional and social arrangements. Although highly controversial in his arguments, and subject to many mis-understandings when dealing with eighteenth-century material, Martin Bernal has quite rightly identified the early nineteenth century as the period in which race became a central issue in historiography (*Black Athena: The Fabrication of Ancient Greece* (1987)). See also Vlassopoulos' discussion of the role of Greek historiography in the nineteenth-century development of the categories of 'East' and 'West', and hellenocentrism (*Unthinking the Greek Polis*, 2, 17–47). This is not to say Grote himself was what we would term a racist, but that he and other 'liberal' writers were part of an increasingly racialised discourse. As Jenkyns comments, 'many Victorians liked also to explain history in racial terms' (*Victorians*, 166; see also 167–8). See Bayliss, this volume.

[166] 'On Mitford's History of Greece'.

[167] 'Grote's *History of Greece*', *The Spectator*, 4 April 1846, 327–8.

historians in a sinister manner. Yet this was not the case in the eighteenth century, and the Persians were the frequent subject of admiration and even eulogy.[168] Once again, the hellenocentrism which still plagues our definitions of Ancient History emerges as another aspect of Grote's legacy. Mitford's admiration for the Persians would not have shocked his readers in the late eighteenth century; those of the following generations, however, were considerably less charitable to the descendants of Cyrus the Great. As the cases of both Macedon and Persia show, eighteenth-century writers displayed a much more open-minded approach to ancient societies beyond Athens, and, perhaps, can serve as a useful corrective to the shortcomings of the modern discipline.

These and many other issues reveal the ways in which nineteenth-century assumptions define and formulate the discipline. Even the sources we use are determined, in part, by Victorian preferences.[169] Thus, much of the revisionist work in modern scholarship is unwittingly battling Grote's legacy. Subjects from the role of slaves and women in Athenian democracy, to reassessing post-classical Greek history and the civilisations of the Near East, and re-evaluations of 'minor' authors, are emerging at the forefront of the modern discipline. In these subjects we see that the eighteenth-century historians are sometimes much closer to modern opinion than those of the nineteenth. To recognise this is to understand

---

[168] Eighteenth-century understandings of Persia were based, primarily, on Herodotus and Xenophon, who are not entirely negative in their portrayals. Xenophon's *Cyropaedia* remained a highly popular text, and was still consulted as a thesis on political leadership. See I. Macgregor Morris, '*Creating the Enlightenment Prince*: Maurice Ashley's Translation of the *Cyropaedia* of Xenophon', in M. Zebrowski (ed.), *Ancient Greece in Eighteenth-Century Britain: Essays on Translation and Commentary in a Tradition of Philosophy, Politics, and Culture* (a special edition of the *Annals of Scholarship*) (forthcoming). Xerxes, the Persian king whose reign Mitford was hoping to discuss, was at times portrayed in a rather sympathetic manner, even in Richard Glover's *Leonidas* (1737). See Macgregor Morris, *Age of Leonidas*.

[169] Grote, Neihbuhr, and Macaulay, set the agenda for the judgement and dismissal of sources. While eighteenth-century writers used an often bewildering range of material, they sought to dismiss what Macaulay described as 'extravagant representations of Plutarch, Diodorus, Curtius, and other romance writers of the same class' ('On History', 60). Plutarch and Xenophon, perhaps the two most widely read classical authors of the eighteenth century, were the principal victims. While few modern scholars would suggest Justin, for example, as a serious source for classical Greek history, it cannot be denied that such a reduction of the canon inevitably reduces the diversity of opinion within scholarship. As Carsten Lange shows in this volume, the ways in which certain sources are prioritised over others can have far reaching, and often negative effects on the work we do as historians. See also Bayliss, *Life After Demosthenes* (forthcoming).

their enduring relevance, and the nature and history of our discipline. A final example will suffice to summarise the negative impact much nineteenth-century criticism had on the development of the discipline, and the condescension with which they destroyed the reputation and legacy of the eighteenth century. Having castigated Mitford for his lack of interest in the literary relics of the fifth century, Macaulay goes on to concede that Mitford did, indeed, admire Homer; but this was, he adds condescendingly, 'principally, I am afraid, because he is convinced that Homer could neither read nor write'.[170]

In judging the historical scholarship of the eighteenth century by the academic standards of the twenty-first, we are committing an act of gross anachronism and precluding the possibility of understanding or learning from it. Moreover, to judge this scholarship by the prejudices of the Victorians, which is what, in essence, many are doing, is quite simply preposterous. We should not read Grote for an understanding of Mitford. And we should not judge historians of the eighteenth century by contemporary standards. Indeed, to do so for Grote would reveal, as Bayliss has highlighted, implications which would make modern readers most uncomfortable.[171]

Yet the standard approach appears to be to excise Grote for being a product of his time, and to condemn Mitford and Gillies for being a product of theirs. Rather, we should recognise that the value of these historical works lies in the very fact that they are products of a different age and context, and that their assumptions and prejudices are so different to our own. So successful was the nineteenth-century demolition of these writers, that none feel the need to return to them. But, in reading Grote and Macaulay out of their context, we see only one side of the debate, and surmise the views of their opponents from their comments alone. The historians of the eighteenth century are mere shadows in the later writers' texts, insubstantial and ultimately inconsequential. It is little wonder, therefore, that they are no longer read nor understood.

The eighteenth century was the period of 'Enlightened History', a concept closely related to philosophy. 'Philosophy', Pocock argues, 'in

---

[170] Macaulay, 'On Mitford's History of Greece'; Jenkyns describes Macaulay's displaying of a 'magnificent condescension' to certain eighteenth-century historians (*Victorians*, 78).
[171] In addition to the issues of race, there are also the issues of Grote's sympathy with neo-Malthusianism that is noted, without comment, by Kahn ('Plato', 51). A darker side of the legacy of Utilitarianism is discussed by Ruth Richardson in *Death, Dissection and the Destitute* (London, 1987).

the eighteenth-century sense deeply affected the writing of history', later adding that this philosophy was 'a state of mind rather than a system of thought'. Integral to this was 'the capacity to read texts critically'.[172] In these ways, the historiography of the eighteenth century was a key part of the intellectual currents of the Enlightenment. The notion that this historiography was in any way philosophically barren, as Grote implied of Mitford, is simply untenable.[173] There is a continuity between the eighteenth-century writers and Grote which he and his contemporaries were at pains to deny. We have already seen the many ways in which Grote echoes Mitford – from his political partisanship to his curious orthography. Turner observes that

> Grote's history was … conceptually a direct descendent of the earlier study. Both writers conceived their histories for contemporary political polemics, and both distorted their evidence and arguments to that end … Grote embraced as his own many, though by no means all, of the political virtues that Mitford espoused.[174]

Moreover, the ways in which Grote *differed* from Mitford are reminiscent of another eighteenth-century engagement with antiquity: the very veneration which Macaulay had castigated in his 1828 essay, 'On History'. Grote envisioned Cleisthenes as an 'almost Rousseauistic legislator', and democracy as a 'vehicle for moral transformation',[175] which 'infused into the Athenian mind a true liberal spirit'.[176] Grote's Lycurgus was Cleisthenes. And while he openly rejected the strict obedience of the former, his lawgiver's transformation of the Athenian 'spirit' echoes what Mably claimed to be Lycurgus' greatest achievement: transforming the 'manners' of the people.

Thus here we see the twin critiques of the eighteenth-century writers, devised by Macaulay and Grote, collapse. Grote did not reject the two extremes of eighteenth-century historiography outlined above: he followed, or perhaps was a product, of them both.[177] While he certainly adopted differing perspectives and approaches, much of what he wrote was a development of eighteenth-century ideas. This is not, nor should it be, a criticism. All great historians build upon the work of their predecessors.

---

[172] Pocock, *Barbarism and Religion*, vol. 1, 121; vol. 2, 21, 25.
[173] Ceserani argues that 'Gillies and Mitford histories counted as philosophical histories' ('Modern Histories of Ancient Greece', 13).
[174] Turner, *Greek Heritage*, 214–15.
[175] Turner, *Greek Heritage*, 222, 226.
[176] Demetriou, *Grote*, 94.
[177] Turner adroitly remarks that Grote 'employed Rousseau's thought eclectically and unsystematically as he did that of so many other Continental writers' (*Greek Heritage*, 221).

Rather it is to dismantle the myth of Grote as the first historian. It is to situate him within the longstanding tradition of Greek history; a tradition which he, for his very political purposes, sought to deny.

These politics, however, gave his work a different dimension to that of Mitford. Mitford's *History* is not as blatantly political as that of Grote; that is to say, it was not conceived in the single-minded pursuit of a political ideal. Rather, Mitford wrote in light of general philosophical, political and intellectual principles which he developed throughout his life.[178] He was certainly eccentric at times, but his prejudices are based upon heartfelt principles. While Mitford wrote as he did because he believed it to be true, Grote wrote as he did because he was pursuing a political vision. We should not let our sympathy for Grote's vision blind us to the possible virtues of Mitford's honesty. It would not be unfair to say, that while Mitford was critical, Grote was dogmatic.

None of this is to deny the genuineness of Macaulay's or Grote's aspirations for political reform, or indeed the significance of Grote's contribution to the study of ancient Greece. Rather, it is to reconsider the ways in which these aspirations coloured their historical understanding and have had far reaching implications on the modern discipline, and to recognise the richness provided by the heritage of our discipline. It would be quite foolhardy to reassess Grote by rejecting his work wholesale, as he did with Mitford, or to replace the current understanding of the historiography of ancient Greece – which can roughly be summarised in saying that everyone before Grote was wrong – with one which merely claims the opposite. Rather, this piece is an admittedly polemical call to re-address the foundations of the discipline of ancient history, to take the appreciation of historiography back to writers who held quite different prejudices from our own.

It is here, perhaps, that the historians of the eighteenth century might still serve a purpose to historians of the ancient world. Much as Macaulay suggested that Mitford could serve as an antidote to the panegyric of his predecessors, instead I suggest that the historians of the eighteenth century could, perhaps, serve as the antidote to the assumptions of the

---

[178] Pocock has analysed these influences for the case of Gibbon (*Barbarism and Religion*, vol. I, passim) and a parallel could be drawn for Mitford. Like Gibbon, he was greatly influenced by his time serving in the Hampshire militia, the fruits of which could be seen in his passionate contributions to militia debates of the late eighteenth century (*A Treatise on the Military Force, and particularly the Militia, of the Kingdom.* (n.d.)); and, again like Gibbon, he formed many of his ideas on the continent. (see I. Macgregor Morris, 'William Mitford', in *Eighteenth-Century British Historians* (New York, 2007), 240–5).

discipline as it stands today. In his summation of the 'virtues' of Mitford, Byron included 'wrath and partiality', adding that, he considered these virtues in a writer, for 'they make him write in earnest'.[179] If this essay appears to be written in such 'earnest', then it can only be added that both Mitford and Grote wrote in such a way. Their Histories were polemical, in that the political drove much of their scholarship and shaped many of their conclusions. Yet this should not negate their value as works of history. Their concerns, political or otherwise, gave rise to new critiques, and were always situated within larger debates. It was within these very debates and discourses that the study of ancient history was born, and gained the relevance which would drive it forward. To ignore or to dismiss them is to deny the origins and nature of our discipline, and the opportunity to understand it.

---

[179] Notes to *Don Juan* 12.19.

# Bibliography of Primary Material

The following bibliography presents a list of historical works, by order of date of publication, concerned with the ancient world, works which included a substantial historical element, and those which contributed to the study of ancient history. The list does not pretend to be exhaustive, but is intended to illustrate development of the breadth and variety of the material produced, and the ways in which these works developed.

Machiavelli, N., *Discorsi sopra la prima deca di Tito Livio* (1531).
Mexia, P., *Istoria Imperial y Cesarea* (1547).
Sigonio, C., *Regum, consultum, dictatorum ac censorum Romanorum Fasti* (1550–5).
De Grouchy, N., *De comitiis Romanorum libri tres* (1555).
Sigonio, C., *Fasti consulares ac triumphi acti* (1556).
Panvinio, O., *Fasti et triumphi Romani* (1557).
Sigonio, C., *De antiquo iure civium Romanorum* (1560).
Glotz, H., *Græcia, sive Historiæ urbium et populorum Græciæ ex antiquis numismatibus restitutæ* (1567).
Bodin, J., *Six Livres de la République* (1576).
Cragius, N., *De Republica Lacedaemoniorum* (1593).
Pighius, S., *Annales Magistratuum et Provinciarum* (1599).
Mexía, P., *The Historie of all the Roman Emperors beginning with Caius Iulius Caesar, and successiuely ending with Rodulph the second now raigning* (1604).
Bellenden, W., *Ciceronis Princeps* (1608).
Bellenden, W., *Ciceronis Consul, Senator, Senatusque Romanus* (1612).
Raleigh, W., *The Historie of the World in Five Books* (1614).
Pighius, S., *Annales Romanorum*, ed. A. Schottus (1615).
Coeffeteau, N., *Histoire Romaine depuis le Commencement de l'Empire d'auguste, jusqu'a Licinius* (1621).
Cluverius, P., *Italia Antiqua* (1624).
Bellenden, P., *De Tribus Luminibus Romanorum* (1633).
Mexia, P., *The Imperiall historie: or The Lives of the Emperours, from Iulius Caesar, the first founder of the Roman Monarchy, unto this present yeere* (1623).

Milton, J., *A Defence of the People of England* (1651).
Ross, A., *The History of the World the Second Part in six books, being a Continuation of Famous History of Sir Walter Raleigh, Knight* (1652).
Milton, J., *A Second Defence of the People of England* (1654).
Harrington, J., *The Commonwealth of Oceana* (1656).
De Saumaise, C., *De re militari Romanorum* (1657).
Laurenbergi, J., *Joannis Laurenbergi Graecia Antiqua* (1660).
Howell, W., *The Elements of History from the Creation of the World, to the Reign of Constantine the Great* (1670).
Sandy, G., *Sandy's Travels* (1673).
Moret de la Fayolle, P., *Histoire de la République Romaine* (1675).
Spon, J., *Voyage d'Italie, de Dalmatie, de Grèce et du Levant* (1678).
De Broé, S., *Histoire de Triumvirates* (1681).
Wheeler, G., *A Journey into Greece* (1682).
Turner, J., *Pallas Armata. Military Essayes of the Ancient Grecian, Roman, and Modern Art of War. Written in the years 1670 and 1671* (1683).
Gronovius, J., *Dissertatio de Origini Romuli* (1684).
Perizonius, J., *Animaadversiones Historicae* (1685).
De Broé, S., *The History of the Triumvirates* (1686).
De Tillemont, L-S., *Histoire des empereurs et autres princes qui ont régné pendant les six premiers siècles de l'Église* (1690–8).
Tourreil, J., 'Préface Historique', in *Harangues de Démosthène* (1691).
Walker, O., *The Greek and Roman History illustrated by Coins and Medals* (1692).
Arrhenius, J., *Dissertatio gradualis de Græcia triumphante* (1693).
Graevius, J.G., *Thesaurus antiquitatum Romanarum* (1694–99).
Echard, L., *The Roman History from the Building of the City to the Perfect Settlement of the Empire by Augustus Caesar* (1695).
Echard, L., *The Roman History from the Settlement of the Empire by Augustus Caesar, to the Removal of the Imperial Seat by Constantine the Great* (1698).
Echard, L., *An Abridgement of Sir Walter Raleigh's History of the World* (1698).
Skunk, C., *Tribuni Militum Consulari Potestate* (1697).
Gronovius, J., *Thesaurus Graecarum anitquitatum* (1697–1702).
Brunell, N., *De Tribunis Romanae Plebis* (1698).
Moyle, W., *An Essay on the Lacedæmonian Government* (1698)
Potter, J., *Archaeologia Graeca* (1698).
Wotton, W., *A History of Rome, from the Death of Antoninus Pius, to the Death of Alexander Severus* (1701).

Swift, J., *A Discourse on the Contests and Dissensions between the nobles and commons in Athens and Rome with the consequences they had upon both those States* (1701).
Dodwell, H., *De Veteribus Graecorum Romanorumque Cyclis* (1701).
Le Bruyn, C., *A Voyage to the Levant: or, Travels in the principal parts of Asia Minor* (1702).
Kennet, B., *Romae Antiquae Notitia* (1703).
Echard, L., *The Roman History from the Removal of the Imperial Seat by Constantine the Great, to the Taking of Rome by Odacer and the Ruin of the Empire in the West & from the Ruin of the Western Empire to its Restitution by Charlemagne* (1704).
Graevius, J.G., *Thesaurus antiquitatum et historiarum Italiae* (1704–25).
Echard, L., *The Roman History from the Restitution of the Western Empire by Charlemagne, to the taking of Constantinople by the Turks* (1705).
Anon., *The Agreement of the Customs of the east Indians with those of the Jews and other Antient People* (1705).
Stanyan, T., *The Grecian History* (1707–39).
Hind, T., *The History of Greece* (1707).
Perizonius, J., *Dissertatio de Historia Romuli et Romanae Urbis Origine* (1709).
Vertot, R.-A., *Histoire des révolutions de la République Romaine* (1719).
Stanhope, J., *A Memorial sent from London by the late Earl Stanhope, to the Abbot Vertot at Paris. Containing the following questions, relating to the constitution of the Roman Senate* (1721).
Vertot, R.-A., *The History of the Revolutions that Happened in the Government of the Roman Republic,* trans. J. Ozell (1722).
De Pouilly, L.-J., 'Dissertation sur l'incertitude de l'histoire des quatre premiers siecles de Rome', *Histoire et Mémoirs de l'Académie Royale des Inscriptions et Belles-Lettres VI* (1722), 14–29.
Sallier, C., 'Discours sur les premiers monuments historiques des romains', *Histoire et Mémoirs de l'Académie Royale des Inscriptions et Belles-Lettres VI* (1722), 30–51.
Sallier, C., 'Second discours sur la certitude de l'histoire des romains', *Histoire et Mémoirs de l'Académie Royale des Inscriptions et Belles-Lettres VI* (1722), 52–70.
Sallier, C., 'Troisieme discours sur la certitude de l'histoire des quatres premier siecles de Rome', *Histoire et Mémoirs de l'Académie Royale des Inscriptions et Belles-Lettres VI* (1722), 115–34.
La Croze, M.V., *Histoire du Christianisme des Indes* (1724).
Catrou, F. and Rouille, J., *Histoire Romaine* (1725–37).
Catrou, F. and Rouille, J., *The Roman History*, trans. J. Ozell. (1725).

Lafitau, P., *Moeurs des Sauvages Amériquains comparées aux moeurs des premieres temps* (1725).
Ozell, J., *Mr. Ozell's Defence Against the Remarks Publish'd by Peele and Woodward, under the name of the translators, on his translation of the Roman history* (1725).
Vico, G., *Principii di una scienza nuova d'interno alla natura delle nazioni* (1725).
Moyle, W., *An Essay upon the Constitution of the Roman Government* (1726).
Newton, I., *The Chronology of Ancient Kingdoms Amended* (1728).
Catrou, F. and Rouille, J., *The Roman History*, trans. R. Bundy (1728–37).
Chishull, E., *Antiquities Asiaticae* (1728).
Gordon, T., *Political Discourses in the Works of Tacitus* (1728).
De Varenne, B., *Histoire de Constantin le Grand, Premier Empereur Chrétien* (1728).
Burges, D., *A Short Account of the Roman Senate* (1729).
Ozell, J., *No I. of the Herculean Labour: or, the Augæan stable cleansed of its Heaps of Historical, Philological and Geographical Trumpery* (1729).
Echard, L., *Histoire Romaine Depuis La Fondation de Rome jusqu'a la translation de l'empire par Constantin*, trans. D. de Larroque and P. Desfontaines (1730–42).
Rollin, C., *Histoire ancienne des Egyptiens, des Carthaginois, des Assyriens, des Babyloniens, des Medes et des Perses, des Macédoniens, des Grecs* (1730–1738).
Horsely, J., *Britannia Romana* (1732).
Sigonio, C., *Opera omnia edita et inedita* (1732–7).
Montesquieu, *Considérations sur les causes de la grandeur des Romains et de leur decadence* (1734).
De la Nauze, L.J., 'De la loi des Lacedemoniens, qui defendait l'entree de leur pays aux etrangers', *Histoire et Mémoirs de l'Académie Royale des Inscriptions et Belles-Lettres* XII (1734), 159–76.
Stukeley, W., *Geographia Classica: The Geography of the Ancients* (1736).
De Beaufort, L., *Dissertation sur l'incertitude de l'histoire des cinq premiers siècles de l'histoire Romaine* (1738).
Hooke, N., *The Roman History From the Building of Rome to the Ruin of the Commonwealth*, vol. I (1738, 1751, 1757).
Hooke, N., 'Remarks on the History of the Seven Roman Kings', in *The Roman History From the Building of Rome to the Ruin of the Commonwealth*, vol. I (1738), i–xl.
Rollin, C. and Crevier, J.-B., *Histoire Romaine* (1739–1750).

Bonamy, P.-N., 'Dissertation sur l'Origine des Loix des XII Tables', *Histoire et Mémoirs de l'Académie Royale des Inscriptions et Belles-Lettres XII* (1740), 27–99.
Middleton, C., *The History of the Life of M. Tullius Cicero* (1741).
Saxius, C., *Miscellanea Lipsiensia Nova I* (1742), 40–79.
Saxius, C., *Miscellanea Lipsiensia Nova II* (1743), 409–95.
Saxius, C., *Miscellanea Lipsiensia Nova III* (1744), 620–712 and 743–9.
Anon. *A Dissertation upon the Constitution of the Roman Senate, by a Gentleman* (1743).
Gordon, T., *Political Discourses, in The Works of Sallust* (1744).
Hooke, N., *The Roman History From the Building of Rome to the Ruin of the Commonwealth*, vol. II (1745, 1751, 1757).
Hooke, N., 'Dissertation on the Credibility of the first 500 years of Rome', *The Roman History From the Building of Rome to the Ruin of the Commonwealth*, vol. II (1745), i–xxxiii.
Middleton, C., *A Treatise on the Roman Senate* (1747).
Montesquieu, *De l'esprit des lois* (1748).
Mably, G.B. de, *Observations sur les Grecs* (1749).
Crevier, J.-B., *Histoire des Empereurs Romains, depuis Auguste jusqu'a Constantin* (1749–55).
De Beaufort, L., *Dissertation sur l'incertitude de l'histoire des cinq premiers siecles de l'histoire Romaine, nouvelle edition, revue, corrigee et augmentee* (1750).
Jablonksi, P.E., *Pantheon Aegyptiorum* (1750–2).
Terrasson, A., *Histoire de la Jurisprudence Romaine* (1750).
Chapman, T., *An Essay on the Roman Senate* (1750).
De Burigny, J-L., *Histoire des révolutions de l'empire de Constantinople* (1750).
Mably, G.B. de, *Observations sur les Romains* (1751).
Blackwell, T., *Memoirs of the Court of Augustus* (1753–63).
Gast, J., *The Rudiments of the Grecian History, from the First Establishment of the States of Greece, to the Overthrow of their Liberties in the Days of Philip the Macedonian* (1753).
Voltaire, *Essai sur les moeurs et l'esprit des nations* (1756).
Le Beau, C., and Ameilhon, H.-P., *Histoire du Bas-Empire, en commençant a Constantine le Grand* (1756–1811).
Macquer, P., *Annales Romaines, ou Abrégé Chronologique de l'histoire Romaine, depuis la fondation de Rome, jusqu'aux Empereurs* (1756).
Hooke, N., *Observations on 1. The Answer of M. L'Abbé de Vertot to the late Earl Stanhope's Inquiry, concerning the Senate of Ancient Rome, Dated December 1719. II. A Dissertation upon the Constitution of the Roman*

Senate, by a Gentleman, Published in 1743 III. A Treatise on The Roman Senate, by Dr.Conyers Middleton, Published in 1747. IV. An Essay on the Roman Senate, by Dr Thomas Chapman, Published in 1750 (1758).

Spelman, M., *A Short Review of Mr. Hooke's Observations concerning the Roman Senate and the Character of Dionysius of Halicarnassus* (1758).

Hamilton, W., *A Short Review of Mr. Hooke's Observations concerning the Roman Senate and the character of Dionysius of Halicarnassus* (1758).

Le Roy, D., *Les Ruines des plus beaux monuments de la Grèce* (1758).

Montagu, E., *Reflections on the Rise and Fall of the Antient Republicks* (1759).

De Brosses, C., *Du culte des diex fétiches* (1760).

De Beaufort, L., *Histoire de Cesar Germanicus* (1761).

Rousseau, J.-J., *Du contrat social* (1762).

Stuart, J. and Revett, N. *Antiquities of Athens* (4 volumes: 1762, 1787, 1794, 1816).

Alletz, P.A., *Abrégé de l'histoire grecque depuis les temps heroiques, jusqu'à la réduction de la Grèce en province romaine* (1763).

Heyne, H., *Quaestio de causis fabularum seu mythorum veterum physicis* (1764).

Hooke, N., *The Roman History From the Building of Rome to the Ruin of the Commonwealth,* vol. III (1764).

Mably, G.B. de, *Observations sur l'histoire de la Grèce* (1766).

De Beaufort, L., *La Republique Romaine* (1766).

Mathon de la Cour, C.J., *Par quelles causes et par quel degrés les loix de Lycurgue se sont altérées chez les Lacédémoniens jusqu'à ce qu'elles ayent été anéanties* (1767).

Ferguson, A., *An Essay on the History of Civil Society* (1767).

De Gourcy, F.A.E., *Histoire philosophique et politique des loix de Lycurgue* (1768).

Roberston, W., *The History of Ancient Greece* (1768).

Mably, G.B. de, *Doutes proposés aux philosophes économiques sur l'ordre naturel et essentiel des sociétés politiques* (1768).

D'Hancarville, P., *Collection of Etruscan, Greek and Roman Antiquities from the Cabinet of the Hon. William Hamilton …* (1768–76).

Goldsmith, O., *The Roman History from the Foundation of the City of Rome, to the Destruction of the Western Empire* (1769).

Vauvilliers, J.-F., *Examin historique et politique du gouvernement de Sparte* (1769).

Turpin, F.H., *L'Histoire du gouvernement des anciens républiques* (1769).

Hooke, N., *Discours et reflexions critique sur l'histoire et le gouvernement de l'ancienne Rome,* trans. L. Hooke (1770–84).

Hooke, N., *The Roman History From the Building of Rome to the Ruin of the Commonwealth,* vol. IV (1771).
Millot, C., *Élémens d'histoire générale* (1772).
Chastellux, F.-J. de, *Essai sur la félicité publique, ou Considérations sur le sort des hommes dans les différentes époques de l'histoire* (1772).
Guys, P., *A Sentimental Journey Through Greece* (1773).
Bryant, J., *A New System, or Analysis of Ancient Mythology* (1774).
Seran de la Tour, *Histoire du tribunat de Rome, depuis sa creation jusqua la reunion de sa puissance a celle de l'empereur Auguste* (1774).
Wood, R. *An Essay on the Original Genius and Writings of Homer: with a comparative view of the ancient and modern state of the Troade* (1775).
Gibbon, E., *The Decline and Fall of the Roman Empire* (1776–1788).
Smith, A., *An Inquiry into the Nature and Causes of the Wealth of Nations* (1776).
Young, W., *The Spirit of Athens* (1777).
Gillies, J., *The Orations of Isocrates, and A Discourse on the History, Manners, and Character of the Greeks, from the Conclusion of the Peloponnesian War to the Battle of Chaeronea* (1778).
Bowyer, M., *An Apology for some of Mr Hooke's Observations concerning the Roman Senate* (1782).
Gast, J., *History of Greece from the Accession of Alexander of Macedon till its Final Subjection to the Roman Power* (1782).
Ferguson, A., *The History of the Progress and Termination of the Roman Republic* (1783).
Astle, T., *The Origin and Progress of Writing* (1784).
Mitford, W., *History of Greece* (1784–1810).
D'Hancarville, P., *Recherches sur l'origine, l'esprit et les progrès des arts de la Grèce* (1785).
De Bouchaud, M.-A., *Commentaire sur la Loi des Douze Tables* (1787).
Bellenden, W., *Gulielmi Bellendeni Magistri Supplicum Libellorum Augusti Regis Magnæ Britanniæ, & De Statu Libri Tres,* ed. S. Parr (1787).
Barthélemy, J.-J., *Voyage du jeune Anacharsis en Grèce* (1787).
De Septchênes, Le Clerc, *Essai sur la religion des anciens Grecs* (1787).
Parr, S., *A Free Translation of the Preface to Bellendenus; containing animated strictures on the great political characters of the present time* (1788).
De Pauw, C., *Recherches Philosophiques sur les Grécs* (1788).
Savary, C., *Letters on Greece* (1788).
Gillies, J., *View of the Reign of Frederick the Great with a Parallel between that Prince and Philip II of Macedon* (1789).
Mably, G.B. de, *De la legislation* (1789).

Schiller, F., 'Die Gesetzgebung des Lykurgus und Solon', in *Thalia. Herausgegeben von Schiller*, 11 (1790), 30–82.
Volney, C.-F., *Les Ruines, ou méditations sur les révolutions des empires* (1791).
Chevalier, J.-B., *Description of the Plain of Troy* (1791).
Guéroult, P., *Constitutions des Spartiates, des Athèniens et des Romains* (1792).
Hereford, C., *The History of Rome: from the foundation of the city by Romulus, the death of Marcus Antonius* (1792).
Gast, J., *History of Greece: Properly so called* (1793).
Heeren, A.H.L., *Ideen über Politik, den Verkehr, und den Handel der vornehmsten Völker der alten Welt* (1793–6).
Dupuis, C., *Origine de tous les cultes ou la Religion universalle* (1794).
Drummond, W., *A Review of the Governments of Sparta and Athens* (1794).
Maurice, T., *Indian Antiquities* (1794–1800).
Adams, J., *A View of Universal History, from the Creation to the Present Time* (1795).
Heyne, C., *Opuscula academica IV* (1796).
Condillac, E.B. de, *Histoire ancienne et moderne* (1797).
Chateaubriand, F.R., *Essai historique, politique et moral sur les révolutions anciennes et modernes, considérées dans leurs rapports avec la Révolution Française* (1797).
Dallaway, J., *Constantinople Ancient and Modern* (1797).
Estlin, J., *The Nature and Causes of Atheism* (1797).
Heeren, A.H.L., *Geschichte der Staaten des Altertums* (1799).
Morritt, T., *Vindication of Homer* (1799).
Bryant, J., *Observations on Morritt's Vindication of Homer* (1799).
Priestley, J., *A Comparison of the Institutions of Moses with those of the Hindoos and Other Ancient Nations* (1799).
Manso, J.C.F., *Sparta. Ein Versuch zur Aufklärung der Geschichte und Verfassung dieses Staates* (1800–5).
De Tracy, D., *Analyse raisonée de l'Origine de Tous les Cultes* (1804).
Gell, W., *Topography of Troy* (1804).
Cockburn, W., *Remarks on a Publicaton of M. Volney called 'The Ruins' etc* (1804).
Dulaure, J., *Des Cultes qui ont précédé et amené L'ídolatrie et l'adoration des figures humaines* (1805).
Cumberland, G., *Thoughts on Outline, Sculpture, and the System that Guided the Ancient Artists in Composing their Figures and Groups* (1806).

Leland, T., *History of Philip, King of Macedon, Now Corrected* (1806).
Levesque, P., *Histoire critique de la République romaine* (1807).
Gillies, J., *History of the World: Comprehending the latter ages of European Greece, and the History of the Greek kingdoms in Asia and Africa, from their foundation to their destruction* (1807).
Niebuhr, B., *Römische Geschichte* (1811).
Douglas, F., *An Essay on Certain Points of Resemblance Between the Ancient and Modern Greeks* (1813).
Leake, W., *Researches in Greece* (1814).
Wilkins, W., *Atheniensa, or, Remarks on the Topography and Buildings of Athens* (1816).
Beaufort, F., *Karamania or A Brief Description of the South Coast of Asia Minor and the Remains of Antiquity* (1817).
Knight, R.P., *An Enquiry into the Symbolic Language of Ancient Art and Mythology* (1818).
Dodwell, E., *A Classical and Topographical Tour Through Greece* (1819).
Müller, K.O., *Geschichten Hellenischer Stämme und Städte* (1820).
Leake, W., *The Topography of Athens* (1821).
Maclaren, C., *A Dissertation on the Topography of the Plain of Troy* (1822).
Müller, K.O., *Die Dorier* (1824).
Leake, W., *Journal of a Tour in Asia Minor* (1824).
Van Kampen, N.G., *Geschiedenis van Griekenland* (1827).
Leake, W., *On the Demi of Attica* (1829).
Droysen, J., *De Lagidarum regno Ptolemaeo rege* (1831).
Arundell, F., *Discoveries in Asia Minor* (1834).
Fellows, C., *An Account of the Discoveries in Lycia* (1841).
Thirlwall, C., *The History of Greece* (1835–44).
Arnold, T., *The History of Rome* (1838).
Grote, G., *A History of Greece; from the earliest period to the close of the generation contemporary with Alexander the Great* (1846–1856).
Hofmann, F., *Der römische Senat zur Zeit der Republik* (1847).
Niebuhr, B., *Lectures on the History of Rome*, trans. L. Schmitz (1849).
Fellows, C., *Travels and Researches in Asia Minor* (1852).
Niebuhr, B., *Lectures on Ancient History, From the Earliest Times to the Taking of Alexandria, Comprising the History of the Asiatic Nations, the Egyptians, Greeks, Macedonians and Carthaginians*, L. Schmitz (ed.), translated by Dr Marcus Neibuhr (1852).
Mommsen, T., *Römische Geschichte* (1854–6).

# Bibliography of Secondary Material

Ahn, D., 'The Politics of Royal Education: Xenophon's *Education of Cyrus* in Early Eighteenth-Century Europe', *The Leadership Quarterly*, Special Issue: Views from Humanities, 19 (2008).

Angelomatis, H., *The Eve of the Greek Revival: British Travellers' Perceptions of Early Nineteenth-Century Greece* (London, 1990).

Ataç, C.A., 'Imperial Lessons from Athens and Sparta', *History of Political Thought*, 27 (2006), 642–60.

Augustinos, O., *French Odysseys: Greece in French Travel Literature* (Baltimore, 1994).

Ayres, P., *Classical Culture and the Idea of Rome in Eighteenth-Century England* (Cambridge, 1997).

Baker, K.M., 'A Script for the French Revolution: the Political Consciousness of Mably', in Baker (ed.), *Inventing the French Revolution: Essays on French Political Culture in the Eighteenth Century* (Cambridge, 1990), 86–106.

Baker, K.M., 'Transformations of Classical Republicanism in Eighteenth-Century France,' *The Journal of Modern History*, 73 (2001), 32–53.

Bayliss, A.J, *Life After Demosthenes: Democracy and Oligarchy in Early Hellenistic Athens* (forthcoming).

Berland, K.J.H., 'Bringing Philosophy down from the Heavens: Socrates and the New Science', *Journal of the History of Ideas*, 47 (1986), 299–308.

Bernal, M., *Black Athena: The Afro-Asiatic Roots of Classical Civilisation*, 2 vols. (London, 1987–91).

Bolgar, R., *The Classical Heritage and its Beneficiaries* (Cambridge 1954).

Borza, E. (ed.), *Classics and the Classical Tradition* (University Park, PA., 1973).

Bridenthal, R., 'Was There a Roman Homer? Niebuhr's Thesis and Its Critics', *History and Theory*, 11 (1972), 193–213.

Bugh, G.R. (ed.),*The Cambridge Companion to the Hellenistic World* (Cambridge, 2006).

Burstein, S.M., 'New Ways of Being Greek in the Hellenistic Period', in W. Heckel and L.A. Tritle (eds.), *Crossroads of History: The Age of Alexander* (Clairemont, California, 2003), 217–42.

Buxton, J., *The Grecian Taste* (London, 1978).
Calder, W., and Trzaskoma, S. (eds.), *George Grote Reconsidered* (Hildesheim, 1996).
Cartledge, P., 'Introduction' to P. Cartledge, P. Garnsey and E. Gruen (eds.), *Hellenistic Constructs: Essays in Culture, History, and Historiography* (Berkeley, 1997), 1–19.
Cartledge, P., 'The Socratics' Sparta and Rousseau's', in S. Hodkinson and A. Powell (eds.), *Sparta: New Perspectives* (Swansea, 1999), 311–27.
Ceserani, G., 'Modern Histories of Ancient Greece: genealogies, contexts and eighteenth-century narrative historiography' (Version 1.0), Princeton/Stanford Working Papers in Classics (2008).
Ceserani, G., 'Narrative, Interpretation, and Plagiarism in Mr. Robertson's 1778 History of Ancient Greece', *Journal of the History of Ideas*, 66 (2005), 413–36.
Chamoux, F., *Hellenistic Civilization*, translated by M. Roussel (Oxford, 2003).
Christ, K., 'Arnaldo Momigliano and the History of Historiography', *History and Theory*, 30 (1991), 459–67.
Clarke, G.W. (ed.), *Rediscovering Hellenism: the Hellenic inheritance and the English Imagination* (Cambridge, 1988).
Clarke, M.L., *Greek Studies in England, 1700–1830* (Cambridge, 1945).
Cohler, A.M., *Montesquieu's Comparative Politics and the Spirit of American Constitutionalism* (Lawrence, 1988).
Constantine, D., *Early Greek Travellers and the Hellenic Ideal* (Cambridge, 1984).
Cornell, T., 'Ancient History and the Antiquarian Revisited: Some Thoughts on Reading Momigliano's Classical Foundations', in M. Crawford and C. Ligota (eds.), *Ancient History and the Antiquarian, Essays in Memory of Arnaldo Momigliano* (London, 1995), 1–14.
Crawford, M., and Ligota, C., *Ancient History and the Antiquarian: Essays in Memory of Arnaldo Momigliano* (London, 1995).
Degner, U., *Bilder im Wechsel der Töne: Hölderlins Elegien und 'Nachtgesänge'* (Heidelberg, 2008).
Demetriou, K.N., 'In Defense of the British Constitution: The theoretical implications of the debate over the Athenian Democracy in Britain, 1770–1850', *History of Political Thought*, 17 (1996), 280–97.
Demetriou, K.N., *George Grote on Plato and Athenian Democracy* (Frankfurt, 1999).
Demetriou, K.N., 'Historians on Macedonian Imperialism and Alexander the Great', *Journal of Modern Greek Studies*, 19 (2001), 23–60.
Demetriou, K.N., 'Bishop Connop Thirlwall: Historian of Ancient Greece', *Quaderni di storia*, 56 (2002), 49–90.

Enenkel, K., De Jong, J. and Landtsheer, J. (eds.), *Recreating Ancient History* (Leiden, 2002).
Erasmus, H., *The Origins of Rome in Historiography from Petrarch to Perizonius* (Assen, 1962).
Erskine Hill, H., *The Augustan Ideal in English Literature* (London, 1983).
Finley, M.I., *Democracy Ancient and Modern* (London, 1973).
Gay, P., *The Enlightenment: An Interpretation*, 2 vols. (London, 1966–70).
Gribbin, W., 'Rollin's Histories and American Republicaniam', *William and Mary Quarterly*, 29 (1972), 611–22.
Guerci, L., *Libertà degli antichi e libertà dei moderni: Sparta, Atene e i 'philosophes' nella Francia del Settecento* (Naples, 1979).
Güthenke, C., *Placing Modern Greece: The Dynamics of Romantic Hellenism* (Oxford, 2008).
Hall, J., *Hellenicity: Between Ethnicity and Culture* (Chicago, 2002).
Hammond, N.G.L., *A History of Macedonia* (Oxford, 1972).
Hammond, N.G.L., *A History of Greece*, third edition (Oxford, 1986).
Hansen, M.H., *The Tradition of Ancient Greek Democracy and its Importance for Modern Democracy* (Copenhagen, 2005).
Hansen, M.H., 'The Tradition of the Athenian Democracy A.D. 1750–1950', *Greece & Rome,* 39 (1992), 14–30.
Hay, D., *Annalists and Historians, Western Historiography from the VIIIth to the XVIII Century* (London, 1977).
Highet, G., *The Classical Tradition* (Oxford 1949).
Hodkinson, S. and Macgregor Morris, I. (eds.), *Sparta: Classical Tradition* (forthcoming).
Hodkinson, S., *Comparing Spartan Militarism* (forthcoming).
Hodkinson, S., 'Five Words that Shook the World: Plutarch, Lykourgos 16 and appropriations of Spartan communal property ownership in eighteenth-century France', in N. Birgalias, et. al. (eds.), *The Contribution of Ancient Sparta to Political Thought and Practice* (Athens, 2007), 417–31.
Hutton, C.A., 'The Travels of 'Palmyra' Wood in 1750–1', *Journal of Hellenic Studies*, 47 (1927), 102–28.
Israel, J., *Radical Enlightenment: Philosophy and the Making of Modernity* (Oxford, 2001).
Israel, J., *Enlightenment Contested: Philosophy, Modernity, and the Emancipation of Man* (Oxford, 2006).
Jenkyns, R., *The Victorians and Ancient Greece* (Oxford, 1980).
Leffter, P., 'French Historians and the Challenge to Louis XIV's Absolutism', *French Historical Studies*, 14 (1985), 1–22.

Leffler, P., '"The Histoire Raisonée", 1660–1720: A Pre-Enlightenment Genre', *Journal of the History of Ideas*, 37 (1976), 219–40.

Leigh, R.A., 'Jean-Jacques Rousseau and the Myth of Antiquity in the Eighteenth Century', in R. Bolgar (ed.), *Classical Influences on Western Thought AD 1650–1870* (Cambridge, 1979), 155–67.

Levine, J., 'Edward Gibbon and the Quarrel between the Ancients and the Moderns', *The Eighteenth Century*, 26 (1985), 47–62.

Levine, J., *Humanism and History: Origins of Modern English Historiography* (Ithaca, 1986).

Levine, J., *The Battle of the Books: History and Literature in the Augustan Age* (Ithaca, 1991).

Levine, J., *Between the Ancients and the Moderns: Baroque Culture in Restoration England* (Yale, 1999).

Levine, J., 'Ancients and Moderns and the Origins of Modern Critical Historiography', *Intellectual News*, 8 (2000), 83–91.

Levine, J., 'Jonathan Swift and the Idea of History', in D. Todd and C. Wall (eds.), *Eighteenth-Century Genre and Culture* (Newark, 2001), 79–95.

Macgregor Morris, I., 'To make a new Thermopylae: Hellenism, Greek Liberation and the Battle of Thermopylae', *Greece & Rome*, 47 (2000), 211–30.

Macgregor Morris, I., 'Richard Glover: A Reassessment', *Eighteenth-Century World*, 1 (2003), 46–52.

Macgregor Morris, I., 'The Paradigm of Democracy: Sparta in the Enlightenment', in T. Figueira (ed.), *Spartan Society* (Swansea, 2004), 339–62.

Macgregor Morris, I., 'William Mitford', in J. Jenkins (ed.), *Dictionary of Literary Biography 336: British Eighteenth-Century Historians* (2007), 240–5.

Macgregor Morris, I., '*Shrines of the Mighty*. Rediscovering the Battlefields of the Persian Wars', in E. Bridges et al. (eds.), *Cultural Responses to the Persian Wars: Antiquity to the Third Millennium* (Oxford, 2007), 231–64.

Macgregor Morris, I., 'The Refutation of Democracy? Socrates in the Enlightenment', in M.B. Trapp (ed.), Socrates From Antiquity to the Enlightenment (Aldershot, 2007), 209–27.

Macgregor Morris, I., '*From Ancient Dreams to Modern Nightmares*: Classical Revolutions in Enlightenment Thought', in A. Montoya, et. al. (eds.), *Lumières et histoire* (forthcoming).

Macgregor Morris, I., 'Liars, Eccentrics and Visionaries: Early Travellers to Sparta and the Birth of Laconian Archaeology', in W. Cavanagh (ed.), *Sparta and Laconia: From Prehistory to Premodern* (London, 2009), 387–95.

Macgregor Morris, I., 'Creating the Enlightenment Prince: Maurice Ashley's translation of the *Cyropaedia* of Xenophon', in *Ancient Greece in Eighteenth-Century Britain: Essays on Translation and Commentary in a Tradition of Philosophy, Politics, and Culture* (a special edition of the *Annals of Scholarship*), ed. M. Zebrowski (forthcoming).

Macgregor Morris, I., *The Age of Leonidas: Hellenism and the Classical Tradition in the Enlightenment* (forthcoming).

Marchand, S., *Down From Olympus: Archaeology and Philhellenism in Germany 1750–1970* (Princeton, 1996).

McCuaig, W., 'Sigonio and Grouchy: Roman Studies in the Sixteenth Century', *Athenaeum*, 74 (1986), 147–83.

Meehan, M., *Liberty and Poetics in Eighteenth-Century England* (London, 1986).

Millar, F., *The Roman Republic in Political Thought* (London, 2002).

Momigliano, A., 'Ancient History and the Antiquarian', *Journal of the Warburg and Courtauld Institutes*, 13 (1950), 285–315.

Momigliano, A., 'Perizonius, Niebuhr and the Character of Early Roman Tradition', *Journal of Roman Studies*, 47 (1957), 104–14.

Momigliano, A., 'George Grote and the study of Greek history', in A. Momigliano (ed.), *Studies in Greek Historiography* (London, 1969), 56–74.

Momigliano, A., 'J.G. Droysen Between Greeks and Jews', *History and Theory*, 9 (1970), 139–53.

Momigliano, A., 'An Eighteenth-Century Prelude to Mr Gibbon', in *Sesto Contributo alla storia degli studi classici e del mondo antico* (Rome, 1980), 251–60.

Momigliano, A., 'Niebuhr and the Agrarian Problems of Rome', *History and Theory*, 21 (1982), 3–15.

Momigliano, A., 'The Rediscovery of Greek History in the Eighteenth Century: The Case of Sicily', in *Settimo Contributo Alla Storia Degli Studi Classici E Del Mondo Antico* (Rome, 1984), 133–53.

Momigliano, A., 'Tacitus and the Tacitist Tradition', in *The Classical Foundations of Modern Historiography* (Berkeley, 1990), 109–31.

Moore, J., 'Periclean Preston – Public Art and the Classical Tradition in Nineteenth-Century Lancashire', *Northern History*, 40 (2003), 299–323.

Mossé, C., *L'Antiquiteé dans la Révolution francaise* (Paris, 1989).

Nelson, E., *The Greek Tradition in Republican Thought* (Cambridge, 2004).

Oake, R., 'Montesquieu's Analysis of Roman History', *Journal of the History of Ideas*, 16 (1955), 44–59.

Orwin, C., 'Rousseau's Socratism', *Journal of Politics*, 60 (1998), 174–87.
Osborn, J.M., 'Travel Literature and the Rise of Neo-Hellenism', *Bulletin of the New York Public Library*, 67 (1963), 279–300.
Phillips, M., 'Reconsiderations on History and Antiquarianism: Arnaldo Momigliano and the Historiography of Eighteenth-Century Britain', *Journal of the History of Ideas*, 57 (1996), 297–316.
Pocock, J.G.A., *Barbarism and Religion*, 4 vols (Cambridge, 1999–2005).
Pocock, J.G.A., 'Classical and Civil History: The Transformation of Humanism', *Cromohs* 1 (1996), 1–34.
Potts, A., *Flesh and the Ideal: Winckelmann and the Origins of Art History* (London, 1994).
Raizis, M.B., 'Philhellenism in English Literature 1780–1830', in A. Noe (ed.), *Der Philhellenismus in der westeuropäischen Literatur* (Amsterdam, 1994), 111–32.
Raizis, M.B., 'The Origin and Culmination of Shelleys Philhellenism', in S. Coelsch-Foisner (ed.), *Trends in English and American Studies* (Lewiston, 1996), 189–204.
Rawson, E., *The Spartan Tradition in European Thought* (Oxford, 1969).
Richard, C., *The Founders and the Classics: Greece, Rome, and the American Enlightenment* (Harvard, 1995).
Ridley, R., *Gibbon's Complement: Louis de Beaufort* (Venice, 1986).
Ridley, R., 'Machiavelli's Edition of Livy', *Rinascimento*, 27 (1987), 327–41.
Ridley, R., *The Historical Observations of Jacob Perizonius* (Rome, 1991).
Ridley, R., 'The Forgotten Historian, Laurence Echard and the First History of the Roman Republic', *Ancient Society*, 27 (1996), 277–315.
Ridley, R., 'Leges Agrariae: Myths Ancient and Modern', *Classical Philology*, 95 (2000), 459–67.
Roberts, J.T., *Athens on Trial: The Anti-Democratic Tradition in Western Thought* (Princeton, 1994).
Sampson, G., Macgregor Morris, I., Moore, J., 'Nathanial Hooke', in J. Jenkins (ed.), *Dictionary of Literary Biography 336: British Eighteenth-Century Historians* (2007).
Seed, J., *Dissenting Histories: Religious Division and the Politics of Memory in Eighteenth-Century England* (Edinburgh, 2008).
Shklar, J.N., 'Rousseau's Two Models: Sparta and the Golden Age', *Political Science Quarterly*, 81 (1966) 25–51.
Shipley, G., 'Recent Trends and New Directions', in G.R. Bugh (ed.), *The Cambridge Companion to the Hellenistic World* (Cambridge, 2006), 315–26.
Spencer, T., *Fair Greece, Sad Relic* (Bath, 1974).

Spencer, T., 'Robert Wood and the Problem of Troy in the Eighteenth Century', *Journal of the Courtald and Warburg Institutes*, 20 (1957), 75–105.
St. Clair, W., *That Greece Might Still Be Free* (London, 1972).
Stanford, W.B., *Ireland and the Classical Tradition* (Dublin, 1976).
Steinberg, M., 'The Twelve Tables and Their Origins: An Eighteenth-Century Debate', *Journal of the History of Ideas*, 43 (1982), 379–96.
Stern, B., *The Rise of Romantic Hellenism in English Literature* (Menasha, 1940).
Stromberg, R., 'History in the Eighteenth Century', *Journal of the History of Ideas*, 12 (1951), 295–304.
Sweet, R., *Antiquaries: The Discovery of the Past in Eighteenth-Century Britain* (Cambridge, 2004).
Turner, F., 'British Politics and the Demise of the Roman Republic: 1700–1939', *Historical Journal*, 29 (1986), 577–99.
Turner, F., *The Greek Heritage in Victorian Britain* (Yale, 1981).
Velema, W., 'Ancient and Modern Virtue Compared: De Beaufort and Van Effen on Republican Citizenship', *Eighteenth-Century Studies*, 30 (1997), 437–43.
Vidal-Naquet, P., *Politics Ancient and Modern* (Cambridge, 1995),
Vlassopoulos, K., 'Sparta and Rome in Early Modern Political Thought', in. S. Hodkinson and I. Macgregor Morris (eds.), *Sparta: Classical Tradition* (Swansea, forthcoming).
Vlassopoulos, K., *Unthinking the Greek Polis* (Cambridge, 2007).
Wagstaff, J.M., 'Pausanias and the Topographers: the Case of Colonel Leake', in S.E. Alcock, J.F. Cherry, and J. Elsner (eds.), *Pausanias: Travel and Memory in Roman Greece* (Oxford, 2001), 190–226.
Ward, A., 'The Tory View of Roman History', *Studies in English Literature 1500–1900*, 4 (1964), 413–56.
Whedbee, K.E., 'The Tyranny of Athens: Representations of Rhetorical Democracy in Eighteenth-Century Britain', *Rhetoric Society Quarterly*, 33 (2003), 65–85.
Wood, E.M., 'Democracy: An Idea of Ambiguous Ancestry', in J.P. Euben, J.R. Wallach, and J. Ober (eds.), *Athenian Political Thought and the Reconstruction of American Democracy* (1994), 59–80.
Wright, J.K., *A Classical Republican in Eighteenth-Century France: The Political Thought of Mably* (Stanford, 1997).
Wright, J.K., 'Conversations with Phocion: The Political Thought of Mably', *History of Political Thought*, 13 (1992), 391–415.

# Index

absolutism, 9, 14, 38–41, 43–4, 49
Actium, Battle of, 115–36, 210
Agrippa, Marcus, 119, 121, 131
Albania, 169–70, 178, 181
Alexander the Great, 13, 220, 221–2, 224–5, 228–9, 231, 233–4, 236–7, 240–4
Ali Pasha, 126, 169–70, 176, 180–1, 230
Antonius, Marcus (Mark Antony), 115–36, 222
Aristotle, 11, 34, 62–64, 77, 237–8
Arnold, Thomas, 183, 261, 271
Ashley, Maurice, 38–9
Asia Minor, 24–5, 27, 170, 222, 229–30, 235
Athens (Attica), 8, 11, 13, 19, 21, 23, 35, 41, 45, 49–54, 57–85, 149, 172–3, 180, 182, 196, 217, 221, 223, 230–1, 239, 241, 243, 245, 254–67, 271–5, 277–81, 283–4, 286
Athens-Sparta debate, 223, 239, 263, 283
Baalbec, 17, 24
Barthélemy, Jean–Jacques, 258, 283
Bentham, Jeremy, 255, 261–2, 271
Bianchini, Francesco, 18, 22, 142, 143
Bolingbroke, Henry St John, 1st Viscount, 35–40, 42–4, 52–3
Bonaparte, Napoleon, 23, 49, 82, 170, 243, 258; *see also* Napoleonic Wars
Brutus, 206, 209

Bulwer-Lytton, Edward, 254, 261
Burke, Edmund, 5, 61, 87, 100, 106, 108–11, 276
Byron, George Gordon, Lord, 21, 26, 124–5, 174, 271, 273, 280, 289
Caesar, Julius, 173, 190, 194, 196, 205–6, 208–10, 213
Capitoline marbles, 18, 142–3, 189
Cassius Dio, 116–17, 120–1, 126–9, 131–6, 217
Cato, 201, 206, 209–10, 236
Catrou, François, 4, 142, 191, 198–200, 210–11
Chateaubriand, François-René, vicomte de, 258, 264, 269–70
Cicero, Marcus Tullius, 9, 18, 33–5, 37, 47, 142, 190, 201, 205–6, 209, 217, 241
Cleopatra, 115–36, 222
Clinton, Henry, 271
Constant, Benjamin, 49, 84, 259–61, 263, 265, 267, 270, 280
Constantine the Great, 13, 94, 211
Constantinople, 211, 231–2
Coxe, William, 38, 55
Crevier, Jean Baptiste Louis, 117–21, 123, 130–2, 135–6, 188, 210–11
Cyrus the Great, 37, 39–43, 54–5, 286
Cyrus the Younger, 35
Davenant, Charles, 45–8, 51–2
de Beaufort, Louis, 9, 200, 202, 203, 207–8, 213

de Pauw, Cornelius, 63, 77, 82, 226, 234–5, 239–42, 251, 254, 258, 261–2, 265–6, 276, 280
de Tillemont, Louis-Sébastien, 193–4, 197
Demosthenes, 66, 223–4, 226, 234, 237, 241, 250, 254, 284–5
D'Hancarville, 4, 6, 28, 137, 139–67
Diderot, 4, 28, 139, 144, 146, 251
Dilettanti, Society of, 13, 28, 158, 160, 170
Dionysius of Halicarnassus, 200, 203–5, 217
Dodona, 174–177
Dodwell, Edward, 20–1, 26–7, 180
Douglas, Frederick, 231–2
Droysen, Johann, 219–21, 223
Dryden, John, 12, 14, 270
Dupuis, Charles, 5, 28, 154, 157, 162–5, 167
Echard, Laurence, 188, 191–5, 197–8, 200, 207
Egypt, Egyptians, 23, 118–21, 124, 127–9, 135–6, 138, 143–4, 147, 151, 173, 221, 225
Epirus, 170, 172, 174–5, 182, 225, 230, 232, 234–5
Etruscans, 149, 150
Fénelon, François, 10, 12, 38, 42–3, 283
Ferguson, Adam, 8–9, 29, 241, 217, 239, 247, 251
Filmer, Sir Robert, 35, 38, 43
Frederick, Prince of Wales, 36, 42, 52, 64
Frederick II of Prussia, the Great, 227–8, 236, 239
French Revolution, 15, 57, 78, 82–3, 87, 109–10, 112, 163, 215, 217, 269–70, 276

Gast, John, 221, 223–5, 228, 234–8, 240, 245–6, 252
Gell, Sir William, 4–5, 21, 25, 180
George III, 55, 65, 99, 239, 276
Gibbon, Edward, 9, 11, 15–16, 27, 87–112, 187–8, 214–15, 239, 247, 289
Gillies, John, 59–60, 65, 127–8, 136, 221, 223–4, 227–8, 234–6, 238–9, 242–6, 252–3, 271, 276, 281, 285, 287–8
Glover, Richard, 12, 15, 26, 59, 68, 265, 286
Goldsmith, Oliver, 60, 122, 208, 212, 217, 225–7, 234, 238, 253
Gracchi, 10, 196, 199, 205–9
Grote, George, 6, 85, 223, 228–30, 234–5, 238–9, 244–9, 252–7, 260–3, 265–90
Hamilton, Alexander, 216, 261–2
Hamilton, Gavin, 19, 22, 153
Hamilton, Sir William, 23, 139–41, 146–53, 156, 158, 162, 166
Harrington, James, 34, 38, 46, 53–4, 63, 83, 196, 264
Helvetius, Claude Adrien, 239, 251
Herodotus, 15, 35, 158, 173, 227, 252–3, 286
Heyne, Christian, 144, 157, 206
Holbach, Paul-Henri, Baron de, 144–5, 154
Hooke, Nathaniel, 4–5, 9–10, 14–16, 121–3, 131, 142, 191, 195, 199–200, 202–9, 211–13, 217
Horace, 18, 129, 142
Hume, David, 8, 44–5, 65, 72, 87, 91–7, 101, 105, 110–12, 137–8, 146, 239, 247, 251, 281
Ioannina, 175, 178–9, 182, 230
Isocrates, 77, 80, 224, 232, 236, 240
Jacobins, Jacobinism, 110, 258, 264, 270

Jacobites, Jacobitism, 5, 16, 40, 44, 50, 199
Johnson, Dr Samuel, 100–1, 204
Knight, Richard Payne, 139–41, 153, 155, 157–65, 167
Kromayer, Johannes, 116–17, 125, 128–36
Lafitau, Joseph–François, 145–6, 159
Leake, William Martin, 24, 27, 125–8, 131–2, 135–6, 169–83, 230–1, 279
Leland, Thomas, 234–6, 245
Leonidas, 26, 258
Liberty, 7–10, 38, 44, 49, 53–4, 62, 64–5, 71–3, 75, 83, 97, 104, 223–4, 226, 238–44, 259, 263, 266
Locke, John, 26, 38, 82
Louis XIV, 10, 36, 40, 42–3
Lycurgus, 231, 263–4, 278, 288
Mably, Gabriel Bonnot de, 59, 63, 69, 71, 77, 82, 214–15, 221, 223–4, 234–40, 242–6, 251, 263–5, 267, 270, 278, 281, 283–4, 288
Macaulay, Thomas Babington, First Baron, 57, 237, 255, 261, 266–72, 274–6, 281–3, 285–9
Macedonia, Macedonians, 118, 170, 181, 192, 216, 219–46, 285, 286
Machiavelli, 33–5, 37, 40, 46–7, 52, 62, 73, 83, 189–90
Madison, James, 216, 261–2
Marathon, 26, 61, 173
Middleton, Conyers, 204–5
Mill, James, 255, 265, 272
Mill, John Stuart, 256–7, 262, 270–3, 275, 277, 279, 281, 284–5
Millot, Claude, 252
Milton, John, 196, 209
Mitford, William, 16, 57, 60, 64, 85, 221, 226, 234–40, 252–4, 260–1, 267–83, 285–90

Mommsen, Theodor, 132, 135, 187
Montagu, Edward, 214, 253, 276
Montesquieu, Charles de Secondat, baron de, 33, 54, 57, 59–60, 63–73, 75–9, 82–3, 85, 122, 189, 214–15, 218, 251, 262, 276
Moyle, Walter, 45–8, 51, 204
Napoleonic Wars, 80, 164, 169, 243; *see also* Bonaparte, Napoleon
Newton, Sir Isaac, 202
Nicopolis (Michalitsi), 124, 126–7
Niebuhr, Barthold, 134, 187–9, 193, 199, 201, 203, 206–209, 215, 217–18, 223, 229–30, 237–8, 244–5, 247–8, 271
Octavian (later Augustus), 115–36, 212
Ozell, John, 191, 198–9, 211
Palmyra, 5, 17, 24
Pausanias, 25–27, 151, 172–3
Perdiccas, 244–5
Pericles, 11–12, 52, 74–6, 79, 231, 258, 284
Persia, 35, 40–3, 54–5, 67, 144, 151, 216, 234, 236–7, 285–6
Persian Wars, 13, 26, 61, 67, 69–70, 75, 80, 83, 173
Philip II, of Macedon, 222–5, 227–229, 231–41, 244–5, 285
Philip V, of Macedon, 242
*philosophes*, 6, 14, 138–9
Pighius, Stephanus, 142, 190–1, 200, 211–12
Plato, 11, 34–5, 50, 81
Pliny, 18, 142
Plutarch, 71, 77, 116–22, 125, 127, 129, 132–6, 159, 217, 228, 233, 241–2, 269, 271, 286
Polybius, 9, 71, 176, 217, 222
Pompeii, 18, 189
Pompey, 115, 124, 206, 213, 225

Pope, Alexander, 12, 204
Priestley, Joseph, 87, 95–112, 163
Ptolemies, 22, 135, 143, 221–2, 227–8, 241
Quarrel of the Ancient and Moderns, 8, 59, 239, 250–1, 256, 260
Raleigh, Sir Walter, 190, 192, 195, 200, 209
Ramsay, Andrew, 43–4, 144
Rawlinson, George, 129, 131, 160, 222, 229–30, 234
Revett, Nicholas, 13, 21, 23
Robertson, William, 60, 223, 225, 234–5, 237, 239, 242, 245–6
Rollin, Charles, 59, 62, 82–83, 116–17, 120, 188, 200, 208, 210–11, 213, 216–17, 233, 237, 250–2, 264, 276, 283
Rousseau, Jean-Jacques, 33, 63, 69, 189, 214, 239, 251, 254, 257, 261, 278, 288
Sallust, 212, 217
Salonica, 182, 230–1
Schiller, Friedrich, 251
Seleucids, 22, 143, 222, 225, 227, 241
Shaftesbury, Anthony Ashley-Cooper, Third Earl of, 7, 12, 38, 67
Shakespeare, William, 115–16, 125
Shebbeare, John, 50, 52, 54
Shiletto, Richard, 239, 274, 279
Smith, Adam, 5, 7, 48, 99, 239
Socrates, 33–3, 45, 81, 263, 266, 280
Solon, 11, 76–7
Sparta, 11, 35, 41, 49, 52, 54, 59, 63–6, 77, 81–8, 171, 221, 223, 239, 243, 256–61, 263–6, 271–3, 276–8, 280–1, 283–5

Stanyan, Temple, 72, 224–5, 234–5, 237, 239–40, 250–1, 253, 276
Strabo, 24–5, 27, 176
Stuart, James, 12, 13, 19, 35, 121–2, 131
Sulla, 206, 209
Swift, Jonathan, 196, 203, 206, 217
Tacitus, 9, 35, 65, 212, 217
Thermopylae, 26, 174, 235
Thessaly, 170, 179–10, 182, 225, 230, 232, 235
Thirlwall, Connop, 228, 234–5, 254–5, 261
Thucydides, 15, 18, 34–5, 52, 54, 74, 175, 183, 239, 253
Tourreil, Jacques de, 66–7, 221, 223, 233, 249–51
Townley, Charles, 19, 21–2, 139–41, 152–3, 157, 161, 164
Troy, 5, 17, 25, 151
Utilitarians, 255–6, 261–2, 265–7, 270–3, 275, 279
Vertot, René-Aubert, 193, 197–8, 200, 203–4
Virgil, 18, 133, 142
Volney, Constantin-François, comte de, 6, 28, 163, 167
Voltaire, François-Marie Arouet, 63, 189, 214, 236, 239, 266, 280
von Ranke, Leopold, 134
Walpole, Horace, 108, 205, 258
Winckelmann, Johann, 24, 28, 63, 67, 139, 141, 146–8, 150–1, 165–6, 251
Wood, Robert, 5, 17, 24–6, 66, 146
Xenophon, 33–55, 65, 77, 81, 286
Xerxes, 285–6
Young, Sir William, 49, 69–85, 251, 253, 257–8, 261–2